Contents

Introduction

Walkthrough

Forest Temple

Goron Mines

Lakebed Temple

Arbiter's Grounds

Snowpeak Ruins

Temple of Time

City in the Sky

Palace of Twilight

Hyrule Castle

Adventure Appendix

Nintendo GameCube Version

A dark power is sweeping over Hyrule.

The denizens of the twilight realm, banished long ago by the three goddesses, hold the land within their grip.

Hyrule's sole hope:

Link, a young farmhand from neighboring Ordona Province. Only by joining forces with the mysterious Midna and harnessing the power of twilight to assume bestial form will Link fulfill his destiny and restore light to the world.

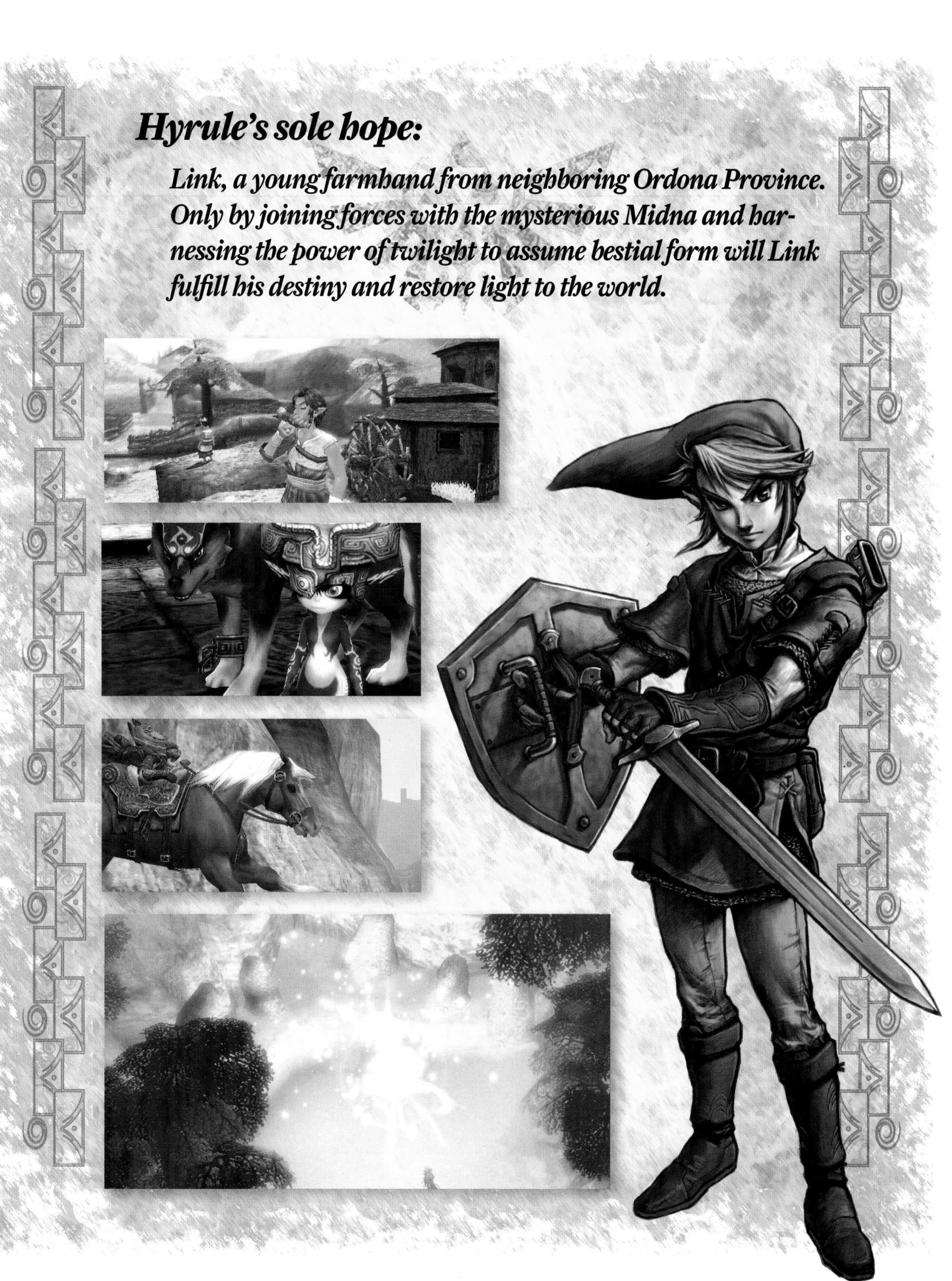

Take Control

You are Link: hero, horse rider, fisherman, and slayer of shadow beings. Hyrule's destiny is in your hands.

Wii Controller Layout

The Legend of Zelda: Twilight Princess requires use of both the nunchuk and the remote. Generally speaking, the nunchuk allows you to control Link's body movement and the camera, and the remote lets you use weapons and items.

Nunchuk

Holding For right-handers

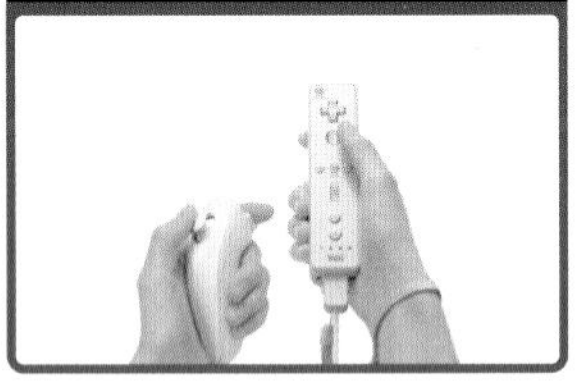

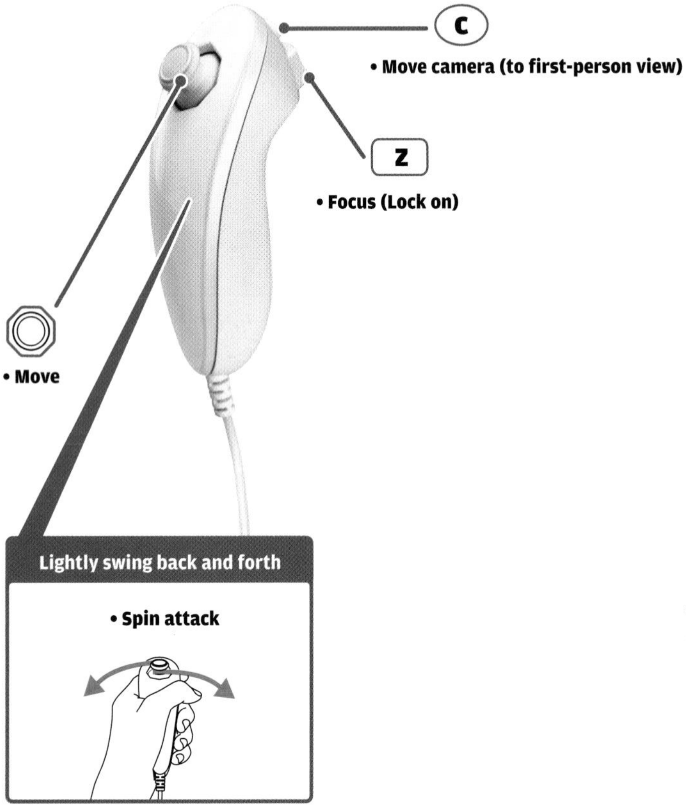

C
- **Move camera (to first-person view)**

Z
- **Focus (Lock on)**

- **Move**

Lightly swing back and forth
- **Spin attack**

Wii Remote

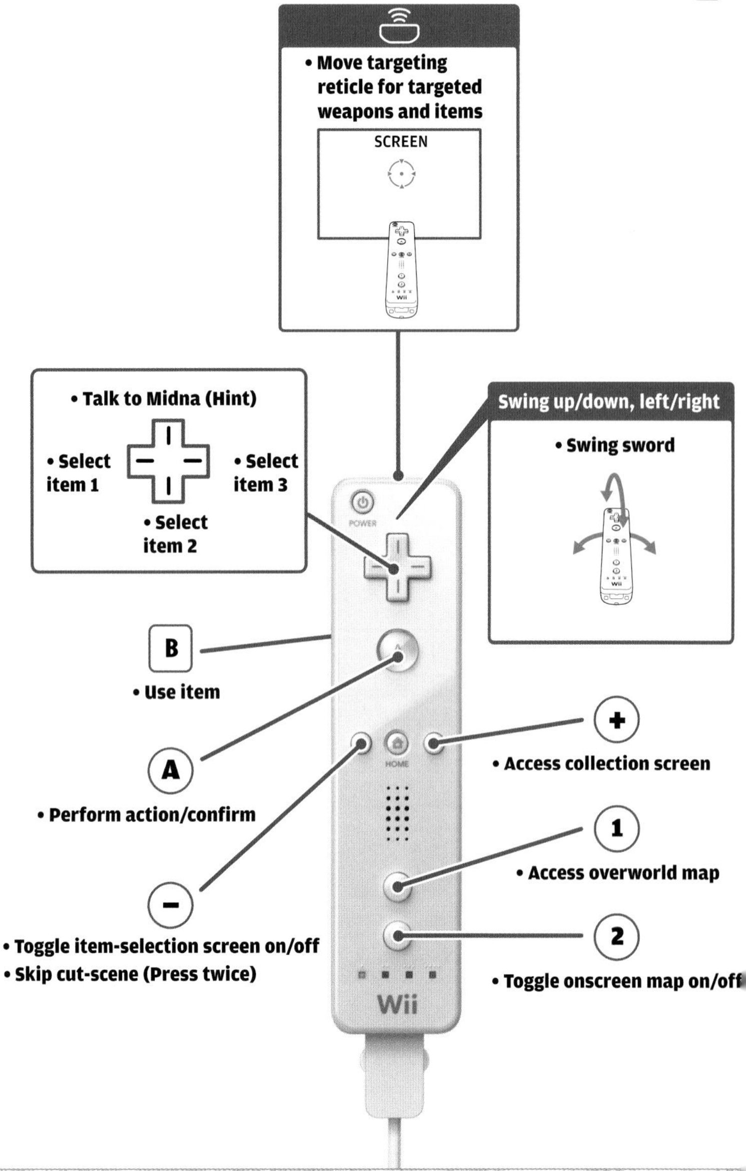

- **Move targeting reticle for targeted weapons and items**

- **Talk to Midna (Hint)**
- **Select item 1**
- **Select item 3**
- **Select item 2**

Swing up/down, left/right
- **Swing sword**

B
- **Use item**

A
- **Perform action/confirm**

−
- **Toggle item-selection screen on/off**
- **Skip cut-scene (Press twice)**

+
- **Access collection screen**

1
- **Access overworld map**

2
- **Toggle onscreen map on/off**

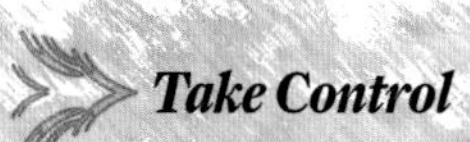

Harness the Power of Man and Beast

As you explore the land and take on every manner of foe, Link will transform between a young hero and a wolf. You'll use similar control schemes for both characters, with a few variations. The human Link is more nimble in the way he moves, and he can manipulate weapons and items. The canine uses special senses and carries a passenger, Midna, who has her own powers. Midna's laugh (heard on the remote's speaker) signals that she has advice or help to offer you.

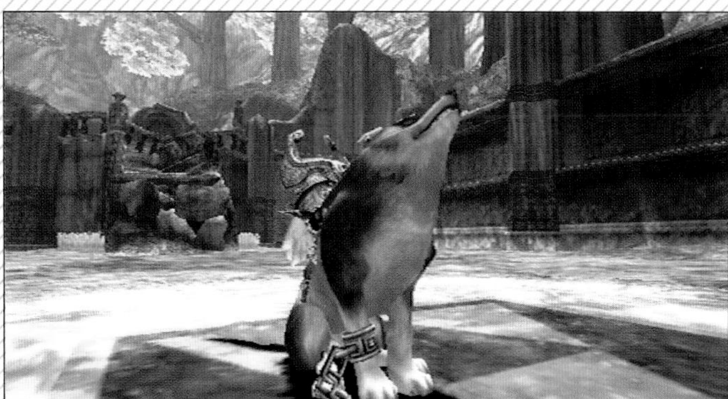

Get Moving

The nunchuk's Control Stick triggers Link's general movements. The control diagrams that accompany each of the following move descriptions show you how to manipulate the Control Stick and additional buttons.

Got to Walk Before You Can Crawl

Link jogs at a healthy pace as you manipulate the Control Stick in the desired direction. Press A to make him roll. When you reach small tunnels, press A to make the hero crawl. Press Z to make the camera swing behind him at any time.

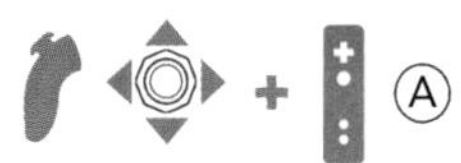

Know Your Limits

Link can walk on even ground and on certain slopes. On some steep slopes he can start up but will soon slide down. Other slopes are too steep for him to even try climbing.

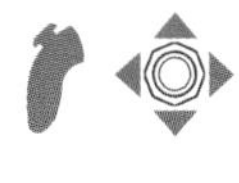

Step Up

Link can step onto short platforms and walls, and pull himself up onto taller objects. All you have to do is move the hero to the object. He'll stop for a moment when he reaches it, but if you continue pushing him in the same direction, he'll step up or climb.

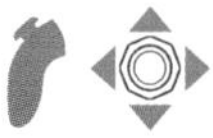

Take a Flying Leap

Link is capable of jumping over some gaps. Run him past the edge to make him jump automatically. If the gap is narrow enough, he'll land on his feet well past the edge on the other side.

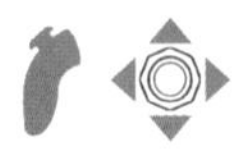

Jump and Grab

In some cases, the platform that you want Link to jump to is higher than the starting platform. If the gap between the platforms is narrow enough, Link will jump, grab the edge on the other side, and pull himself up.

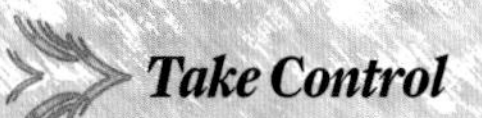

Wide Gap, Short Jump

If a gap is just wider than the distance Link can leap, he'll grab the ledge with one hand then pull himself up.

Leap Left, Leap Right

When your enemies attack, it pays to be able to get out of the way. A sidestepping jump keeps your foes guessing. Press and hold Z, hold left or right on the Control Stick, then press A on the remote.

Flip Out

A backflip works similarly to Link's sidestepping jump. Hold Z to correct the camera, hold down on the Control Stick, then press A. You'll watch Link fly back, flip, and land on his feet.

Come in for a Landing

Link can jump off any ledge. If the drop is short, he'll land gracefully. If it's long and he lands square on his feet, Link will take a little damage.

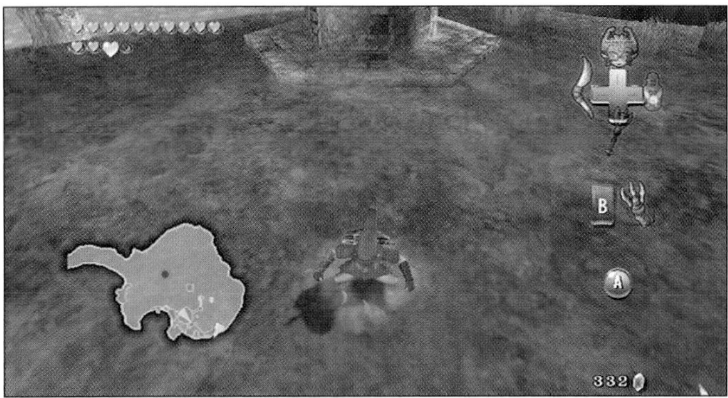

Jump, Tuck, and Roll

By rolling after a long drop, Link can avoid a hard landing. Press away from the ledge with the Control Stick to have Link continue to move forward mid-drop. The hero will absorb the impact with a smooth maneuver.

Push Up and Out

Climbing out of a pool or a patch of quicksand is similar to climbing onto an object. Guide Link to the edge of the pool and keep pushing to have him climb up to dry land.

Wall-Crawl

Some vertical surfaces, such as vine-covered walls and nets, are scalable. Push toward the wall to start climbing. If the scalable surface is out of Link's reach (as in the illustration), he won't climb.

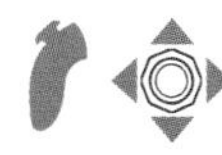

Hang in There

If you walk slowly off a ledge, Link will drop, then grab onto the ledge. A solid wall below will give him footholds; without a wall, he'll dangle. Press left or right to have Link move along the ledge.

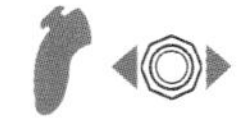

The All-Around Action Button

When a situation calls for a special type of interaction, the A Button is usually your answer. Most of the time, when a simple button press is required an A Button prompt will appear. In other situations, you'll use the Control Stick in combination with the A Button to pull off a more complex move.

Ⓐ

Press A

Walk up to a small object and press A to pick it up. Press A again to set it down. Run, then press A to throw the object. If an item is too large to carry but you can still push it, press A to hold onto it, then push with the Control Stick. The A Button also allows you to open doors, crawl into small spaces, talk to characters, open chests, and read signs.

An Introduction to Sword Fighting

The real strength of Wii control is motion sensitivity. Most of Link's fighting moves take advantage of that feature. While Link is swinging, spinning, and pulling off special techniques, you'll be participating with similarly active maneuvers.

Slice

Think of the remote as the hilt of Link's sword. Move it left and right or up and down with a slicing motion. (Alternatively, you can Z-target and swing to do vertical slices.) The hero will respond with his own sword swipes. If he doesn't have his sword drawn when you start swinging, he'll draw it automatically.

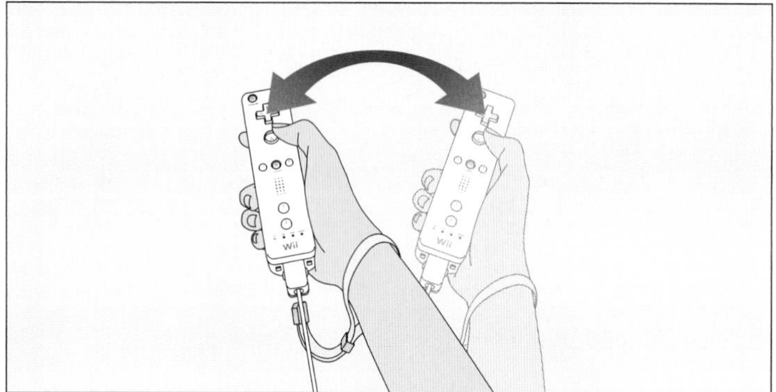

Spin Attack

Link's spin attack is a full-body move. Shake the nunchuk quickly left and right. The hero will turn 360 degrees in a split second, his sword hitting every target within range. After the move, a spark will travel from the sword base to tip, indicating Link is ready to swing again.

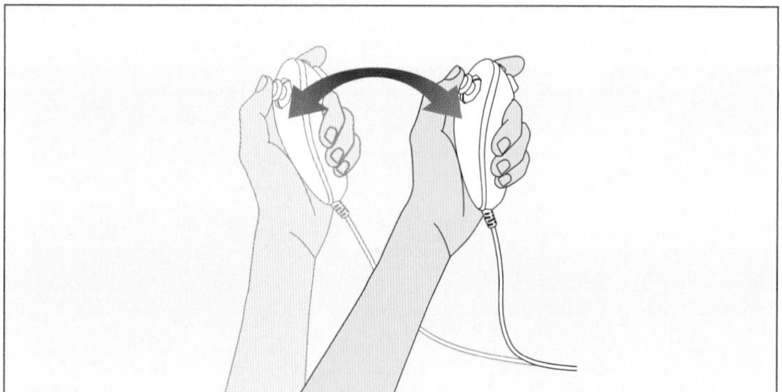

Jump Attack

Leaping forward then using all his weight to bring the sword down, Link is capable of dealing a lot of damage with his jump attack. Press and hold Z to target the closest enemy, then press A to leap and attack. The move is about four times the strength of a standard slice.

Stab

Link can surprise his enemies with a powerful stabbing move. Press and hold Z to home in on your target, hold up on the Control Stick, then slice with the remote. The hero will respond by making a thrusting motion.

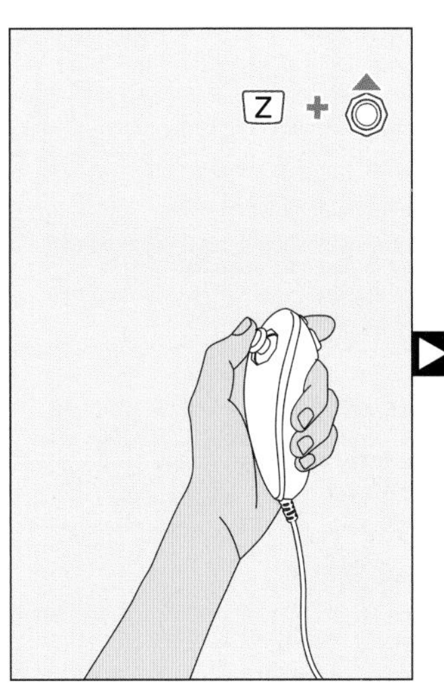

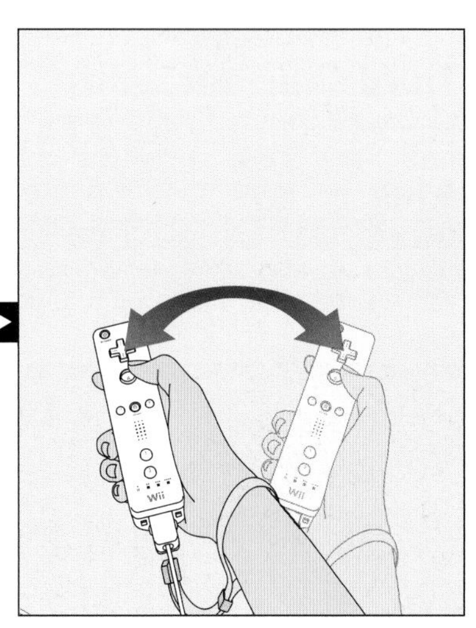

On-the-Job Training

You can discover seven hidden skills over the course of your adventure by visiting Howling Stones (in your canine form), then locating a golden wolf in your human form. The wolf will turn into a soldier then teach you a new move. You can go to the Howling Stones in any order, but you'll learn the moves in a strict progression.

First Skill: Ending Blow

The first hidden skill that you'll learn is a finishing move. After you've managed to stun your target with a few standard blows, target the beast on the ground by holding Z, then press A. Your enemy won't have a chance as Link leaps, then plants his sword.

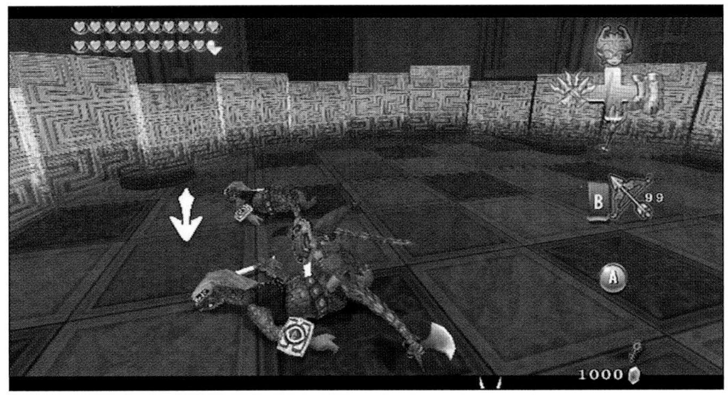

Second Skill: Shield Attack

The Shield Attack is useful for stunning enemies and knocking enemy projectiles back to their source. While Z-targeting an enemy, thrust the nunchuk forward; Link will lunge with his shield, striking the targeted foe and thus leaving it vulnerable to attack.

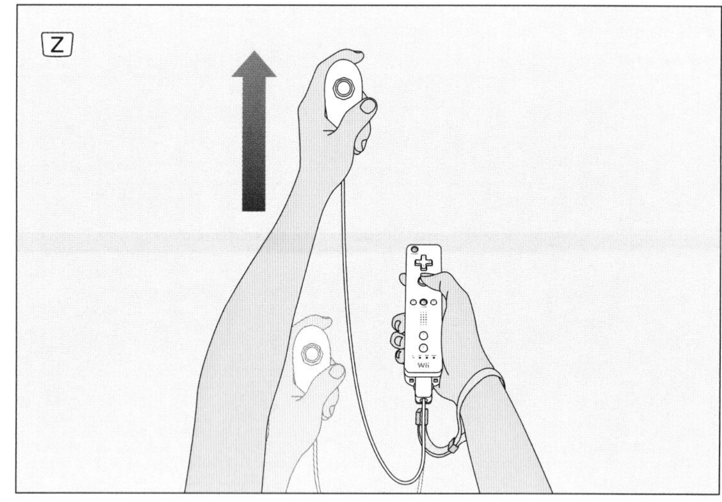

Third Skill: Back Slice

Some enemies are heavily armored in front; use the Back Slice to strike their vulnerable backsides. Target an enemy with the Z Button, then hold left or right on the Control Stick and hit A once to sidestep, then quickly hit A again to roll, and swing the remote to attack.

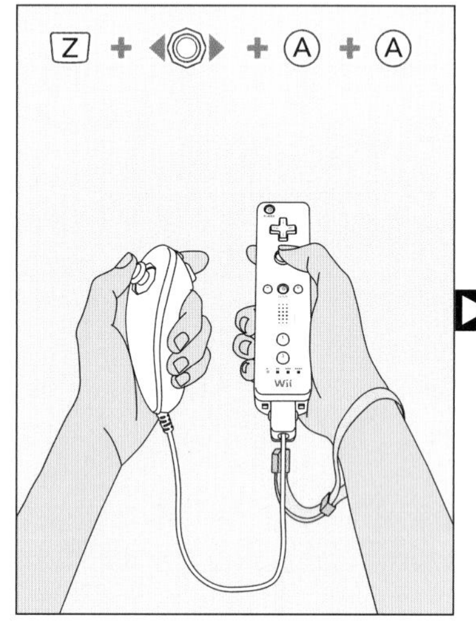

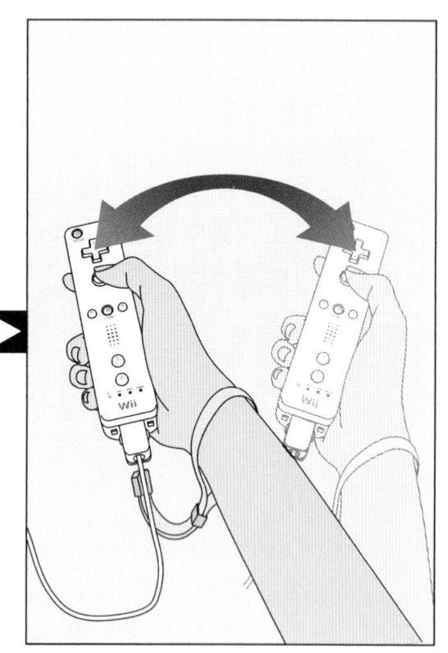

Fourth Skill: Helm Splitter

You'll need the Helm Splitter to pierce some enemies' defenses. First strike an enemy with the Shield Attack to stun it, then press the A Button to pounce over the enemy and strike it on the head. Follow up the Helm Splitter with additional attacks to maximize the effect.

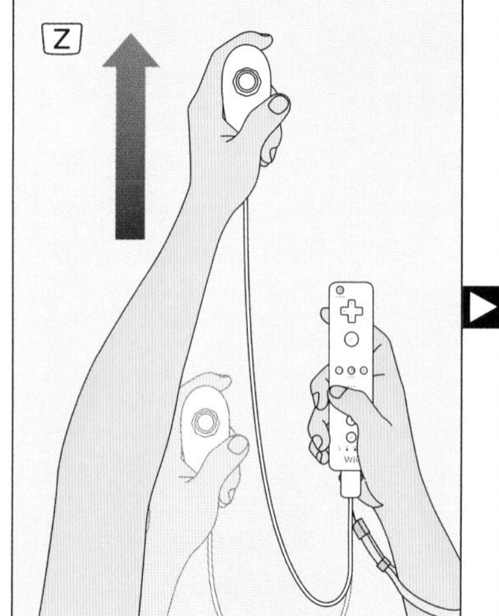

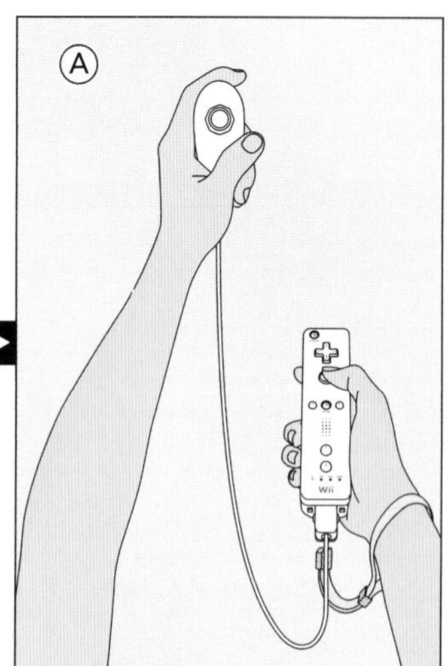

Fifth Skill: Mortal Draw

The Mortal Draw is easy to execute, but it can leave you vulnerable. To use this technique, sheath your sword and don't Z-target any enemies. As an enemy prepares to strike, hit A (you'll see an onscreen indicator) to draw your blade for a devastating surprise attack.

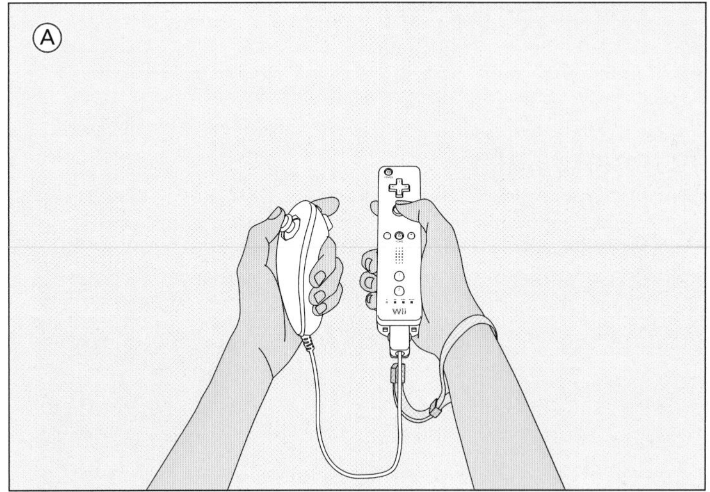

Sixth Skill: Jump Strike

The Jump Strike is an even better version of Link's excellent jumping attack. To activate the Jump Strike, Z-target an enemy then hold down the A Button until a glimmer goes up your blade. Release A to perform a spinning jump attack that takes out all nearby foes.

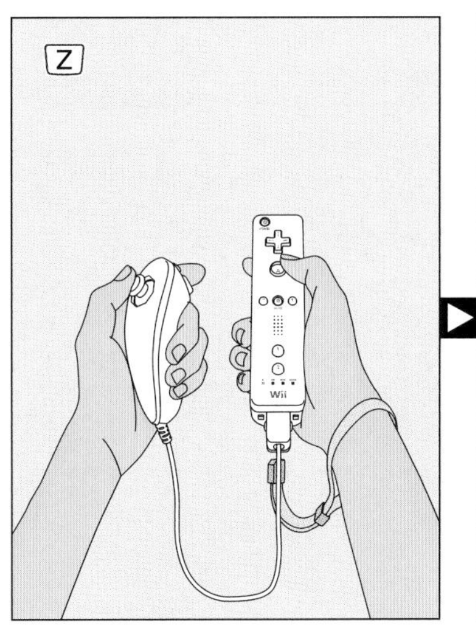

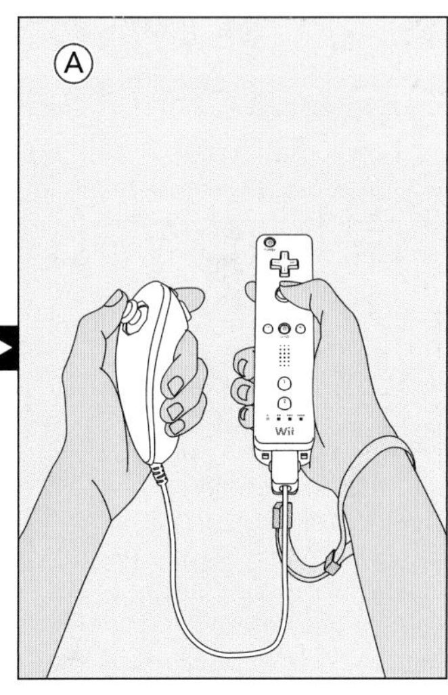

Final Skill: Great Spin

The last hidden skill, the Great Spin, is a variation on the regular spin attack; it's more powerful and possesses a much greater attack radius. However, you can use it only when your hearts are full. Execute the move by shaking the nunchuk back and forth while at full health.

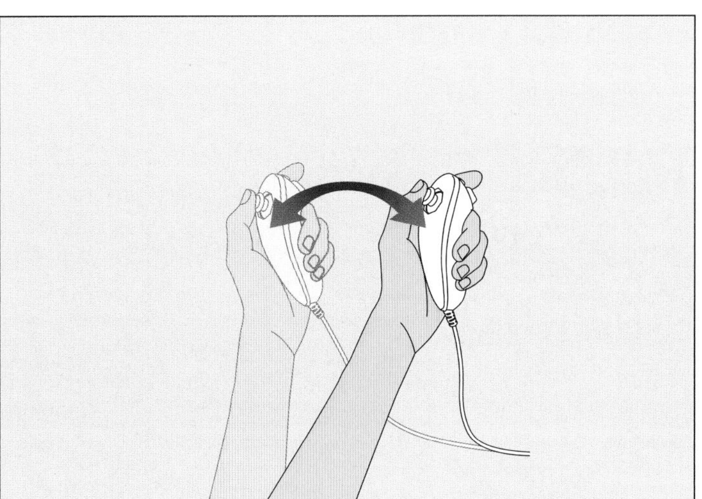

Targeting View

When you're using items like the slingshot, Hero's Bow, Gale Boomerang, and Clawshot, an over-the-shoulder perspective lets you aim your shots more accurately. (The fairy cursor can also help you aim.) This technique is useful for hitting distant enemies or objects.

Point and Click

After equipping an item that utilizes the targeting view, press and hold the B Button to wield the item. Point at the screen with the remote to aim the shot, and adjust your view with the Control Stick on the nunchuk. Release B to fire, or press A to return to normal view.

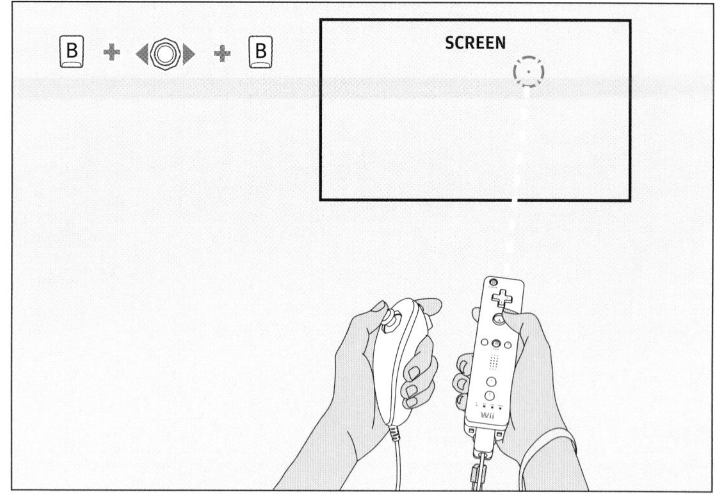

Riding Your Horse

Hyrule is a huge place, but it's a breeze to navigate thanks to your trusty steed, Epona. She'll get you where you want to go fast and can jump over obstacles. Like when you're on foot, you can attack with your sword by swinging the remote, do a spin attack by shaking the nunchuk, lock onto enemies by pressing Z, and use items by hitting B.

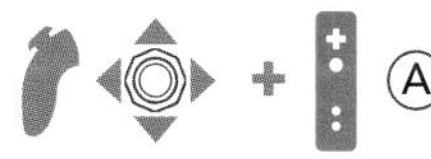

Giddy Up!

After mounting Epona with A, press the Control Stick up, left, or right to move in that direction, and dash by pressing A. To slow Epona down, hold down on the Control Stick then press A to dismount. You can also attack by swinging the remote to do a sword slash, shaking the nunchuk back and forth for a spin attack, and pressing B to use your items.

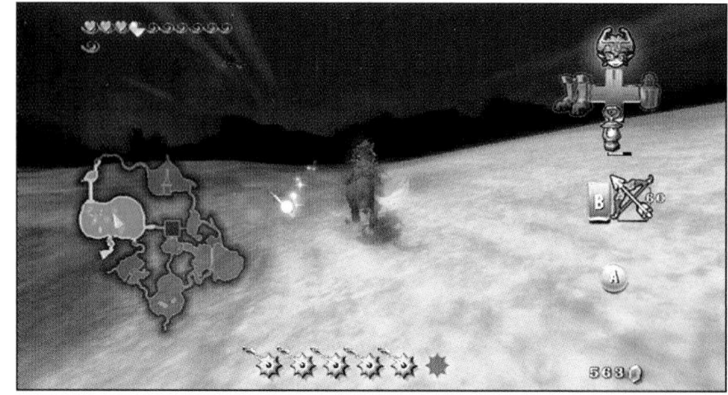

Bobber-Fishing

Link gets the bobber-equipped fishing rod early in the game. Its ability to catch fish is limited since you have to use it from the shore, but it's a great rod for beginners. While bobber-fishing, you can use bait such as bee larva to try to make a more desirable catch.

Sinking Feeling

Equip the fishing rod to B and press the button to cast. When you see the bobber submerge, pull the remote into an upright position. You'll get a message if the fish is biting. Continue to hold the remote up to land the fish. You can use bait by equipping both the rod and bait, and pressing the Control Pad direction that the bait's assigned to.

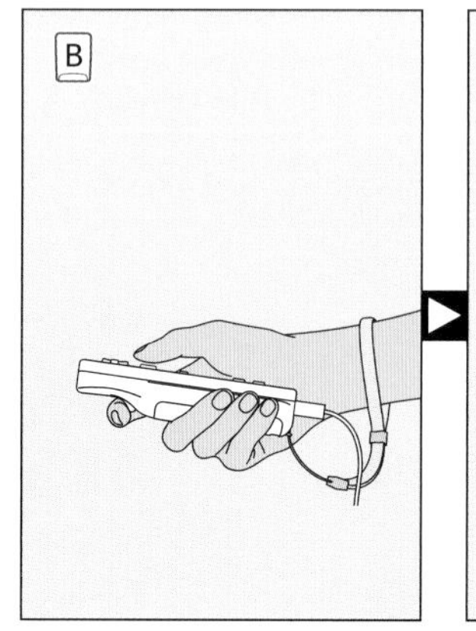

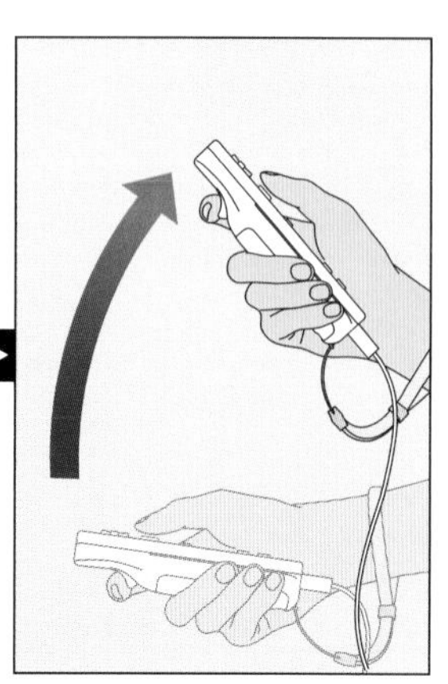

Lure-Fishing

After Link saves Lanayru Province, he'll have the opportunity to enjoy some relaxing lure-fishing at Hena's Fishing Hole. Lure-fishing is more complicated than bobber-fishing, and there are several lures to choose from.

Fish On!

Lure-fishing is performed from a boat. Use the Control Stick to move the boat, then when you've reached a good fishing spot, press B to ready your rod and use the Control Stick to aim. When you're facing the desired direction, hold A and raise the remote to an upright position, then snap the remote forward and release A to cast.

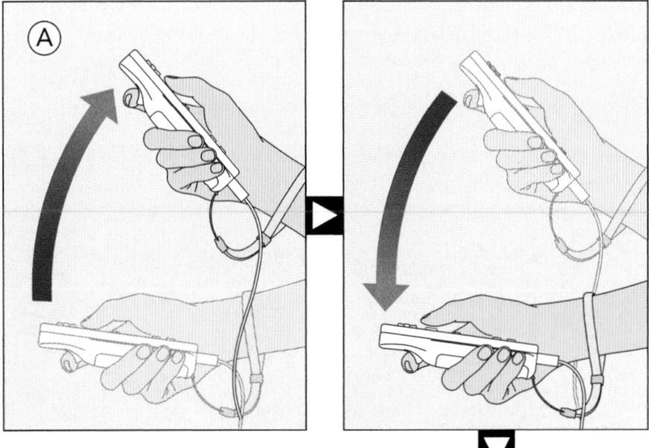

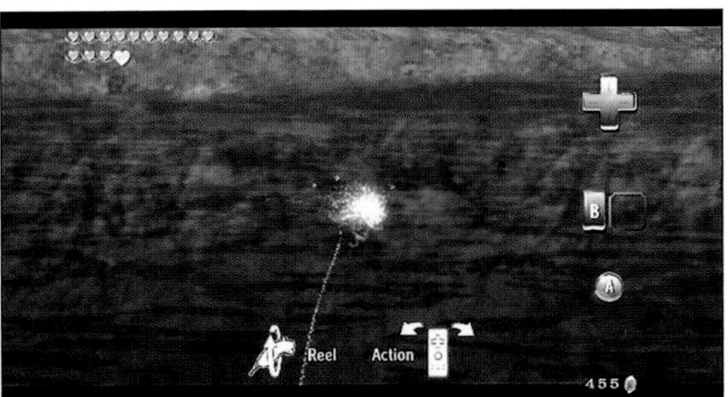

Once the line has been cast, attract fish by moving the remote from side to side. Before you cast, you can change lures to better attract different types of fish.

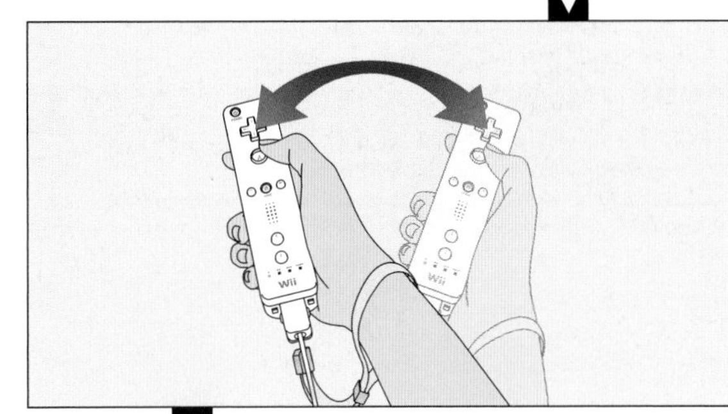

When you see a fish bite (look for the "set hook" signal at the bottom of the screen), quickly snap the remote into an upright position to hook the fish. Reel it in by holding the nunchuk sideways and making a circular reeling motion. If the fish jumps, lower the remote so it doesn't throw the hook, then raise it again when it returns to the water. When the fish nears the boat and you see the onscreen prompt, press A and B together to land your catch.

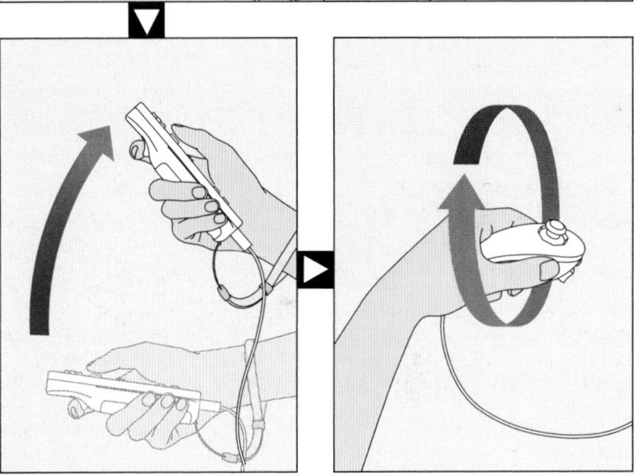

Basic Wolf Controls

When Link gets transformed into a wolf, he loses the ability to use his items, but controlling his movements remains largely the same. Later in the game, Link will be able to change from man to wolf at will and use whatever form best suits the situation.

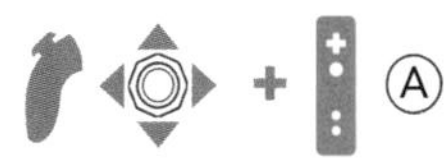

Walk on the Wild Side

Even though Link has changed forms, his movements are familiar: simply use the Control Stick to move Link in the desired direction. Press A while the wolf is running to make him dash. If you dash into a wall, you might knock something loose.

Four-Legged Climb

Link has the same climbing abilities in canine form as he has in human form. He can walk up slopes of a certain angle, but if an incline is too steep he'll slide backward. If a slope is so sheer that it is practically straight up and down, the wolf won't even attempt to climb.

Rope Trick

Having a low center of gravity, the wolf is able to balance on tightropes. As long as you guide him in a straight line, he'll walk the rope with ease.

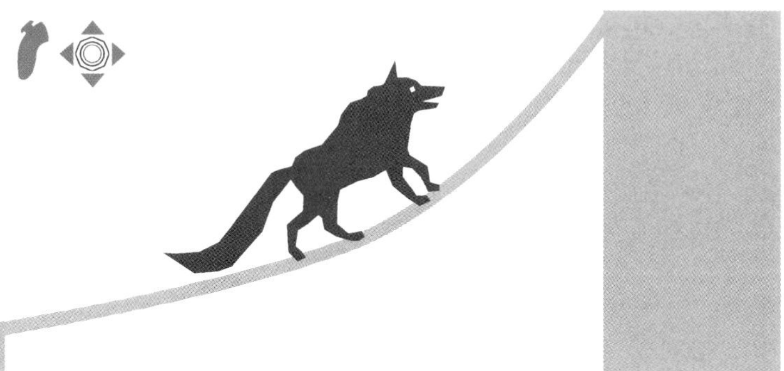

Over the Top

You may not want your real-life pet to climb on the furniture, but you'll be glad to know that Link's wolf form can climb onto any object that his human form can. Press forward with the Control Stick. The wolf will do the rest.

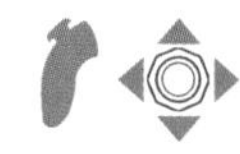

Clear the Gap

Like Link's human form, the wolf can jump over fairly wide gaps. Neither form is better at clearing a jump, but the wolf form is capable of landing more gracefully than the human form, without hanging over the edge.

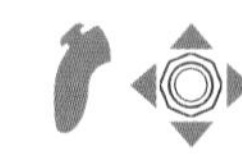

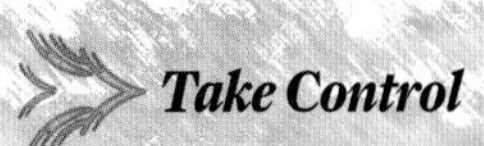

Jump and Skitter

When faced with a gap-spanning leap in which the second platform is higher than the first, the wolf will grab onto the ledge with his front paws then pull himself up.

Get out of the Pool

Like human-form Link, the wolf is capable of climbing out of pools and quicksand patches. Lead him to the edge then push him up onto solid ground.

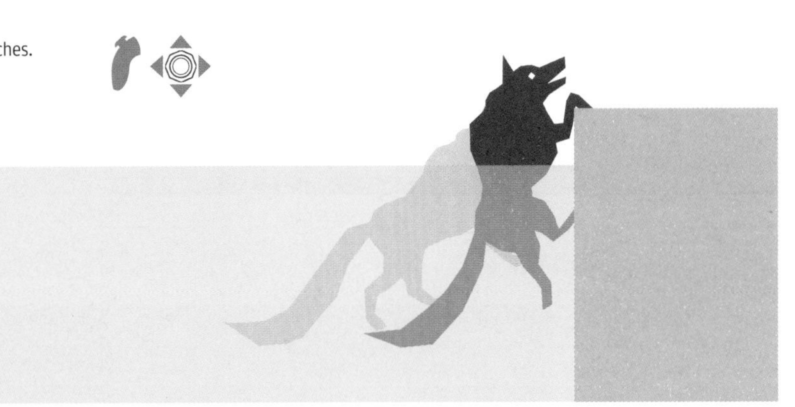

Talk to the Animals

The wolf Link can carry off several simple interactions with aid from the A Button, just like the human Link. They include talking to other animals—even ones that might normally be prey to a scary-looking wolf.

Press A

Press A to talk to critters, pick up small objects, and hold onto large objects. By manipulating the Control Stick, you can have the wolf push an object that he's holding onto. While you're running out in the open, you'll move just a little quicker with a short dash by tapping A.

Dig Up Hyrule

Wolf Link does another thing that you probably don't want your real-life pet to do. He digs. Press down on the Control Pad to have him scratch the surface. If you're using his canine senses to detect a prize in the dirt, you'll know exactly where to dig.

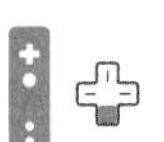

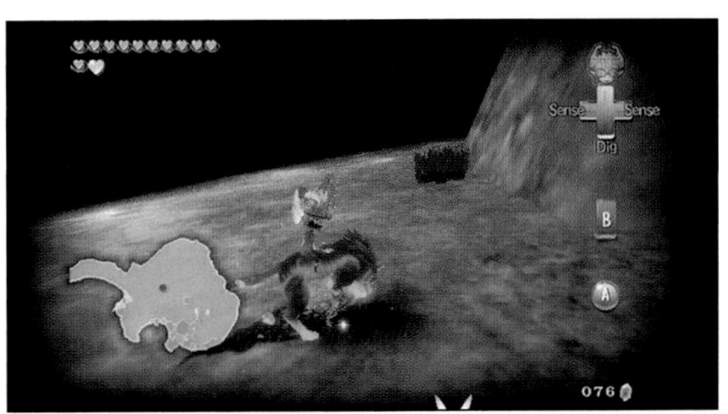

Dog Bites Monster

The basic attack moves for Link in wolf form mirror the moves Link makes in human form. There are wolf-equivalent attacks for the human's standard slash, spin attack, and jump attack.

Bite

You're one mean canine. Any enemy that gets in your way is going to have to deal with your fangs. Slash left and right with the remote as you would the sword to make the wolf lunge forward and bite hard.

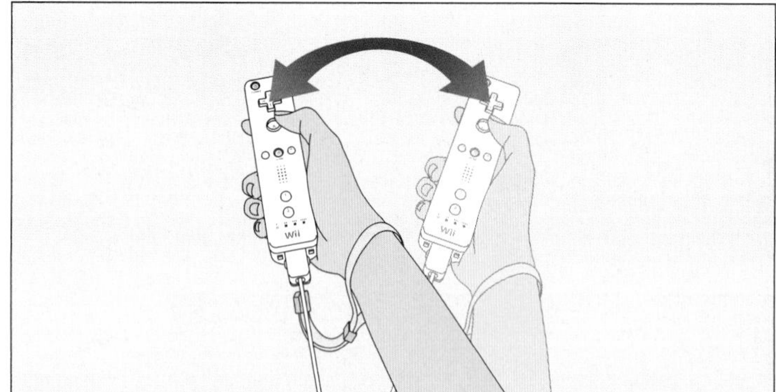

Spin Attack

The human Link spins with his sword to slash all enemies that surround him. The wolf hits the enemies with his body while he spins. Shake the nunchuk left and right to pull off the move. A sound from the remote indicates the spin attack is ready to use.

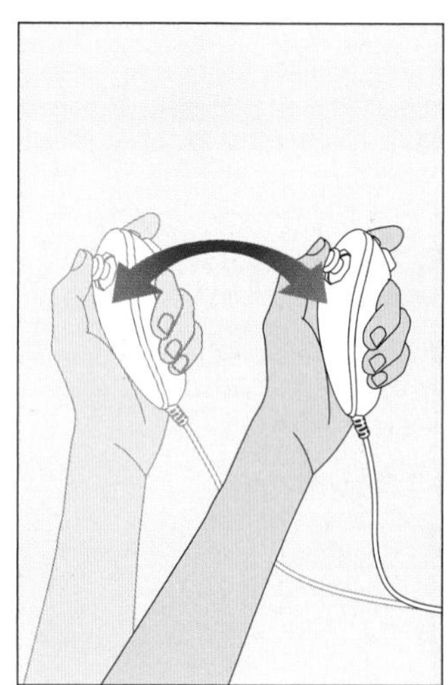

Jump Attack

Pouncing and going for the jugular is always a popular move with vicious beasts. Wolf Link leaps and bites after you Z-target an enemy then press A. In some situations the dog will hold onto the target, allowing you to press A repeatedly for a sustained attack.

Dealing with Dark Energy

Midna and canine Link work together on a special attack that is effective against shadow creatures. Press and hold B to create a dark energy force, targeting all enemies in the circle. When you release the button within the time limit, Link will attack every marked enemy in one move.

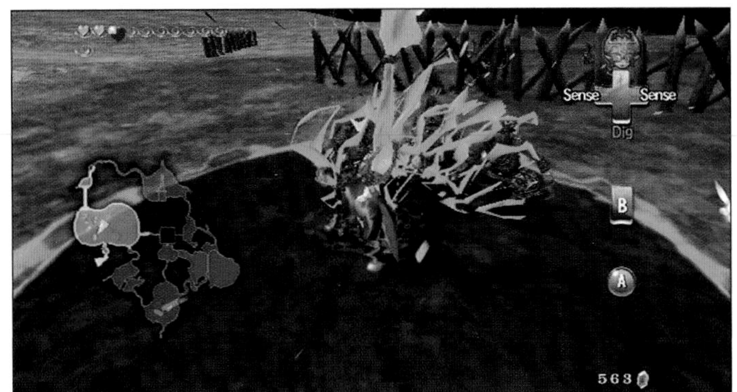

Animal Instincts

A heightened sense of smell and the ability to see in the dark allow canine Link to sense items, paths, and enemies that human Link cannot see. Press left or right on the Control Pad to initiate the wolf's senses.

See the Unseen

With senses engaged, your field of vision will be limited, but in the immediate area—where you can see your surroundings—you'll be able to detect buried items, Poes, and the scents of certain targets.

Giggle and Go

Midna is a mysterious creature with an odd sense of humor. When she laughs (by way of the remote's speaker), press up on the Control Pad to call to her. She'll offer advice or some other kind of help. Even if she doesn't laugh, she usually has something to say. She can also warp you to open portals.

Dial Long Distance

When you're standing at the edge of a wide gap and Midna gets your attention with a chuckle, press up on the Control Pad; she'll fly across the gap. Hold Z to target her and press A to leap to her. If she flies away, press A again to make another jump.

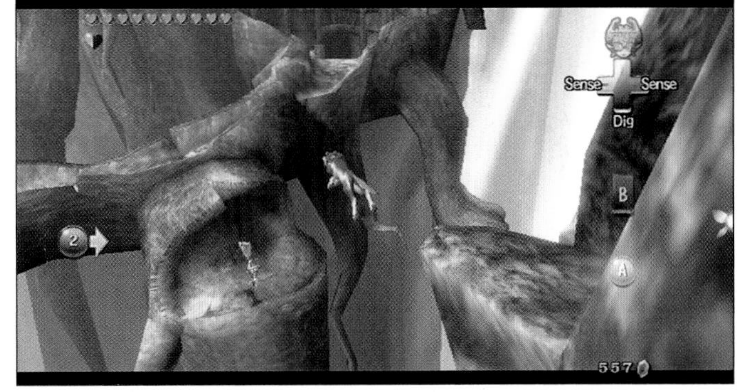

Beautiful Noise

Howling is another useful wolf activity. It figures in to your lessons in hidden skills. After you learn a song at a Howling Stone, you'll join in a duet with the golden wolf. (See page 160.)

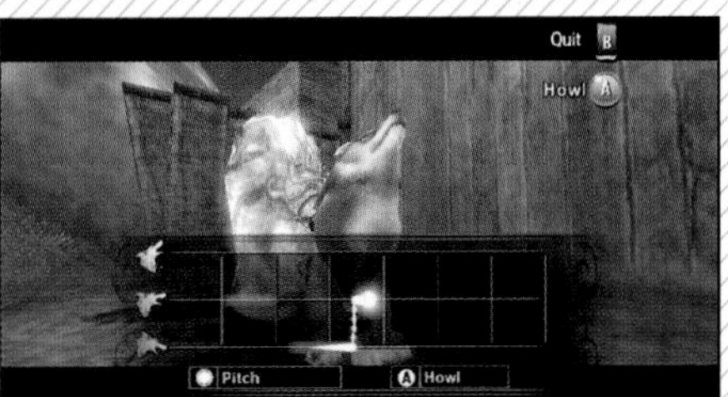

Tools of the Trade

You're never left empty-handed in a Legend of Zelda adventure. Here's what you'll find as you explore Hyrule.

Weapons and Tools

Lantern and Lantern Oil

A gift from Lantern Oil salesman Coro, the lantern lights dark places, burns barriers (such as spider webs), and even wards away a poisonous fog. Use it to light every torch you see. Torchlight can trigger special events. Lantern Oil keeps your lantern burning. Conserve it by putting your lantern away when it's not needed. Buy a bottle of oil from Coro.

Gale Boomerang

Found in the Forest Temple, the Gale Boomerang provides a twist on the classic Legend of Zelda boomerang. It creates mini tornadoes that spin turnstiles and carry items. You can target as many as five objects with a single boomerang toss.

Iron Boots

The Iron Boots cause you to move at a snail's pace. Luckily, you can take them off in an instant. When you're wearing the boots, you'll sink to the bottom of flooded areas and stick to magnetic surfaces, you can even walk on charged walls and ceilings.

The Versatile Adventurer

Many of your tools have multiple purposes. You can use them to get past barriers and dispatch enemies. The ball and chain, for example, demolishes ice walls and giant barrels, and it does a pretty good job of knocking enemies for a loop, too. The Spinner and Clawshot are transportation items primarily, but they sting foes on contact. Experiment with your tools—you may find new uses for them.

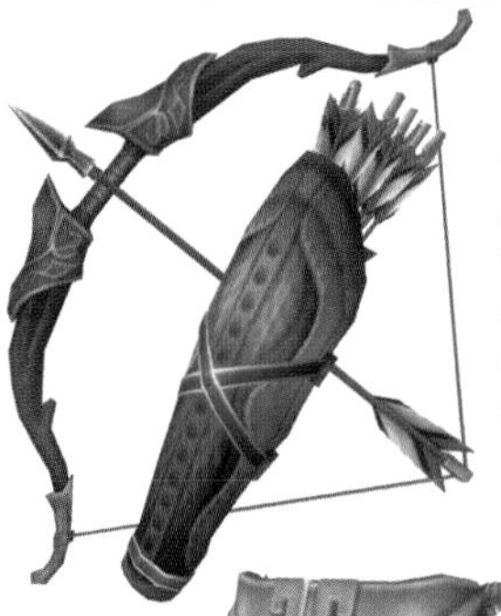

Hero's Bow

When you want to defeat enemies or slice ropes from a distance, the Hero's Bow is your item of choice. Using the Wii remote, your shots are always dead-on. The standard quiver that comes with the bow holds 30 arrows. Two replacement quivers hold 60 and 100 arrows. Combining arrows with bombs will give you explosive bomb arrows.

Hawkeye

Giving you the sharp vision of a bird of prey, the Hawkeye acts as a telescope when you use it by itself, and as a sniper's scope when you combine it with the bow.

Clawshot and Double Clawshots

Similar to the Hookshot, which dates back to A Link to the Past, the Clawshot sends out a claw and a chain then reels you in after it hooks onto certain objects, allowing you to cross wide gaps, climb tall structures, and retrieve objects. The Double Clawshots give you more grappling versatility, letting you use one Clawshot to dangle from a spot while you use the other one to grapple to another spot.

Spinner

A mix between a gear and a top, the Spinner allows you to float over dangerous surfaces (such as quicksand), ride on tracks, and activate certain mechanisms. It also packs a punch that will stun some enemies.

Ball and Chain

You'll walk slowly while lugging the ball and chain, but you'll also be able to punch through big obstacles and bigger enemies.

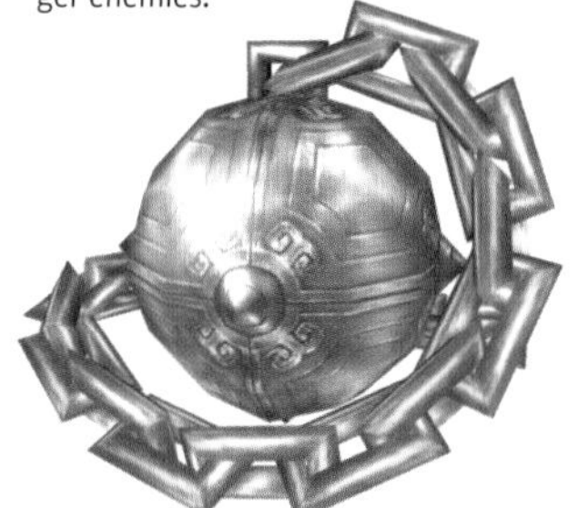

Dominion Rod

The Dominion Rod is built for just one purpose, but quite a purpose it is. With it, you can bring life to certain inanimate objects then have them follow your every move. It's a must-have item in the Temple of Time.

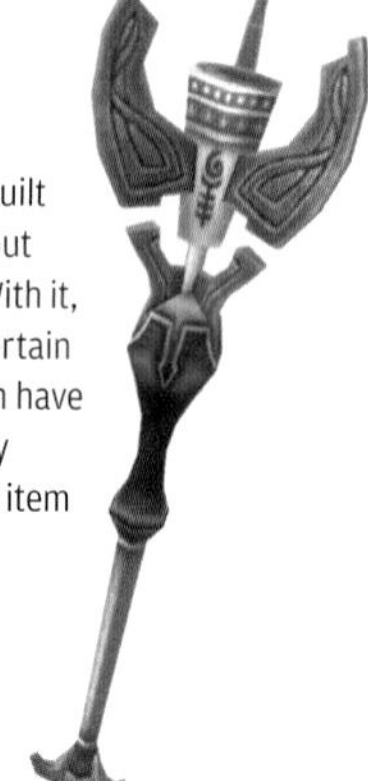

Bombs

Big explosives with short fuses are Legend of Zelda standbys. You can use them to create openings in cracked walls and floors, and destroy certain boulders. They're also useful for defeating several foes at once. Set them down, toss them, or send them flying with the Hero's Bow (in combination with arrows) or with the Gale Boomerang to make a strong impression on enemies and obstacles.

Bomb Bag

You can't carry bombs unless you have a Bomb Bag: one type of bomb per bag. The Giant Bomb Bag upgrade doubles the capacity of your Bomb Bags.

Water Bombs

The fuses of standard bombs don't burn underwater. In Zora's Domain and Kakariko Village, you'll collect bombs that work above and below the water's surface.

Bombling

You can throw any type of bomb, but only Bomblings can move on their own. Equipped with spiderlike legs, the bomblings skitter across surfaces, then explode.

Fishing Rod

Your Wii remote becomes a fishing rod. You'll catch fish to trigger events and add to your fish journal.

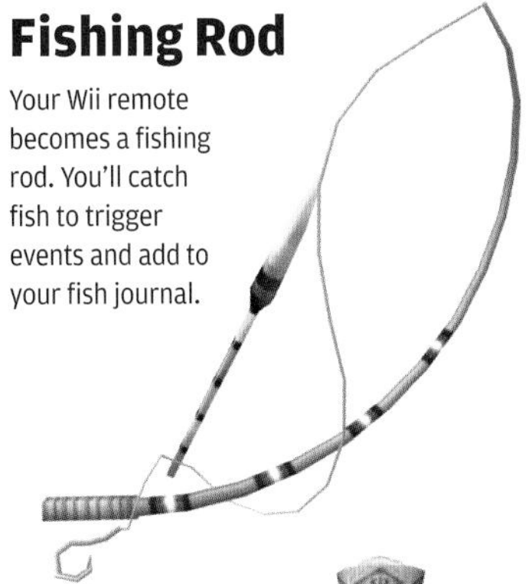

Bee Larva

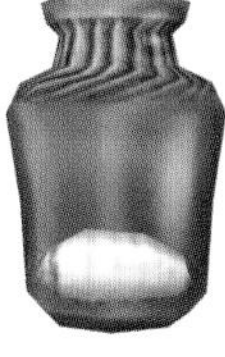

Knock a beehive to the ground so you can scoop up bee larva. Use it to replenish hearts and as fish bait.

Worm

Using your canine senses, you'll always know where to dig for items. You might just uncover a worm. Use it to catch fish.

Coral Earring

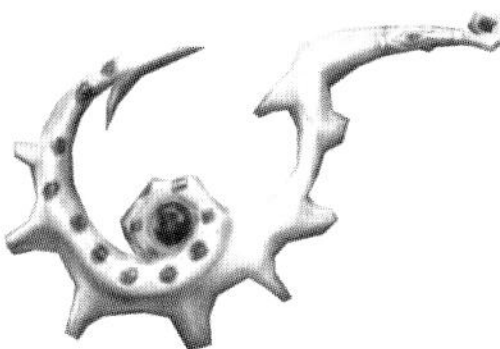

Prince Ralis of Zora's Domain wears an earring made of the type of coral that the red Reekfish nibble on. On your way to the Snowpeak Ruins, you'll collect the unusual piece of jewelry from the prince and use it to pluck one of the rouge beauties from the water.

Horse Call

For most of your adventure, you'll be able to call Epona only where a certain type of grass grows. After you help Ilia regain her memory, however, you'll earn a porcelain call that allows you to whistle for your steed from any outdoor location.

Rupees and Wallets

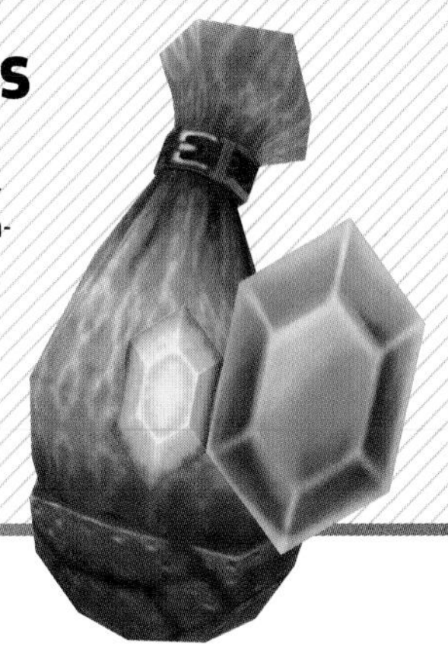

You can trade shiny rupees for goods and services in Zelda's kingdom. The jewels come in seven denominations, each a different color. At the start of your adventure, you'll be able to hold as many as 300 rupees in your regular-sized wallet. Two wallet upgrades—the Big Wallet and the Giant Wallet—will let you hold 600 then 1,000 rupees at a time.

Health Items

Heart Containers and Pieces of Heart

A line of hearts at the top of the screen represents your health. The more full hearts you have, the healthier you are. The line is three hearts strong at the beginning of the adventure, and will increase by one with every Heart Container you collect. You'll earn full containers for victories over dungeon bosses, and collect Pieces of Heart that are scattered all over the kingdom. Five pieces make a full heart.

Fairies

Scoop up a fairy with an empty bottle and keep it in your inventory. If you are damaged to the point where all of your hearts are empty, the fairy will pop out of the bottle and replenish your energy. If you don't want to wait until the last moment, you can uncork the bottle to release the fairy at any time.

Chu Jellies

Chu Jellies have the same effect as potions of corresponding colors. A Red Chu Jelly, for example, replenishes health, just as a Red Potion would. The two exceptions to the rule are Purple Chu Jellies (a random effect) and Rare Chu Jellies (full health and temporarily increased attack power). Additionally, Yellow Chu Jelly can be substituted for Lantern Oil to fuel your lantern.

Fairy Tears

You can receive Fairy Tears as a gift from Jovani and find them in springs after your Cave of Ordeals adventure. Fairy Tears fill your hearts and increase your attack power temporarily.

Dungeon Items

Keys

Locks and keys are the bread and butter of Legend of Zelda adventures. The most common keys are the Small Keys found in dungeons. You can use a Small Key from a given dungeon in any of that dungeon's Small Key locks. Additionally, every dungeon has a Big Key that unlocks the boss room. (In Snowpeak Ruins, however, it's called the Bedroom Key.) You'll also find keys outside dungeons, and each key is for a specific lock.

Map and Compass

Every dungeon holds a map and a compass. The map shows you the full dungeon layout, displaying already-explored rooms with a green hue. The compass reveals the locations of the boss room, treasure chests, and items related to mission objectives.

Ooccoo and Ooccoo Jr.

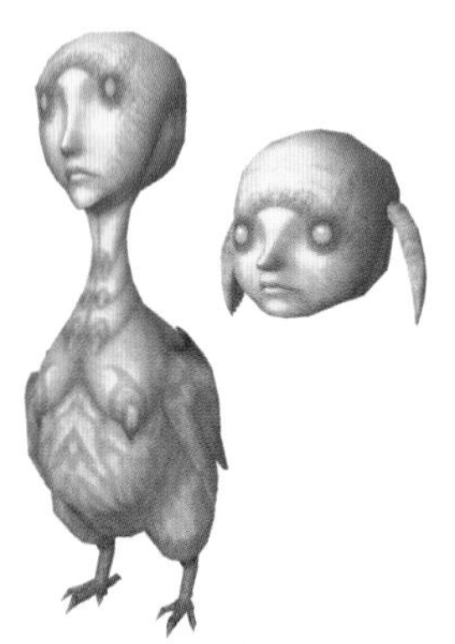

The Strange sky being Ooccoo wanders around the kingdom's dungeons. Once you find her, use her to warp to the dungeon exit. You'll get Ooccoo Jr. in the bargain. When you're ready to return to the place where you warped from, use Junior. He'll bring you to his mother.

Documents

Letters

The postman pops up often, especially when you are between missions. He delivers letters that let you know about events around Hyrule. Sometimes they point you to new missions. Sometimes they inform you about new items available in shops.

Auru's Memo

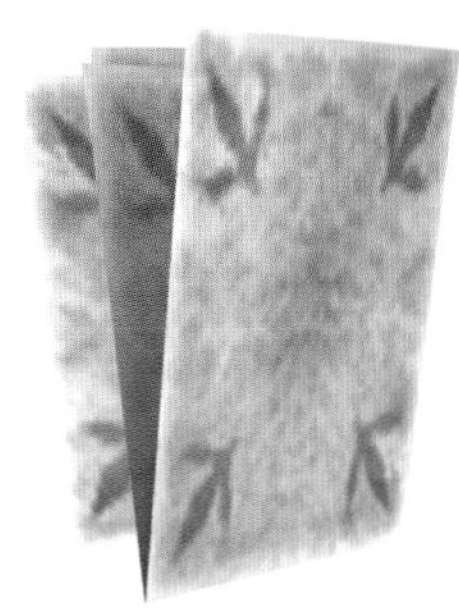

You can use the document that you receive from adventurer Auru to convince cannon operator Fyer to offer you a new destination in the eastern desert.

Ashei's Sketch

Part of the quest that leads you to Snowpeak Ruins, Ashei's sketch depicts a yeti holding a Reekfish. After you show the sketch to Prince Ralis, he'll give you the Coral Earring, which you'll use to catch a Reekfish of your own.

Renado's Letter

Renado's letter is one piece of the puzzle that leads you to reviving Ilia's memory.

Invoice

Telma will give you another piece in the puzzle relating to Ilia's memory.

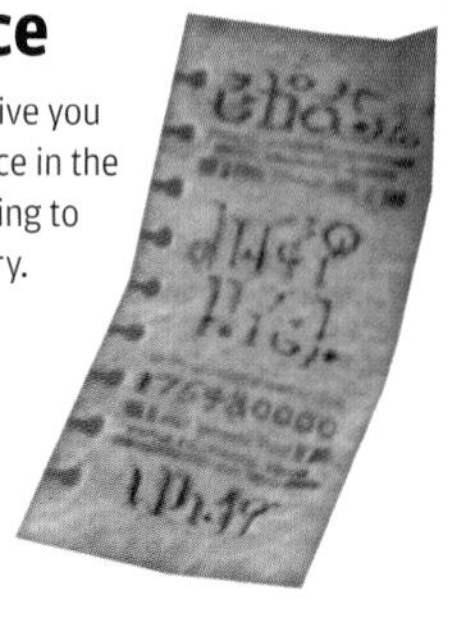

Keep Track of Puzzle Pieces

Monkeys rule the Forest Temple. You'll find them all over the place and free them from wooden cages. After you find all of them, you'll gain access to the boss room. Other dungeons are populated with similar special characters or items. Snowpeak Ruins has cannonballs, for example, and the Temple of Time has a large statue that you will guide to its final destination. Ooccoo and items that are specific to the mission appear on the map after you collect the compass.

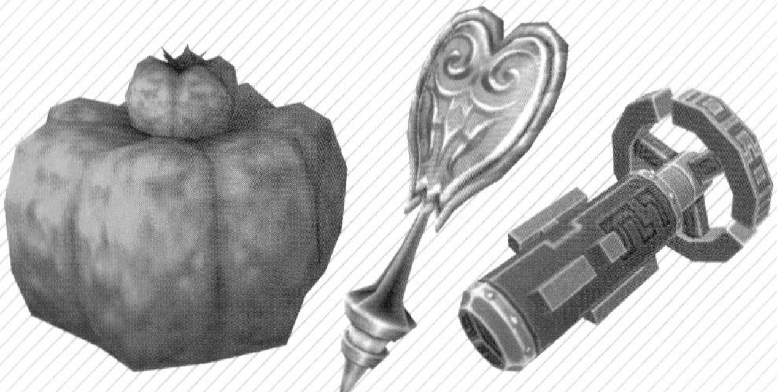

Equipment

Wooden Sword

The first sword that you will receive is a gift from Ordon craftsman Rusl. You'll use it for training and on a short mission to save one of the village children and a monkey from forest creatures. You'll pass it on to the youngster before the real adventure begins.

Ordon Sword

Meant to be a gift from Ordon to Hyrule, the Ordon Sword is a good, sturdy weapon that will help you get through more than a few scrapes. It'll be your go-to blade for your journey through the first three dungeons.

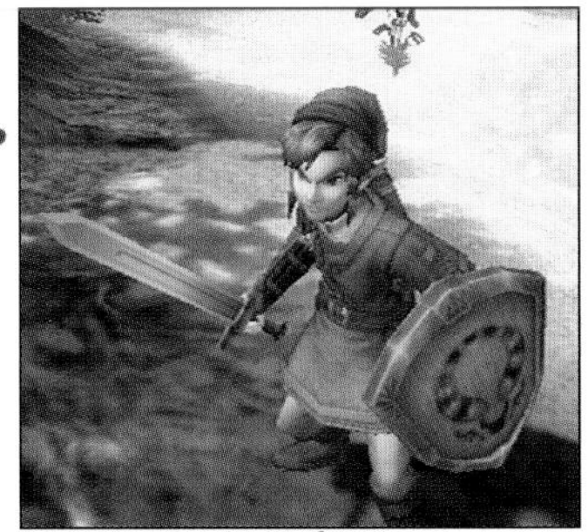

Master Sword

A legendary weapon blessed by the spirits of Hyrule, the Master Sword will be yours after you venture into the Sacred Grove. Not only will it give you the strength to overcome your enemies, but it will act as a key to enter the Temple of Time.

Light Sword

A Master Sword upgrade comes your way after you liberate two Sols from the Palace of Twilight. It is more powerful than the original version of the sword and capable of burning away a fog made from Shadow Crystals. It glows brightly in the twilight realm.

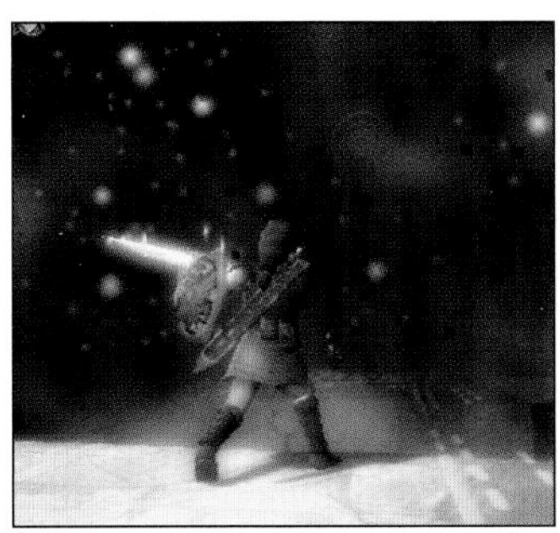

Ordon Shield

While doing a favor for Midna, you'll take the Ordon Shield from Jaggle's home in your canine form. The shield provides good protection against enemy attacks, but will burn up if hit by fiery projectiles.

Wooden Shield

Possessing the same protective (and flammable) qualities as the Ordon Shield, the Wooden Shield replaces your first shield after it goes up in flames.

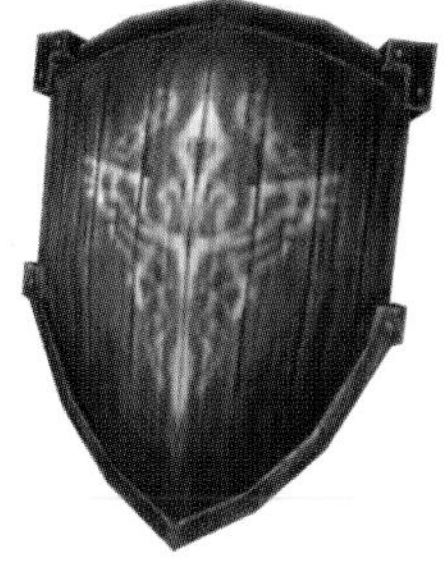

Hylian Shield

More expensive than the Wooden Shield but well worth the price, the Hylian Shield is the last one you'll need. It provides strong protection against enemy attacks and is fireproof.

Hero's Clothes

The signature green costume of the legendary adventurer and a gift from the spirit of Faron, the Hero's Clothes identify you as Link, hero of Hyrule.

Zora Armor

Part armor, part scuba gear, a gift from the Zora queen allows you to swim freely and breathe underwater. It's mandatory equipment for your mission in the Lakebed Temple.

Magic Armor

The Magic Armor will make you invincible as long as you have rupees (which deplete as you wear the armor). When you're out of rupees it is heavier than the Hero's Clothes, so the item (which you can purchase at Malo Mart's Castle Town branch) will make you move much slower than normal.

Bottles

Empty Bottle

Sure, the adventurer needs swords, shields, bows, and arrows, but there's also no denying the value of a good container. Most bottles that you acquire will contain something initially. Once you use the contents, though, you'll be able to scoop up other items with the bottle.

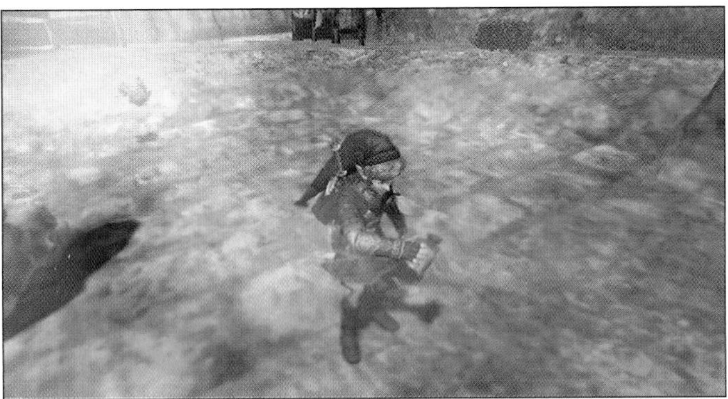

Milk

You can hold two milk portions per bottle. A single portion of milk replenishes three hearts. The first bottle you get (from Sera in Ordon Village) will be half full of milk.

Red Potion

The standard healing potion of Hyrule replenishes eight hearts. Unlike a fairy in a bottle, though, you'll have to use a Red Potion before you lose all of your energy. A warning sound indicates when you are low on energy.

Blue Potion

An all-around great potion to take into challenging situations late in your adventure, the Blue Potion replenishes all of your hearts.

Water / Hot Springwater

Can't wait for the Ordon pumpkins to grow naturally? Scoop up some water and pour it on a little gourd. The plant will grow to picking size instantly. Water from the hot springs of Death Mountain has healing powers, but only if you drink it within a few minutes of collecting it.

Nasty Soup

The broth in Coro's pot will affect your health, sometimes regenerating it just a little, sometimes causing damage. If you're feeling brave, scoop up and slurp down a bottle of the stuff.

Yeto's Soups

While you're working your way through the Snowpeak Ruins, you'll cross paths with the male yeti, Yeto, several times and add ingredients to his pot. Before you contribute to the cooking, his Simple Soup will regenerate two hearts. Add a pumpkin to make it Good Soup then slurp it to regain four hearts. After you add goat cheese, the concoction will become Superb Soup, which will regenerate eight hearts.

Quest Items

Fused Shadows

The objects that you'll go after in the adventure's first three dungeons are of special importance to Midna. They'll assist her in helping you fight the forces of evil.

Shadow Crystal

Midna will use the Shadow Crystal to transform you between your canine and human forms. If you try to transform within view of bystanders, she'll tell you to go where no one can see you.

Mirror Shards

The pieces of the Mirror of Light are crucial to restoring the kingdom and vanquishing the creatures of the darkness. You'll discover them in four special places.

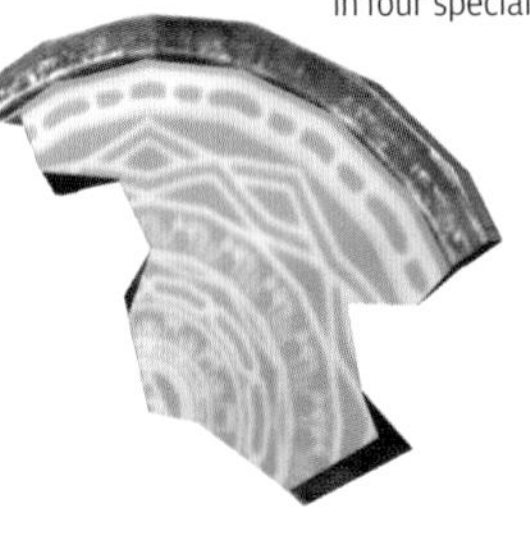

Wooden Figure

While you attempt to jog Ilia's memory, you'll trade for a series of meaningful items. Among them is a wooden figure.

Ilia's Charm

Along with the wooden figure, the invoice, and Renado's letter, Ilia's charm is part of the series of items that you will barter for while working to revive Ilia's memory.

Collections

You'll reap great rewards and make two Castle Town residents happy by maintaining item collections.

Bugs

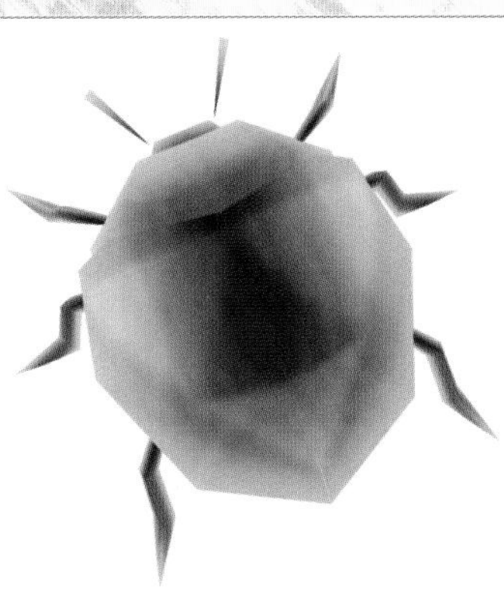

The Queen of the Bugs

Though she might be delusional, Agitha will help you finance your adventure by providing you with wallet upgrades. All you have to do for her is collect 24 Golden Bugs. You'll find Agitha's castle on the Castle Town south road, southeast of the central square. Bring her one bug and she'll give you the Big Wallet. Bring her all 24 to get the Giant Wallet.

Bug Hunt

There are 24 bugs in all; that's male-female pairs of beetles, butterflies, stag beetles, grasshoppers, phasmids, pill bugs, mantises, ladybugs, snails, dragonflies, ants, and dayflies. If you see a glint of gold, chase after it. Once you grab the bug, it will appear in your Golden Bug collection.

Complete the Set

Agitha will give you a rupee reward for every bug that you pass along to her. The first bug in every pair is worth 50 rupees. The second is worth 100 rupees. It's good that Agitha also gives you bigger wallets, because you'll need them to hold all of that cash.

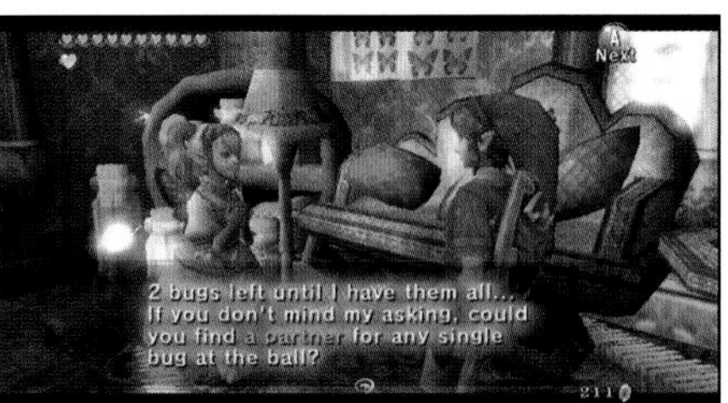

Poes

A Man without a Soul

As you venture through Telma's Bar to the Hyrule Castle sewer in your canine form, you'll happen across the shell of a man, Jovani. He has lost his soul to greed. Bring him 20 Poe Souls. He'll reward you with a bottle full of Fairy Tears. Later he'll ask you to bring him 60 Poe Souls.

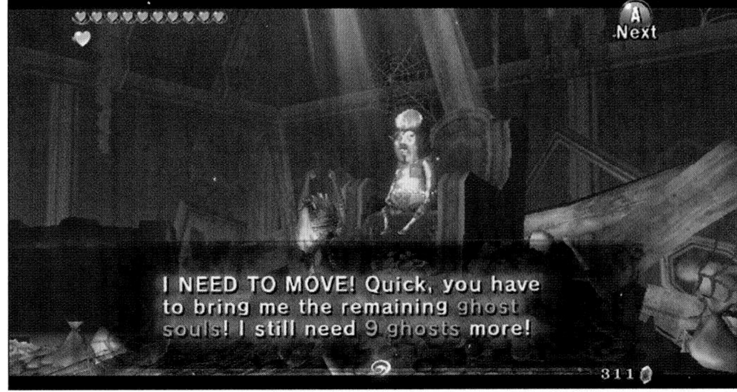

Ghost Hunter

When you see a floating lantern, use your canine sense to reveal a Poe. Attack the ghost, then remove its soul after you've knocked it to the ground.

Using the Guide

Driving back the darkness is no easy task. Before setting out, prepare yourself with Player's Guide basics.

Walkthrough
The step-by-step walkthrough describes where to go and what to do. The numbered paragraphs correspond to numbered locations on the map.

Boss Strategy
Each dungeon is punctuated by a dramatic boss battle. Use the tactics in these boxes to finish off Link's toughest foes.

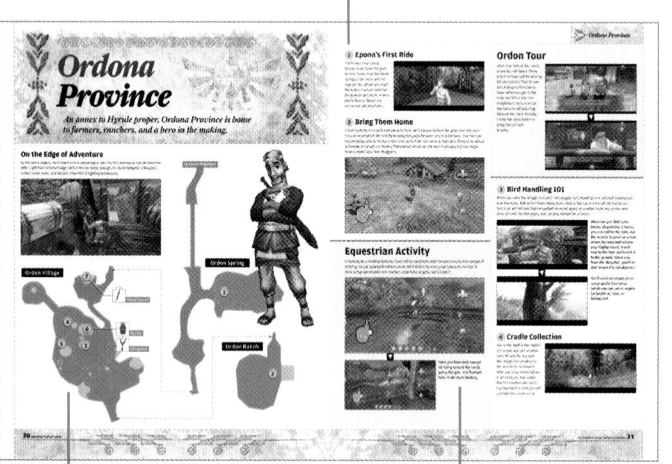

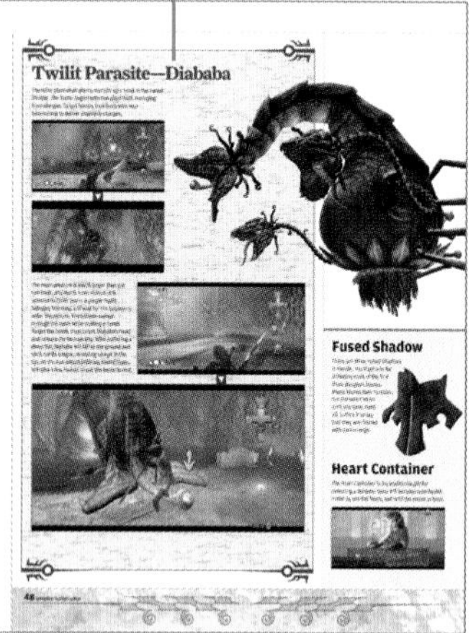

Maps
Maps show you the layout of each region and dungeon, including locations of significant items. The numbers correspond to walkthrough tips.

Special Tips
Tips in shaded boxes focus on a variety of useful subjects, such as mastering new moves, fighting certain foes, and obtaining optional items.

Items
Link will find many weapons and items throughout his quest. Entries like this describe how each important item is used.

Make the Most of the Maps

To get the most from the maps, turn to the back page of this book for a complete key to the icons that appear throughout the walkthrough. In addition, this guide includes specialized maps that identify the locations of all the Pieces of Heart (p. 144), Poe Souls (p. 153), Golden Bugs (p. 156), and Howling Stones (p. 160). If you need guidance for the GameCube version of Twilight Princess, consult the complete game maps starting on p. 170. The GameCube maps are mirror images of the Wii maps, so if you're using the walkthrough for the GameCube version east and west will be reversed.

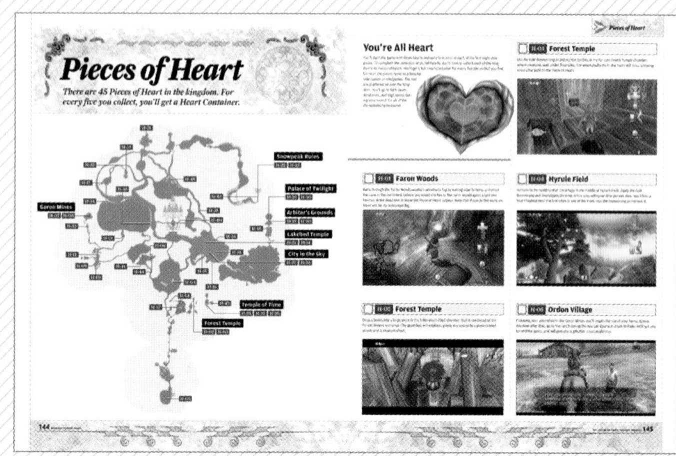

Forest
Temple

Ordona Province

An annex to Hyrule proper, Ordona Province is home to farmers, ranchers, and a hero in the making.

On the Edge of Adventure

As the story begins, ranch hand Link is preparing to take his first journey to Hyrule Castle to offer a gift from Ordon Village. Before he can leave, though, he must complete a few jobs, collect some items, and master a handful of fighting techniques.

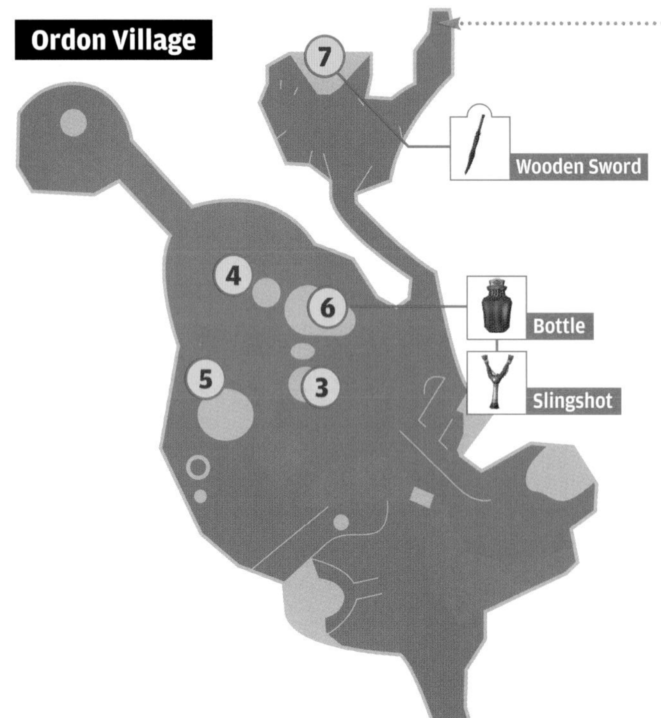

1 Epona's First Ride

You'll need your steed, Epona, to aid Fado the goat herder. Epona is at the forest spring to the north with village girl Ilia. When you reach the water, pluck a reed from the ground and use it to whistle for Epona. Mount the horse and ride into town.

2 Bring Them Home

Travel south to the ranch and speak to Fado. He'll ask you to herd the goats into the barn. You can accomplish the task by keeping the goats between you and the barn. Start by making sweeping runs at the far end of the ranch, then narrow in on the barn. (Press A to whoop and make the goats run faster.) The animals will enter the barn in groups, but you might have to round up a few stragglers.

Equestrian Activity

Following your herding exercise, Fado will set up fences and introduce you to the concept of dashing. As you approach a fence, press the A Button to encourage Epona to run fast. If she's at top speed when she reaches a low fence or gate, she'll jump it.

Once you have had enough of riding around the ranch, jump the gate. You'll return later to do more herding.

Ordon Tour

After your time at the ranch, a new day will dawn. Three kids from town will be waiting for you outside. They'll mention a slingshot for sale in town. When you get to the shop, you'll find that the shopkeeper, Sera, is not in the mood to sell anything because her cat is missing. Follow the steps below to bring the cat back to Sera.

3 Bird Handling 101

When you enter the village, you can't miss Jaggle. He's standing on a tall bluff, looking out over the water. Talk to him from below then climb to the top of the bluff. He'll point out Sera's cat and tell you that he spotted some tall grass on another bluff. Hop to the next piece of land, pick the grass, and use it to whistle for a falcon.

Wherever you find grass blades shaped like a falcon, you can call for the bird. Use the remote to point at a hive across the way and release your flighty friend. It will soar to the hive and knock it to the ground. (Once you have the slingshot, you'll be able to use it to hit objects.)

You'll need an empty jar to scoop up the bee larva, which you can use to replenish health or, later, as fishing bait.

4 Cradle Collection

Hop to the bluff in the middle of the lake and pick another reed. Whistle for the bird then target the monkey on the rock in the northwest. After you let go of the falcon, it will bring you the cradle that the monkey was carrying. Hop back to solid ground and take the cradle to Uli.

5 Gone Fishing

Uli will give you a fishing rod as a reward for returning her cradle. Cross the midvillage bridge and walk to the dock on the far side of the mill. You'll see Sera's cat nearby. Drop a line and catch a couple of fish. The cat will steal the second one and take it to Sera's shop.

Press the B Button to initiate a cast. Flick the remote forward (as if you were actually casting with a fishing rod) to send the line out. The bobber will float to the surface, then sink to indicate that you have a bite.

Once the bobber's top red line is submerged, pull up with the remote and hold it steady. A message will tell you that a fish is hooked. You'll claim your prize in a matter of seconds. Later on, you'll use a lure rod for more-advanced fishing.

6 Shop for the Slingshot

With Sera's cat back where it belongs, return to the shop. Sera will give you a bottle of milk and offer to sell you any of three items. Purchase the slingshot for 30 rupees.

The Bottle

Sera's gift to you is a bottle half full of milk. While the milk is good to have, the bottle itself is an even better prize. You can use it to scoop up anything from Chu Jelly to fairies. In total, there are four bottles to find.

Cash and Carry

Rupees make the world go 'round. You'll need them throughout your adventure to pay for goods and services. The crystals come in seven colors, each representing a different denomination. The slingshot will cost you 30 rupees.

Rupees are often hidden in tall grass. You can find them by running through the fields or, when you have a sword, by slicing the blades of grass.

Pots, pumpkins, and even rocks can hold rupees. Pick up the objects and toss them. When they land, they'll break and potentially yield cash.

The Slingshot

Return to your home with the slingshot in hand. The village kids will ask you to demonstrate your slingshot skills. With the weapon mapped to the B Button, press and hold the button to bring up the targeting reticle. Release the button to fire.

7 Your First Real Target

Rusl left an item for you inside your house. There's a spider on or near the ladder that leads to the front door. Use the slingshot to hit the arachnid before you attempt to climb the ladder.

The Wooden Sword

The item that Rusl left for you is a Wooden Sword. The kids will ask you to demonstrate a few techniques. You'll use a dummy as your target as the kids give you tips on how to pull off each move. The most challenging move is a jab. Hold Z to target the dummy, then press up on the Control Stick and slice with the remote.

Faron Province

Out of Ordon and into the big world, the adventure heats up when you enter Faron Woods.

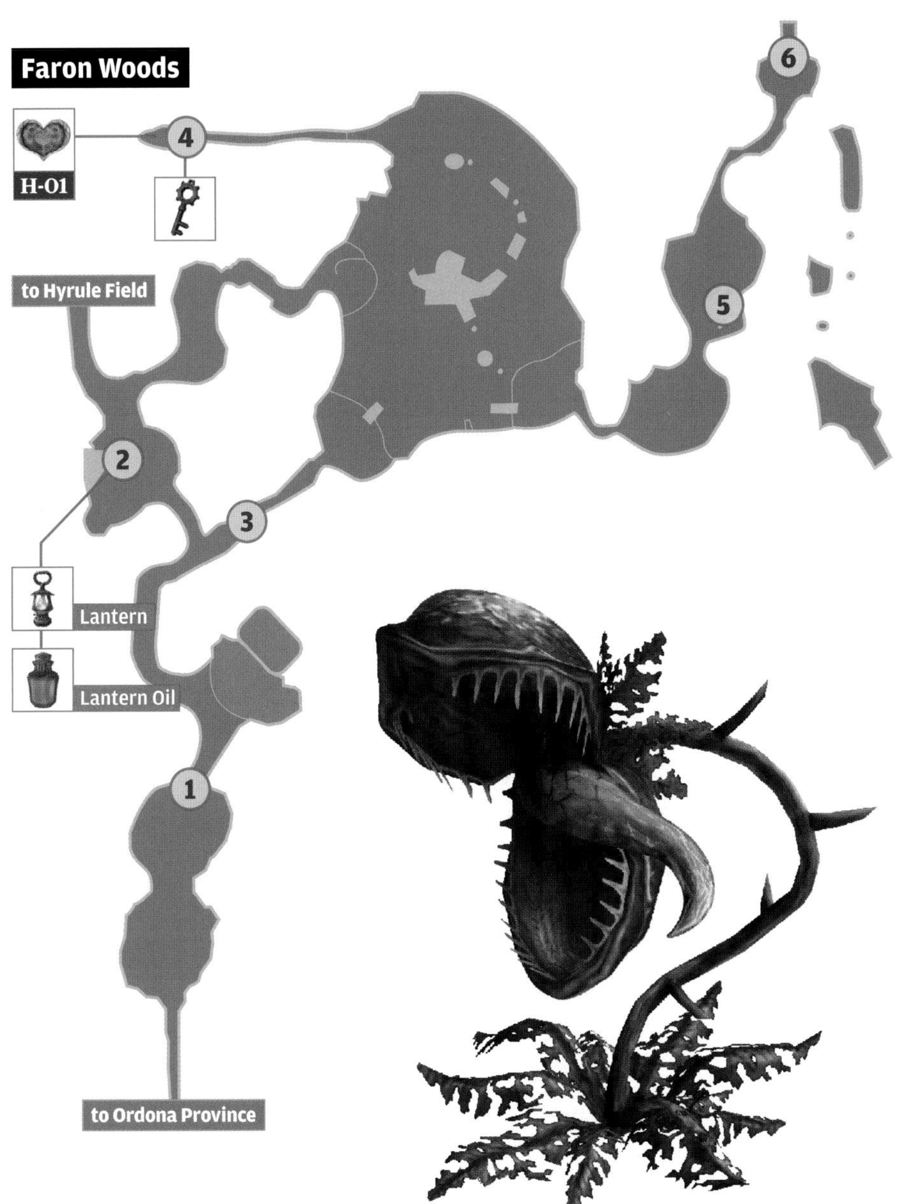

1 Link to the Rescue

Talo and Malo have run after a monkey. Climb onto Epona and head north. If you leave without her, use a blade of grass at the spring to call her. Jump a fence after you cross a bridge, advance to the Forest Temple path, then dismount. You'll discover Talo's wooden sword just inside the cave.

Monster Mash

The cave holds bats, rats, and killer plants. You'll perfect your sword-slashing techniques there. Press Z to target individual enemies, and swing away. The standard slash and A-Button-triggered jump attack are fast and effective.

2 Seek Enlightenment

A sign outside of the Forest Temple path's cave warns that it's too dark inside to venture in without a light, and a spider web inside keeps you from advancing until you have fire on your side. Venture northwest from the cave entrance to grab the lantern.

The Lantern

Coro will provide you with a lantern and offer to sell you Lantern Oil. Use the light to see in the darkness, ignite torches, and burn spider webs. Watch your oil supply and conserve fuel by putting the lantern away when you don't need it.

3 Return to the Darkness

With the lantern in hand, go back into the cave. Take on each enemy as it comes and light the cave's torches to get a better look at your surroundings.

4 Two Treasures

When you emerge from the cave, you'll see two red-marked destinations on the Faron Woods map. Chase after the item in the northwest section first. It's a Small Key in a chest. While you're there, light two torches to reveal another chest, which holds a Piece of Heart.

5 Midadventure Supplies

On your way to freeing Talo, you can stop for a moment and purchase Lantern Oil or Red Potions from a bird-operated shop outside the Forest Temple.

Coro Sheds Light on Your Adventure

Coro is an entrepreneurial shop owner. He'll offer you the lantern for free, then sell refills for 20 rupees and (later) a bottle full of oil for 100 rupees. Once you've used the oil, you can reuse the bottle for any purpose that you see fit.

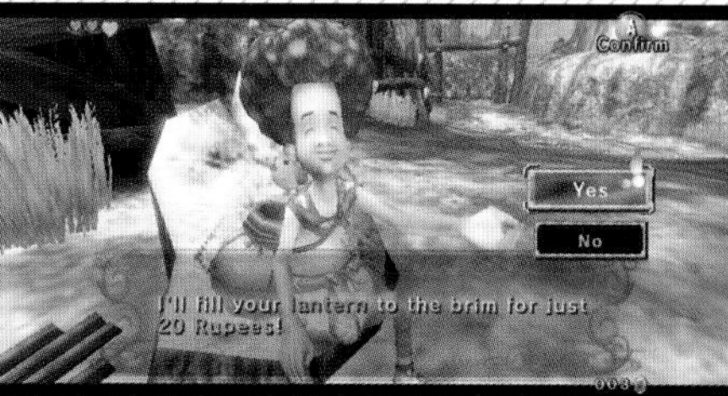

The Best Defense Is Offense

As you explore Faron Woods and beyond, you'll begin to encounter more-dangerous enemies. The armed ones pose a particular threat. Since you don't own a shield, you won't have any defensive options. Attack aggressively instead.

When you're going up against armed enemies, be sure to use Z-Button-triggered targeting. If you're surrounded by foes, shake the nunchuk to perform a spin attack.

When you're targeting an enemy, you can dodge by pressing left or right on the Control Stick and pressing the A Button. Early on, you'll find that attacking quickly is a better option than spending time trying to dodge enemies.

Take Heart

It's not a Legend of Zelda adventure without Heart Containers. You'll earn a container for every dungeon-ending boss you defeat, and for collecting Pieces of Heart. In earlier adventures, it took four pieces to complete a container. In this one it takes five pieces.

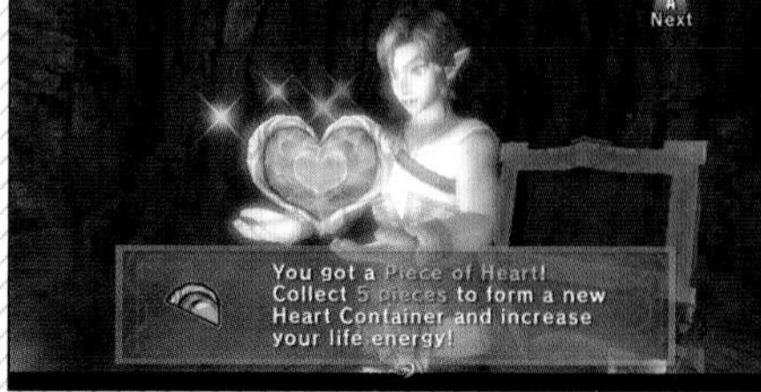

Take a Penny, Leave a Penny

Trill's Shop near the Forest Temple operates on the honor system. If you press the A Button to check the goods in the offing, you'll see that they have recommended prices, but you can get away with paying less—or nothing at all. If you leave without paying, the bird that runs the place will peck at you, making it difficult to steal anything else.

6 Come to Talo's Aid

Both Talo and the monkey that he was chasing are captives on the steps of the Forest Temple, guarded by armed enemies. Bash the baddies, then dismantle the captives' cage with a spin attack.

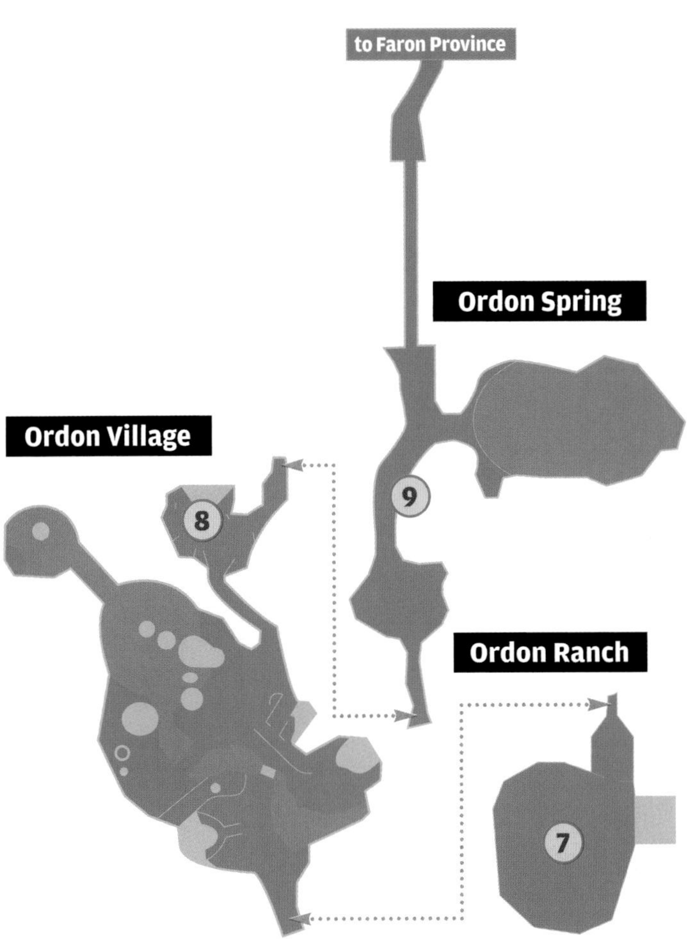

7 Three-Minute Run

Upon your return to Ordon, you'll engage in more goat herding. Call Epona then get started. The time to beat is three minutes. If the activity takes more time, you'll still advance but Fado will remark on your lack of speed.

8 Sword Exchange

Following your conversation with Ilia and the mayor, the girl will take Epona to the forest spring. Talo won't let you follow Ilia until you give him your sword.

9 Horsing Around

Unhappy with the way that you've treated Epona, Ilia is seeing to the horse's health. You must have Epona to set out on your journey, however.

Talk to Colin through the locked gate. He'll tell you to enter the area through a tunnel. Backtrack south to a small clearing and locate the tunnel. It has one turn, to the left.

Enter the Darkness

Everything will change in an instant. One moment you'll be talking to Ilia. The next you'll be out cold, with Ilia gone—taken by marauders. After you wake, you'll chase after the enemies but find a strange dark force field instead.

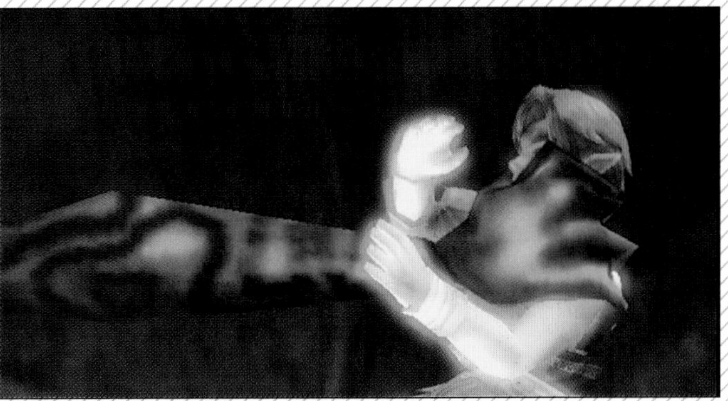

In the middle of the woods you'll approach a wall of darkness, and without warning you'll be pulled inside.

Link's Transformation

A new chapter in the story begins with Link in wolf form. It's the first of several lupine transformations. To help you through the change is a playful twilit being. She will aid you with clues and guidance. You're in a cell, in shackles. The twilit being will cut the chains, but you'll have to get out of the cell on your own.

Twilight Castle

What is the darkness that has fallen over the land? Where are you? The only way to find out is to explore.

Castle Rooftops

Castle Sewers

Dungeon

1 2 3 4 5 6 7 8

1 A Great Escape

There's a pile of debris in the southeast corner of the cell. Attack it by swiping the remote or shaking the nunchuk. Destroying the debris will expose a hole under the bars. Press down on the Control Pad to dig your way out.

Get a Clue

You're in the domain of your strange companion. If you press up on the Control Pad, she'll offer some advice. When you hear her laugh (through the remote's speaker), call her to receive additional assistance.

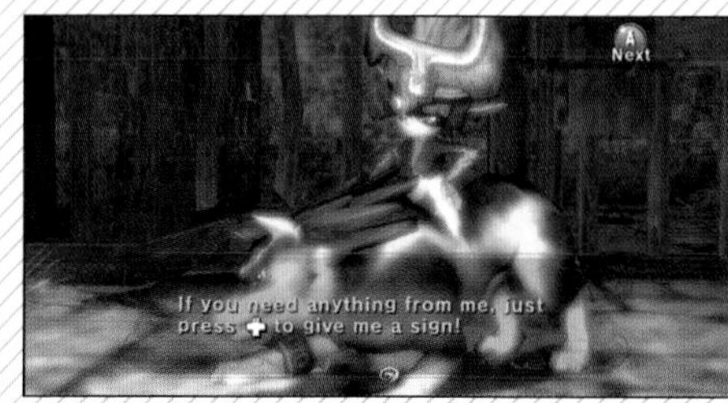

2 Enter the Sewers

When you step into the next cell over from the one where you were kept, the twilit being on your back will produce a hand that reaches out for a dangling handle. Press Z to target the handle, then press A to bite it. You will open a grate to the sewer.

A Helping Hand

Your partner has a phantom hand that can point at objects that you can manipulate. At crucial moments, when you've targeted an item that you can bite, the hand will appear. Press A (as if you were attacking the object) to interact with it.

Activate Canine Senses

There are spirits nearby, but they can't see you. You can see them, though, by using your senses. When you spot a floating light, press left or right on the Control Pad to investigate.

Hungry Like the Wolf

You have nearly as many attack options in wolf form as you do in human form. Swipe the remote to bite enemies. To jump, press A when an enemy is targeted. Shake the nunchuk to activate a spinning attack.

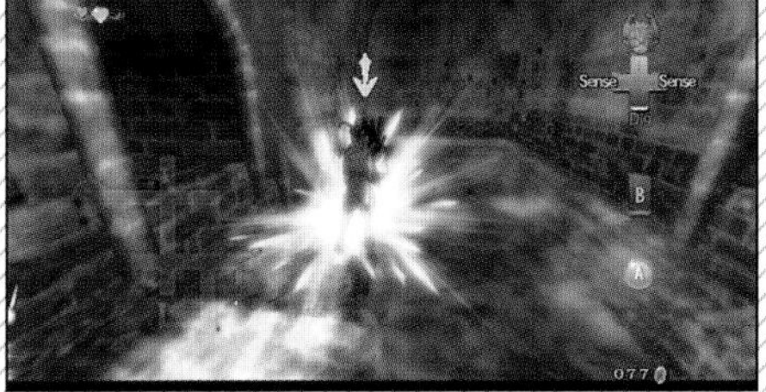

3 Flood the Sewers

The dungeon's main intersection is blocked by spikes on the floor. Pull a chain south of the spikes to bring in water, then swim over the spikes.

When you approach the chain next to the metal door, press Z to target it. Press A to have your partner pull it and lift the gate. Water will rush into the sewer.

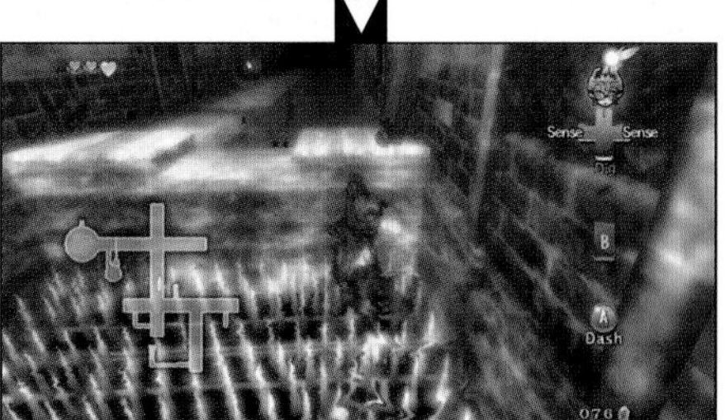

With the water level high, you'll be able to swim across the main intersection and access the sewers' northern area.

4 Follow the Twilit Being

When you approach the gate in the area's northwest corner, your companion will float through the bars. If you haven't pulled a chain to lower the water level in the northeast corner, do so (Z-target the chain and press A). Then crawl through a hole on the floor, near the bars.

5 Spiral up the Tower

The spiraling steps of a tower lead out of the sewers. You can cross small gaps by yourself, but you'll need help from your companion to make big jumps. At one section, where the gap is far too wide to jump, you'll walk a rope to the other side.

Teach a Dog New Tricks

Certain gaps look too wide for you to jump. If you try to cross them on your own, you'll fall. When you get to the edge, your passenger will laugh. Press up on the Control Pad to watch her float across the gap, then Z-target her and press A to jump.

6 Reach New Heights

At the top of the stairs, battle a gaggle of bats then jump to a door at the top of the tower with your companion's assistance.

After the bats are defeated, climb onto a block near the closed door. The twilit being will laugh. Let her help you reach the top of the tower.

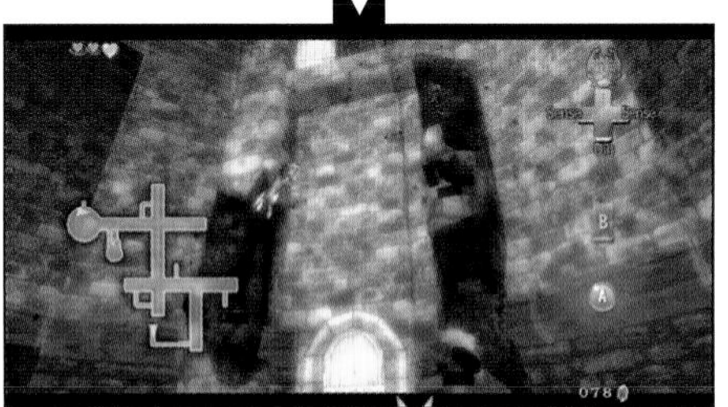

Press up on the Control Pad to have your partner float to the next destination. Z-target her, then press A four times to follow a zigzag path to the open door at the top.

7 Travel on the Rooftops

While you're walking on the roof, you'll sense a spirit who will say that this place is Hyrule Castle, and that there are winged creatures in the area. Push a crate to access a high perch (or hop from the crate), and keep moving forward. When you're about to fight the flying creatures, position yourself in an open area far from a ledge. Target the beasts and hit them with A Button attacks.

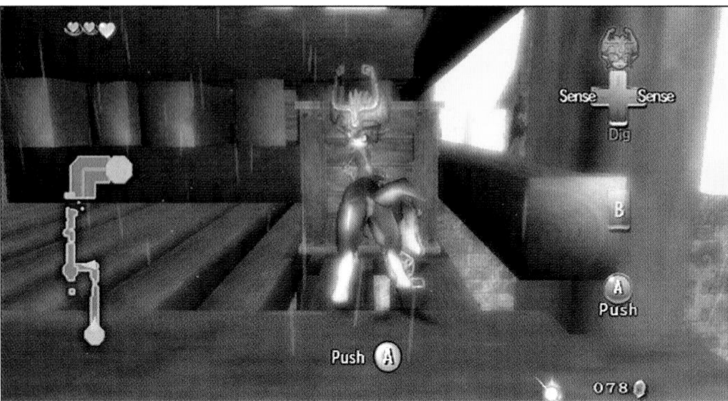

8 The Last Long Gap

You'll see a wide gap on the map. When you reach it, walk to a wooden platform to the right. Your companion will guide you to the roof's peak. Battle two more creatures while you walk along the narrow path, and advance to the tower.

The Princess and the Partner

Inside the tower, you'll finally reach the person that your companion wanted you to meet. She'll identify your partner as Midna and, in dramatic fashion, show herself as Princess Zelda.

Twilight Falls

This was once the kingdom of Hyrule. Overtaken by the king that rules the twilight, however, it became mired in darkness and full of lost souls. The princess will show you what has became of the kingdom, and let you know that it needs your help. After you leave Princess Zelda, Midna will lead you outside, remind you that you need to save the children of Ordon, and send you back to the village.

Ordona Province, Part 2

The twilight has not touched Ordon, but the villagers are still wary. They will not welcome a beast.

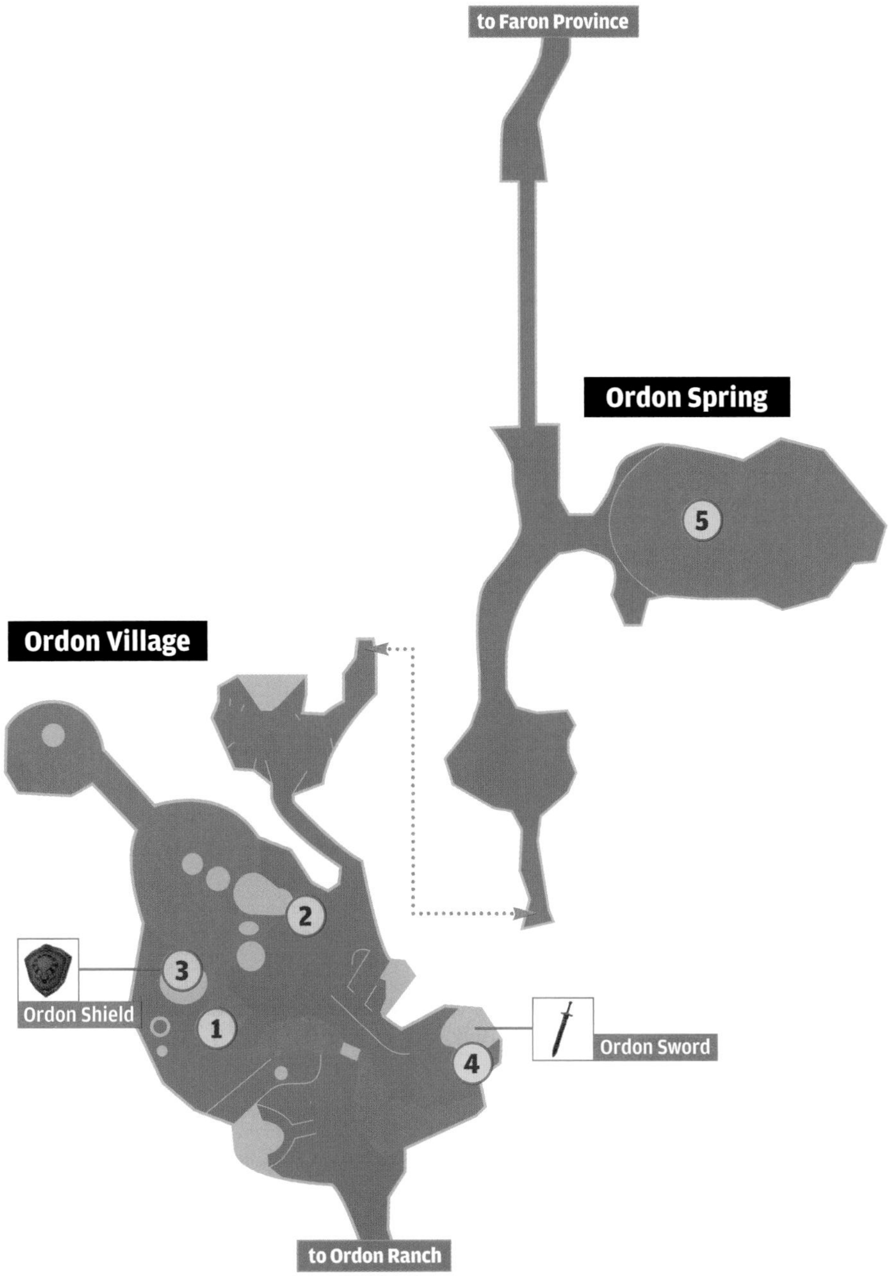

to Faron Province

Ordon Spring

Ordon Village

Ordon Shield

Ordon Sword

to Ordon Ranch

A Hero in Wolf's Clothing

Though you're not in the twilight realm anymore, you are still in canine form. Midna will keep you that way until you complete a task for her. The villagers, who have already endured an attack by monsters, will stay away from you. You can find solace by talking to other animals.

1 On the Hunt

Midna will help you right the wrongs that have fallen on the land. But first she wants weapons. Cross the bridge to the west side of Ordon Village. You'll see Bo and Jaggle. Sneak through the tall grass to listen to their conversation about a sword and a shield. The shield is in Jaggle's storage loft. Midna will point out an open window on the second floor and suggest that you jump up to it. But where to start? Head to the area around Sera's shop.

2 Monster!

Sera's husband, Hanch, will see you from the bluff near the shop as you skulk about town, and he'll attempt to sic the falcon on you. Run to the shop's far side. There, Midna will help you hop onto the roof. Jump to Hanch's bluff to scare Hanch away. That perch will give you a view of the windmill and a good approach to Jaggle's house. Midna can help you jump to the windmill then to the roof of the house. Walk through the open window.

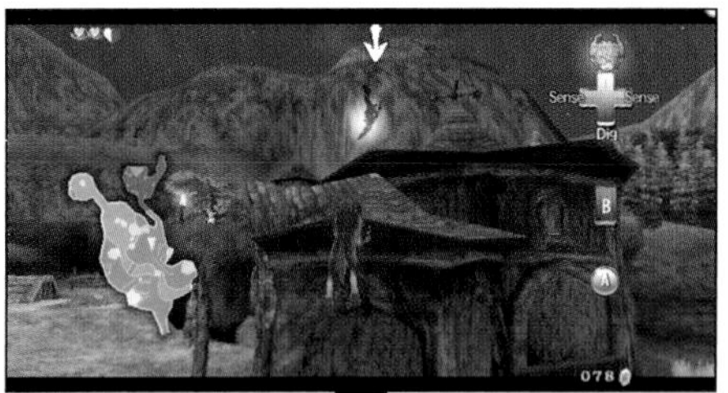

3 Shake It Loose

Climb onto the table in the middle of the house and let Midna help you jump up to the storage loft. The shield is hanging on the wall between two curtains. Dash into the wall (by pressing A) twice to knock the shield to the ground. Grab it then use the loft window to exit.

4 It's a Gift

Rusl and Uli are outside, suspicious of the creatures that have been causing havoc. You'll hear Rusl say that a sword—meant to be a gift to Hyrule—is inside the house. Avoid the humans, walk to the east side of the house (near the pumpkins and chickens), and use your senses to find a place to dig under the wall to get into the building.

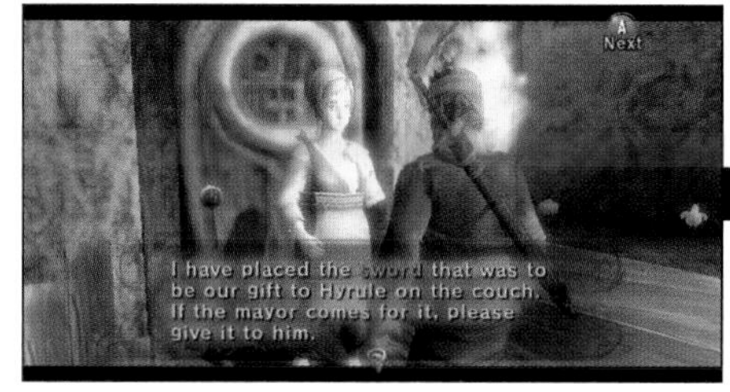

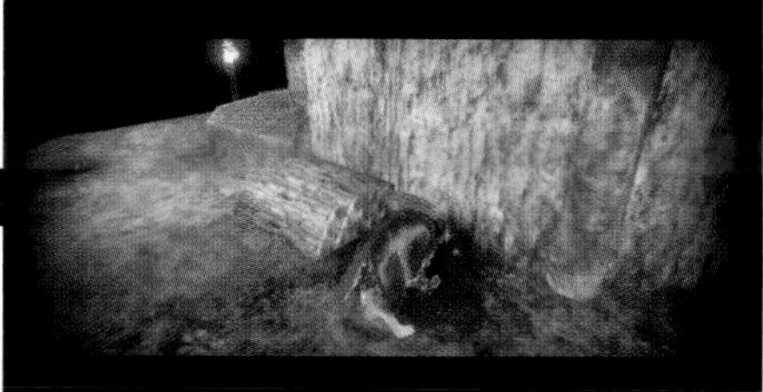

Dig Up Hyrule

One of the advantages of being a wolf is that you always know where to dig. With your senses engaged (press left or right on the Control Pad), look for shiny spots on the ground. Press down to dig. You'll find hearts, rupees, and tunnels.

5 Out from the Shadows

When you return to the spring, you'll face the first of many shadow beings: creatures who create phantom barriers, forcing you to fight. Later, when you battle groups of them, you'll have Midna's help. For now it's just you and one of the creatures. Jump onto the beast and press A repeatedly to maul it.

A Spirit of the Light

After you defeat the creature from the darkness, you'll meet a creature from the light. This light spirit, Ordona, is one of four who protects Hyrule. Your new quest is to help the spirits save the kingdom by returning the lost light to them. Ordona will tell you that, if you revive the light spirit in Faron Woods, you will return to your original form. Go north.

Faron Woods

Faron's light is scattered throughout the area. By collecting the Tears of Light, you'll revive the forest spirit.

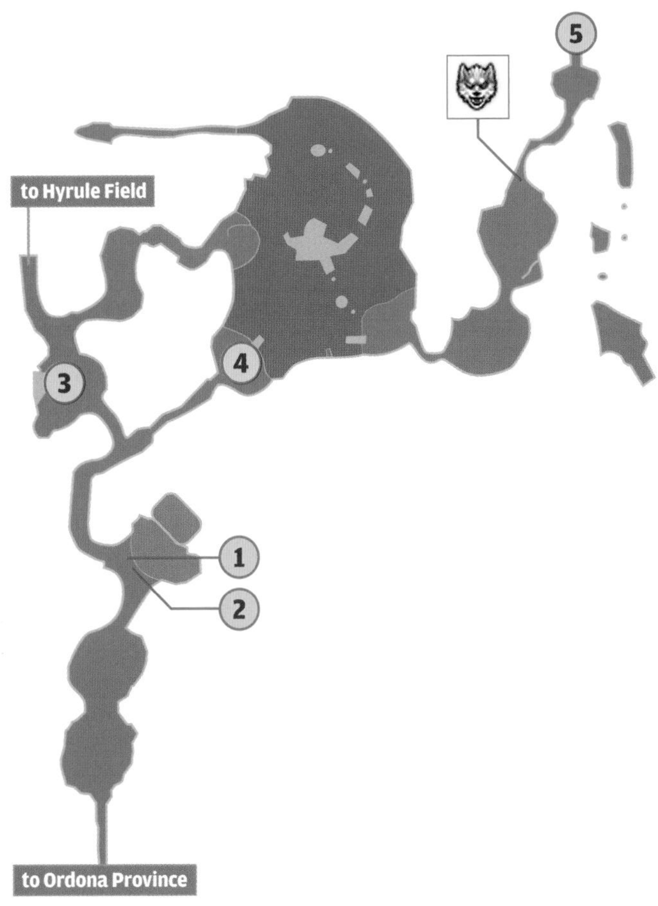

1 Twilight Trio

You'll meet three shadow beings early in your trip through the woods. You must hit the last two in one fell swoop to vanquish the group. To do so, you will require Midna's help. Press and hold B to envelop them in dark energy.

Group Dynamics

Midna's power, which allows you to target several creatures at once, is a must for battling shadow beings. As you hold B, a dark circle will grow around you. Touch your enemies with the circle to paint them as targets. After you let go, the attack will begin.

2 A Light Quest

Following your battle versus shadow beings, you'll meet another light spirit. This one will give you the Vessel of Light and ask you to find 16 tears that cut through the darkness.

Sense the Insects

The Tears of Light have been captured by creatures that you can detect by using your canine senses. Consult the map. Each tear is represented by a white dot. When you're in the right place, use your senses to root out a bug. Defeat it then collect the tear.

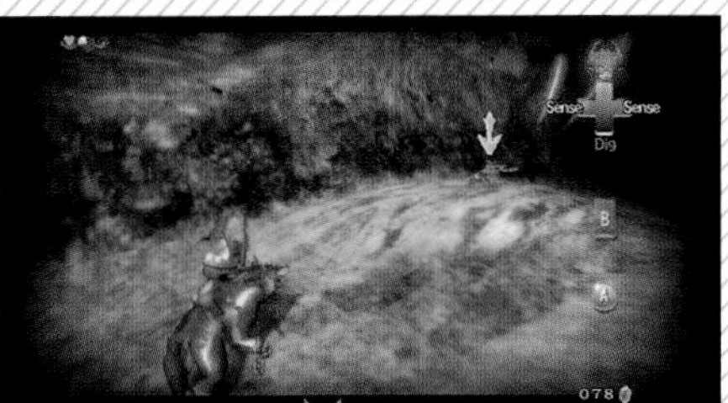

Tears of Light Locations

Faron Woods

Start the Extermination

1 & 2 Though you can sometimes detect the dark insects that hold the tears without using your canine senses, you can really see them with your senses engaged. They let out a sparkling aura. Defeat a pair of insects on the path, wait for them to explode, then collect their tears.

Visit Coro's House

On your way up the path, you'll watch two bugs scurry under the forest-path gate. You'll fight them later. First find the bugs at Coro's place.

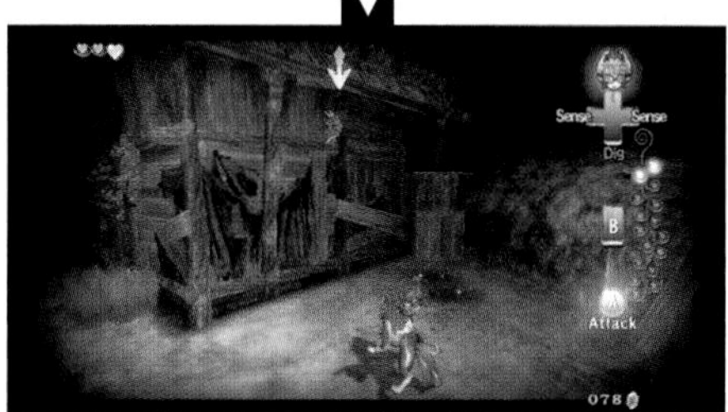

3 There's a bug on the outside of the building. Run into the structure to knock the insect to the ground.

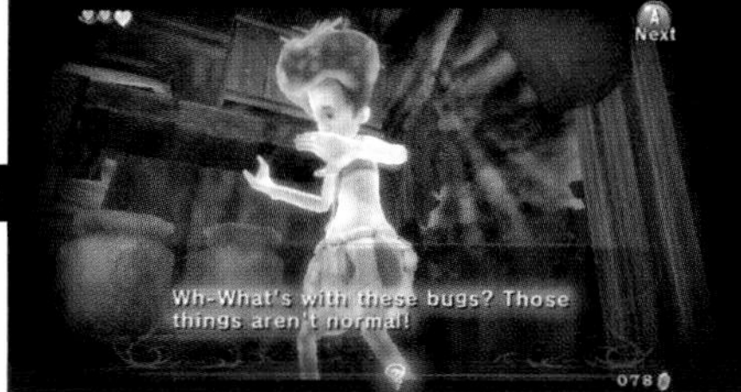

4 & 5 Walk up the ramp south of Coro's house. When you get to the edge, Midna will giggle. Have her help you jump from the ramp to the second-floor window. Drop to the floor, then listen to Coro's spirit. The bugs will pop from their hiding spot. Defeat them then collect the tears.

6 & 7 Head back to the gate before the forest path and use your senses to detect a place where you can tunnel through to the other side. Once there, defeat two more insects. As is the case with all of the bugs, you'll notice that the blue lights they release hover out of reach for a few seconds. Wait for them to drop so you can collect them before you move on.

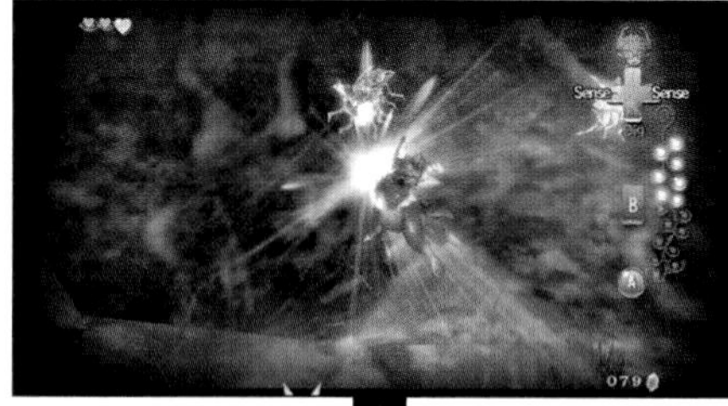

8-12 When you reach the clearing in the middle of the forest, you'll detect two insects on a rock wall. Run into the wall or use Midna's B-Button-triggered ability to knock them down. Then attack. A poisonous fog keeps you from walking on the forest floor. You'll need Midna's help to cross it. Near the place where you fought the insects, climb onto a flat rock. Midna will titter, signalling that she can help you jump over the fog and into the trees. You'll find three more bugs in a large, hollowed-out stump.

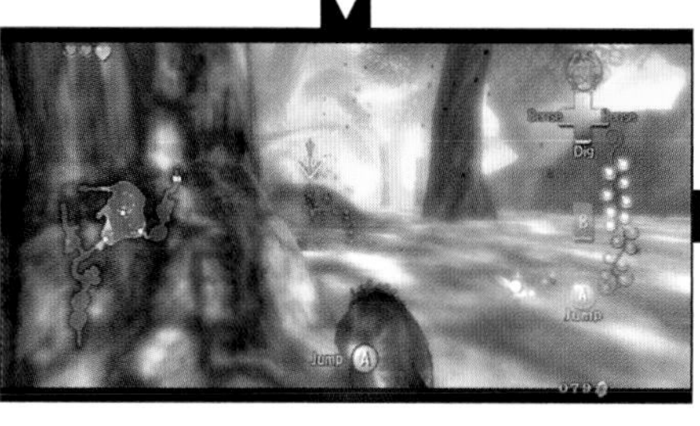

13 & 14 While you're crossing the clearing (and keeping an eye open for more dark insects), you'll find that the sections where Midna guides you can be dangerous. A few sections are seeded with killer plants. In another section, the path is sometimes blocked by a swinging log. Jump when the log is out of the way. When you reach the other side, dig up a pair of insects.

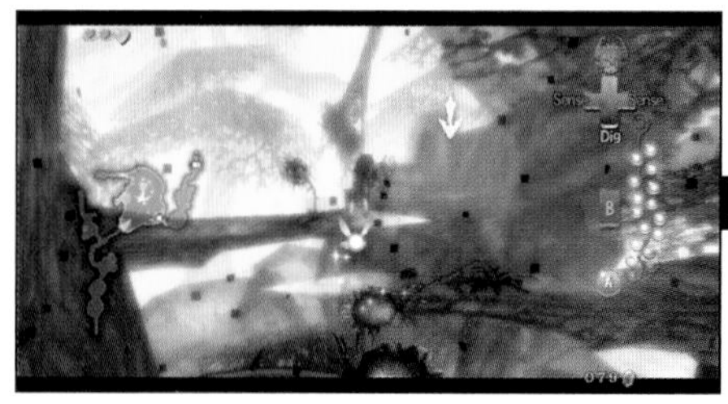

One Then Two

Once you emerge from the clearing, you'll face three more shadow beings. One of them is separate from the others. Defeat the loner first, then go after the pair.

15 & 16 The final pair of insects is on the steps to the Forest Temple, tormenting a monkey spirit. After you defeat the insects then collect their tears, you'll be transported to the place where you collected the Vessel of Light.

A Spirited Reunion

You've finished a task for forest spirit Faron as a wolf. Now you can continue your quest as a young man: the hero Link, complete with the signature green tunic, sword, and shield. Faron will thank you and point you to the Forest Temple.

The Fully Equipped Adventurer

With the sword and shield that you collected for Midna in hand, you're ready to take on a world of nasty beasts. Now that you have a shield, you won't have to dodge every enemy. Use it in combination with the sword to vanquish your foes.

3 Coro Has the Key

You can't dig under the forest-path gate in human form, and you can't jump over it without a horse. Talk to Coro. He'll give you the key and offer to sell you a bottle of Lantern Oil.

4 Follow the Monkey

The clearing is still covered by poisonous fog. When you reach it, a monkey will steal your lantern and walk into the fog, burning a path through the fog with the flame. Follow the creature and defeat enemies along the way. Pick up the lantern after the monkey drops it.

You've Got Skill

Over the course of your adventure, you'll have the opportunity to learn seven hidden skills from a golden wolf who transforms into a knight called the Hero's Spirit. Your first meeting with the teacher will net you the Ending Blow, a finishing move that you can use on stunned enemies.

5 Fire Away

A web is blocking the Forest Temple entrance. That should not be a deterrent for you. Use the lantern to burn the blockage, then put the lamp away to conserve fuel.

Forest Temple

Get ready to go ape. Monkeys rule the Forest Temple. You'll enlist their help and battle one bad baboon.

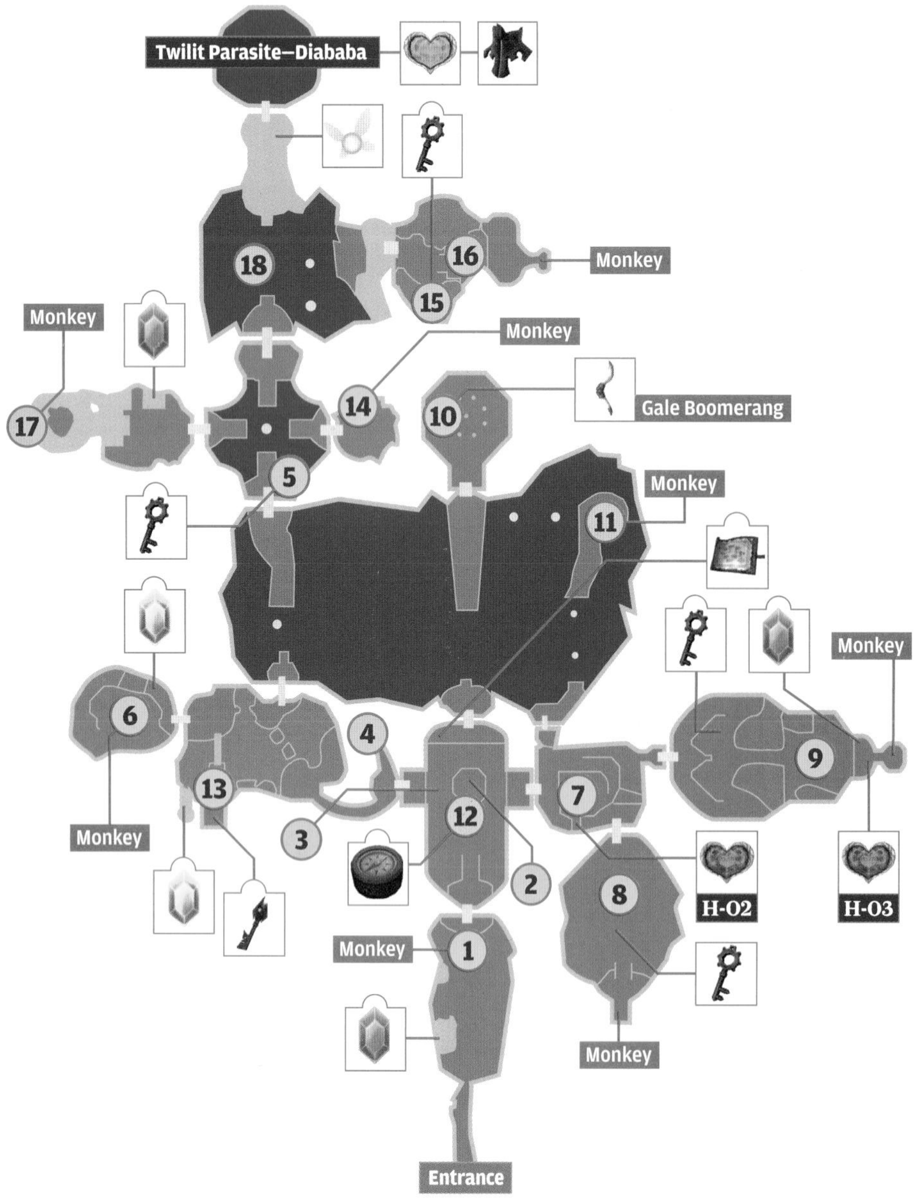

Twilit Parasite—Diababa

Gale Boomerang

Monkey

Monkey

Monkey

Monkey

Monkey

Monkey

Monkey

Monkey

H-02

H-03

Entrance

1 Free the First Monkey

You'll find one of several caged monkeys in the temple's first area. As soon as you destroy her cage, she'll climb a vine-covered wall then encourage you to follow her. Pluck spiders from the vines with your slingshot before you go.

2 Cross Over for Treasure

A huge spider waits for you on a platform. Attack its backside with several fast slices or a jump attack. Once the spider is gone, light the platform's four torches to make a set of stairs appear. Climb the stairs then collect the dungeon map from a treasure chest.

3 Start Swinging

The monkey will lead you to the room to the north. After you watch the dungeon's baboon use a boomerang to cut down a bridge, you'll return to the previous chamber. Your simian pal will offer assistance in getting over a gap.

4 Acquire Explosives

Spiderlike enemies are common in the Forest Temple. You could turn them into bombs by slicing them with your sword, but then you'd have to put your sword away before you picked them up. That wastes time. Let them hit your shield instead.

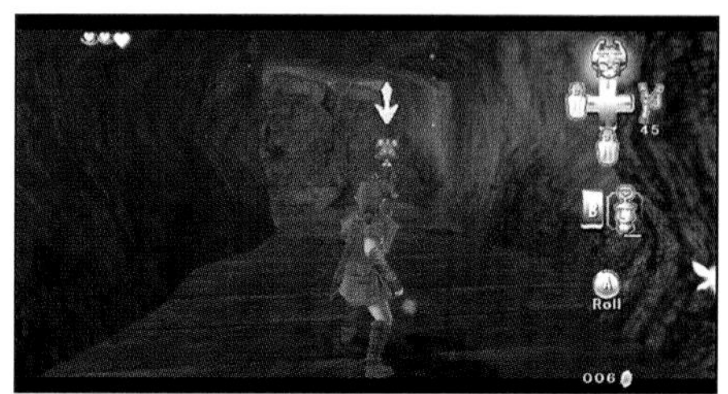

Warped Creature

Use the explosive enemy to break through a weak section of wall. In the alcove on the other side, you'll find Ooccoo, a strange being who will offer to warp you to the dungeon entrance at any time.

5 First Things First

Your pal will encourage you to go west to a locked door, but you'll actually have to go north first to get the key. You'll find it in a chest after you cross a rotating bridge. Return to the monkey, defeat a hanging spider, then move on to the west.

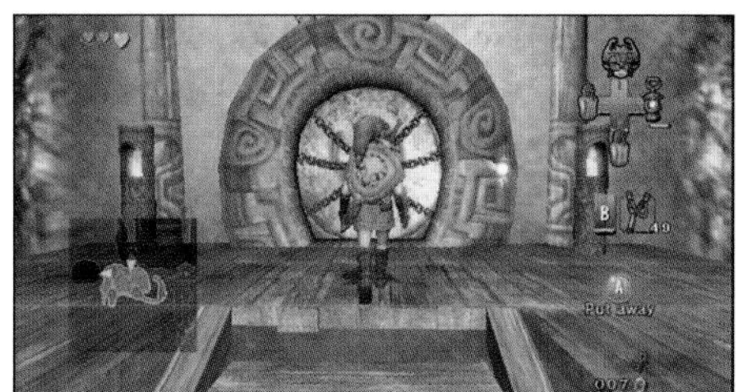

6 Crash Course

Another caged monkey waits on a pillar in the room on the temple's west side. Run into the pillar three times to knock it over. The fall will break the cage. After a short battle against new foes, you'll use both monkeys to swing over a gap then escape the room.

7 Prune the Plants

Deadly plants of two varieties make the room east of the main chamber dangerous. Slice the large Baba Serpent before it chomps you, and feed bombs to two vase-shaped man-eaters for access to the next room to the east, and a Piece of Heart.

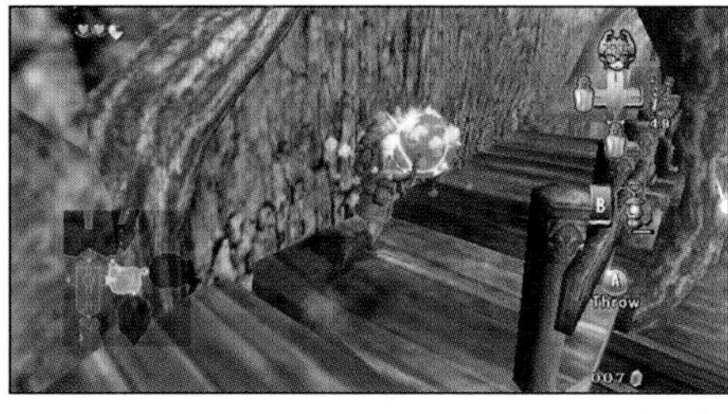

Use your shield to hit a spiderlike creature and produce a bomb. Toss the bomb over a nearby gap to deal with a huge plant. Take another bomb over the gap and use it to destroy a boulder for access to the passage east.

Pluck spiders from a vine-covered wall, then climb the vine to gain access to another bomb-producing creature. Toss the bomb into a gap to destroy the plant below. That'll give you access to a Piece of Heart.

8 More Plant Problems

You'll face off with another dangerous growth in the southeastern room. After you enter the chamber, a plant will swallow a key. Target the roaming bud, dodge when it lunges at you, and counter with a jumping attack. After it's gone, use a bomb to do away with the rest of the growth, collect the key, then free the monkey.

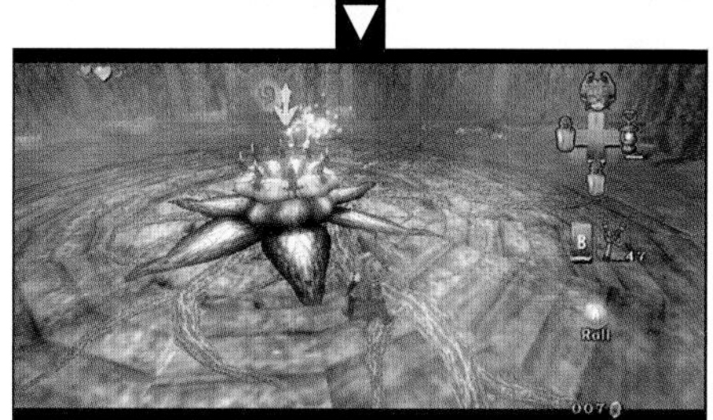

With the plant's head gone, you'll be free to destroy the body with a bomb. Toss the explosive at the plant then collect the key that it leaves behind.

9 The Creatures under the Floor

East of the killer-plant chamber, you'll see a monkey in a locked cage. Hit a pole to knock a chest to the ground. Collect the key then advance east. Swim across the gap to avoid the enemies that lurk under some tiles. Light the lanterns to make steps appear, then climb up to the monkey. Return to the room later with the boomerang to collect a Piece of Heart.

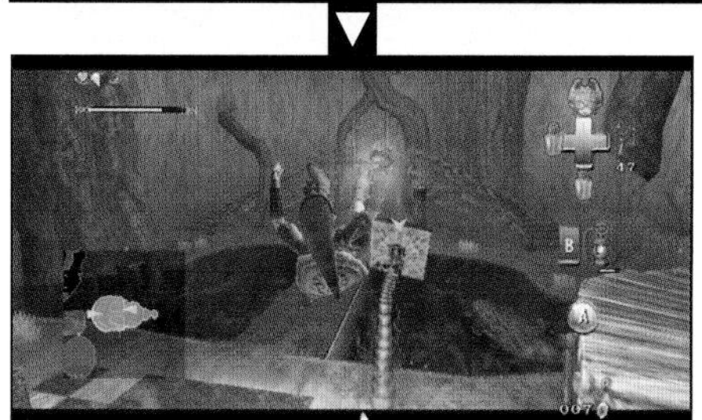

Avoid any tiles that have enemies under them. If you stand on an enemy's tile, you'll be thrown. Defeat the spider that drops in front of the cage by targeting its backside.

10 Battle for the Boomerang

With four monkeys in tow, cross the wide gap in the center of the temple's largest room. In the chamber directly to the north, you'll fight the baboon who has the boomerang. The monkey hops from post to post, sometimes stopping to toss his weapon. After your enemy lets go of the device, run into the baboon's pillar. A square hit will knock the monkey to the ground. Target its behind.

After you've knocked the baboon off its post, target its red behind and hit it with A-Button-triggered jumping attacks. Watch for the roaming plants that the monkey has freed from their vines—they could surprise you with a lunging attack.

The Gale Boomerang

Your new boomerang is the most versatile comebacker in the Legend of Zelda series. It creates a whirlwind as it flies, and it can target more than one object at a time. Want to move an out-of-the-way object from one place to the next? Point at the object and press Z to target it. Point to the destination and press Z again. Then let go of the boomerang. It will fly to the object then carry the item to the destination. You can target up to five points at a time. In addition to carrying items and creating gusts of wind, the boomerang stuns enemies.

11 Release a Whirlwind

Use the Gale Boomerang to spin a turnstile above the exit and raise the gate in front of the door. Leave the room then spin two bridges to cross a gap in the east. You'll discover a monkey in a cage that is suspended by webbing. Hit the webbing with a boomerang shot. The cage will fall and the monkey will scramble.

12 The Way to the Compass

Return to the central room—the one south of the temple's largest chamber—and use the boomerang to free a treasure chest from webbing. Open the chest to collect the compass.

The Compass and the Map

With the compass and your map, you can identify the location of every chest in the dungeon. Spend some time to accumulate wealth. In the Forest Temple, the compass and map will also reveal monkey locations.

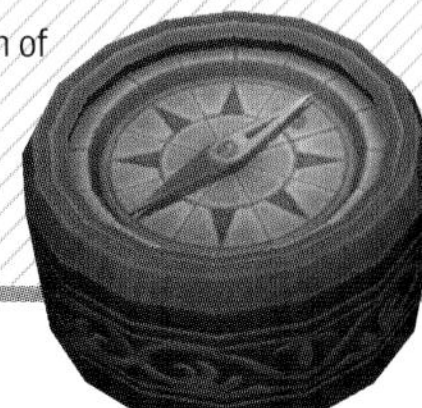

13 Zig and Zag

Travel west to the large gate and four turnstiles. A light path on the ground connects the turnstiles in a zigzag pattern. Use the boomerang to hit the turnstiles in that pattern to make the gate open. You'll collect the Big Key from the treasure chest on the other side.

The Big Key

Big Keys are a Legend of Zelda mainstay. Small Keys work as skeleton keys for small locks. The Big Key opens just one door per dungeon: the one leading to the boss's chamber.

14 In the Hole

Travel north past the west side of the temple's largest chamber. Hit the turnstile with a boomerang blast to straighten out the bridge section. When you're on the bridge, hit the turnstile again. The bridge will span east and west. Go east to a room where there are spiders and three holes in the floor. Burn the web that covers the hole on the northern side. After you fall through the hole, you'll land on a stump, next to a caged monkey. Destroy the cage to free your new friend.

15 Monkey House

Rotate the bridge so it spans north and south, and go north to the room that houses the saved monkeys. Manipulate the room's bridges to reach the east side. Target the spiders on the east wall's vines, then climb to the top of the room. Go east to the next room.

There's a bomb-producing creature on an island at the north end of the room. Hit it with the boomerang to retrieve the bomb. Run south and toss the bomb at the large vase-shaped plant. After the plant is gone, you'll have access to a key.

16 Bombs Away

A rock blocks the way to a trapped monkey. Use the Gale Boomerang to carry a bomb to the rock and clear the way.

Target the bomb creature and press Z, then target the large rock and press Z again. Let the boomerang fly. It'll carry the bomb to the rock and the rock will explode, giving you access to the eastern alcove. Fight the enemies in the area by using your boomerang and sword. Look out over the room after the fight and use the boomerang to retrieve another bomb, which you can toss at the boulder in the alcove to free a monkey.

17 One Last Monkey

Use your Small Key to enter the westernmost room. There you'll find creatures under some floor tiles. Hit the tiles with a boomerang shot to expose the enemies, then slice them with your sword. A path on the room's north side leads to the last monkey. Hit two turnstiles with boomerang power to free your little buddy.

18 A Big Swing

With all of the temple's monkeys free, return to the room that houses the simians. They'll form a single swinging line. Hold onto the monkeys to cross a very wide gap.

Bottled Relief

Before you enter the boss's room, look for a fairy in a pot. Either collect the fairy to replenish your health, or bottle it for later.

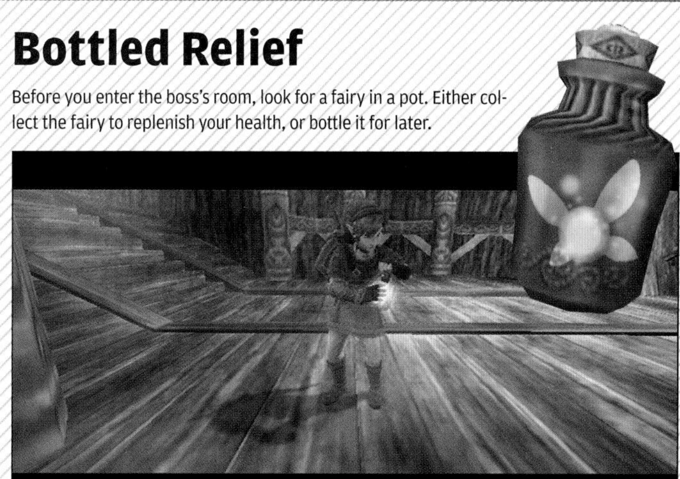

Twilit Parasite—Diababa

The killer plant of all plants rears its ugly head in the Forest Temple. The battle begins with two giant buds emerging from the goo. Target bombs then buds with your boomerang to deliver explosive charges.

The main creature is much larger than the two buds, and much more vicious. It'll attempt to cover you in a purple liquid. Sidestep the mess and wait for the baboon to enter the picture. The baboon swings through the room while holding a bomb. Target the bomb, then target Diababa's head and release the boomerang. After suffering a direct hit, Diababa will fall to the ground and stick out its tongue, revealing an eye at the tip. Hit the eye with thundering sword blows. It'll take a few rounds to put the beast to rest.

Fused Shadow

There are three Fused Shadows in Hyrule. You'll get one for defeating each of the first three dungeon bosses. Midna knows their function, but she won't let on until you have them all. Suffice it to say that they are riddled with dark energy.

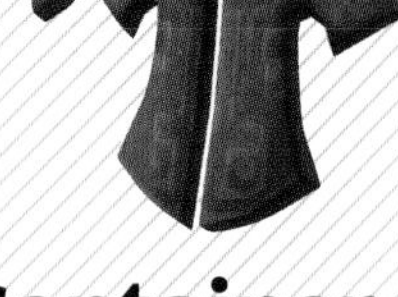

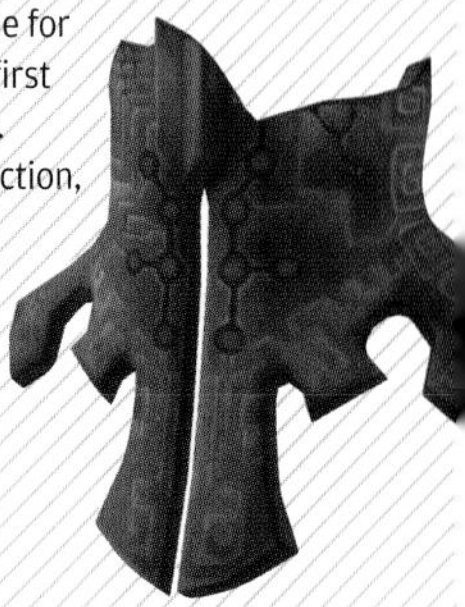

Heart Container

The Heart Container is the traditional gift for defeating a dungeon boss. It'll increase your health meter by one full heart, and refill the meter to boot.

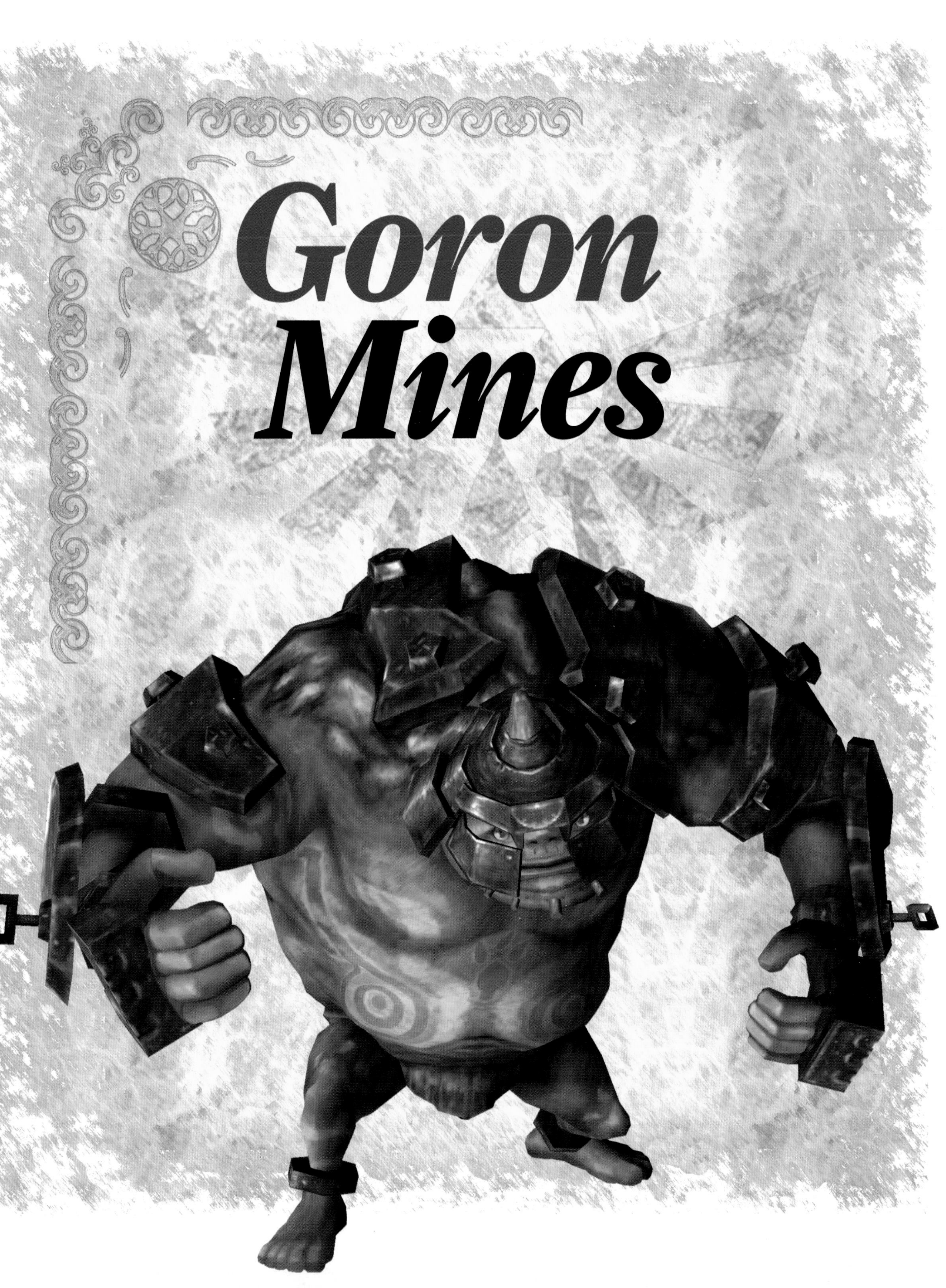

Goron Mines

Eldin Province

Home to Kakariko Village, Eldin Province will be a frequent destination throughout your adventure.

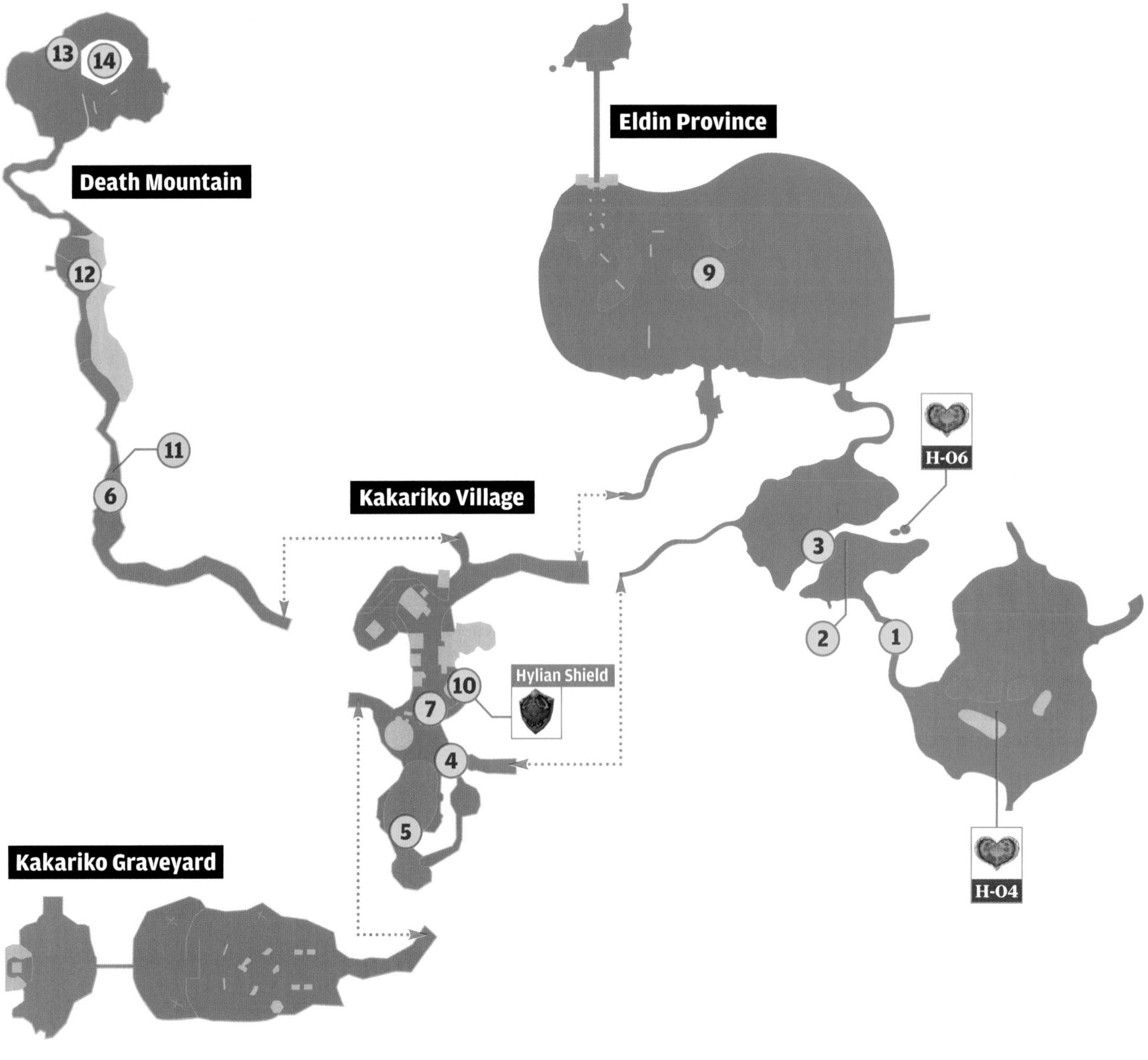

Death Mountain

Eldin Province

Kakariko Village

Hylian Shield

H-06

H-04

Kakariko Graveyard

13 14 12 11 6 9 3 2 1 10 7 4 5

Golden Bugs

You'll spot a glowing bug in one of the trees as you run through the field. Hit the tree to collect the prize. More bugs are scattered throughout the world. Agitha in Castle Town will reward you for finding all of them. See page 156 for the locations of Agitha and all bugs.

The Postman

Since you're on the road, mail would pile up if the postman delivered it to your house. He'll find you in the field and give you letters relating to the quest and side missions.

1 Follow Your Nose

As you travel on foot to the west, you'll collect a letter from the postman. Forge on through a narrow passage to a curtain of twilight. After Midna pulls you through the barrier, you'll change to wolf form. By sniffing Talo's wooden sword on the road, you'll pick up the youths' scent. Use your canine senses to follow the trail.

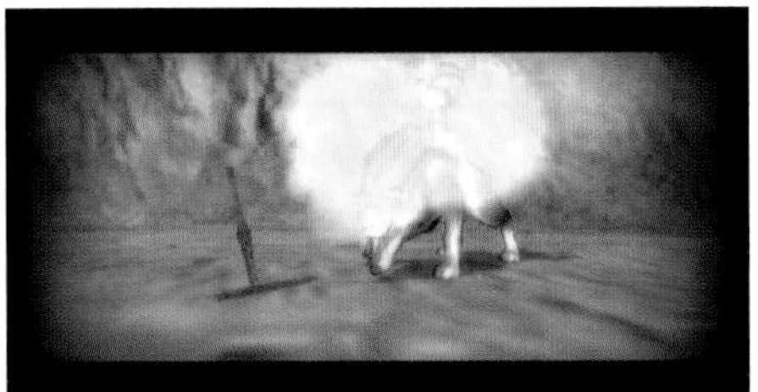

Scents

One great thing about being a wolf is a superior sense of smell. After you sniff a scent, you'll be able to detect the scent's trail by engaging your canine senses.

2 Shadow Fighter

Three shadow creatures block your way. Use Midna's B-Button-triggered dark power to envelop the trio in a circle of darkness, then let go. You'll fell them all with one elaborate attack and open a warp portal.

Travel by Portal

With Midna's help, you can warp to open portals—places where you've defeated shadow beings. You can travel through portals only in wolf form. Once you can transfer forms freely, portal warping will be a big part of your adventure.

3 Floating Bridge

Shortly after you defeat the shadow creatures, you'll find a gorge that has a missing bridge. Midna will explain that you can find the bridge in the woods. After she opens the map, warp to North Faron Woods. The bridge is leaning against a rock wall. Walk up to it and call Midna when you hear her laugh, then use her to warp the bridge to Kakariko Gorge. With the bridge in place, cross it and continue to follow the youths' scent.

4 A Village in Trouble

Using your canine senses, you'll find a place to dig under the Kakariko Village gate. Once you're on the other side, run into the village and defeat three shadow creatures (beating the loner first). Though the village is dark, you will find the spirit Eldin in a glistening pond.

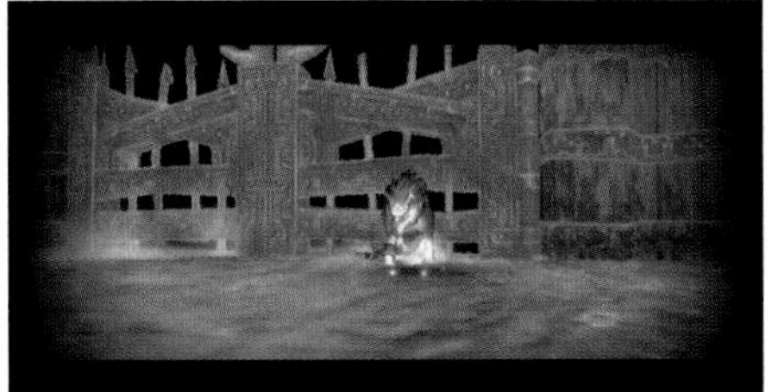

5 World of Tears

The spirit will give you the second Vessel of Light and ask you to fill the vessel's 16 tears with the light stolen by the shadows. To do so, you will have to use your canine senses to hunt down a group of insects, most of which are hidden in the village's buildings.

Insect Identification

The village map shows where some of the insects of darkness can be found (they appear as white dots). The in-game overworld map shows three more insect locations. Start by finding the village bugs, then work your way to the outskirts.

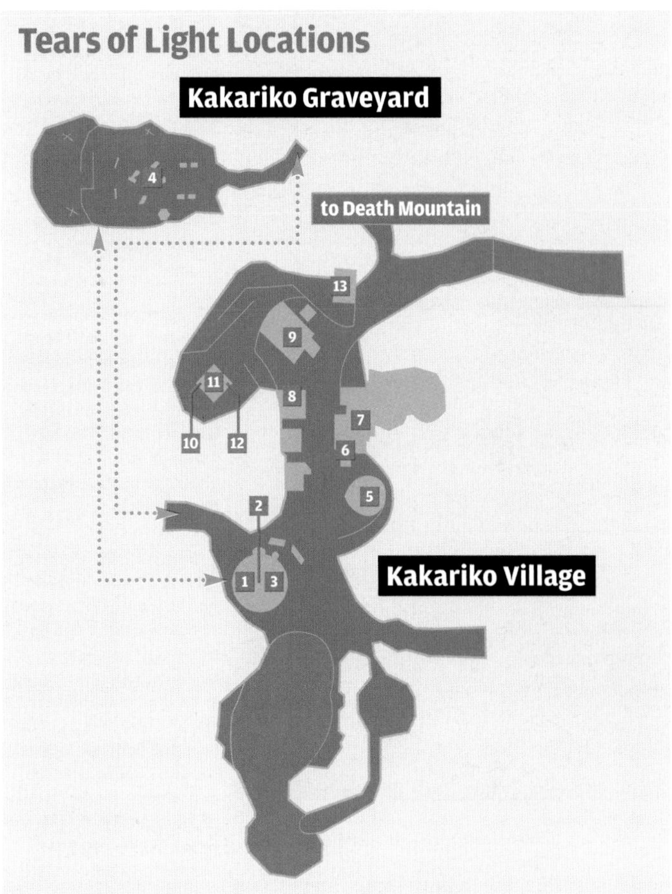

Complete Your Insect Collection

The first insects that you'll come across are in the shaman's house, near the pond. Walk to the tree or the cart at the back of the round building and call Midna after she giggles. She'll lead you up to the roof. Fall through a hole. After a cut-scene, pick up the stick on the floor and light it. Then run around the room to ignite the four candles. The cellar will open.

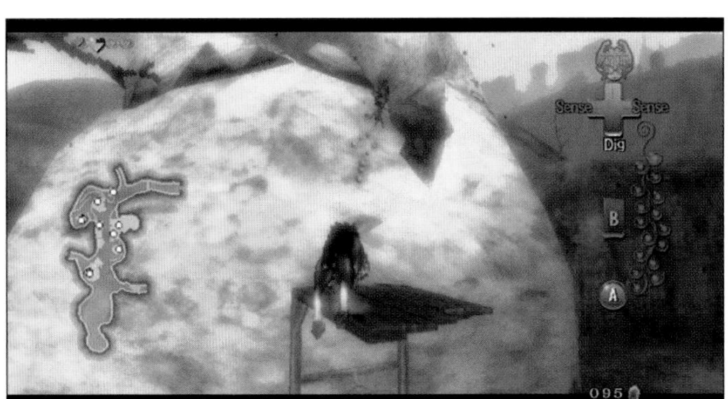

1-3 Once you're in the cellar, activate your senses then attack the three insects in the room. You'll defeat them easily. Collect the blue tears they leave behind, and walk to the room to the north. Midna will lead you up the scaffolding and into the graveyard.

4 You'll spot a dot on the in-game graveyard map. Activate your senses to track the bug. You may have to fight bats on the way. When you reach the bug's location, you'll see a dark spot on the ground. Dig there to expose the insect. Defeat it then collect the blue light.

5 Emerging from the graveyard, walk east to the general store. In the store's side yard, you'll find a passage that leads you inside. Use your canine senses to find another insect, and attack the creature to collect the stolen tear.

6 You'll find a "dead end" sign just south of the general store. Walk past it and up a hill. At the ledge, jump across the gap to the corner of the inn's roof. Enter the inn, pick up a stick from the floor, and light the stick as you jump from a table and past a torch. Use the flaming stick to start the furnace and smoke out an insect that nests in the pipes.

7 As you explore the rest of the inn's rooms, you'll come across noninsect enemies. Make short work of them with targeted attacks, then climb up to the second floor and, with senses engaged, root out another insect.

8 There's a row of boarded-up houses on the west side of town. Climb onto a pen on the southern end of the row, then hop from roof to roof. Fall through a hole in the third house's roof then move a crate to hunt down an insect.

9 Climb to the top of a shack north of Barnes Bomb Shop. Press A to crash through the window of the bomb shop. You'll find the insect behind a dresser upstairs. Run into the dresser to knock it over and expose the bug. After you defeat the insect, climb onto the toppled dresser then up to an opening.

10-12 As you emerge from the upper reaches of the bomb shop and climb to the top of a cliff, follow a bug into the explosives-storage building nearby. Once inside, pick up a stick, light it, and transfer the fire to the furnace. Make your escape while the rest of the building catches fire. The building will explode after you exit, leaving three Tears of Light where there were once bugs.

13 Climb to the top of the ledges northeast of the former explosives hold, then engage your canine senses once you reach the building at the top. You'll find a place to dig at the base of the building, giving you access to the structure's interior and another insect.

Listen to the Goron Guard

There are three insects on Death Mountain. Shortly after you enter the area, you'll discover a steep cliff. Walk up a gentle slope to the left, then let Midna guide you to the top of the cliff with a series of jumps. At the top, use your canine senses to listen to a Goron. He's not happy to be on remote sentry duty.

14 Run north until you reach a series of geysers. Engage your senses then uncover and attack a quickly moving bug. Avoid steam from the geysers as you move. If the hot gas hits you, it will knock you over but it won't cause damage.

Tears of Light Locations

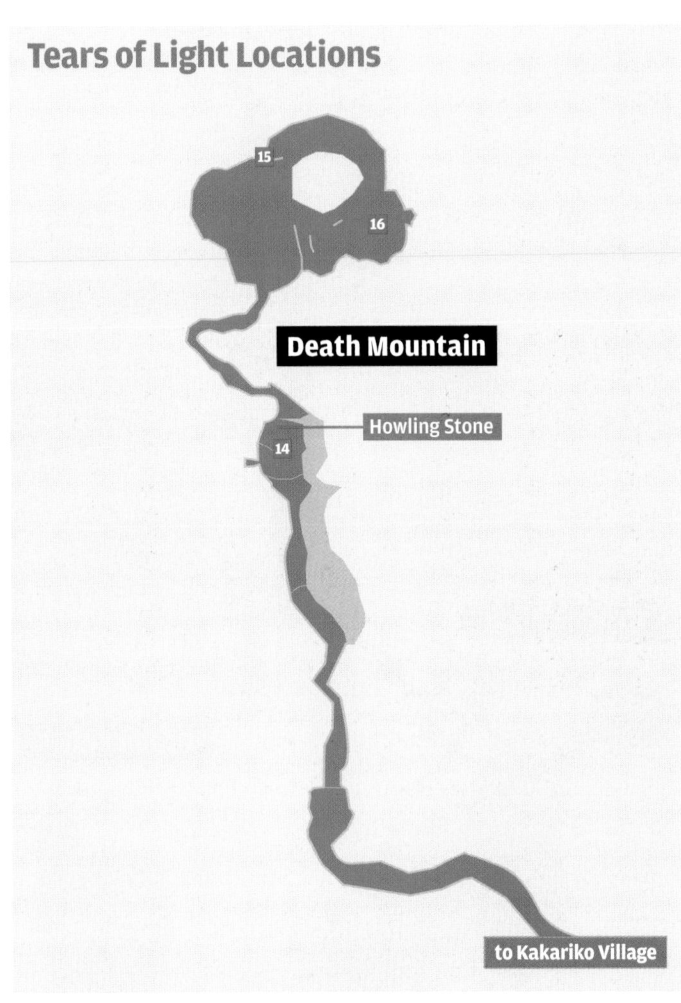

The Howling Stone

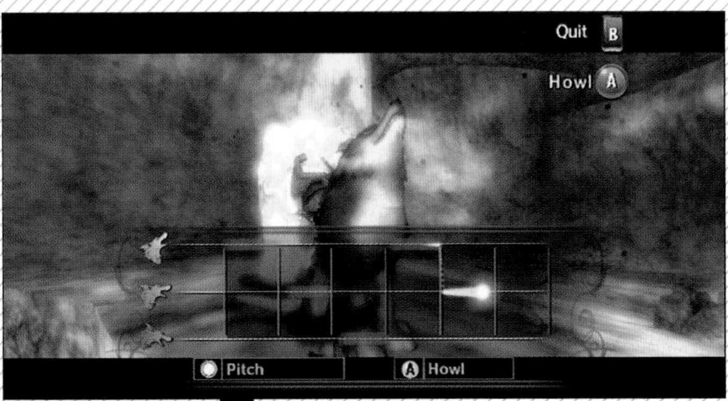

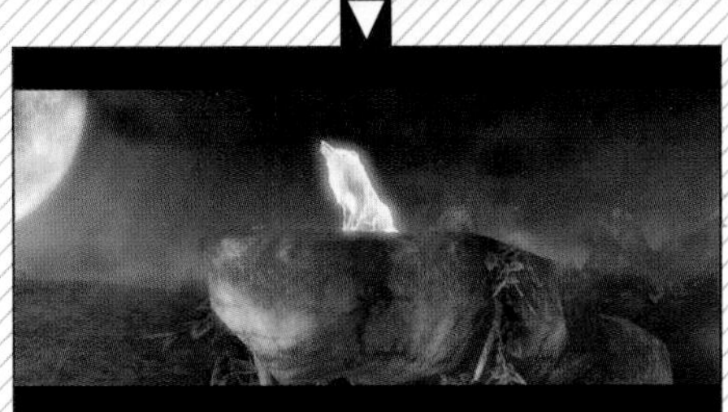

Interact with the stone in the path to learn a new song and get the attention of the wolf who teaches hidden skills. Howl with the wolf. He will tell you to meet him later, in your human form, to learn a skill. His location will appear on the map.

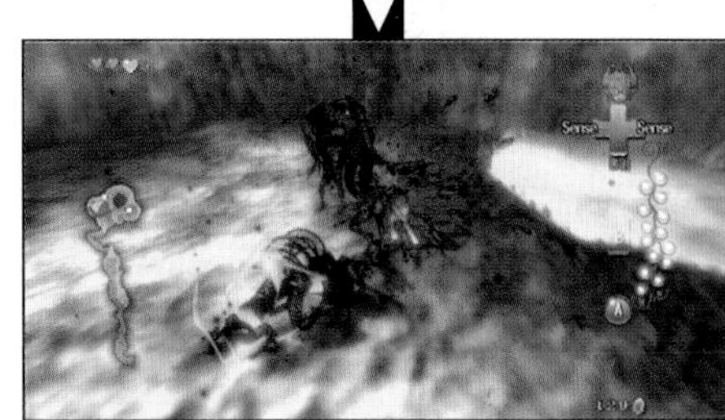

Advancing to the north, you'll encounter four shadow creatures. Three of them are out in the open. Another one is in a maze of force fields. Defeat the beast in the maze first, then attack the farthest away of the final three. Finally, take out the remaining pair with a single attack.

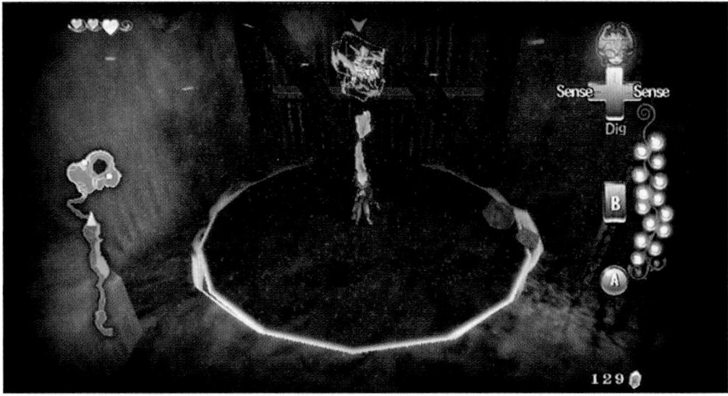

15 Immediately after you defeat the shadow creatures, engage your senses. You'll discover an insect in the area, possibly waiting on a fence. Either run into the fence to knock the insect to the ground, or use Midna's dark energy to stun the creature.

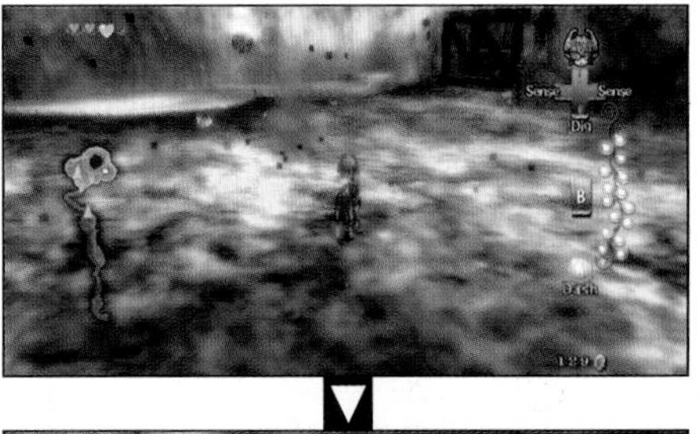

16 Continue along the path, avoiding falling fireballs and steam geysers as you move. You'll enlist Midna's help to jump to new heights a few times, then eventually drop into an area littered with enemies. Once you've defeated the visible creatures, use your senses to find the final insect.

Back to the Tunic

As soon as you fill the Vessel of Light, you'll return to human form and go directly to the village pond, where the spirit Eldin will explain that the Gorons in Death Mountain have the next treasure that you seek. Head north after you speak to Renado, the shaman.

6 Bested by a Goron

On your way up to Death Mountain, you'll encounter a Goron who will roll right for you. He's considerably more powerful than a runaway goat and will knock you off the cliff. Return to the village, where Renado will tell you that you need help from Bo, mayor of Ordon, to learn how to keep a rolling Goron from flattening you.

7 Horsing Around

When you reach the center of town, Epona will barrel through, knocking you to the ground. Mount your steed then follow onscreen prompts and keep Link centered on the horse to stay in the saddle. After you've ridden for several seconds, you'll be able to seize the reins by pressing the A Button.

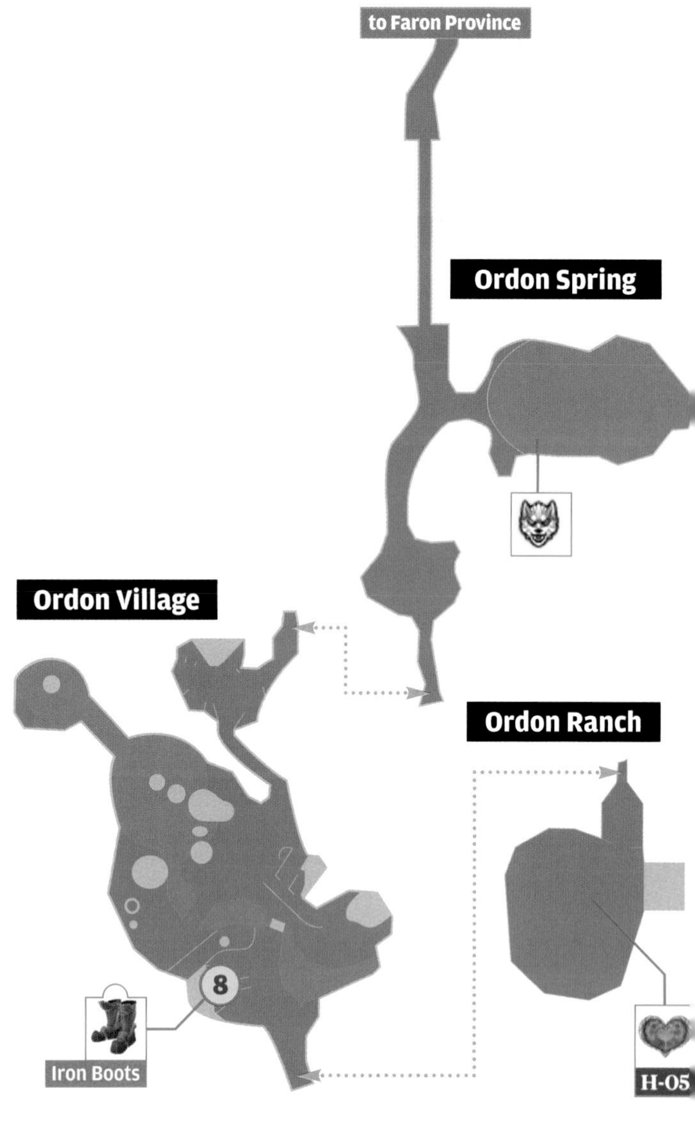

Learn a New Skill

Now that you have a mount, you'll be able to jump the village gate and return to Ordon Village. On your way, you'll receive a new hidden skill, the Shield Attack (an excellent defense against enemies who use projectiles), in the forest spring area where you first saw Ilia and Epona. After you've learned the skill, head for the mayor's house in the village.

8 Earn the Iron Boots

If you're going to put the Gorons in their place, you'll need to learn the techniques of the sumo wrestler. Mayor Bo will school you on the basics. After a warm-up match, you'll wrestle for real. Move, slap, and grab. With victory, you'll earn the Iron Boots.

Following your second victory in the sumo ring, Bo will reward you with the Iron Boots. You'll use them for a variety of purposes in the Goron Mines.

The Iron Boots

Though your pace slows when you're wearing the Iron Boots, the heavy footwear has practical purposes. Wear the boots to stick to magnetic surfaces, sink in water, and walk past steam jets that would knock you over otherwise.

9 The Thundering Herd

On your return to Kakariko Village, you will witness Colin's kidnapping by a group of boar-mounted beasts. Chase them northeast into the field and knock them off their rides.

Defeat the minions when you have the opportunity, but focus on the leader. Speed up, cut him off, target him, then knock off his armor piece by piece.

Your initial victory against the leader of the mounted beasts leads to a joust on the stone bridge. Charge toward your opponent at full speed, swerve left or right as you draw near, then swing your sword when you pass him (a nunchuk-shaking circle swing works best). If you miss, pull back to turn around, then charge again.

10 The Right Shield at the Right Price

When you return to Kakariko Village, you'll discover that youngster Malo has opened his own shop, Malo Mart. The mart's top-shelf item is a Hylian Shield. You can buy it elsewhere, but Malo's price (200 rupees) is the best deal around. Purchase the fire-resistant protector before you head back to Death Mountain.

The Hylian Shield

The Hylian Shield offers much better protection than the Wooden Shield. It can deflect more-powerful projectiles and, unlike the Wooden Shield, it won't burn up.

11 Toss the Goron

Return to Death Mountain with your Iron Boots at the ready. When the Goron who pushed you over the edge tries to do it again, put on the boots. When prompted, press A to stop the Goron, then toss him to either side. You'll repeat the process with other Gorons as you continue up the path.

12 Call for Help

The road to the Goron encampment is dangerous. When you reach a place where archers aim to keep you from progressing, pick up a tall blade of grass and use it to call a falcon. The bird will land on your arm and offer you a way to take out the enemies.

Use your remote to aim at one of the archers, wait for any geysers in the way to die down, then press A to let go of the bird. The falcon will fly straight and knock out the assailant. Repeat the process with the other archers, then look for another blade of grass near the next group of enemies.

13 Spring and Fall

You'll witness two things at the camp: a Goron giving his pal a boost and the crash of a molten boulder. You'll deal with the rock later. For now fight Gorons until they roll up, climb onto them, and use them to launch to the top. Wear the boots to walk through steam blasts.

Healing Waters

On your way to the top of the encampment, you'll come across hot springs. Wade in the water to replenish your health. Near the springs, you'll find a shop where you can buy, among other things, a replacement shield and Lantern Oil.

14 Sumo Showdown

The (relatively) diminutive leader of the Gorons, Gor Coron, will challenge you to a sumo match to test your worthiness as a hero. Strap on the Iron Boots and remember your training. One toss out of the ring is all you need.

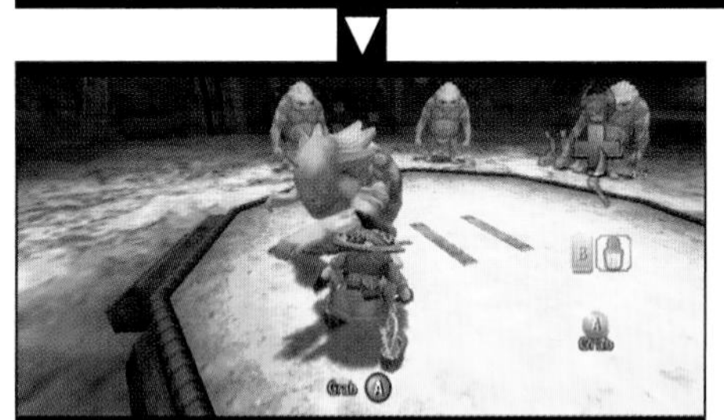

Gor Coron will attempt to stun you with a slap. If he manages to grab onto you, press A repeatedly to wrestle free. When you've got a clean shot, swing at your opponent, grab him, then push him over the edge.

Elevator Operator

The Goron Mines are open to you. However, if you want to explore before you take on your next big challenge, find the elevator in Gor Coron's chamber—it will take you to the rest of the camp. Use your Iron Boots to make it move.

Goron Mines

A troubled Goron leader and a treasure await in the lava-flooded domain of the mine dwellers.

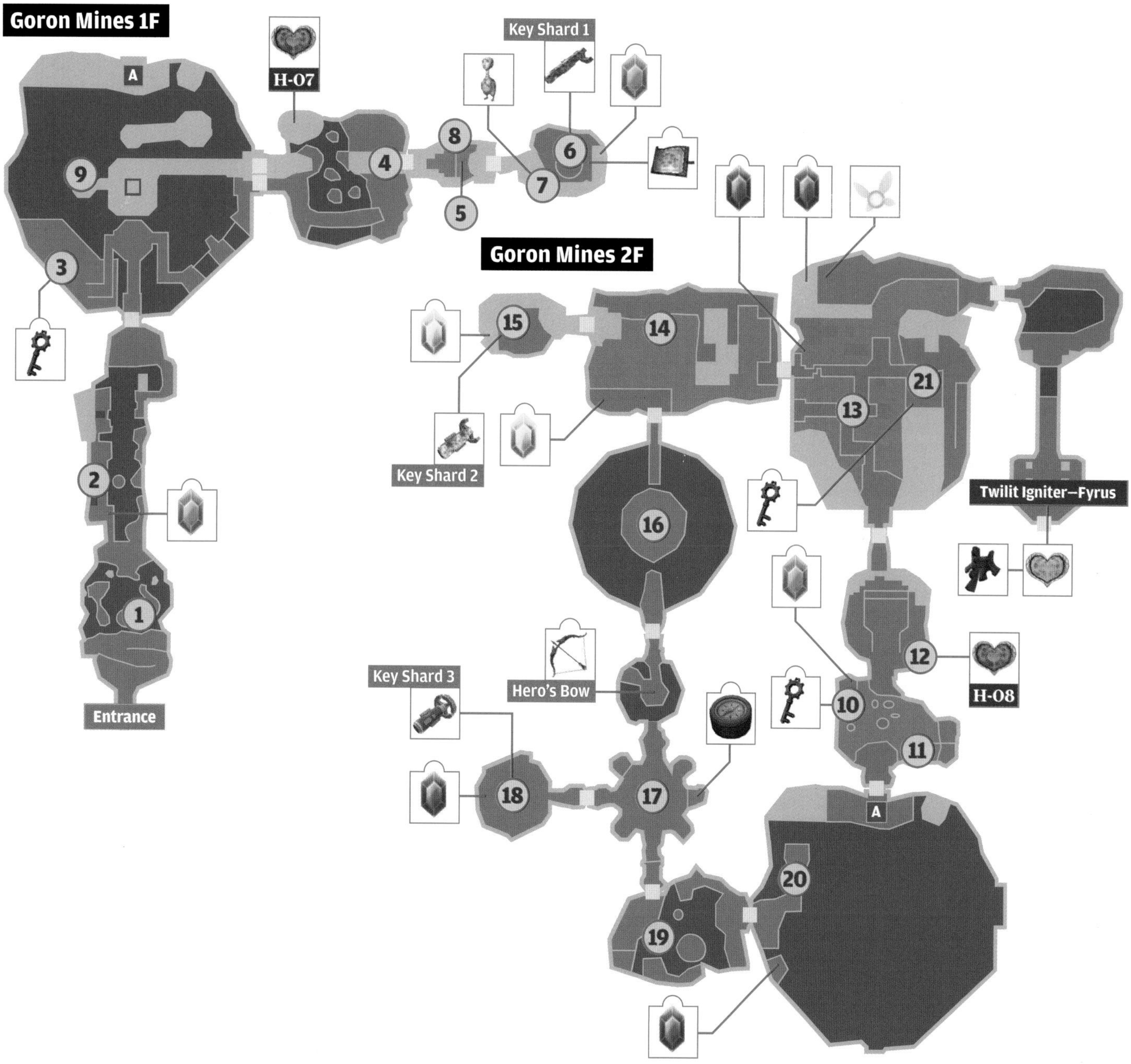

Goron Mines 1F

A
H-07
Key Shard 1
1
2
3
4
5
6
7
8
9
Entrance

Goron Mines 2F

10
11
12
13
14
15
16
17
18
19
20
21
A
Key Shard 2
Key Shard 3
Hero's Bow
Twilit Igniter—Fyrus
H-08

1 Old Faithful

Lava geysers (or as Midna calls them, flame pillars) spit forth molten rock in the lower reaches of the Goron Mines. As you move from ledge to ledge over the open lava river, wait for each geyser to die down before you leap.

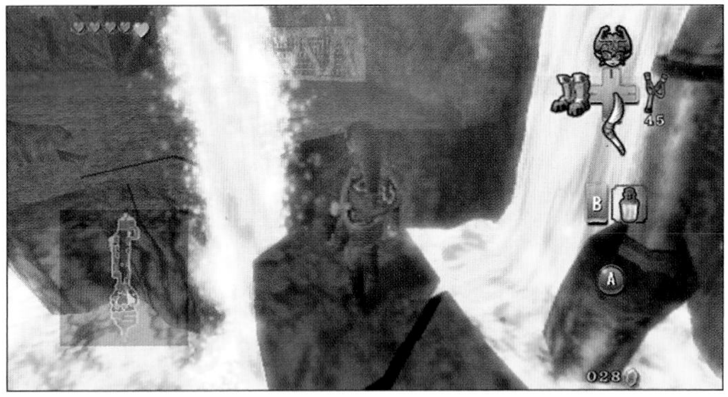

2 Don't Flame Out

The first section of the mine is real adventurer's territory. You'll break wooden barriers with your sword, jump gaps, and outrun balls of flame. When a steady stream of fire blocks your way, look for a switch on the floor, activate it with your boots (turning off the flame temporarily), then take your boots off to run through the passage quickly. As you approach the heavy door at the north end of the first chamber, jump onto the huge platform next to it. Switch to your boots to make the platform drop, causing the door to open.

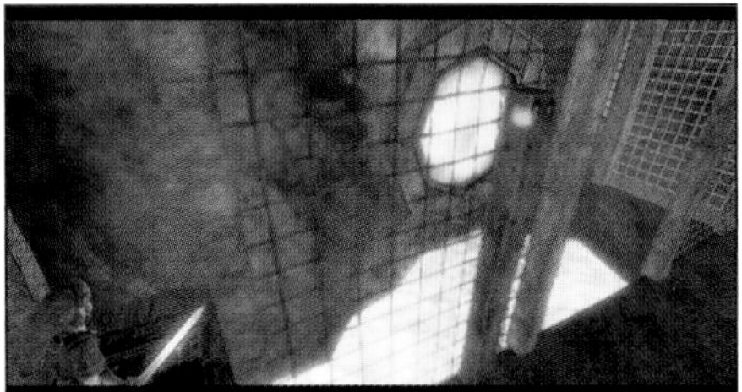

3 Key Finding

When you enter the large round chamber, a cut-scene will focus on the magnet that hangs above the area, but what you want to look at is the treasure chest below. Take the path to the left that leads down to the chest, and open it to reveal a Small Key. Climb back up the ramp, follow the path to the east side of the chamber, and use the key to move on. You'll encounter fire-spitting Dodongos in the next area. Target their tails with sword swipes.

4 Tug-a-Wall

There's a chain attached to a section of wall in the north-east corner. Pull it to make the wall slide. Wait for the flame pillars in the area to drop, then let go of the chain and jump from platform to platform until you reach the passage that the wall was blocking. If you get there before the wall slides back into place, you'll be able to continue along the path.

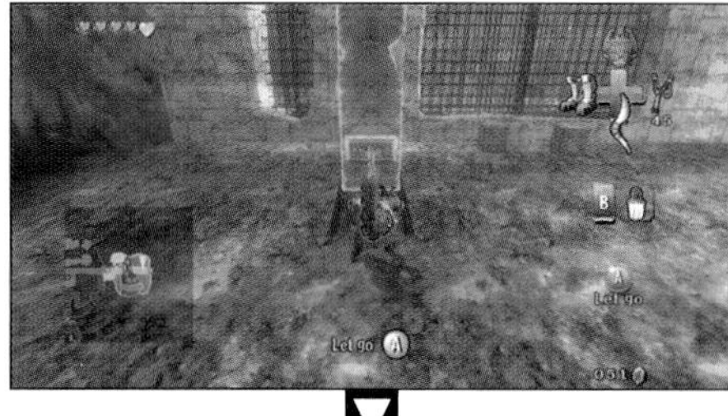

5 Heavy Metal

You'll go from a room flooded with lava to one flooded with water. Jump in. Use your Iron Boots to sink to the bottom (while watching the oxygen meter in the upper-left corner of the screen) and walk to the switch on the floor. The switch will activate a magnet above the pool and pull you toward it, Iron Boots first. Afterward, you'll be able to walk on magnetic blue surfaces, even on walls and ceilings.

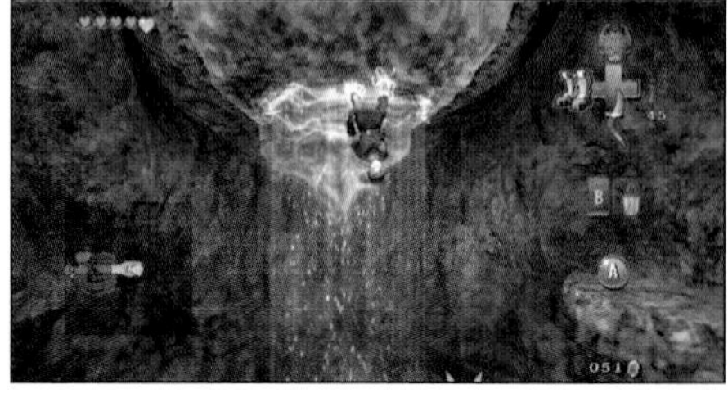

6 Key Assembly

In the room of elder Gor Amoto, you'll learn that the area's Big Key is in three pieces. Gor Amoto will give you the first of the Key Shards and tell you to find two more elders who have shards. The completed key will let you into the room where elder Darbus is being held.

7 The Treasures of Gor Amoto

Behind Gor Amoto, you'll discover a chest that holds the dungeon map, and another one that holds 20 rupees. Climb the ladder and pick up the pot that shakes. Inside the pot you'll find Ooccoo, who'll let you warp out of the mines if you need to leave in a hurry.

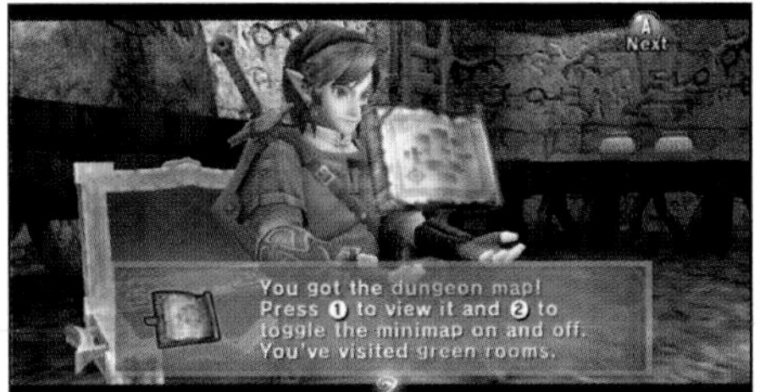

8 Wall Crawl

From the perch where you found Ooccoo, follow the path to the ledge that overlooks the water. You'll notice blue walls to your left and right. Put on the Iron Boots and use them to walk on the wall to reach the ledge and door on the west side of the room. In the next room, which holds a Piece of Heart, activate a magnet switch then walk on the curved path on the ceiling to the west.

9 Magnetic Pull

When you return to the large round chamber that acts as the Goron Mines hub, you'll run to a platform in the middle of the chamber and fight a gang of baddies. After they're gone, stomp the platform's switch to activate a magnet that will carry you over the lava.

10 Underwater Treasure

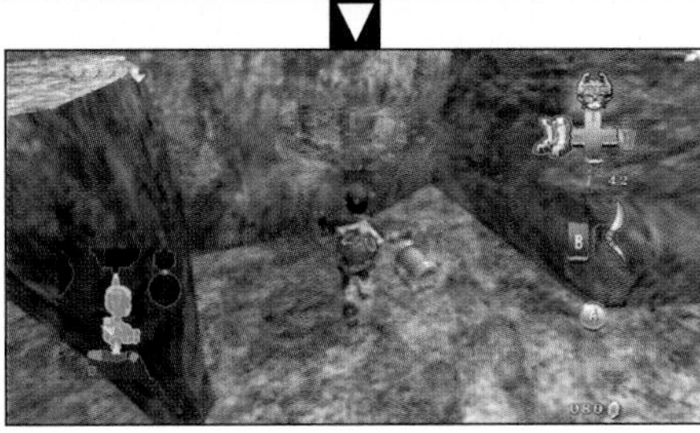

The flooded passage north of the hub houses a group of Tektites. Slice the bugs then drop into the water. Put on your Iron Boots when you get to the pool's northwest corner. When you reach the floor, you'll find a chest that holds a Small Key.

11 Crystal Quest

Swim to the southeast section of the pool, sink to the bottom, push a crate out of the way, then walk into the wire cage. Remove the boots, swim up to the surface, and climb onto dry land.

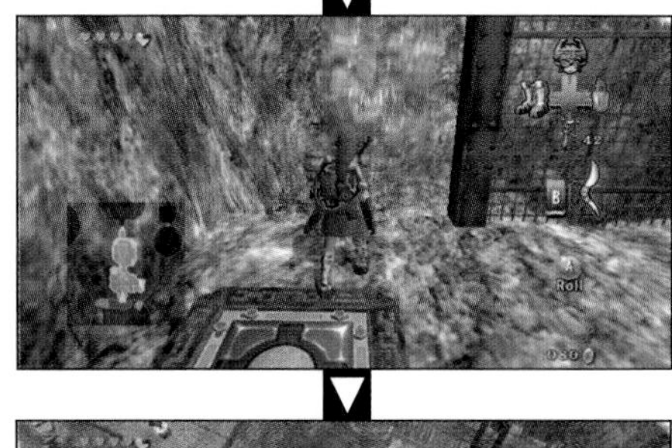

Wearing your Iron Boots, stomp on the platform at the east end of the room to activate a magnet. Use the magnet and a magnetic path to get to the room's highest platform. Walk to the center of the room on the platform, then hit another switch to activate a magnetic stream below you. Drop into the magnetic stream. It will pull you to the west wall, where you'll walk a curved path to a platform. After you drop to the platform and collect some rupees, attack the platform's blue crystal to open the gate at the north end of the room.

12 Heart Bypass

In the room that houses two Beamos statues and a drawbridge, climb up the wall on the east side while wearing your boots, and branch to the right. You'll find a chest that contains a Piece of Heart. Walk the path again, branch to the left, and cut the drawbridge rope with your sword.

13 Avoid the Archers

You'll see three archers at the far end of the mine's central northern chamber. You'll defeat them later. For now, run to the center of the room, collect a Small Key from a chest in the east (avoiding a Beamos), then follow the path west to a locked door. Use the key to continue.

14 Walk and Roll

A long platform revolves at a steady rate. There are three magnetic patches on one side and one on the other side. You'll get to the far end quickly by walking on the side that has one patch (sticking to it while the platform turns), but the three-patch side is a better bet.

15 Another Puzzle Piece

Gor Ebizo will greet you and give you the second Key Shard in the northwest corner of the mines. He'll also tell you that a new weapon is almost in your grasp. Collect a 10-rupee piece from a treasure chest, climb a ladder, and follow a path to the upper portion of the last room that you were in. Turn to the right and use your boots to walk a magnetic path to the door on the room's south side.

16 Catch the Guardian Off Guard

The round room on the west side of the mine houses a guardian who will stop at nothing to protect his territory. His weak spot is his belly. Get close to him, take a few swipes, and attack his stomach when he raises his arms.

After you hit the guardian's gut a few times, he'll ball up and roll toward you. That's your cue to put on the Iron Boots. Face the creature, press Z to put the camera behind you, and wait for the monster to approach. Press A to grab him when he gets close, then toss him left or right. When you've thrown him into the lava three times, you'll win.

The Hero's Bow

You'll find the Hero's Bow in the chamber south of the guardian's room. Collect it, equip it, and use it to cut the rope that holds up the drawbridge to the south.

17 Disarm the Turrets

Continuing your journey south, you'll enter a room full of inactive Beamos statues. When you reach the Beamos at the south end, it (and the rest of them) will come to life. Fire an arrow at the south turret's red light. Return to the other Beamos statues and knock out their lights, too.

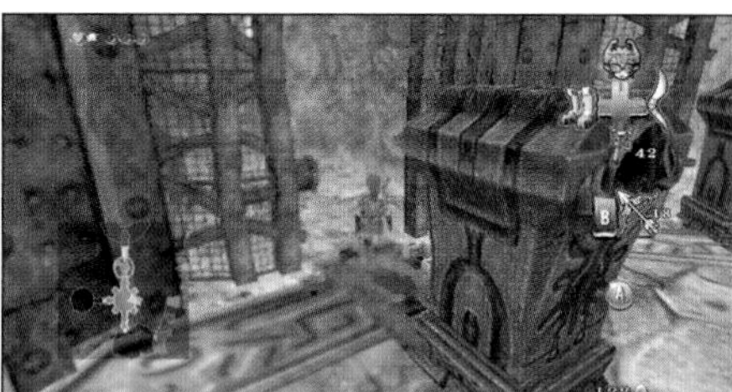

With the turrets out of commission, you can pull them out of the way and walk around them. Go to the other side of the turret that's due east of your location to find the compass.

18 The Puzzle Complete

Those Goron elders aren't easy to find. But by entering the room to the west of the turret-filled chamber, you will discover the third one and collect the last Key Shard. You now have the Big Key. Collect a 50-rupee piece from the room's chest, then return to the turrets.

19 Your Aim Is True

As you advance along the path south of the turret chamber, you'll reach a wire fence. Roll into it to knock it over. Before you start to jump onto the small islands in the lava, use your bow to hit the enemies that are above the islands.

When you get to the gate at the north end of the room, you'll find a switch on the ground that will activate a magnet and pull you to the ceiling, where a Dodongo waits. To make the battle easy, target its tail from below with your bow before you go to the ceiling. While you're walking on the ceiling, you'll come within view of the crystal that opens the room's gate. Hit it with an arrow, then drop to the floor and advance.

20 Turn North at the Hub

You'll find yourself in the west side of the main room's upper reaches. Collect a rupee prize to the south and use an arrow to cut down a drawbridge to the north. There you'll trigger a magnet on a crane that will carry you to the room's north end. Head north from there.

21 Archery Practice

When you return to the archer-guarded room, stop moving and target all of the creatures that you can see, then advance to the east side of the room.

Approach the Beamos that was once protecting a Small Key and use an arrow to shoot out its red light. Pull the Beamos to reveal a passage to the room's upper level.

Target more archers from the upper level (target the explosive barrels for easy kills) and advance to a switch that triggers a magnet on a crane. From there, drop to a platform.

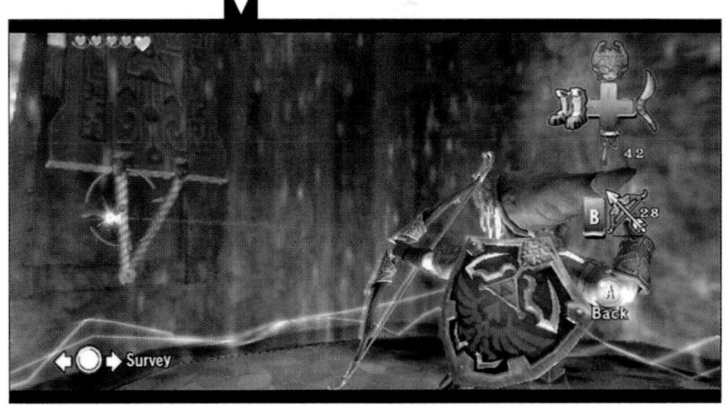

Put on your boots to let the magnet pick you up. It'll take you to the drawbridge in the room's northeast corner. Target the drawbridge's rope. After the drawbridge opens, drop to it and move on.

Healing Help

Before you cross the drawbridge, explore the platform in the northeast corner. Break boxes and barrels and free a fairy. Scoop up the fairy with an empty bottle.

Twilit Igniter—Fyrus

After you endure another battle against archers and make another drawbridge open, you'll head off to the boss's chamber. Patriarch Darbus is not feeling like himself. He's been possessed by a fiery being, and the only way to make him return to normal is to defeat his new form. Midna will tell you that the shiny object on the monster's forehead is its true eye. Hit it with arrows.

After you score a direct hit, the beast will walk around dazed. Run behind him and grab one of the chains that he's dragging. Put on your Iron Boots for traction then pull the chain. If you manage to tighten it, Fyrus will trip and fall, and his fire will go out. If you don't have any luck felling the beast by dragging his chain, you'll knock it to the ground eventually by hitting its shiny spot with enough arrows. Once the beast is on the ground, run up to its luminescent weak point and hit it with your sword. You should be able to get in about three quality hits before the creature ignites again and stands up for another round. After a few rounds, you'll defeat the creature for good and earn another Fused Shadow for Midna and another Heart Container for yourself. As a reward, Midna will tell you the name of the king of twilight: Zant.

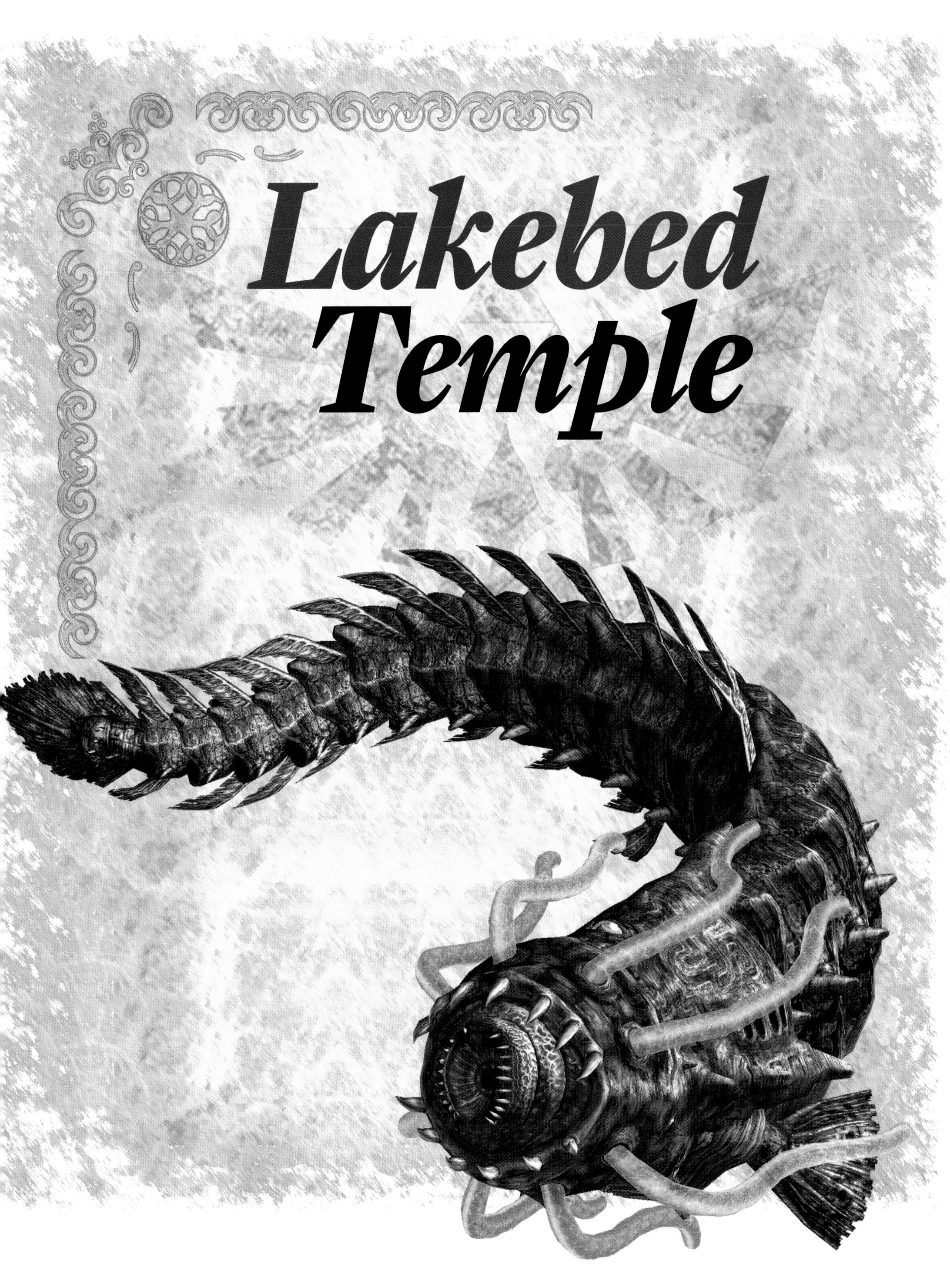

Lakebed Temple

Lanayru Province

Lanayru Province is home to the aquatic Zora people and the waters of Lake Hylia. Hope you're ready for a swim.

1 An Explosive Offer

By the time you've conquered the Goron Mines, the Barnes Bomb Shop in Kakariko Village will be back in business. If you try to purchase bombs, Barnes will offer you a special deal—a Bomb Bag with 30 bombs for 120 rupees. Take Barnes up on his offer.

Bombs

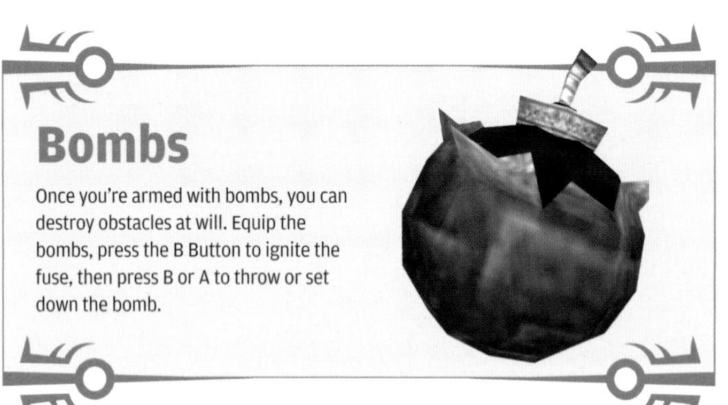

Once you're armed with bombs, you can destroy obstacles at will. Equip the bombs, press the B Button to ignite the fuse, then press B or A to throw or set down the bomb.

Hawkeye

The Hawkeye functions like binoculars and lets Link see great distances. Combined with the bow, it works like a sniper's scope—perfect for hitting distant enemies. To find it, head to the north part of town and get a boost from the Gorons to the upper levels. Atop the high tower, you'll find Talo, who asks you to participate in an archery game. Whether you hit the last target or not, the Hawkeye will become available in Malo's store. (If you do hit the target you'll receive a Piece of Heart.) You'll also eventually receive a letter that clues you in on the new item for sale.

Go Long with the Bomb

As the shopkeep indicates, you can combine the arrows with bombs from the equip menu—first equip the bow, then highlight the bombs and press the Z Button. Once you enter Hyrule Field, you'll get a letter from the shopkeep explaining the process, but if you use the explosive arrows before you leave Kakariko Village you can acquire a Piece of Heart.

To the left of the Spirit Spring, you'll see a bluff that has three boulders on top. Shoot the boulders with the explosive arrows to reveal a Piece of Heart, then use the Gale Boomerang to retrieve the treasure. You can explode a lower group of boulders to reveal a path to another Piece of Heart.

2 Back to the Bridge

Make any desired purchases in Kakariko Village then ride Epona north through Hyrule Field and across the stone bridge. Bomb the boulders that block the path. When you blow up the boulders, the bridge will break and twilight-realm creatures will fall from the sky. You don't need to fight them now if you don't want to. If you choose to fight them, use Link's spin attack to finish them all at once.

3 It's in the Bag

Shortly after Midna helps you penetrate another curtain of twilight and you return to wolf form, you'll find Ilia's bag. Forget the youths' scent and learn Ilia's scent.

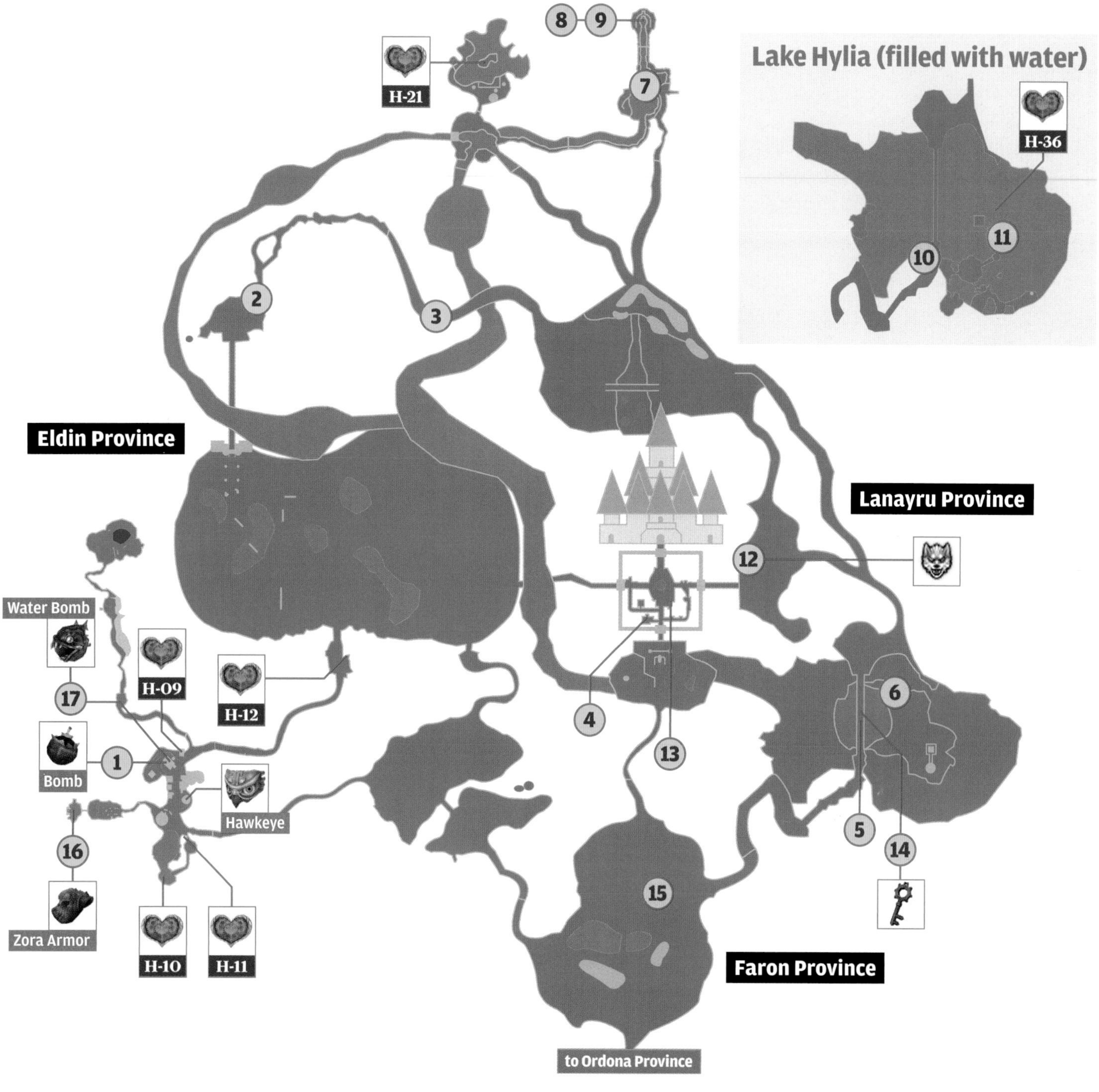

Lake Hylia (filled with water)

H-36 10 11

8 9 7 H-21 2 3

Eldin Province

Lanayru Province

12

Water Bomb 17 H-09 H-12 1 Bomb Hawkeye 16 Zora Armor H-10 H-11

4 13 6 5 14 15

Faron Province

to Ordona Province

4 The Nose Knows

Follow the scent all the way to Castle Town. Eventually it will lead you to Telma's Bar, where Ilia is caring for a Zora child. Listen to her and the nearby group of soldiers.

With all the spirits roaming Castle Town, it's easy to get distracted. Stick to following Ilia's scent.

You'll learn from the soldiers that something's amiss at Lake Hylia. Check their map to see where trouble's brewing, then head there via the town's eastern exit.

5 Jump off a Bridge

Continue east after you exit the town. While you're crossing the Great Bridge of Hylia, you'll be ambushed by an enemy that lights the bridge on fire. Climb onto one of the boxes and use it to jump over the rail.

6 Monster—It's the Only Way to Fly

After recovering from your fall, listen to the Zora soldiers then listen to Fyer near his shack. He'll spot a monster prowling the edge of the lake. When you head after the monster, it mounts a giant bird creature and attacks.

Dodge the rider's flaming arrows, and when the bird monster swoops down and attempts to grab you, jump-attack it with the A Button. Keep pressing the A Button to inflict damage. Eventually you'll knock the rider off the bird; defeat the rider with standard attacks.

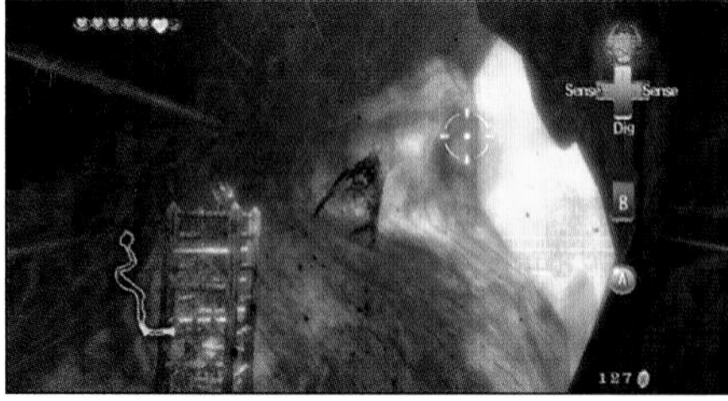

After you defeat the rider, Midna will take the bird creature's reins. Control the creature by pointing the Wii remote in the direction you want to move, and dash with the A Button. Dodge the flaming arrows and falling rocks, and don't crash into the scaffolding.

7 The Frozen Falls

When you reach the base of Zora's Domain, you'll see why the water isn't flowing: everything's frozen! Ascend the frozen waterfall by summoning Midna and repeatedly pressing A to jump from ledge to ledge. If you see a shaking icicle, let it fall before you proceed.

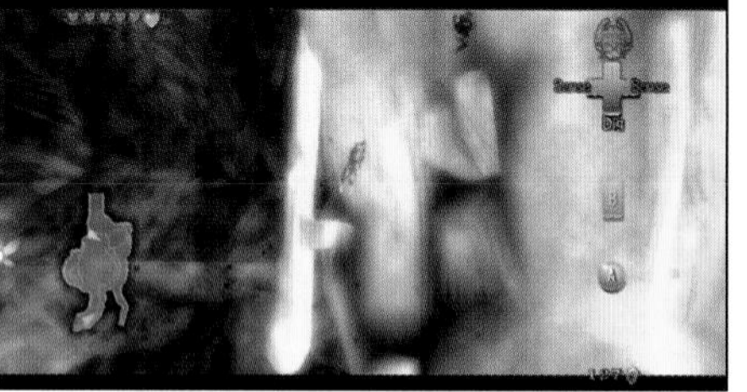

8 Triple Threat

As you approach the Zoras' throne room, you'll encounter three shadow creatures. First circle around to the left and slay the single creature that's protected by the barrier, then use your multienemy attack to take out the other two monsters.

9 Rock On, Dude

The Zoras are frozen beneath the ice, so use Midna's warping ability to warm them up. Warp to Death Mountain then check in with Midna when you're near the huge rock that fell earlier. Warp the rock back to Zora's Domain to melt the ice.

10 Off the Deep End

After you exit Zora's Domain, dive into the water and follow the river back to Lake Hylia. You'll wind up at the Spirit Spring. Talk to Lanayru to get the third Vessel of Light.

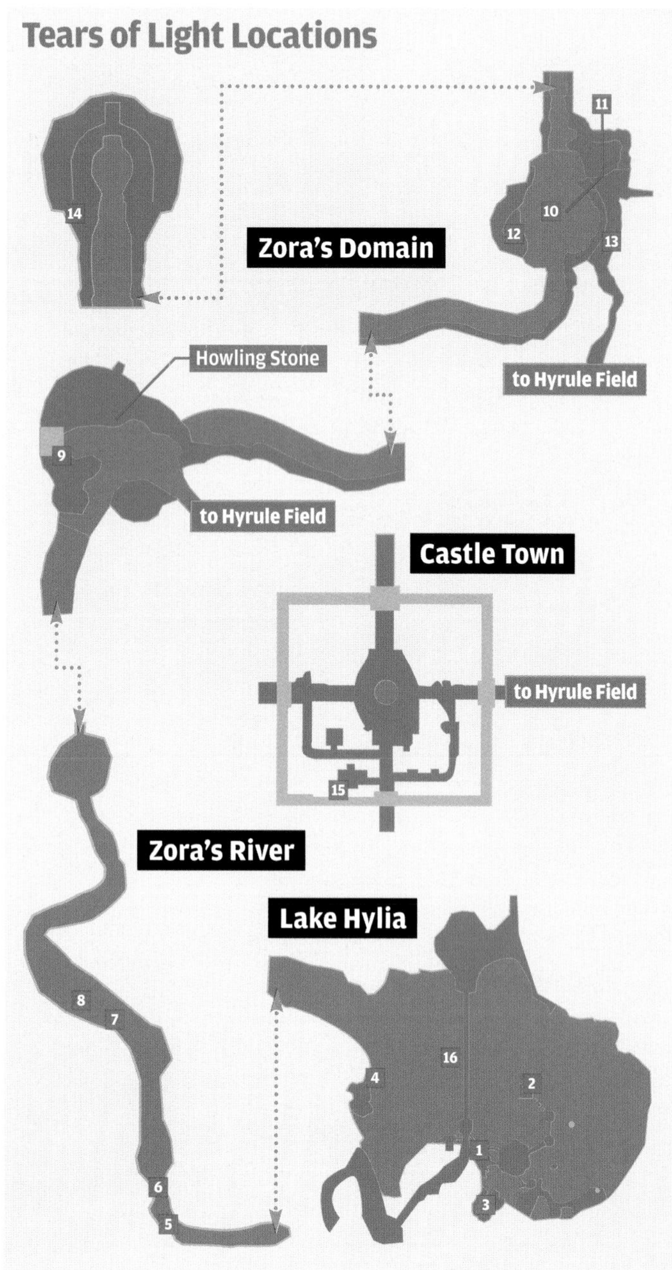

Lakeside Extermination Service

1 You'll encounter the first bug as soon as you exit the Spirit Spring. Follow the wooden bridge to your right and switch to sense mode to dispose of the creature.

2 When you head across the circular island, you'll encounter three more shadow beasts. Defeat them and continue on to Fyer's shack. You'll find a flying bug near the back of the shack. Avoid the bug's attack when it swoops down, then counter with an attack of your own.

3 South of the round island is a series of disconnected islands. Jump from island to island, using dash jumps to clear the gaps. If you miss a jump and fall in the water, you'll have to swim back to dry land near the wooden bridge. When you reach the high ground, dig up and defeat the insect.

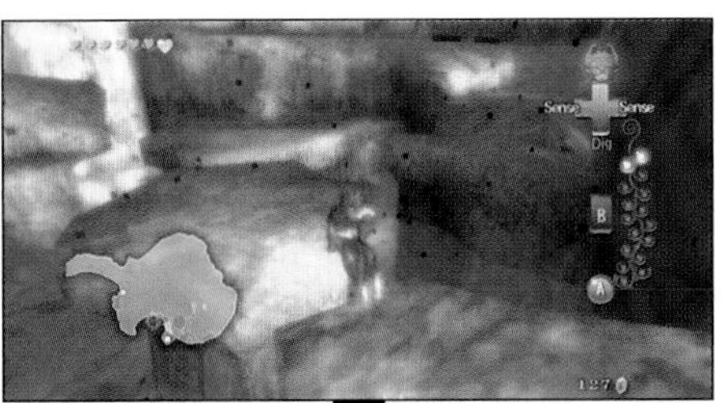

More Unfriendly Skies

4 Head to the western edge of Lake Hylia, where you'll find the fourth shadow bug. After beating the bug, howl near the fanlike plant to summon the giant bird monster you rode earlier. It's your ticket to catching the next four bugs.

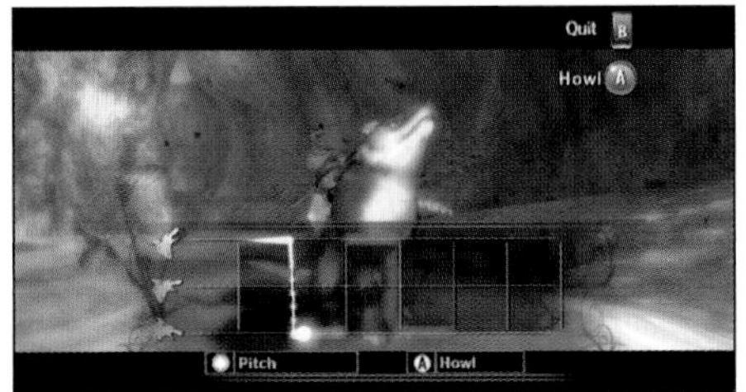

5-8 Activate sense mode as you fly through the cavern in the grip of the bird creature. When you get close to one of the bugs, lock onto it with the Z Button, and dash into it when it's not electrified to destroy it. If you miss any of the bugs, fly through the cavern again to take care of the stragglers.

9 Listen to the spirit near the boat-rental cabin—a bug will appear. Destroy it to claim your ninth tear. Before you seek out the remaining bugs, locate the nearby Howling Stone.

Stone by the Stream

You'll find a Howling Stone north of the boat-rental cabin. If you match the howl sequence, the swordsman will appear near the castle to teach human Link a new skill.

10 & 11 Follow the path next to the river to re-enter Zora's Domain. You'll find two more bugs in the center of the pool. Stand on one of the floating leaves, and jump-attack the bugs. You can't hurt them while you're in the water.

12 On the western shore of the pool, you'll encounter another bug. Dig it up if necessary and defeat it to collect another tear.

13 Use Midna to jump from ledge to ledge and climb the canyon wall. Partway up, you'll find a path leading south. Jump the gap to reach the path, and defeat the bug you'll find.

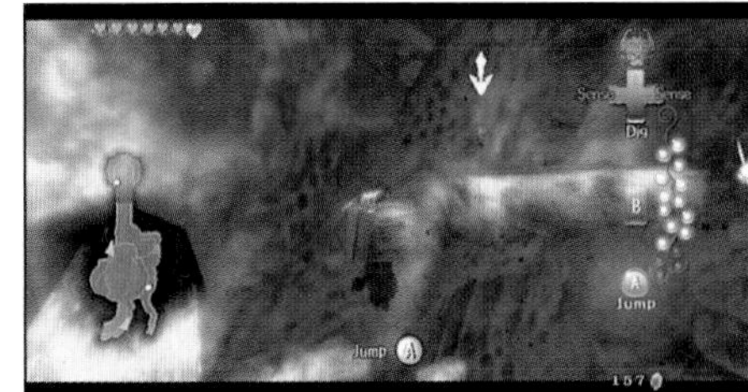

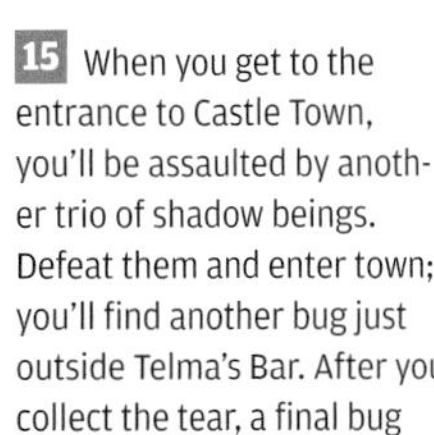

Follow the trail of rupees to find the path to the 13th bug. Midna won't offer to help you clear the gap; you can make the jump on your own.

14 One of the bugs is on a wall in the throne room. Ram the wall to knock the bug loose, then defeat it to claim its tear. Afterward, retrace your steps to Zora's River. Jump into the southeast-flowing river to take a shortcut back to Hyrule Field. From there return to Castle Town.

15 When you get to the entrance to Castle Town, you'll be assaulted by another trio of shadow beings. Defeat them and enter town; you'll find another bug just outside Telma's Bar. After you collect the tear, a final bug will appear at Lake Hylia. Use Midna to warp there.

The Mother of All Bugs

16 The final tear is held by a giant insect boss. Like its smaller counterparts, the boss attacks with electrified swooping charges. Dodge the charges and use your jump attack to hurt the boss when the electricity subsides.

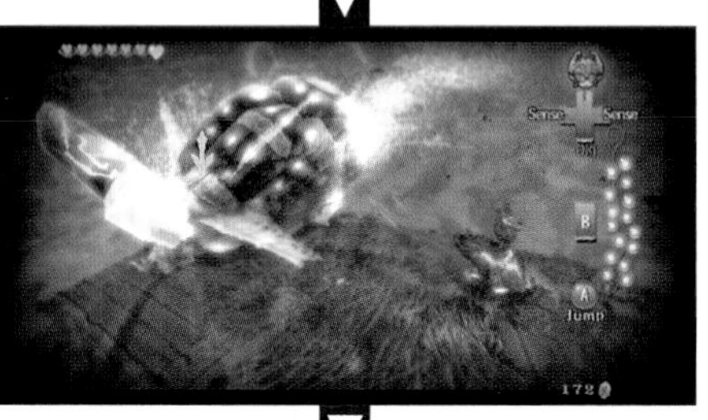

After you damage the boss, the bug will submerge and swim through the water in an attempt to damage you with its electrical charge. Stay on land unless you need to dodge an attack, and wait for the boss to resume its airborne assault.

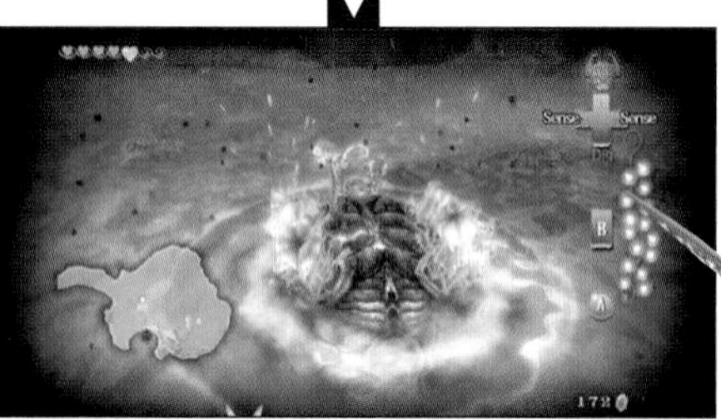

Once you've hit the boss several times, it will fall into the water on its back. Leap onto the creature's belly and use your charged multienemy attack to hit all its weak points at once.

The Third Light Spirit Returns

After you've defeated the boss and collected the Tears of Light, light will be restored to Lanayru Province. The Light Spirit Lanayru will show you the location of the next Fused Shadow, but will also give you a warning in the form of a Hyrulian history lesson.

11 Prepare for Launch

You can't visit the Lakebed Temple without proper underwater gear, so talk to Fyer and try his attraction—it's the only way out of the lake basin. Once you've landed topside, you can play Falbi's minigame before heading back to Hyrule Field.

A Fowl Trip

Falbi's Flight-by-Fowl minigame lets you float down to the lake via Cucco, collecting rupees and attempting to land on a set of tiered platforms. Each tier has a different reward (from top to bottom): 100 rupees, a Piece of Heart, 50 rupees, 20 rupees, and 10 rupees.

12 Backstabber

If you activated the Howling Stone near Zora's Domain, you'll find the golden wolf to the right of the Castle Town entrance. Face the ghostly warrior to learn the Back Slice.

Minigames are the Bomb

As you enter Castle Town, the mailman will deliver a letter notifying you that two new minigames have opened near Zora's Domain: Iza's Rapid Ride and Hena's Fishing Hole. If you want to carry multiple types of bombs, visit Iza's Rapid Ride. To get there, proceed to the section of Hyrule Field north of the town and travel to the northernmost point, where you can bomb open the cave to Zora's Domain. From there, follow the river south until you reach a cabin. After you defeat some shadow creatures outside of the cabin, Iza will ask for your help blowing up some rocks. When you accomplish the task you'll get an extra Bomb Bag, allowing you to carry multiple types of bombs at once. If you ride the rapids again and score 25 points or more, you'll win a Giant Bomb Bag upgrade, which makes your current Bomb Bags hold twice the number of bombs. While you're in the area, you should also visit Hena's Fishing Hole. If you snag the Piece of Heart on the precipice while fishing, it's yours to keep.

Take the Scenic Route

Now that you've freed Castle Town from the darkness, the place is bustling with activity. Before you head to Telma's Bar, take some time to get acquainted with the town. There are several points of interest, including the STAR minigame, Fanadi (the fortune teller), and Agitha (the bug-obsessed little girl). If you have one of the bugs Agitha is looking for, she'll give you a Big Wallet that holds 600 rupees. You can also donate money to the preacher, but you'll need to contribute 1,000 rupees before reaping any benefit.

Castle Town

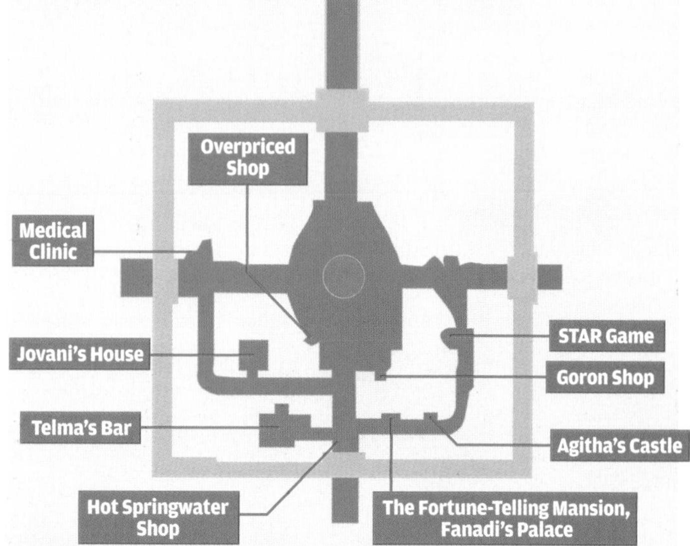

13 Goron Goods

Gorons have set up shop in the southeast section of Castle Town's courtyard. Each Goron has a different item to sell you. The big Goron on the first floor will sell you a Hylian Shield. If you didn't buy one in Kakariko Village, get it now.

14 Battle on the Bridge

Telma and Ilia need to go to Kakariko Village, and it's up to you to get them there. The first obstacle is another boar-riding enemy on the bridge, but this time the enemy is well-armored and will deflect your sword attacks. Charge forward on Epona, and as you get close to the enemy, switch to your bow and aim between his shields. After you hit him a few times, he'll go careening over the edge. In a cut-scene, you'll grab a key that you'll need to proceed.

15 Protect the Wagon

Enemy archers, riders, and flying beasts will try to stop the wagon's progress, but if you stay close you should be able to ward off most of the danger. Use your bow to defeat the archers that fire at you from the hills on either side of the road.

If the enemies light the wagon on fire, you can extinguish the flames by locking onto the wagon and using the Gale Boomerang. Attack the enemy riders with your sword at close range, and with your bow from afar.

Flying enemies are particularly annoying—they will drop bombs that throw the wagon off course. Try to shoot the birds down with arrows, or lock onto them and hit them with the Gale Boomerang.

16 Ghosts of the Zora

After making the trek to Kakariko Village, you'll be visited by the spirit of Rutela. Follow the spirit to the graveyard, through the opening she reveals, and to her husband's grave, where you'll acquire the Zora Armor.

Zora Armor

The Zora Armor has magical enchantments that give the wearer the powers of a Zora—specifically, the abilities to breathe and move freely underwater. However, you'll be more vulnerable to fire and ice attacks while the armor is equipped.

17 Go with the Flow

While you're in Kakariko Village, purchase Water Bombs at the bomb shop. You may have to sell your stock of regular bombs, but the Water Bombs will let you blast a secret shortcut from King Zora's grave to Lake Hylia.

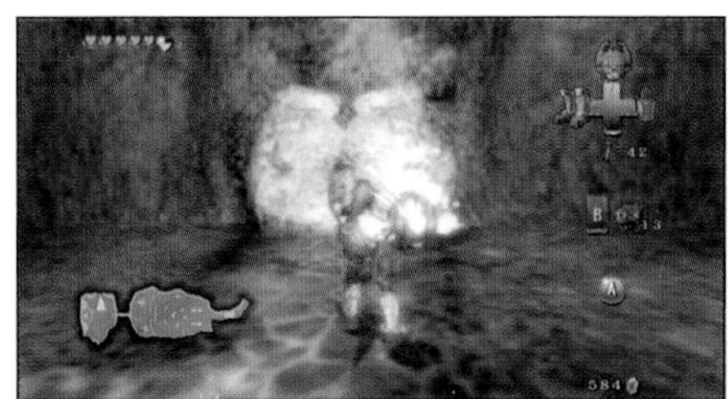

Water Bombs

Water Bombs function like regular bombs, but you can use them on land and underwater. They'll come in extremely handy when you explore the Lakebed Temple.

Lakebed Temple

Beneath Lake Hylia, sluices and hydro-powered machinery protect the Lakebed Temple's secrets.

Lakebed Temple 1F

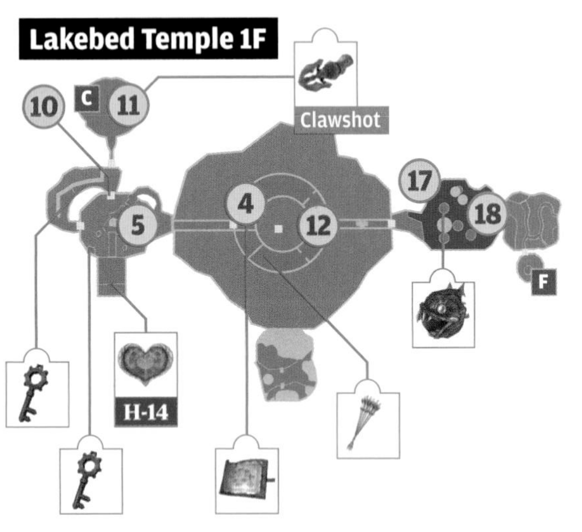

Lakebed Temple 4F

E

Lakebed Temple 3F

Lakebed Temple B1

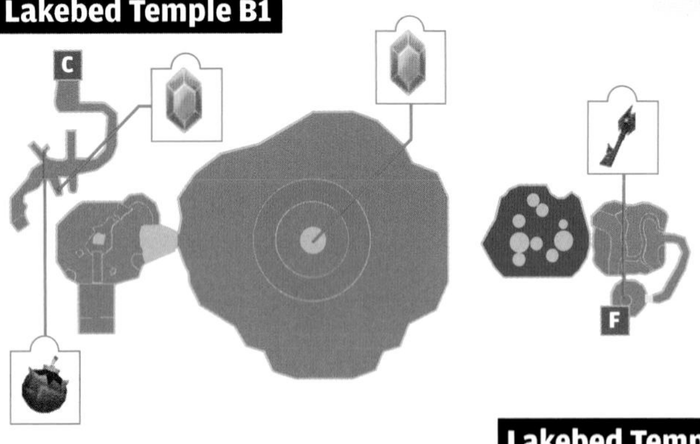

Lakebed Temple 2F

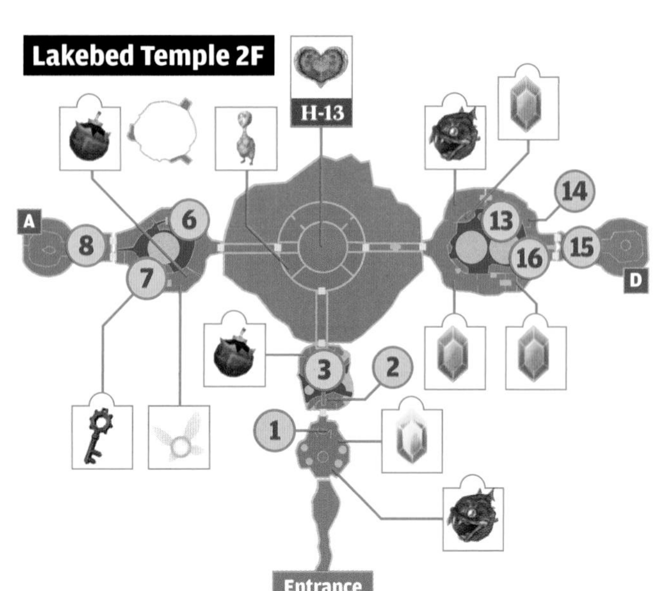

Lakebed Temple B2

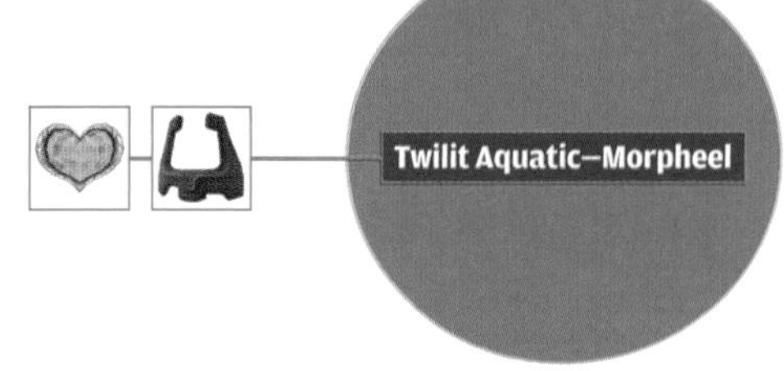

Explosive Entrance

You must use Water Bombs to open the entrance to the Lakebed Temple; if you don't have any, one of the Zoras near the temple entrance will sell you some. Bomb the rock in front of the entrance to cause bubbles to rise, then set another bomb, which the bubbles will carry upward.

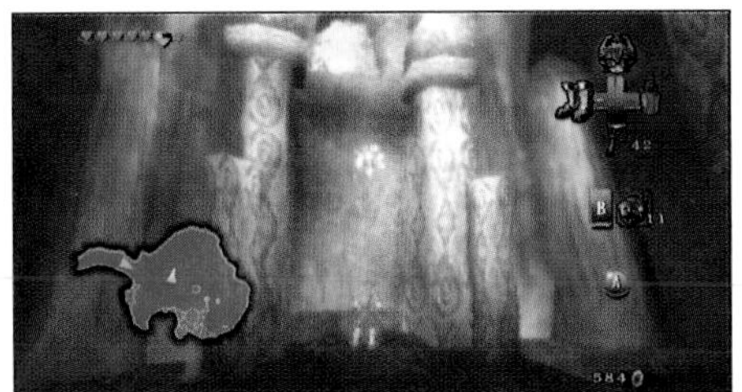

Aquatic Assault

While you're underwater, you won't be able to use most of your equipment, and you won't be able to use your sword while you're swimming. Keep your Iron Boots handy, since equipping them will let you walk on the floor and fight using your sword and shield. Water Bombs should also be a key part of your arsenal. If you find yourself vulnerable against underwater foes, retreat to a position where you can fight on solid ground.

Taste the Chu Jelly Rainbow

Though it sounds gross, you can scoop up the remains of defeated Chus with an empty bottle and save them for later. The effect varies depending on the Chu Jelly's color: red and blue ones restore health, yellow ones fuel your lantern, and purple ones can heal or damage Link.

1 Yank It Down

The gate at the top of the stairs is shut tight, but you can open it by jumping from the ledge and grabbing the lever. Link's weight will pull the lever down and open the gate. You'll encounter several similar devices throughout the temple.

2 Hold on Tite

Use your bomb/arrow combination to shoot the thin necks of the stalactites that are hanging from the ceiling. The stalactites will fall and create platforms that enable you to get across the chamber.

3 Shell Shock

The Helmasaurs are impervious to a frontal attack. Either dodge their charges and hit them on their vulnerable back sides, or use the Back Slice to circle around and hit them where it hurts.

4 Map to the Map

In the large circular room, you can rotate the central stairs by pulling the levers, which will allow you to get to otherwise-inaccessible parts of the room. To reach the dungeon map, head down the stairs and circle around to the south of the room, then jump from the ledge and grab the lever to rotate the staircase. Afterward, head back up the steps and grab the lever on the east side. Head down the stairs and go right to find the map.

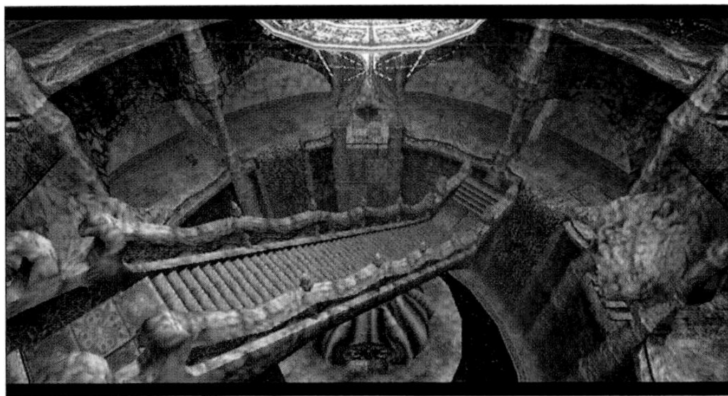

5 Stalactites Are the Key

Take the lower western exit out of the circular chamber and cross the bridge. In the next room, knock down the stalactites with the bomb arrows, then head down the passage to the right. Climb around the central pillar using the vines and drop onto the western ledge.

If you knocked down the most distant stalactite, the broken tip will form a platform on the geyser. Jump from the ledge to the stone pillar, and then to the platform. From there, jump to the pillar that holds the treasure chest. You'll find a Small Key inside the chest.

6 Rise and Fall

Return to the circular chamber and head upstairs. Circle around to the upper western door; you'll find Ooccoo to the door's left. Open the door with the Small Key and cross the bridge to the next chamber. Blast the stalactite near the northern wall to create a step that allows you to reach the vines and climb on top of the wall.

From the top of the wall, jump and grab the lever, which will cause the gate below you to open. Jump down, continue through the chamber, and take the first door to the south.

7 Across the Cog

You'll encounter a lizard warrior in the round room where the giant cog is. After defeating the creature, take the southwest exit then head left to find a treasure chest containing another Small Key.

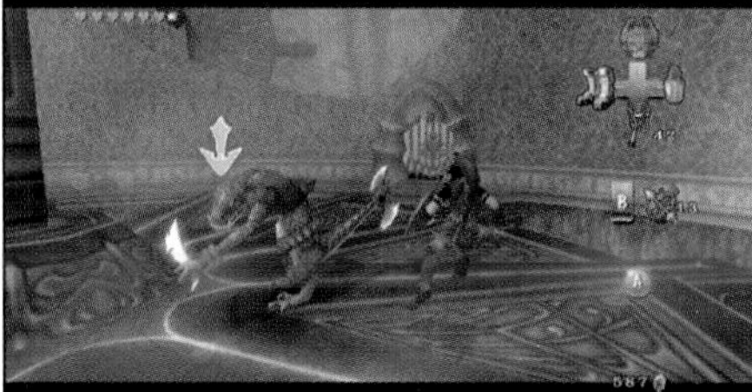

8 Burst His Bubble

Head back through the cog room and turn left. You'll find a boulder blocking your path—destroy it with a bomb. Continue down the hall and enter the next room.

In that chamber an enemy jumps into a bubble to protect itself. Use any type of bomb (or bomb arrow) to destroy the bubble, then attack the foe directly. Once it's defeated, use a Small Key to get through the locked door.

9 Let It Flow

Head to the top of the western tower by taking the spiraling ramp. At the top you'll find an archway. Climb the archway and jump onto the lever to open the sluice and release the water. Follow the water to the bottom of the room.

With the room's lower area filled with water, you can swim over to the large fish statue. Grab the lever that's hanging from the statue to open another sluice.

10 Like Clockwork

Follow the flowing water through the door; you'll end up back in the chamber where you found a Small Key earlier. You can collect a fairy in the area past the waterwheel before entering the door that leads to the room with the huge cog inside. Jump to the lower level and make your way to the door on the east side. From there jump to a moving platform and take the door leading north. Head left and grab a Small Key, then return to the moving platforms. Ride a platform to the western door. In the next room use a Small Key to unlock the door to your left.

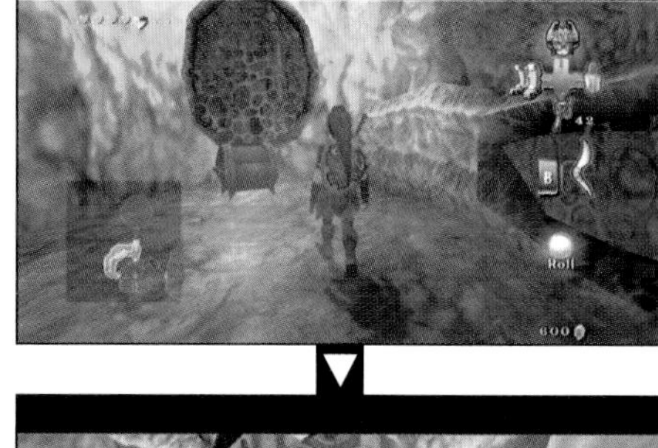

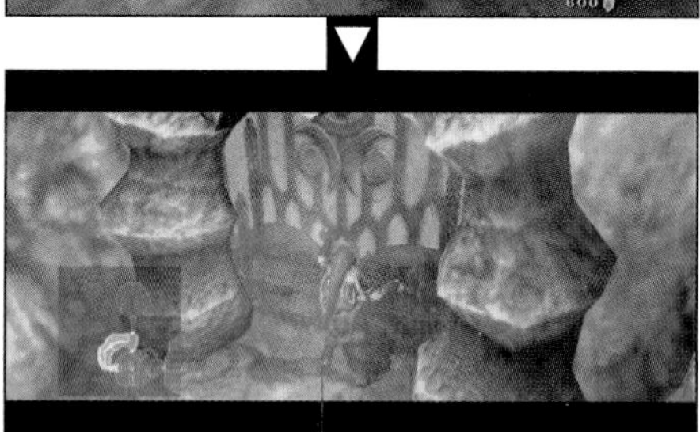

11 Feelin' Froggy

Equip the Iron Boots and enter the water-filled passage. Since you can't hurt the jellyfish, it's best to avoid them, but if you're feeling daring you can explore the side caves and collect some extra rupees. Blow up the boulder with a Water Bomb to proceed through the passage, then swim up to the next chamber. Look at the ceiling like Midna suggests to enter battle against a gargantuan frog.

The huge frog sends a swarm of tadpoles after you; use the spin attack to kill several at once. Once you've destroyed them, the frog will leap into the air and try to squash you. Run away to avoid the attack, then hit its vulnerable tongue after it lands.

When the frog opens its mouth, toss a bomb or bomb arrow into its gullet. The explosion will cause the frog to collapse, again exposing the tongue and allowing you to inflict more damage.

Clawshot

Like the venerable Hookshot of old, the Clawshot is an extendable chain with an attachment on the end that will let you grapple to distant locations. After you've assigned the Clawshot to the B Button, you can target objects and surfaces from an over-the-shoulder view; the targeting reticle will turn yellow if you're aiming at a location you can grapple to. If you grapple onto a ceiling, you can raise, lower, and rotate Link with the Control Stick on the nunchuk. The Clawshot is also extremely useful in combat. It can tear the armor off of the armadillolike foes, pull the green enemies out of their protective water bubbles, and extract the vulnerable center of jellyfish. The Clawshot comes in handy for stunning enemies as well.

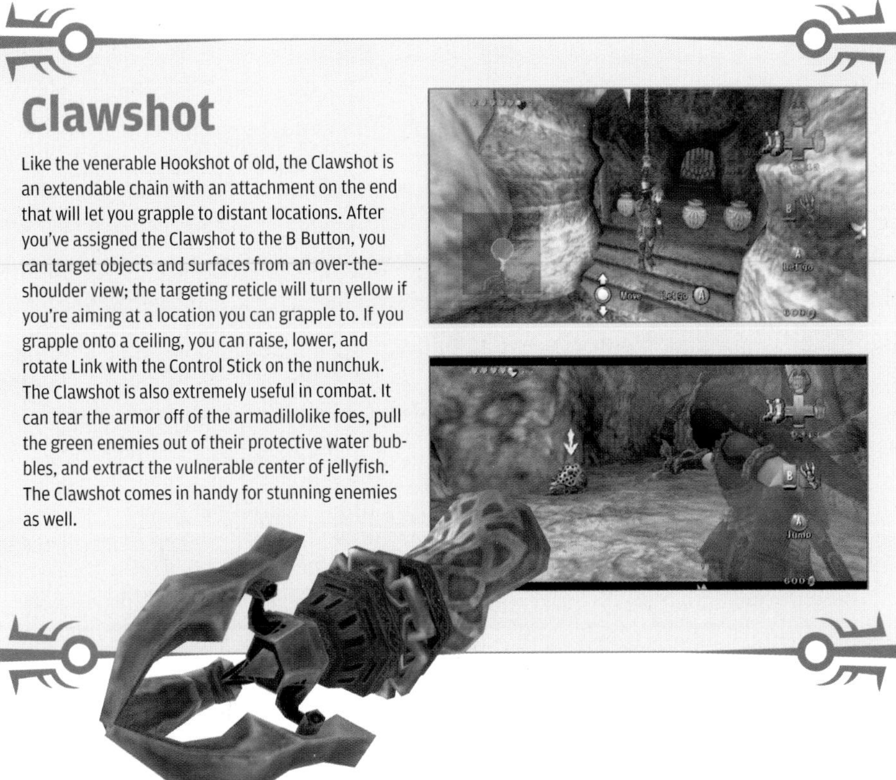

12 A River Runs through It

Using the Clawshot, target the red switch above the doorway in the giant frog's chamber to escape the room. Return to the central round room; now that you have the Clawshot, you can grapple to vines that let you bypass the barriers and maneuver around the chamber freely. Head to the lower east side of the room and hit the red switch with the Clawshot, which will rotate the steps and allow water into the eastern chambers. Follow the flowing water through the eastern door.

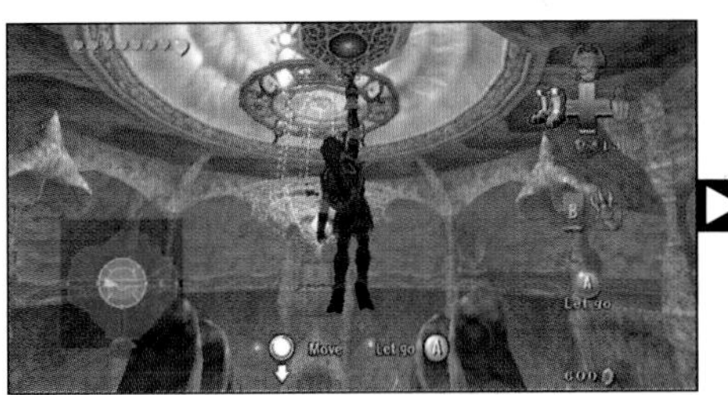

13 From Pillar to Post

After entering the room that contains chained platforms and two giant cogs, grapple the gold-and-red target on the left side of the near cog. Drop to the pillar, get the bombs in the treasure chest, and grapple to the vines on the northern wall. Grapple to the vines to climb up the pillars, then grapple to the vines along the upper northern wall. Drop to the ledge and enter the northern door.

14 Up and Over

Use a bomb arrow to knock down the stalactite that's above the geyser, then ride the platform you've created to the top of the wall. Jump down and grapple to the ledge.

15 Another Watery Rush

Use the Clawshot to grapple to the vines on the ceiling and bypass the barrier. Drop to the floor. Then, as you did in the western tower, ascend the spiraling pathway and pull the lever at the top to get the water flowing.

Large gaps will impede your progress up the spiraling passage; use well-timed grapples to get across. At the top of the tower, unleash the Clawshot to get the compass before heading back down to activate the second lever.

16 Fast Cash

Once the water is flowing in the eastern tower, you can grab some extra treasure before exploring the rest of the dungeon. If you take the right door in the tower, you can obtain some bombs beyond the waterwheel. If you opt for the left door, you can dive into the pool to find 20 rupees. On the other side of the pool, go under the waterwheel and enter the cog room. Cross the cogs and take the southwest door to find more rupees. You can also grapple the gate open to get back to the central circular room.

The treasure chests don't hold anything essential. If you don't need the bombs or rupees, you can head straight back to the central room.

17 Claw Your Way Through

The easiest way into the easternmost chambers is to return to the central room via the left passage from the east tower and re-enter the room that contains the dual cogs. Use the Clawshot to latch onto the near cog, and drop onto the pillar in the middle of the room. From there grapple onto the second cog and drop off when you reach the eastern door.

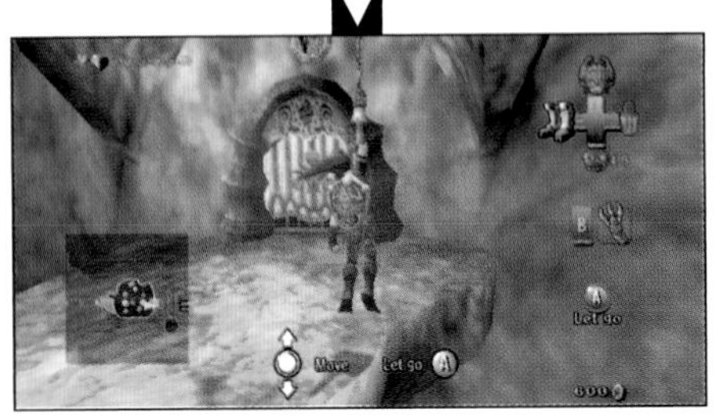

Keep an eye on Link's shadow as he's hanging from the rotating cogs. Drop only when you can see your shadow on a platform below you.

18 Waterlogged Labyrinth

Jump into the water and find a boulder near the middle of the area. Destroy it then go through the newly created passage and equip the Iron Boots to fall to the seafloor. Blow up another boulder in the southeast corner of the chamber. Proceed through the tunnel, then head to the surface and go through the door.

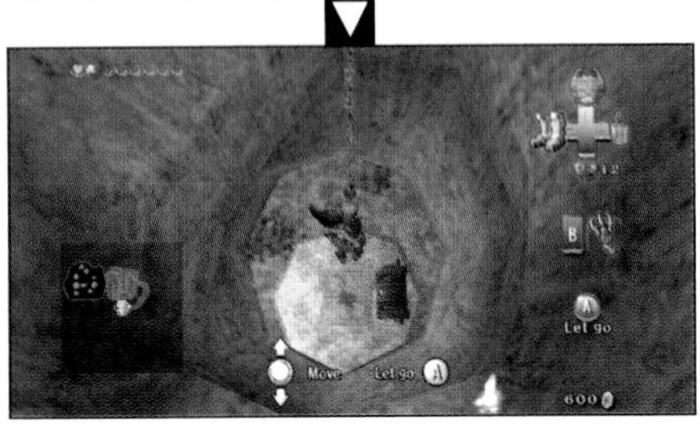

When you use the Clawshot on the switch on the ceiling, a hole will open in the floor. Lower yourself through the hole and retrieve the Big Key from the treasure chest. Jump into the water and follow the underwater passage to make your exit. Afterward, head back to the central chamber.

Twilit Aquatic—Morpheel

After you enter the boss's room from the central chamber, drop to the bottom with the Iron Boots. The boss's weak point is the eyeball inside its tentacles. Stay as far from the boss as you can while remaining in Clawshot range, then grapple the eye out of the tentacles while Z-targeting, and hit it with your sword. If you get caught by one of the tentacles, quickly unequip your Iron Boots, or else you'll be sucked into the boss's mouth repeatedly.

After you pull out and attack the eyeball a couple of times, Morpheel will emerge from its hole and reveal its true form. Unequip the Iron Boots and start swimming. Position yourself above and behind the boss's head, but stay away from its mouth or you'll get sucked in (unless you quickly equip the Iron Boots). When you're in range, Z-target the eye on the back of Morpheel's head and nail it with the Clawshot. A successful hit will pull you onto the creature's head, allowing you to hit it with your sword. After several blows, Morpheel will be defeated.

Z-targeting is the best way to tell if you're in range of Morpheel's eyeball. As soon at the targeting indicator appears, unleash the Clawshot.

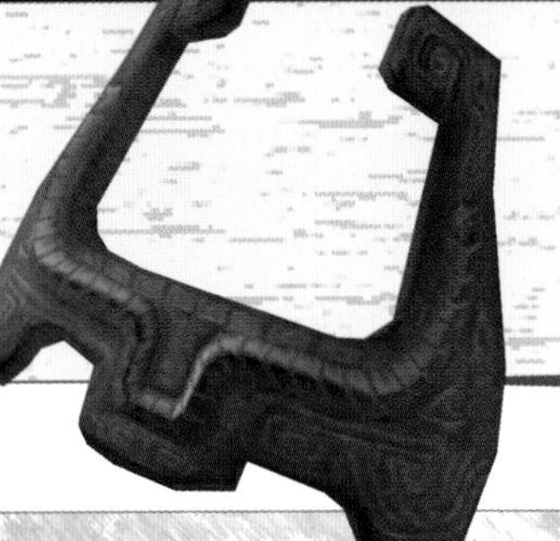

Arbiter's Grounds

Hyrule Castle Town

A confrontation with Zant makes meeting the princess a priority. It won't be easy to reach her in your canine form.

Between Dark and Light

Your success in Lakebed Temple will be followed by much drama. The king of twilight himself, Zant, will meet you and Midna at the Spirit Spring (after a face-off with Lanayru) and chide Midna for thinking that the Fused Shadows could stop him. Using dark magic, he'll embed a crystal in your head and injure your companion.

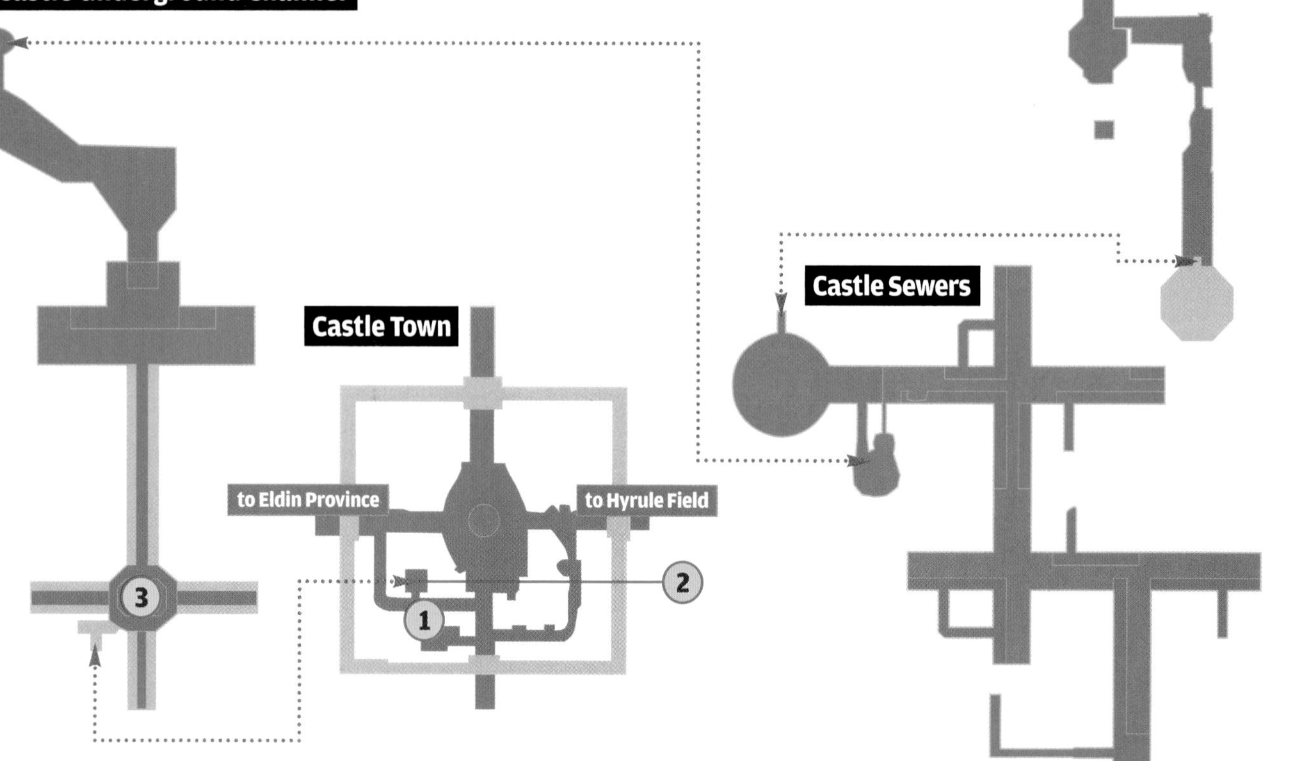

1 No Dogs Allowed

You must speak to Princess Zelda about the developments with Zant and the Fused Shadows. Start by walking into Castle Town. Though the humans are afraid of you (and they'll kick you out of Telma's Bar when you try to enter through the front door), the town's animals are willing to help. Telma's cat, Louise, will lead you through the window and into the castle's waterway. Push a box for a boost up to the opening.

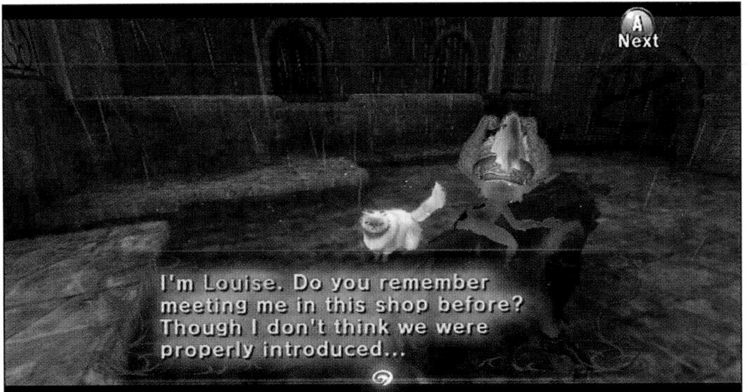

You'll do some tightrope walking above the bar's patrons. When prompted, listen in on their conversations. The ledges that give you access to the ropes are riddled with pots. You can move the pots, but don't let them fall.

2 Soul Sacrifice

At the entrance to the waterway, you'll meet the shell of a man, Jovani, who will ask you to defeat a ghost to return part of Jovani's soul. After you do the deed, Jovani will open the waterway entrance and task you with finding the rest of the Poe Souls.

Steal the Soul

Engage your canine senses and attack the ghost in the room. Once you've knocked it to the ground, you'll have just a couple of seconds to grab the Poe Soul from it before it comes to. Target the object and press A to pull the black sphere away from the ghost. You'll find more Poes later. Track them down in your wolf form. Once you have 20 Poe Souls, return to Jovani for a reward.

3 Flushed Away

Your journey through the waterway will begin at a hub. Walk around the ledge, defeat the rats, then pull a chain. That will open a route to the north. After you float to the castle basement, you'll go up against a pair of spiders—burn their web with a flaming stick. You'll come across another web as you explore the underground. Light torches to ensure that there will be a source of fire when you need it. Engage your senses at the dead end to identify a place where you can dig to the next area.

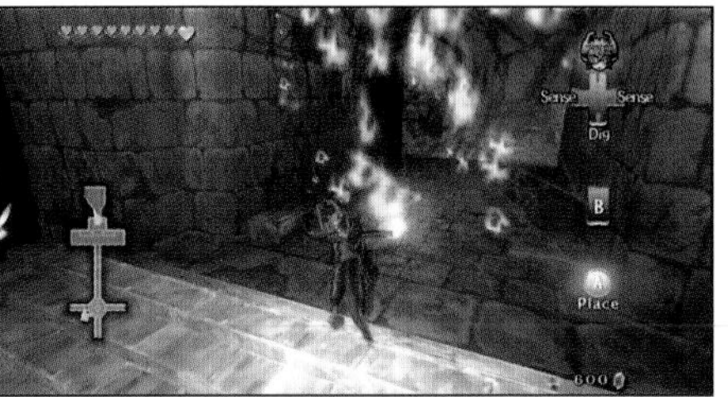

4 The Long Way to the Top

You've been to the castle tower before, but Midna is in no shape to help you reach the top this time. Target and jump on enemies on your way up the spiral staircase. Use ropes to cross wide gaps. Outside you'll deal with strong winds. When the wind blows enough to make a broken bridge span the gap, jump onto the bridge and run across it before the wind dies. You'll jump from a wooden platform to the roof's peak, then follow that narrow path to Zelda's tower.

Zelda will see that you are bound by an evil force and tell you to go back to Faron Woods to find the sword that will transform you back into a hero. Then she'll sacrifice herself to heal Midna's injuries.

Faron Woods

In the woods, near the Forest Temple, you'll find a sacred grove where a great sword lies.

1 A Monkey in Distress

When you reach the area near the Forest Temple, you'll find a monkey surrounded by enemies the likes of which you have not seen in Faron Woods. You'll defeat them with ease, then learn about another section of forest on the other side of a cliff.

2 Unexplored Faron Woods

Climb atop the stump east of the monkey and let Midna guide you to the area on the other side of the cliff. You'll hop across wide gaps then cross bridges and ropes to get to your destination. After Midna leads you across several gaps, you'll fight off a group of bats. Move on to two rotating bridge sections.

Once you reach the second section, let it rotate so that it points east-west, then exit to the east. Avoid the swinging logs as you walk over the two successive tightropes. You can stop on a rock between the ropes to wait for the second log to swing out of the way.

Howl at the Wind

There's a Howling Stone on the far side of the rope-strung gap. Stop there and follow the howling instructions. Howl again with the golden wolf. After the duet, the wolf will show you where to go once you're in human form to learn the next hidden skill.

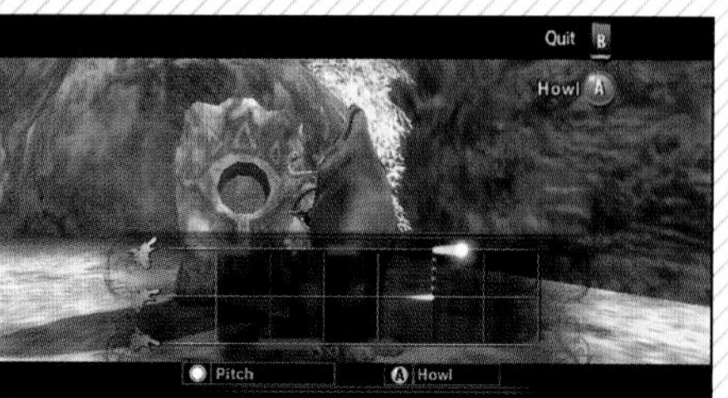

Sacred Grove

You'll do a lot of howling and a little fighting in the Sacred Grove, and finally earn the Master Sword.

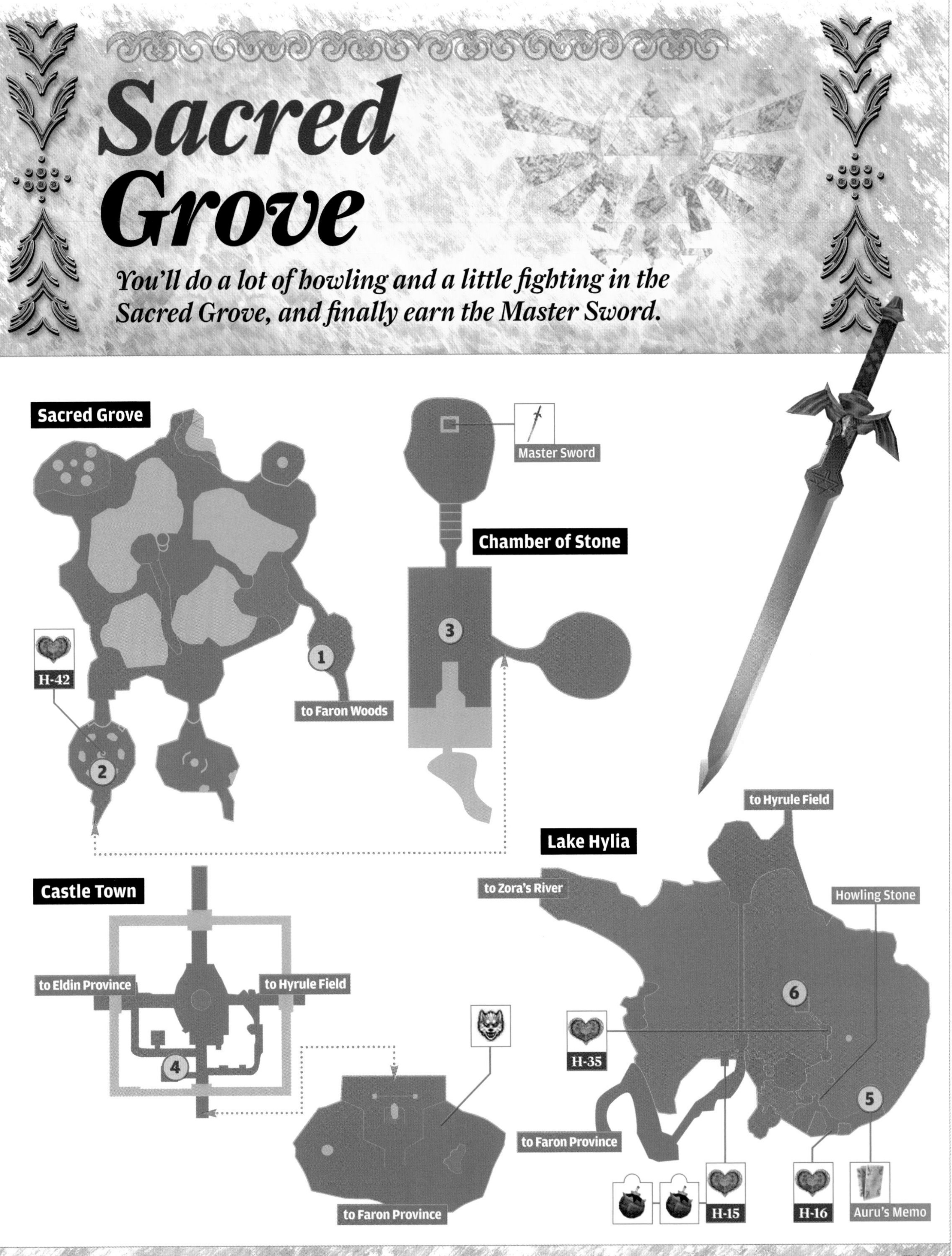

1 Another Howling Stone?

Shortly after you howl with the golden wolf, you'll find a stone that teaches you another song. But, instead of learning another skill, you'll trigger the appearance of the Skull Kid and his skeletal henchmen. Defeat the henchmen using Midna's dark energy, then chase the leader.

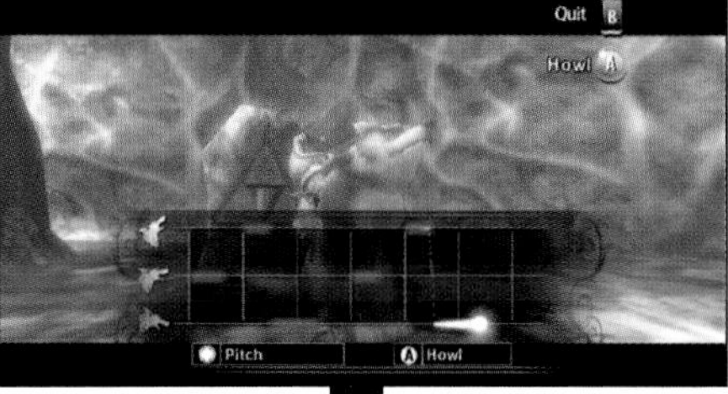

The Skull Kid's followers will continue to regenerate while you search the woods. When you find the leader, bite him. He'll open a new section of the maze and warp there.

2 Growing Forces

After you attack the main baddie a few times, he'll lead you to an arena. Fight his followers then hit the leader while he's busy calling more skeletons. Successful slices will cause your foe to call in increasing numbers of creatures. Eventually, you'll chase away the Skull Kid and a new section will open.

3 Giant Puzzle

At the entrance to the Sacred Grove, you'll howl from a symbol on the ground to make two stone giants come to life on a group of blocks. They'll ask you to lead them to their sentry posts by hopping on the blocks. Jump in the following pattern: left, down, right, right, up, left, up, up, left, down, down, right, and up.

The Master Sword

You'll be drawn to the Master Sword in the Sacred Grove. After you touch it and it accepts you as the hero of the land, you'll return to human form and an artifact that embodies Zant's magic—the Shadow Crystal—will drop to the ground. Midna will explain that the object allows you to turn into a wolf at any time. If you want to transform or warp to a portal, just call Midna.

Buried Treasure

Before you leave the area, return to the Skull Kid arena (to the east), and blast through a rock in the middle of the area. Transform into a wolf, fight for a Poe Soul, then dig. You'll discover a room in which a Piece of Heart appears once all the room's monsters are dead.

Timely Correspondence

Warp to Castle Town then transform back into human form. While you're walking across the bridge to the town proper, the postman will stop and deliver a letter from Telma. She wants to inform you about a group of like-minded adventurers who have gathered at her bar.

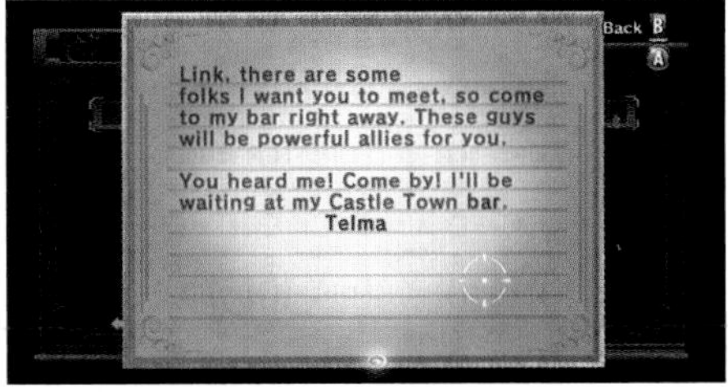

4 Adventurer's Guild

The last time you were in Telma's Bar, you had to sneak in because you were in beast form. This time you can walk right in. Telma will tell you about a group of adventurers who are trying to right the wrongs that have befallen the kingdom. An old man named Auru has gone off to Lake Hylia. Look at the map in the room to see where he is.

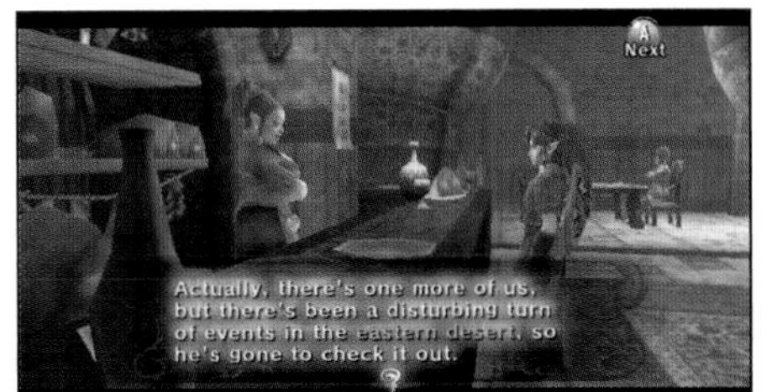

5 Desert Tale

Warp to Lake Hylia and consult your map. Climb to the tower where Auru studies the Gerudo Desert. The old man will tell you about the desert and a cursed mirror. After you tell him that you intend to go to the desert, he'll ask you to give a memo to Fyer.

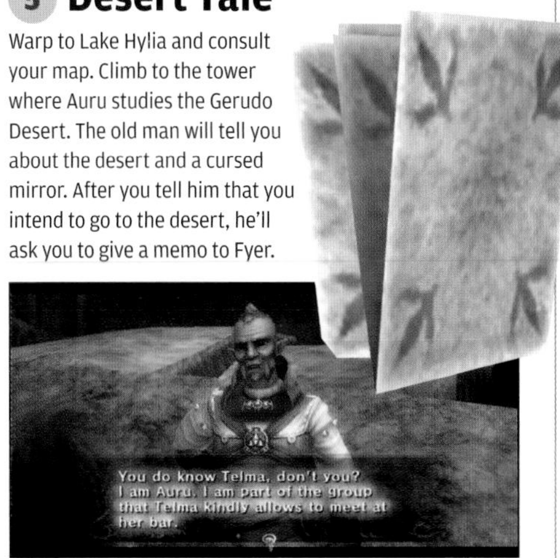

Hone a Hidden Skill

If you howled at the Howling Stone near the Sacred Grove, the golden wolf will be waiting for you south of the castle. Look at the overworld map for a gold dot and go to that location to find the wolf. He'll turn into a soldier and teach you your next skill. Which technique he'll teach depends on how many skills he has already taught to you.

Last Chance for Supplies

It won't be long before you're in another large dungeon, fighting for your life. Before you leave town, stock up on all of the things you need: Lantern Oil, Red Potions, arrows, etc. Now that you have the Clawshot, you should be able to succeed in Castle Town's STAR minigame. Use the Clawshot to grapple onto the cage walls as you zoom around to collect the glowing orbs. Victory will earn you the Big Quiver, which holds as many as 60 arrows.

Go Spelunking

A cave southwest of Auru's tower holds three Poes and a Piece of Heart. Stock up on bombs and Lantern Oil before you venture in there. You'll find more explosives and oil-alternative Chu Jelly inside.

The Wind Calls

There is a Howling Stone between Auru's tower and Fyer's hut. Transform into a wolf there and howl. The golden wolf will move to the Gerudo Desert. Lucky for you, that's where you're headed.

6 A New Flight Path

Go to Fyer's colorful hut (you can't miss it) and show him Auru's memo. Fyer will give you the option to take a flight to an oasis. That's where you want to go.

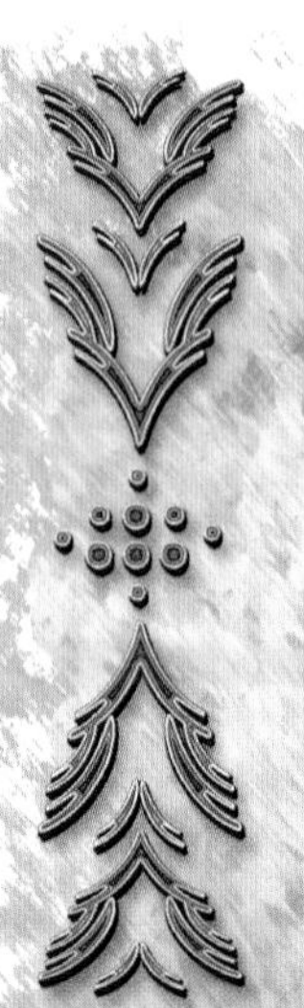

Gerudo Desert

A mysterious mirror awaits in a desert keep. Before you get there you'll deal with boars and lots of baddies.

H-18

1

2

3

4

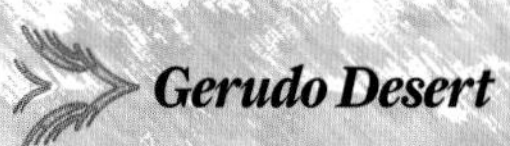

1 Cross the Desert

Landing in the desert makes Midna reflective. She'll tell you about what happened to her people and why she needs the Mirror of Twilight. Your journey continues in the desert's northeast corner. As you make your way there, run around the chasms and watch for enemies.

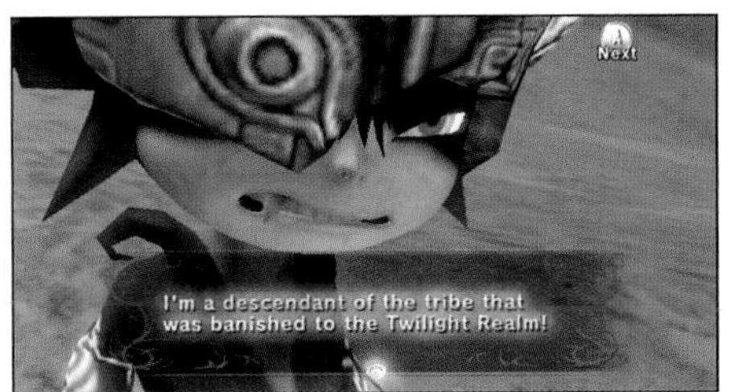

The Missing Link

A stone monolith reaches for the sky in the desert's southwest section. Midna will note that the object appears to be man-made. It's the middle section of the Bridge of Eldin. Use Midna's help to warp it to the span. When you return to the desert and travel to the bridge chunk's former location—the Gerudo Mesa—you'll discover the 50-level Cave of Ordeals (p. 163). You're not equipped to survive the cave yet, but go there later to free some fairies.

2 Catch a Ride

As you approach the building in the northeast, a pair of foes on boars will charge. Hit them both with spin attacks or a Hawkeye-enabled arrow, then mount one of the boars. A big pig doesn't handle as smoothly as a horse does. When you press A to make the animal run faster, it will take off and keep running for about 10 seconds. Use the speed to crash through the fence in the northeast. (You can collect tons of rupees via the boar.)

A New Move

If you howled at the Howling Stone in Lake Hylia, you'll find the warrior with the hidden skills shortly after you crash the gate. Speak to him and learn.

3 Camp Counseling

Go north on foot to the next area. Before you get too close to the camp, use an arrow to knock the archer off the tower. Run inside the gate, head east, and continue the fight. There are many enemies ahead. Lock onto them and swing away.

Inside the camp, you'll see enemies on the ground and on towers. Pick them off with arrows. If one of the foes spots you, a large group of beasts will attack. Zigzag east. Defeat the creature who is roasting a boar to earn a Small Key (you'll use it to unlock the gate in the center of the camp). Swipe at the fire under the boar, then slice the boar to get a Piece of Heart.

4 Brains versus Brawn

The axe-wielding soldier in the middle of the camp looks intimidating, but he moves very slowly. You'll be able make quick work of the creature as long as you keep swinging and moving.

After your victory against the axe-wielding beast, the place will catch fire. Climb onto the boar in the room and crash through the gate. You'll continue to break fences until you reach the exterior of the Arbiter's Grounds. After you climb up the stairs, you'll discover a Poe Soul to the east.

Arbiter's Grounds

The desert dungeon is filled with sand. Don't stop, or you'll sink.

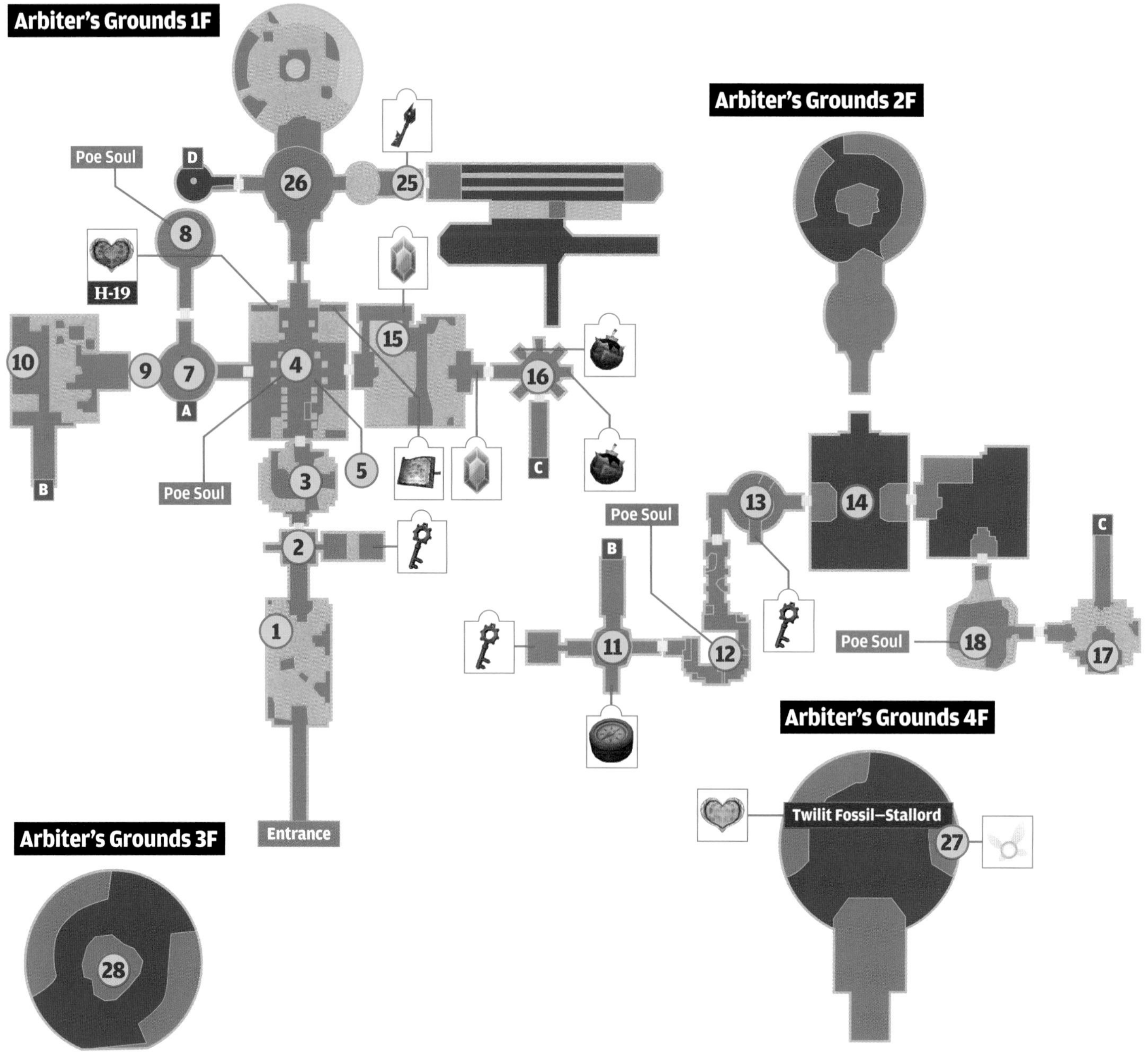

Arbiter's Grounds 1F

Poe Soul
D
26
25
8
H-19
15
10
9
7
4
16
A
5
3
C
B
Poe Soul
2
1
Entrance

Arbiter's Grounds 2F

13
14
Poe Soul
B
C
11
12
Poe Soul
18
17

Arbiter's Grounds 4F

Twilit Fossil—Stallord
27

Arbiter's Grounds 3F

28

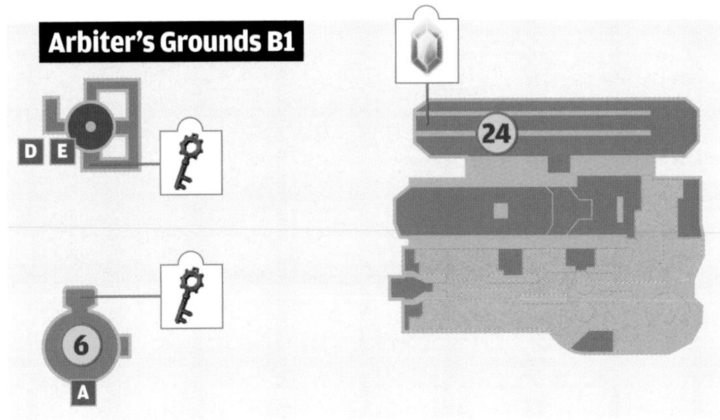

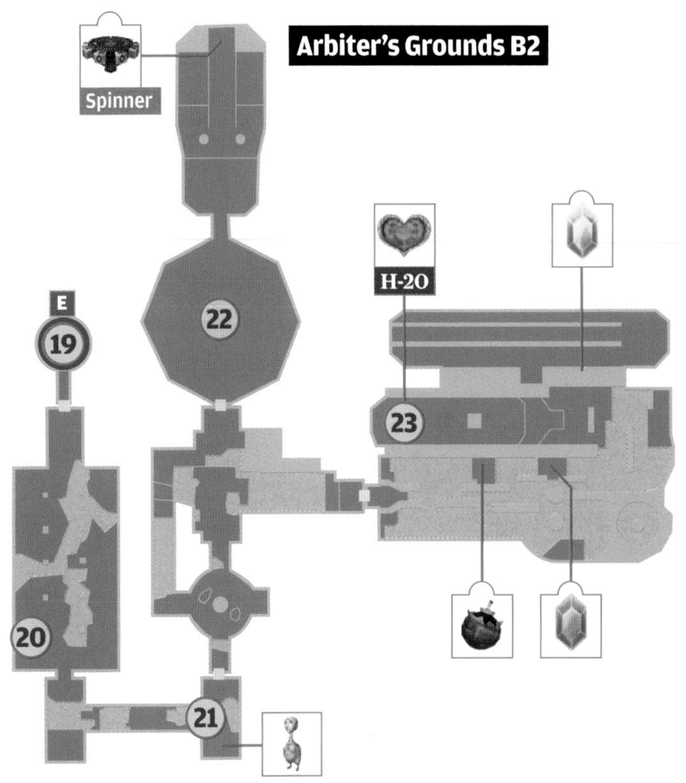

1 Over and Out

You can't stand for long on the first room's sandy floor without being consumed by it. Fire your Clawshot at the east wall's round grate to float over much of the sand. Then jump across platforms and run over short expanses of sand to get to the chamber's northwest corner.

When you have a clear shot at the chain in the northwest corner (while standing on solid ground) hit it with the Clawshot to bring it toward you. Pick it up and pull back. The gate will open.

2 Bugs. Why'd It Have to be Bugs?

There's Lantern Oil to the west of the locked door, and a Small Key to the east (on the other side of a weak wooden barrier). Blast through the barrier then collect the key. Small insects will swarm. Swat them away by using spin attacks.

3 Light and Fight

The dark round room has two unlit torches on the far side. There are sinking-sand holes and an army of skeletal warriors between you and your goal. Use your lantern to light the way to the torches, and perform spin attacks to defeat the skeletons.

4 You've Got Soul

Four Poes appear after you enter the chamber in the middle of the first floor, then three of them leave. Turn into your canine form to take on the remaining ghost. It'll become transparent for a moment following your attack. Wait for it to become solid, then attack again.

5 Ghost Hunter

The Poe that you defeated leaves a trail. Inspect its remains to learn the Poe scent, and follow it to a patch of dirt. Digging will reveal a chain that you can pull to make a set of stairs to the basement appear.

Before you go down the stairs, investigate the room's treasure chests. The one to the east holds a map, and the one to the west holds a Piece of Heart. Use the Clawshot to return to solid ground.

6 Push for a Key

A flat appendage sticks out of the pillar in the round room downstairs. Push it to make the pillar turn and a door open, revealing an alcove that holds a key. A Redead Knight defends the prize. Attack it from afar.

If you get too close to the Redead Knight, it will freeze you with a scream. Attack it from a distance using bomb arrows or hit it with a jump attack in wolf form.

7 Claw Your Way Out

Standing on the north end of the room, engage your Clawshot and look up. Aim the claw at the round grate on the other side of a hole in the ceiling. Release the shot and grapple up through the hole.

8 Another One Bites the Dust

The round room in the northwest houses the second Poe. Engage your canine senses to see it, then defeat it the same way you took care of the dungeon's first ghost.

9 On the Scent

Head back the way you came (turning the pillar again to give you access to the stairs), and engage your senses in the main room to reveal two paths. Follow the path west past the pillar and through the locked door (which you can unlock using your key while still in canine form).

10 Pulling Strings

Go across the north end of the room to the west side, moving across the sand from one solid platform to the next. Move slowly—spikes pop up from the sand in some of the gaps.

Pull the cage east then north to fit it between the raised platforms. Walk up the stairs and hop over the wall to the west. Pull the chain back while walking on top of the cage that you put into place. The chandelier will rise. Let go of the chain then run under the chandelier before it falls.

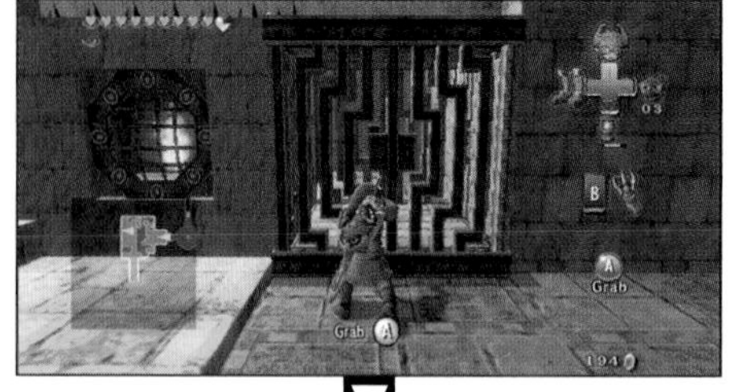

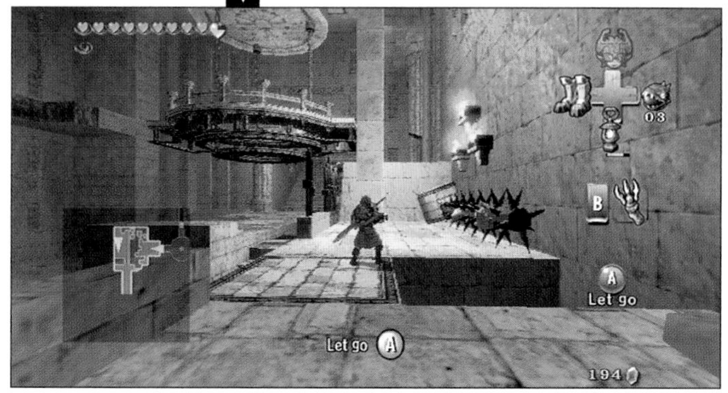

11 The Compass and Another Small Key

Head up the stairs, pass the pillar, and collect the compass. Then return to the pillar and push the part that juts out from it to reveal openings to the east and west. Head west, cut through a wood barrier, and confront another screaming enemy. Once it's out of the picture, open the chest to collect the Small Key.

12 Lost Soul

After you open the locked door to the east, transform into a wolf and take on a group of small skeletons and two screaming Redead Knights. Then follow the scent to a chain under a patch of dirt, and pull it to reveal the dungeon's third Poe.

Engage your senses, dig up a patch of dirt, then pull a chain. You'll move a section of wall to find a Poe. Defeat it the same way you defeated the others.

13 Stealth Rats

Head north then east to a small circular room. Grab the key from the chest on the south side, then engage your senses. There are ghost rats in the room, and some may be on top of you already, weighing you down. Use Midna's dark energy or a spin attack to defeat them.

14 The Last Ghost Trail

Travel east through the locked door to the second floor of the room that houses the Poe lantern. Engage your canine senses to see a scent trail that floats over the room. Follow it to the east, over the chandelier, and into the next room.

15 Lift It, Drop It

Walk down the stairs in the room east of the main chamber, push the cage until it sets into place, then climb and pull a chain to make the chandelier rise. Walk under the chandelier and let it drop. You'll be able to escape to the east.

Pull the chain, walk to the middle of the path, and let the chandelier drop so that it surrounds you. Climb from the center of the chandelier to the east, then continue east through the door.

16 Dead Rising

The eastern room offers a classic Legend of Zelda puzzle. You have to defeat an enemy to make the door on the room's south side open. The catch is that the enemy is a regenerating skeleton. After you reduce it to a pile of bones, destroy the bones with a bomb to do it in for good.

17 Bright Idea

You must light two particular lanterns to escape from the southeast corner room. Light the one that is not in the row, and the one farthest west. (If you ignite the wrong ones, skeletons will rise from the sand and attack you.) After you light the correct ones, a section of wall on the west side of the room will slide out of the way.

18 Split Spirit

After you find the final Poe, it will appear as four ghosts—the real one shines just a little brighter than the others. Identify it, attack it, then steal its soul. When you return to the main room, the gate at the north end will open. Travel north from there.

19 Corkscrew Room

Find the shaft in the northwest section of the first floor. Drop to the platform near the bottom of the shaft and push the center pillar's appendage counterclockwise for two full rotations to make the platform rise to a path that holds a key. Then push the lever clockwise to have the platform sink to the bottom of the shaft. Open the locked door.

20 Rats in the Cellar

Invisible rats, spikes from the ground, and sinking sand are the dangers of the long chamber in the southwest section of floor B2. Use your canine senses to see the rats and glowing outlines of places where spikes will pop up. In the south end of the room, you'll find a chain on the west side of a wall-blocked opening. Clear the area of rats and a screaming Redead Knight, then pull the chain to slide the wall out of the way. Run around the spikes and through the opening.

21 Torture Chamber

Move north through the middle section of floor B2 in human form. You'll have to slice through large groups of swarming bugs, then plant bombs to defeat regenerating Stalfos. Ooccoo waits for you in a pot nearby.

A closed gate on the west side of the round chamber features a spinning spiked pole. Run around the spikes through the opening to the north to take on three Stalfos.

By defeating all three of the regenerating Stalfos, you'll cause the gate in the round room to open. Attack the two Stalfos that are out in the open, then destroy them using bombs once they're just piles of bones. Then cross the sand to the west to fight the third Stalfos. Once the gate is open, return to the round room.

22 Invisible Swordsman

There's a beast in the basement. You'll cause him to attack if you cut one of the ropes that holds his sword. At first it will appear as if the sword is floating by itself. But the swordsman is there—he's just invisible. Use your canine senses to find him.

Engage your senses at the beginning of the fight to see the sword-carrier. Attack him in your canine form until the creature becomes visible and begins to fly around the room.

Return to human form, dodge out the way of the creature's gaseous projectiles, then fire arrows back at him. He'll drop to the ground after a single direct hit.

Strike the creature with your sword once to make him fall to his knees, then follow through with more blows. When he floats up, knock him down again with another arrow.

The Spinner

Link gets a taste of extreme sports with the Spinner, a rotating disk that allows him to float over the sand and follow tracks in the wall. Press A to hop and give the Spinner faster rotation for a moment. When you're not on a track, the Spinner will run out of steam and disappear eventually. Unfortunately, you can't re-engage it while you're walking on sand.

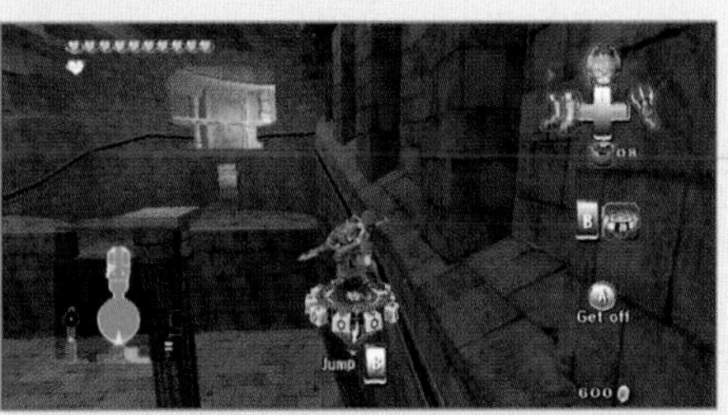

23 Track Down a Piece of Heart

In the basement's northeast-corner chamber, float over the sand with your Spinner to reach the first two treasure chests shown on the in-game map, then ride a track on the right wall to reach a chest that holds a Piece of Heart. There's a Stalfos nearby. Fight it or avoid it.

24 Up and Away

From the chest that held the Piece of Heart, take the track on the north wall to get past the rotating spiked stick, then hop from track to track to make your way to the northern half of the room. When you get to the room's northern section, you'll be headed the wrong way. Stop spinning for a moment, turn around, and follow a track up to the northeastern corner.

25 Hop, Skip, and Fly

Four small spinning spiked devices ride the tracks between the chamber's northeast and northwest corners. Hop from track to track to avoid them. When you reach the other side, you'll have access to the room that holds the Big Key.

26 Get into Gear

A gear-shaped hole in the floor of the room acts as a basement hub. Drop into it with your Spinner, then press B repeatedly to activate a mechanism under the floor. The mechanism turns the outer wall, giving you access to the northern shaft.

27 Bottled Beauty

Ride the track in the northern room as far as it will go. Then slice the skulls in the room with your sword. You'll expose a fairy. Put it in an empty bottle.

28 Center Piece

Your next stop is the middle of the room. Ride the track down to a place that overlooks the part of the center pedestal that juts out. When you're lined up, you should be close to a big broken section of the stairs. Put away the Spinner and jump to the pedestal. You'll likely catch the ledge with one hand. Climb up then use the Spinner in the pedestal's indentation.

Twilit Fossil—Stallord

Run to a giant animal skull in the center of the room. Zant will appear for a moment then use his dark-magic sword to assemble the skeleton, Stallord. This battle is a two-parter. During the first part Stallord will be caught in the mud in the middle of the arena. You can hit the creature's spine with your Spinner. Ride along the track on the arena's perimeter (hopping off the track to avoid contact with spiky mechanisms that also ride the track), and drop to the skeleton when the way is clear. Press B to attack the monster's vertebrae.

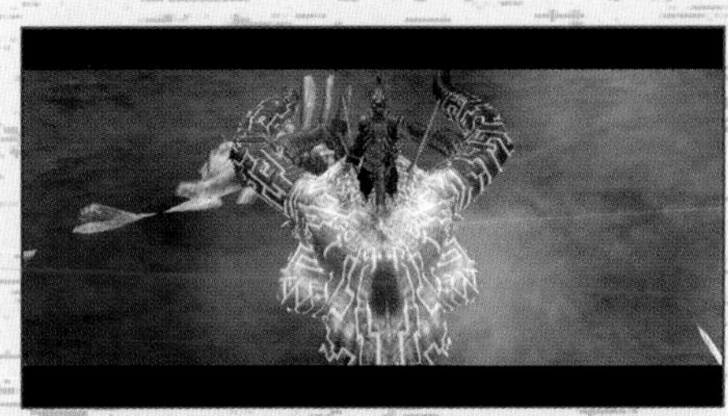

After you hit Stallord's spine a couple of times, the number of minions in the arena will increase. Swerve to avoid them.

Stallord will be reduced to a skull for the second part of the battle. Use your Spinner to raise a pillar in the center of the arena. The skull will come to life and knock you off the structure. There are spiral tracks on both the pillar and the arena wall. Start spinning on the inside track to pursue the skull, then jump between the tracks to avoid Stallord's fireballs. When you're close to the skull, jump to hit it with the Spinner. The creature will drop to the floor. Hit it several times with your sword. You'll win after a few rounds.

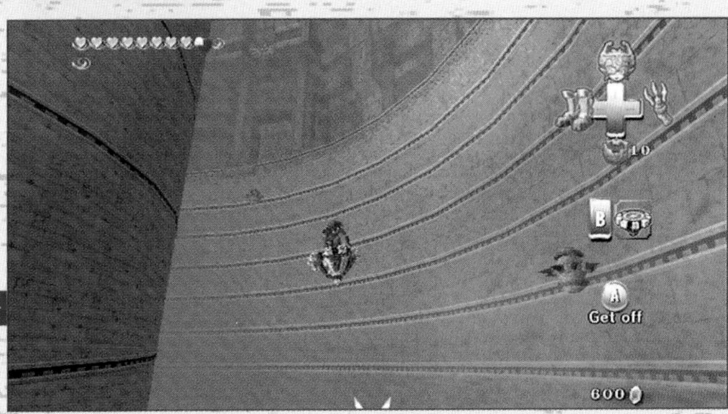

Following every round with Stallord's skull, the foe will add spiky mechanisms to the tracks. Jump to avoid them.

Look into the Mirror

After the battle you'll collect a Heart Container and Midna will let you know that you are close to the Mirror of Twilight. Go outside to investigate.

29 Battle at the Base

Climb to the top of the building to discover a huge statue in the Mirror Chamber. When you get to the base, shadow beings will create a force field around the structure then attack you. In your human form you can hit several of the creatures at once using spin attacks. In your canine form you can do the same by using Midna's dark energy.

30 Top Spin

After your victory against the shadow beings, follow the Spinner track to the top of the statue, then spin in the gear hole at the top to make the Mirror of Twilight (or what remains of it) emerge from the roof.

Mirror Chamber

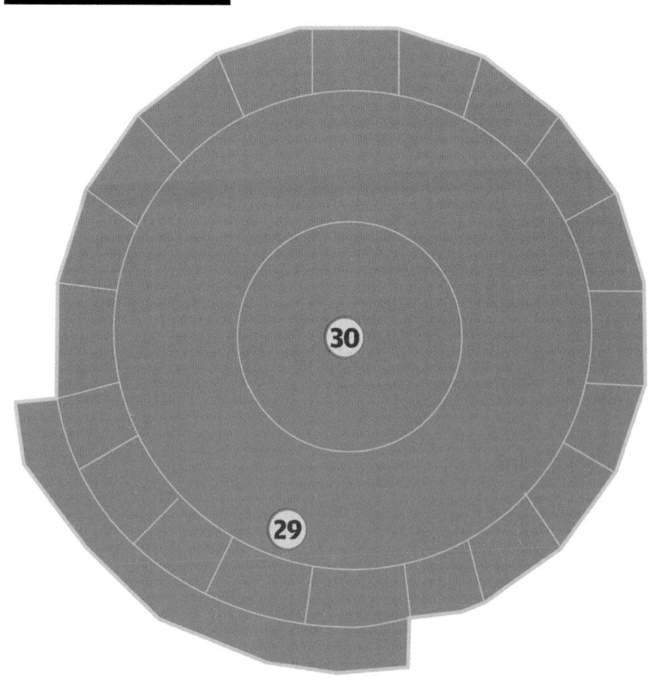

Ganondorf?!

The guardians of the mirror will tell you its history and show you a scene in which the true enemy of Hyrule—Ganondorf—was transported to another realm by the ancient object. Zant has now broken the mirror, and its three pieces are scattered over the land. It's up to you to collect the shards to continue fighting the good fight.

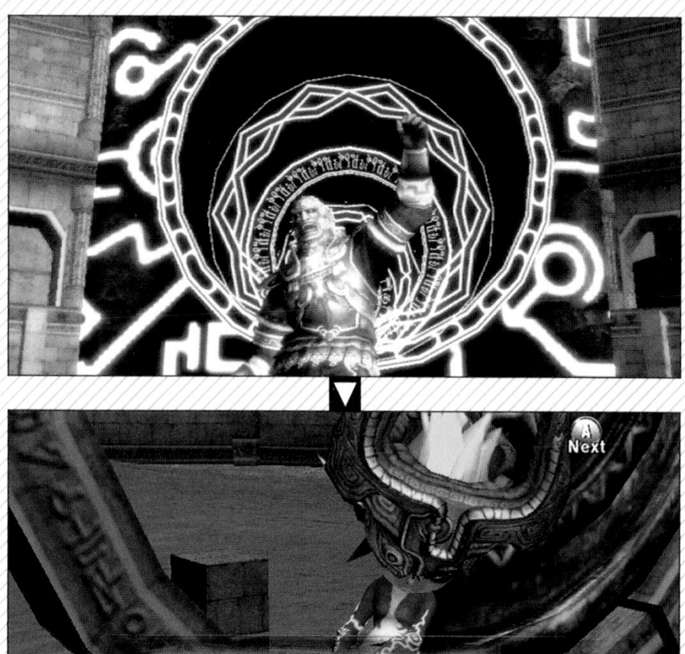

Snowpeak Ruins

Peak Province

A search for information about the mirror will lead you to a fishing expedition and a snowboard run.

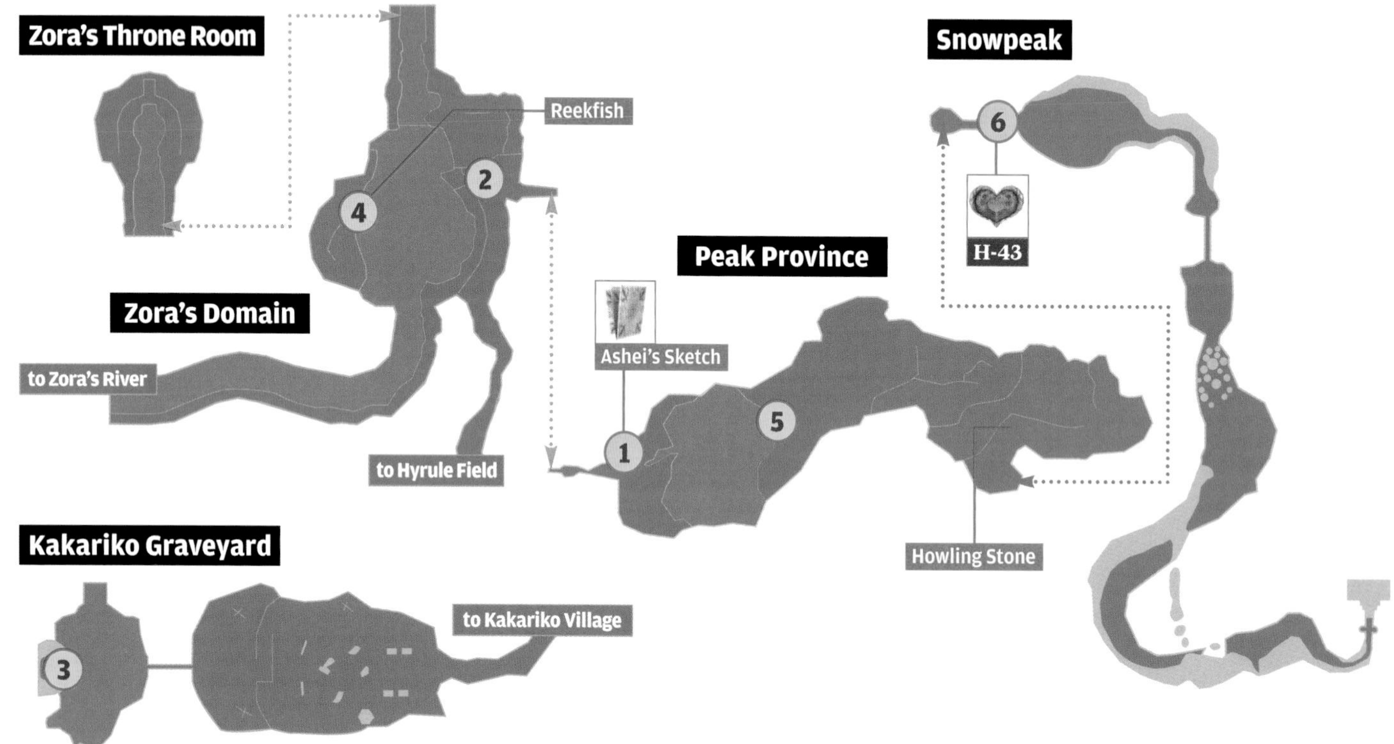

Bomb Letter

As you head into town, the postman will stop you with correspondence from Barnes of Kakariko Village. He's got a new kind of bomb in his shop. Stop by when you have a chance.

1 Telma Tells All

Need information about where to go next? Talk to Telma. Warp to Castle Town and sidle up to Telma's Bar. She'll point you in the direction of Ashei, on the northern mountain. The map in the back room shows Ashei's exact location in Zora's Domain.

2 Fish Story

In Snowpeak the water of Zora's Domain becomes ice. Ashei will start you on a quest for information by giving you a drawing of a yeti and a red fish.

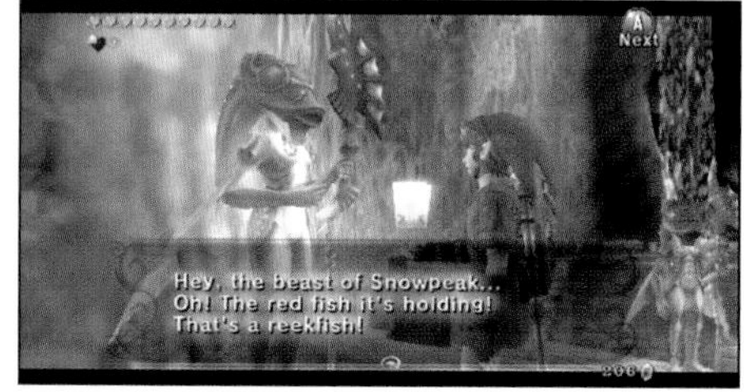

Show Ashei's sketch to the Zoras outside Ashei's cave. They'll tell you that the fish in the illustration is a Reekfish, and they'll tip you off that Prince Ralis knows a few things about the red fish. Seek him out.

3 A Gift from the Prince

Warp to Kakariko Village and seek out Prince Ralis. By speaking to Beth, you'll learn that the prince is in the graveyard. Venture to the west end of the graveyard and crawl through a hole. You'll find the prince near the watery tomb. Show him Ashei's sketch. He'll tell you that the Reekfish is attracted to a specific type of coral, then hand you his Coral Earring as an example. The coral is in the shape of a fishhook. How convenient!

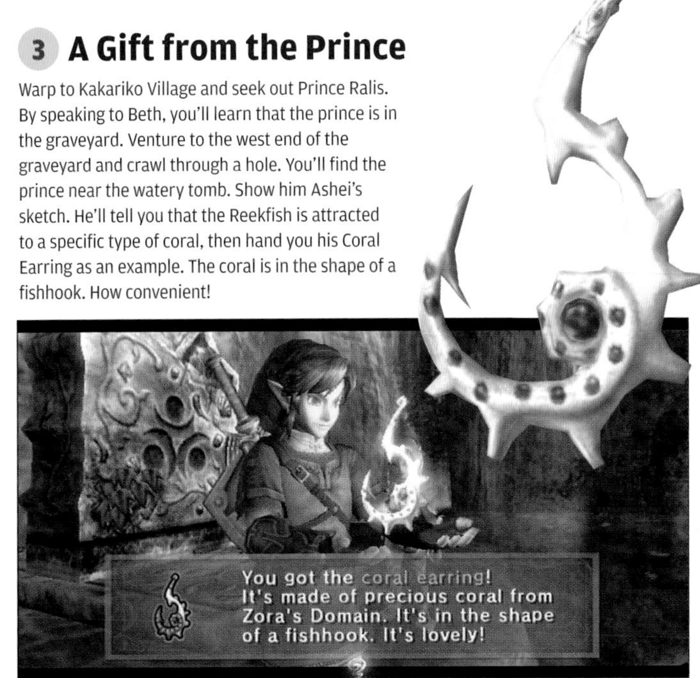

The prince's gift is both an earring and a hook, allowing you to catch Reekfish. After you collect it, the prize will be attached to your fishing pole automatically.

Bomblings

When detonating standard bombs, you either toss them, or set them down and run to avoid damage from the explosion. Bomblings (available at Barnes Bomb Shop) move by themselves (in a straight line) and explode on contact with their target.

4 That Fish Reeks

Prince Ralis will tell you that Reekfish can be found at the basin below the waterfall in Zora's Domain. They swim close to what the prince calls the mother-and-child rocks: two formations that jut out from the water, one larger than the other. Go there, catch a red fish, and sniff it in your wolf form. You'll learn the Reekfish scent.

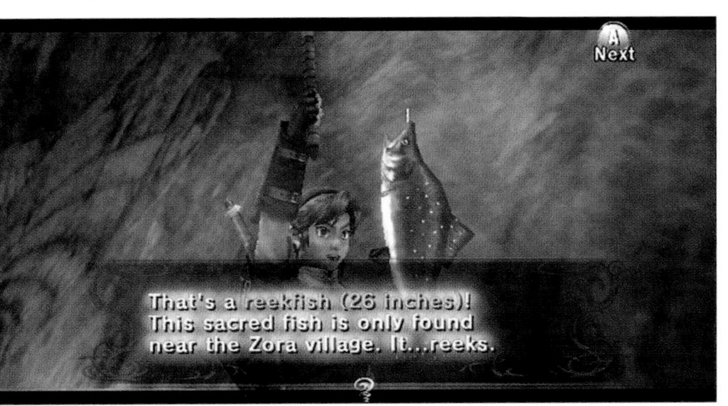

5 On the Reekfish Trail

Your new scent will lead you back to the Snowpeak area, beyond the place where you spoke with Ashei. Your canine form will allow you to sense the Reekfish trail and withstand the cold. Jump on the ice floes and don't fall in the water.

Watch for White Wolfos as you advance. They'll disappear as quickly as they appear. When you get to a short cliff that is topped by a snowbank, run into the cliff to make the snow fall. The cold stuff will form a passage to the top.

Dig under the wall to enter a cave, then transform into your human self. Climb a ladder then a vine. When you get outside, turn back into a wolf. Follow the scent to a battle against shadow beings. After your victory, you'll have a yeti sighting.

Howling Stone Clue

You'll discover a Howling Stone on your way to the Snowpeak summit. Learn the stone's song, then howl it with the golden wolf. He'll then move to a location near Kakariko Village.

6 Yak with the Yeti

Turn into human form before you talk to the yeti, Yeto. After a discussion about the Mirror Shard, he'll invite you to a Reekfish dinner and slide away on a frozen leaf. Run into the tree nearby to knock another leaf to the ground, then slide after him.

Riding a frozen leaf is a lot like riding a snowboard. Lean forward to gain speed. Press A to bend your knees, and release the button to jump. Swing the sword to clear the path of ice blocks and flying enemies.

Mirror Reflection

Walk inside Snowpeak Ruins, then enter the room north of the foyer. The yeti's wife, Yeta, will tell you that she has been ill ever since she and her husband found the Mirror Shard. It's now locked in the bedroom on the third floor, surrounded by monsters.

Snowpeak Ruins

The frozen foes of the Snowpeak Ruins will give you a cold reception. Warm up with some pumpkin soup.

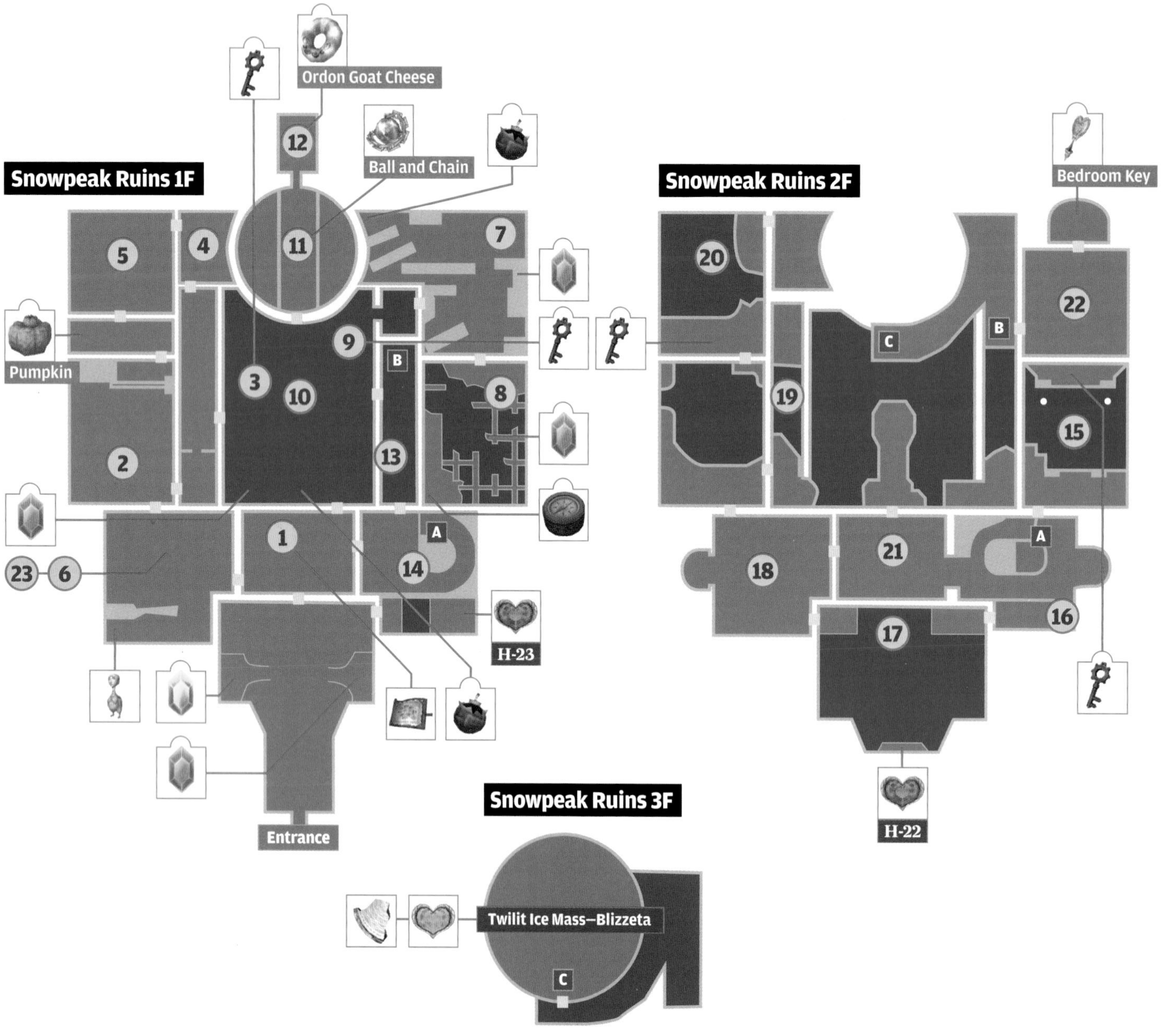

1 Map Quest

Yeta will give you the Snowpeak Ruins map and ask you to find a key for her. The item's location is marked on the map.

Have Some Soup

After you walk through the door to the west, you'll meet Yeto again. He's making soup for his wife. Scoop up some of it for yourself. One serving will replenish two hearts.

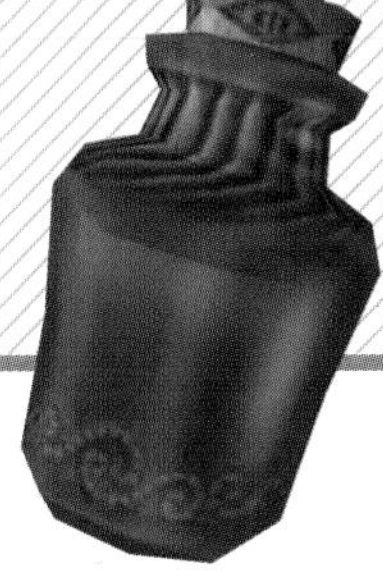

2 Block Slide

There's a block-sliding puzzle in the chamber north of the kitchen. The goal is to slide a block along the slippery surface and onto a switch. Complete the task to open a door.

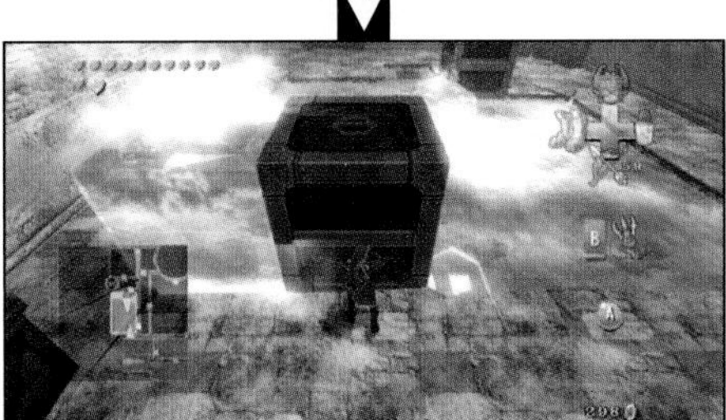

Push the closest block west. Push the other block south then west (so it collides with the first block), then push it south again.

3 Dig under the Wall

There's a crack in the wall of the small room east of the block puzzle. Turn into a wolf then dig under the wall, into a courtyard.

After you do away with a pack of White Wolfos and open a chest that contains rupees, dig up a chest buried in the snow to find a key. Advance west through the door, then north.

4 Slippery Battle

Three Mini Freezards at the north end of the house will freeze you on contact. You can push them with your Clawshot, but you'll have to use your sword to destroy them. With victory, you'll earn passage to the west.

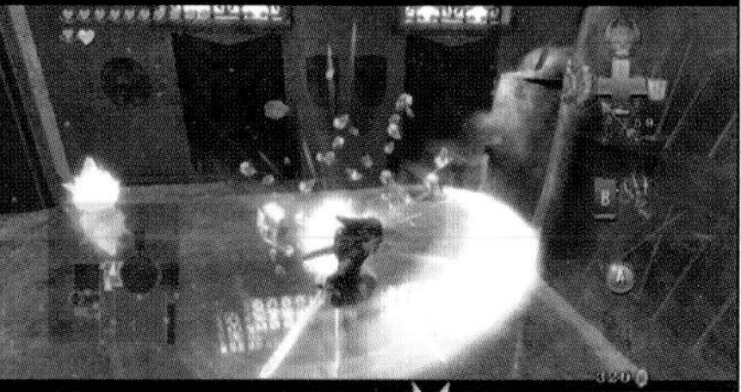

5 Fight for the Pumpkin

You'll fight two icy skeletons on the way to the prize on the house's west side. Hit them with jump attacks and the Jump Strike if you've learned it. You'll make ice cubes out of them after several hits. Move on to the chest and collect the Ordon pumpkin.

6 Great Pumpkin Soup

The item that Yeta sent you to get was a key. You found a pumpkin instead. Travel south, back to the kitchen. Yeto will add the pumpkin to the soup, doubling the broth's heart-regenerating power. Speak to Yeta. She'll give you a new destination and unlock another door.

7 Have a Blast

A Freezard with icy breath blocks your path north. Climb through an opening in the courtyard's northeast corner and drop into an icy maze. Avoid or attack the icy creatures that slide along the maze. Pick up the cannonball and take it to the cannon. Place the ball in the cannon. Turn the device to make it point south, then drop a bomb into the cannon. The cannon will fire and clear the way to a door.

On the way to the cannon, toss the cannonball at the sliding enemies to knock them out. If you lose track of the first cannonball, find others scattered throughout the maze.

8 Compass Directions

The compass is in the southwest corner of the room that is south of the ice maze. Walk on the beams (avoiding the white slippery sections near the edges), hit the path's icy creatures with your Clawshot, and hop over short gaps on your way to the prize.

9 Buried Treasure

Return to the courtyard. The compass will reveal the location of a treasure chest near the northeast corner. After you defeat the White Wolfos in the area, use your wolf senses to dig for the chest.

10 Bring out the Big Gun

Use the key to open the door on the courtyard's east side. Grab a cannonball from the east room and use the room's mechanism to transfer the cannonball into the courtyard. Place it in the courtyard's cannon. Point the cannon at the monster to the north and fire away.

Pull the lever on the west wall of the cannonball room to make the scoop drop. Place a ball in the scoop, then exit to the courtyard and use the mechanism there to retrieve the ball. Head west to the cannon. Turn it so it faces north, then blast the Freezard.

11 Have a Ball

The knight in the room north of the courtyard has the ball and chain. Use the Clawshot to grapple over him as he draws near, then run from him and dodge as he swings the ball toward you. Have your sword at the ready. Run to the other side of the knight while he reels the ball in, and strike his tail.

You likely won't see the knight attack, as you will be running away from him. When you see the ball land, though, that's your cue to run around the beast and hit his tail. You should get in three jumping attacks per round. Victory earns you the ball and chain.

The Ball and Chain

Heavy though it is, the ball and chain is incredibly powerful, allowing you to destroy barriers such as ice walls and suits of armor. You can use it in battle to hit enemies hard, but it's a somewhat limited weapon. You walk very slowly while carrying it, and you're vulnerable while you're reeling it in. It acts as a shield while you carry it, though—it will deflect projectiles.

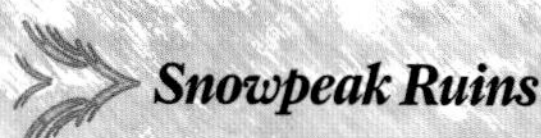

12 Cheesy Prize

The prize for all that fighting is a wheel of Ordon goat cheese! It's definitely not the key that Yeta promised. Add it to the soup (now it'll replenish eight hearts), then talk to Yeta for more instructions.

13 Foreshadowing Shortcut

Before you head up the spiral path on the east side of the first floor, go through the door to the west and push a block out of the way to clear a path that you'll use later.

14 Flatten Frosty

On your way up the spiral path, avoid the caged Freezards' ice breath and look for cage openings wide enough for the ball and chain to fit through. Two hits to each monster will do the job.

15 In the Swing of Things

When you reach the second-floor room north of the spiral path, hit the ice on the west wall to expose a grappling point. Move directly south of the chandelier, then hit it with the ball and chain. Use the chandelier as a platform to access a Small Key.

16 A Hole and a Piece of Heart

Drop a bomb on the weak floor section south of the spiral path. Fall into the hole then collect a Piece of Heart. Use a grappling point to return to the second floor.

17 Swing across the Foyer

When you reach the second floor of the foyer, destroy the ice barrier to expose a grappling point. Use bomb arrows to defeat the enemy across the gap, then use the ball and chain to make the chandelier start moving. Jump, swing, and cross the gap.

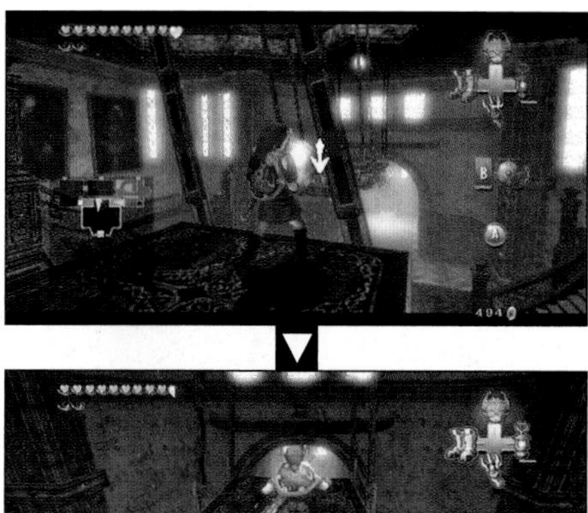

There's a Piece of Heart in a treasure chest on the south end of the foyer. You can get to it by riding on swinging chandeliers. Start on the north chandelier and hit the middle one with the ball and chain. Hop to the middle one then quickly hit the south one so it swings in the opposite direction from the middle one. Hop again, then jump to the chest. If a chandelier loses steam or if you fall, use the grappling point to get back up.

18 Block Party

Defeat the ice creatures in the room west of the foyer, then break ice to reveal a Poe. Take the soul, head north, and drop into the room that contains the sliding blocks. Use the ball and chain to destroy the ice barriers in the puzzle area, then push blocks to the middle switch.

Break the ice on the middle switch and on the frozen block. Push the block that rests on the first switch to move it north. Push the one that was in ice to move it south, west, then north to line it up with the first block that you pushed.

Return to the first block and push it east, south, west, then north to have it rest on the middle switch. That will open a door on the second floor. Climb up the boxes to return to the second floor, then exit to the east.

19 Tough Crowd

As you advance north on the west side of the courtyard's second floor, you'll go up against a trio of powerful ice creatures. Hit them from a distance with your ball and chain. If you fall off the ledge, return through the block-puzzle room.

20 Swing for the Key

Break the ice in the northeast corner of the northwest room to expose a grapple point. Then set a chandelier swinging, hop onto it, make the next chandelier swing, and advance to a Small Key.

21 Cannonball Transfer

Use the key to get to the room between the foyer and the courtyard on the second floor. Defeat two ice creatures by using the ball and chain. Push the blocks on the east wall then move east and run down the spiral path to find a cannonball. Take the ball all the way up the path to the cannon. Point the cannon west and fire it into the room where you started.

Use the mechanism on the north wall to transfer the cannonball to the courtyard. Place the ball in the cannon and aim it at the Freezard in the northeast. Fire away.

22 Church Social

Drop to the cannonball-storage area, work your way around to the ladder in the northeast, climb, then enter the chapel. The enemies pop up as you move through the room. Defeat them all to earn access to the Bedroom Key.

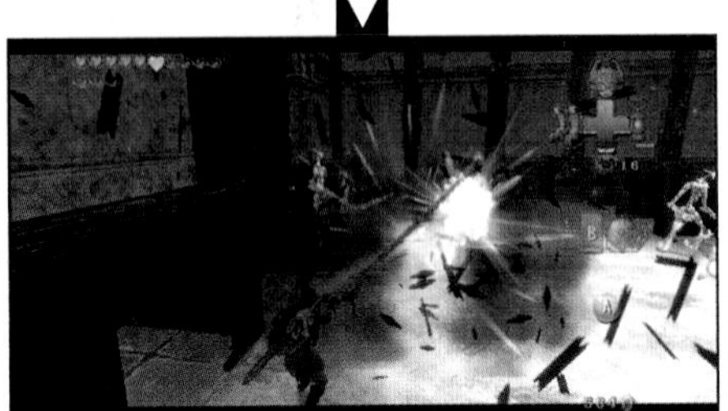

23 Stock Up on Soup

As you leave the church, Yeta will point you in the direction of the boss room. Before you go there, visit Yeto for more health-generating soup.

Twilit Ice Mass—Blizzeta

Yeta has been possessed by the Mirror Shard's magic. She'll grow into a giant ice statue at the beginning of the battle. Hit her with the ball and chain as she glides around the room. She'll shrink with every hit. When she is down to normal size, she'll radiate small ice statues. Dodge them then counter with more ball-and-chain attacks.

For the second phase of her attack, Blizzeta will surround herself with icy spikes and hover above you. You'll be able to tell where the spikes are by looking at their reflections on the shiny floor. The fiend will drop the spikes one at a time. Run to avoid them. Shortly after they drop, the spikes will rise and form a circle that will drop. Try to be out of the circle when that happens. Blizzeta will fall into the circle. Hit her with the ball and chain. You'll win the battle after you score three direct hits.

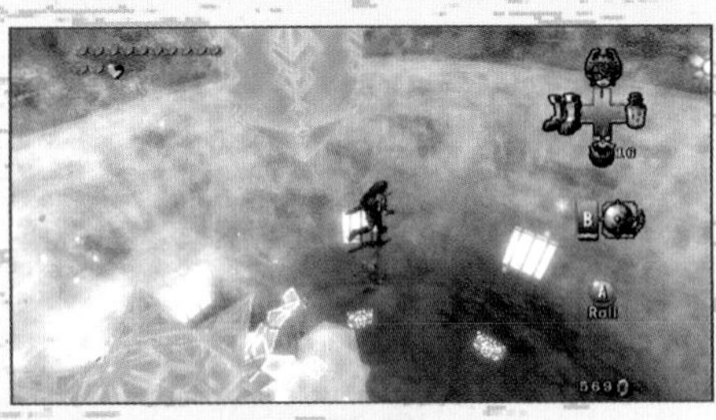

After the individual spikes drop, destroy them. When Blizzeta forms the spike ring, there will be holes where the missing spikes should be. That'll expose the beast.

Temple of Time

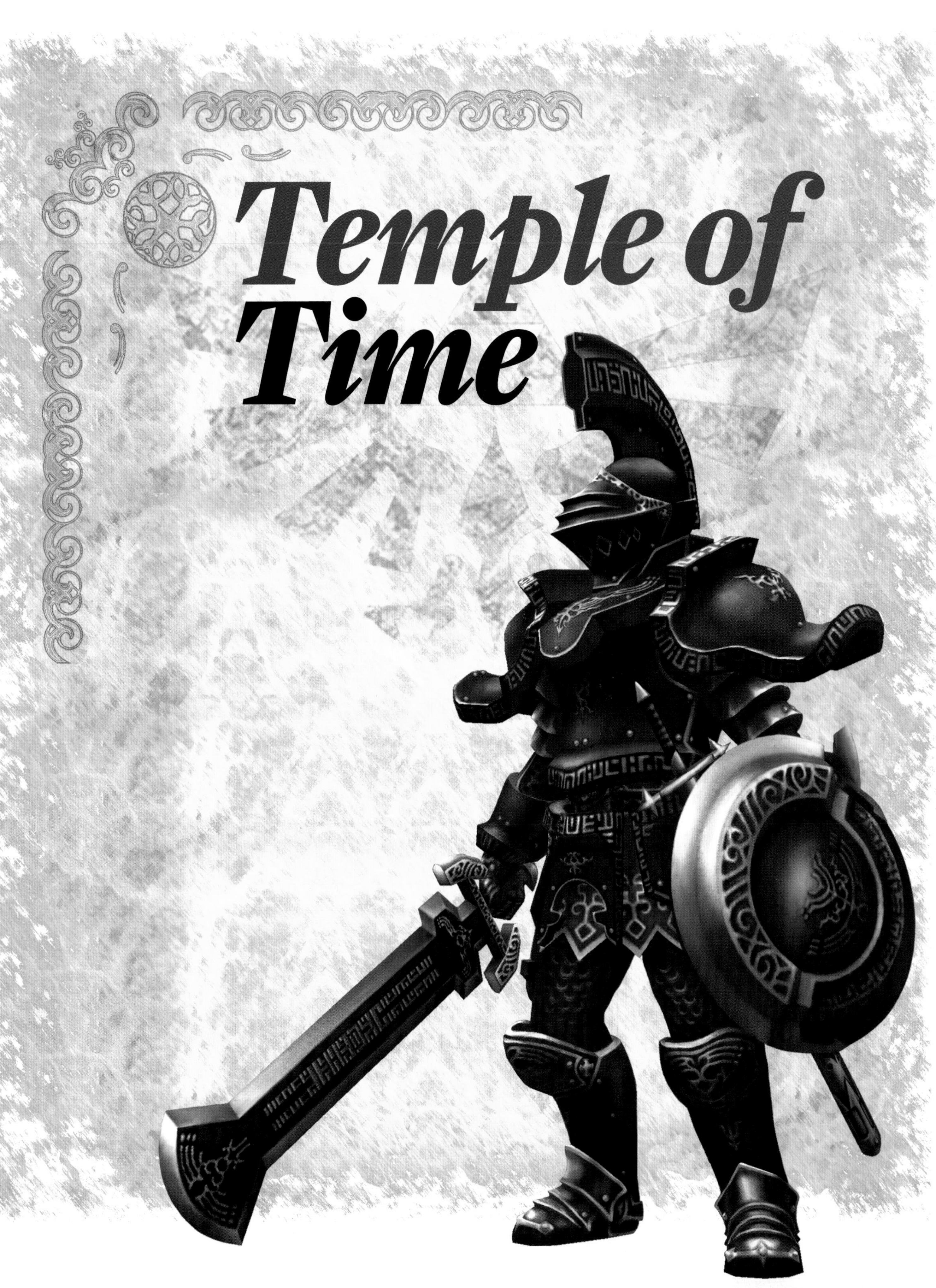

Faron Province

Return to the Sacred Grove for another Master Sword-related quest.

Track Down an Old Friend

Your visits to Telma's Bar are becoming regular occurrences. When you talk to Telma after your Snowpeak Ruins episode, she'll tell you to seek out Rusl. Check the map on the table to see that Rusl is in Hyrule's southern wood, in North Faron.

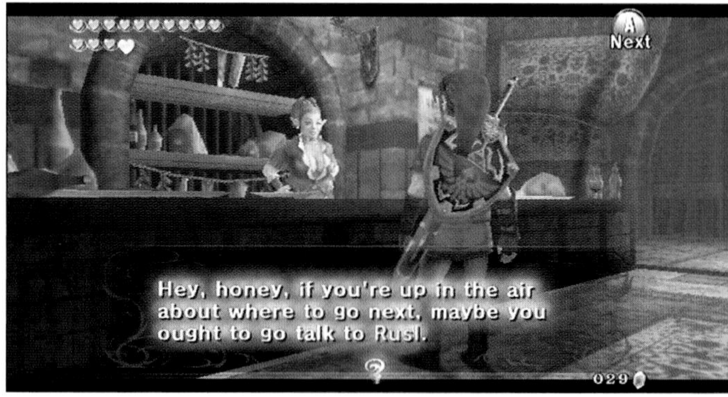

1 Travel by Poultry

Warp to North Faron Woods, change to your human form, then head due north. You'll find Rusl on the same stump from which you began your journey to the Master Sword. He'll explain that an ancient temple on the other side of the gorge holds a secret, and he'll offer you a way to get there: by holding a golden Cucco.

2 Glide to Safety

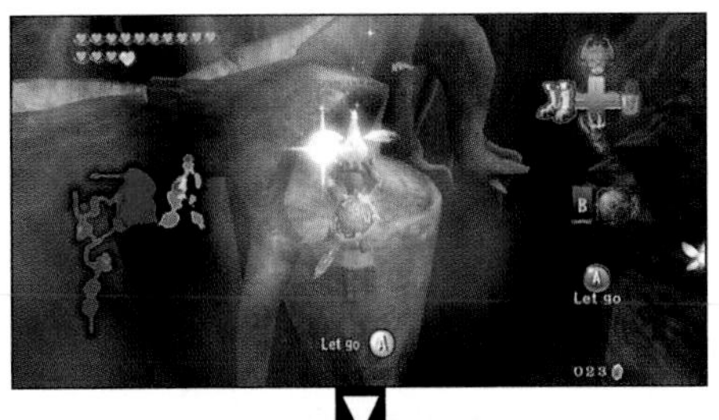

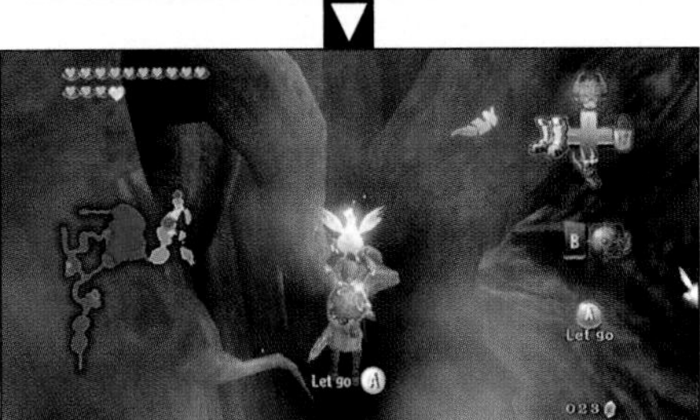

Pick up the Cucco and use it to glide straight across a gap to a ledge. Turn and glide to a root that juts out from the cliff, then turn again and glide to another ledge. From there, you'll walk for a short distance, manipulate a bridge, then glide some more.

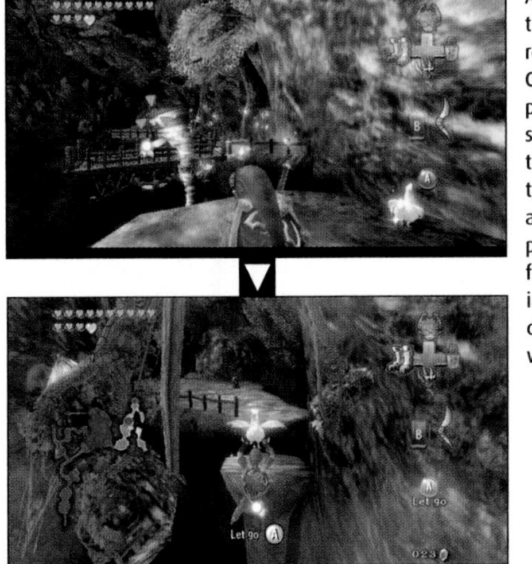

After your initial flight across the gorge you'll overlook a rotating bridge. Drop the Cucco. Use the boomerang to position the bridge so it spans north-south. Pick up the Cucco then swoop over to the bridge. Turn the bridge again and soar to the precipice in the west. Then fly over two more gaps, making sure the swinging logs don't hit you. You'll be done with the Cucco after that.

Sacred Woods

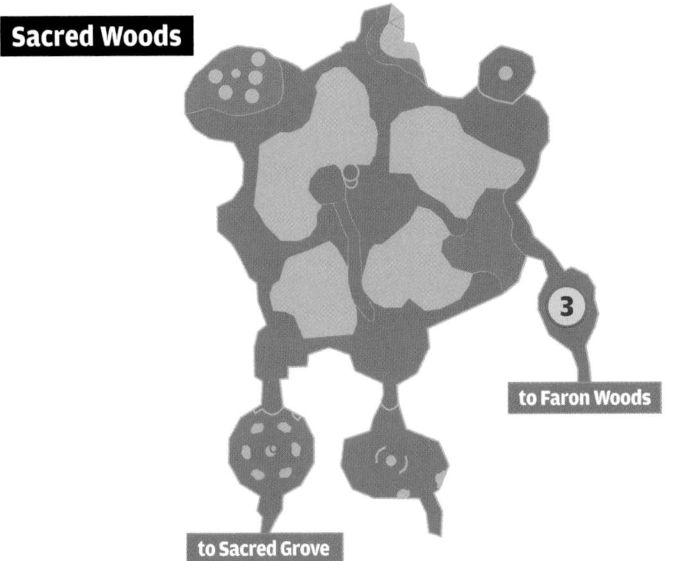

3 Getting the Runaround

On your way to the temple, you'll go up against the Skull Kid and his skeleton followers again, this time in your human form. Make quick work of the followers then search the woods for the little guy. You'll know that you're on the right track when you see lamp light. After finding the scamp and hitting him with your sword or arrows in three locations, you'll drop into an arena for three more rounds. Every time your foe appears, clear the area of skeletons then hit your target with an arrow. After your victory, the kid will lead you to the next area.

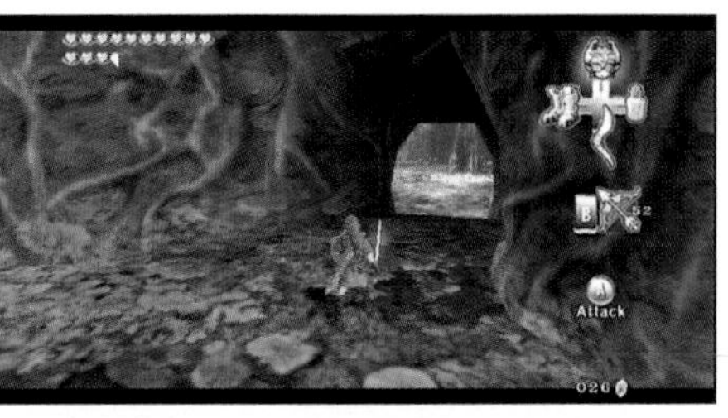

Sacred Grove

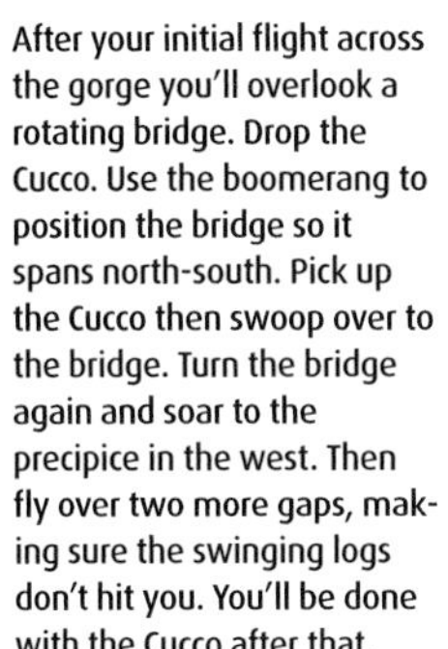
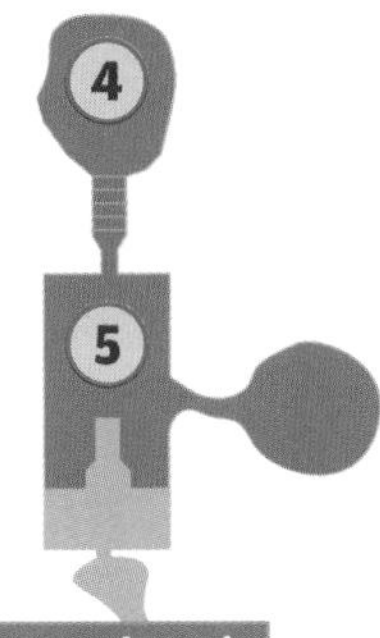

4 Remastered Sword

Push a large block to clear your way. Drop off a ledge and go north to the place where you got the Master Sword. By striking down with the sword where it once rested, you will cause a guardian statue that blocks the entrance to the Temple of Time to disappear. Head south to the entrance.

5 Surprise Attack

On your way to the temple, five shadow beings will drop from the sky. You can choose to fight them as Link or as the wolf. After you knock out the first three, hit the last two with a single blow.

Temple of Time

All marble, stone, and moving platforms, the Temple of Time is an adventurer's dream.

The Sword Is Key

Enter the hallowed hall and run north. You'll discover another place to plant the sword. Doing so will cause a blue-glowing staircase to appear. It leads to the temple proper.

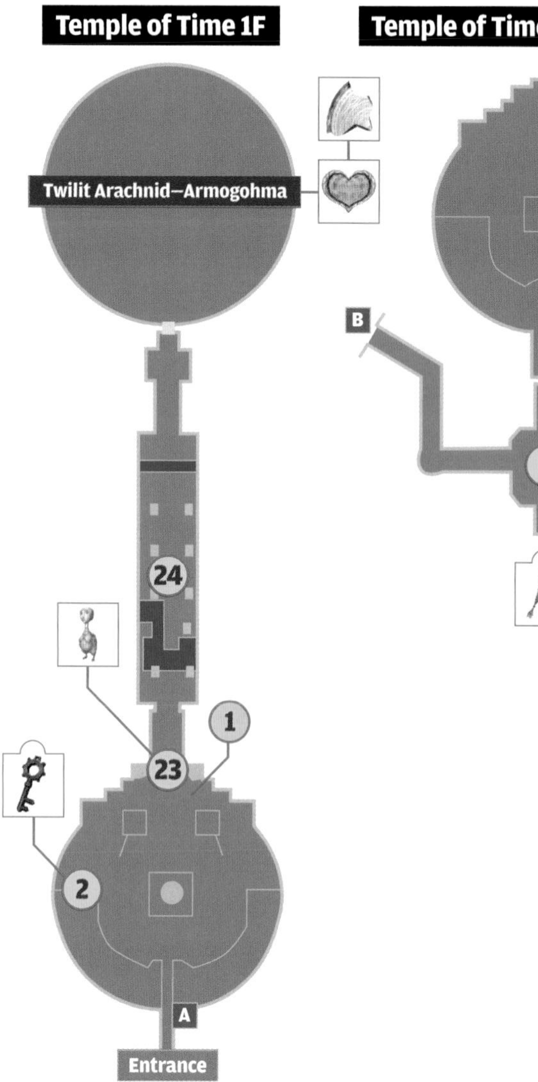

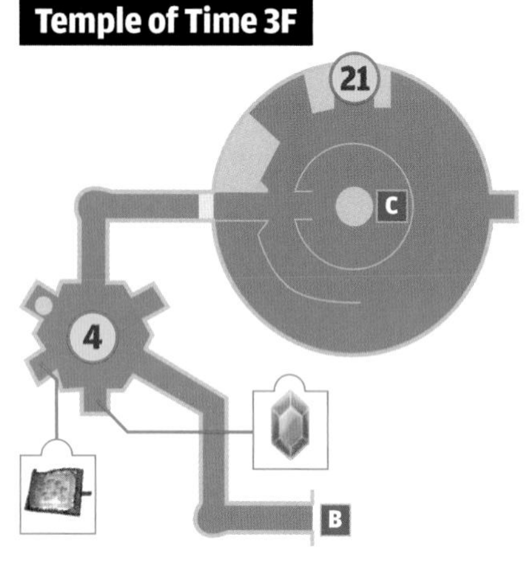

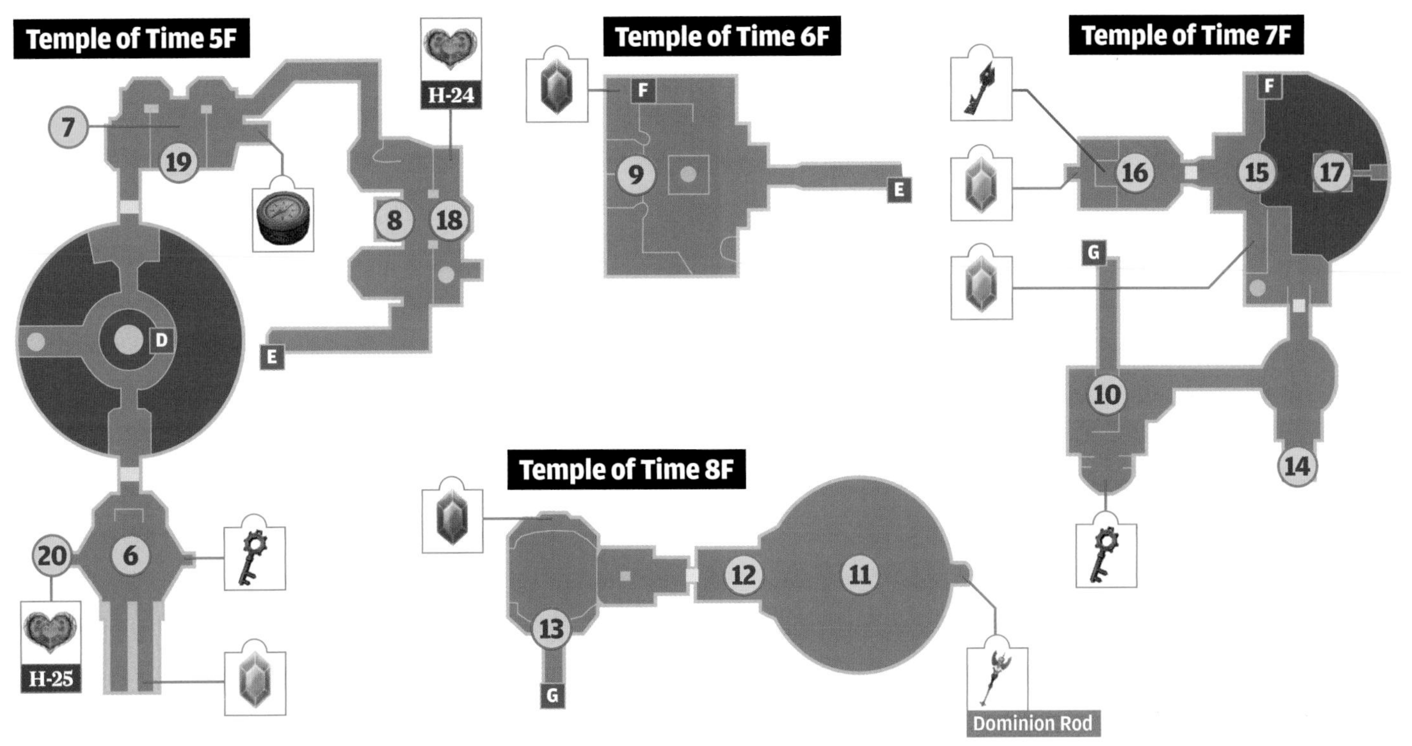

1 Art History

As you approach the grand door of the temple foyer, Midna will comment that there is a statue on one side of the door but not on the other. Use your canine senses to see the ghostly image of the statue that was once in the now-empty place. Your quest: find the statue.

2 Key Finding

There's a small piece of art on the pedestal in front of the door's remaining statue. Put it on the pedestal in front of the place where the missing statue would go. You'll gain access to the stairs. Climb up, then down the other side. Light torches to earn a key.

3 Gate Game

Head south into a chamber that has golden gates. Defeat the enemies but leave at least one pot intact. Place the pot on the switch in the middle of the room to make two gates open and one gate closes. Open the chest that was behind the southern gate. Then go west past the other open gate and hit the pot with an arrow. Gates will open and close again, allowing you to advance west.

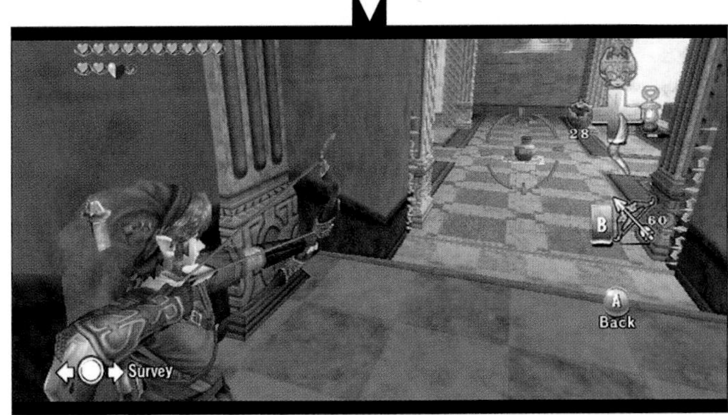

4 Small Battle, Big Map

An Armos statue comes to life as you approach it on the third floor. Work your way around to the other side of the statue and hit the jewel that is on its back. The statue will explode and a chest containing the dungeon map will appear.

5 Platform Pop-Up

Climb up the stairs in the large round room to the fifth floor. Push the arm of the central platform to make the platform sink. Pick up a small statue, put it on the platform, then make the platform rise. Place the statue on a switch near the south door. Find another statue to the west. Put it on the other switch.

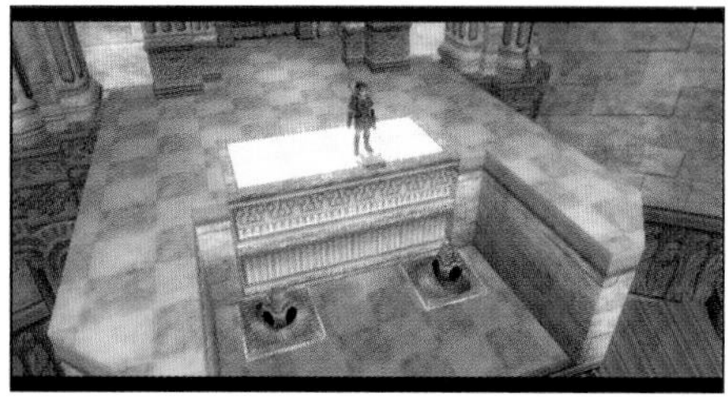

A couple of seconds after you have both statues in place, the white tiles will rise. Make sure that you have a clear path to the tiles when you place the last statue. Then ride the white-tiled platform. It will give you access to the south door.

6 Life and Death

The fifth floor's southern-most room has two Armos statues. You'll want to deal with them one at a time. Walk close to one of them to have it attack you, then hit the jewel on its back to destroy it. Do the same with the other statue. With victory, you will win a Small Key.

7 Sharp Shooter

Hit the green diamond in the room at the north end of the fifth floor to turn the jewel red and make barriers move out of the way. Go to the middle of the room and fire an arrow at the diamond to make the barriers move again, giving you access to the compass.

Collect the compass, then fire another arrow at the jewel. The barriers will move once more, allowing you to exit to the east.

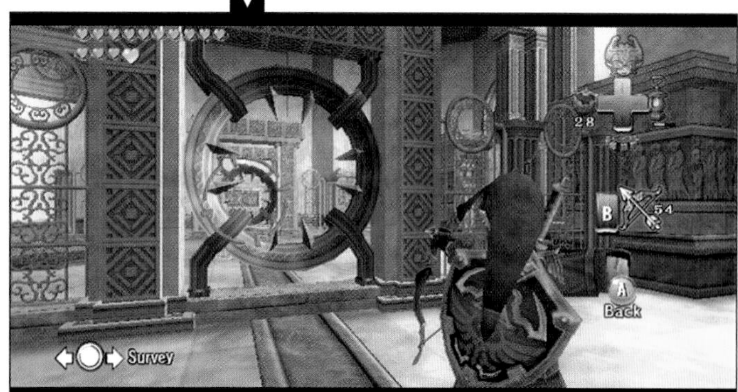

8 Shoot and Slide

The chamber on the east side of the fifth floor will present you with another series of moving barriers that are triggered by a diamond. Round marks on the floor show you where to stand while firing. As soon as the barriers move, be ready to take on armored enemies.

9 Weights and Measures

Climb up the stairs in the chamber at the northeast corner of the seventh floor then step onto a giant scale. Your platform will sink and the other one will rise. Toss the small statue from your platform to the other platform to make them even. Advance to the south.

By defeating every bug in the room, you'll cause a treasure chest (containing a 50-rupee piece) to appear. Use spin attacks or arrows from a distance to clear the chamber.

10 Spikes, Lasers, and Blades

Fire an arrow at the eye of the southern room's Beamos to keep it from blasting you. Run with the flow of the spiked mechanisms to reach the stairs. Climb up, fight three lizardlike enemies, then deal with a spiky roller and a pendulum to get a key in the southwest corner.

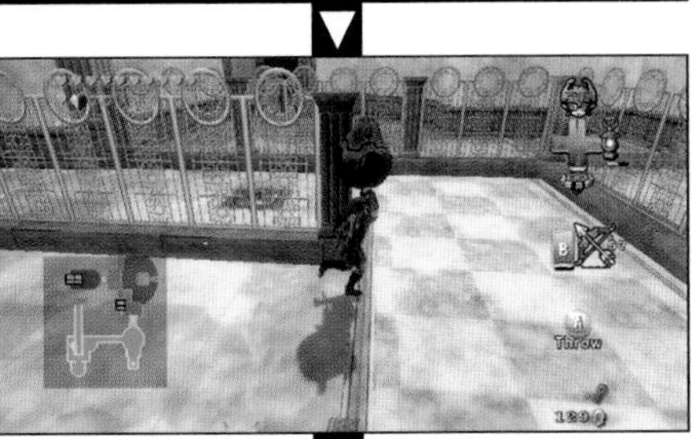

Pick up a small statue in the northwest corner and take it to a switch on the floor. Place the statue on the switch to make an electrical field turn off. Head up the stairs to the north.

There are two Armos statues in the north end of the eighth floor's west room. Before you drop in and make the statues notice you, use arrows to defeat the room's little spiders for a rupee reward. Then fight the statues to make the door to the east open.

11 Knight Moves

Prepare for a two-stage fight against a real swordmaster. It'll be worth the hassle—the reward is the Dominion Rod. Your enemy starts slow, as he is weighed down by armor. Hop out of the way of his lunges, then counter with your own attacks. Hidden skills are very useful here. After you knock off your foe's armor, his speed will increase.

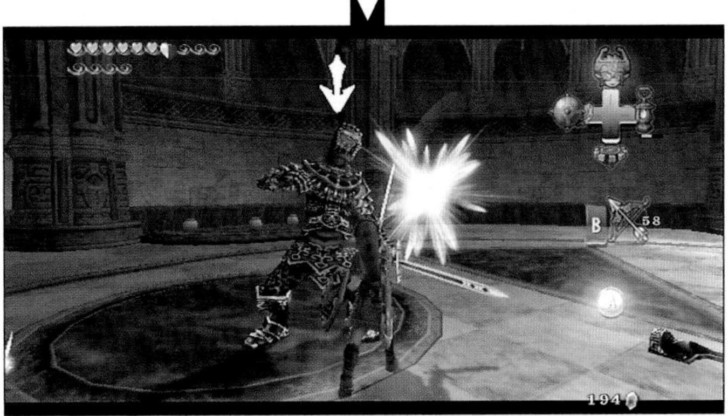

Once your opponent is free of his armor, he'll move quickly, slash without warning, and defend himself with his sword. Try the Back Slice and Mortal Draw skills against him, or circle him without Z-Button targeting (for more speed and maneuverability), listen for him to slash out at you, then target him and start swinging.

12 Statue Found

Grab the Dominion Rod from the chest in the room where you fought the knight, then use it to make the statue on the ledge above you come to life. The statue is the temple's missing piece. Guide it to the disc under the bell-shaped device to make it transfer to the next room.

The Dominion Rod

The Dominion Rod fires energy that brings some inanimate objects to life. They will move as you do. Press the B Button to make the objects attack or jump.

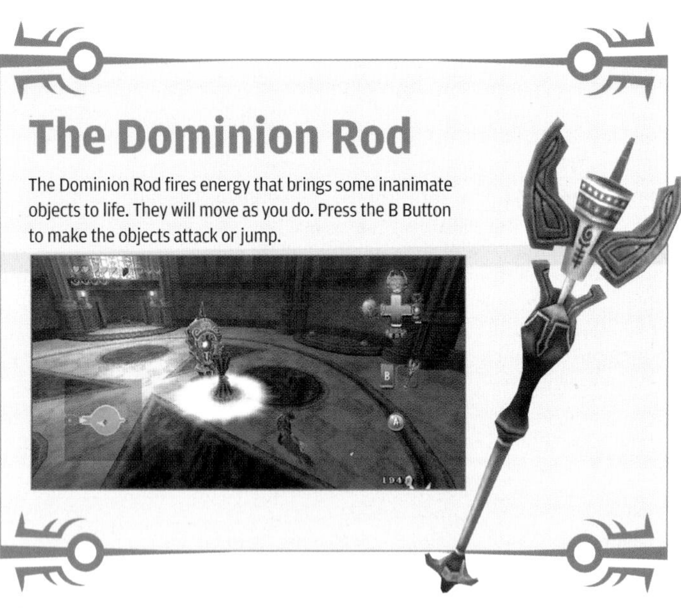

13 Power Through

Press the B Button to have the rod-controlled statue swing its hammer. Use the statue to destroy a golden gate, then clobber the two smaller statues that come to life.

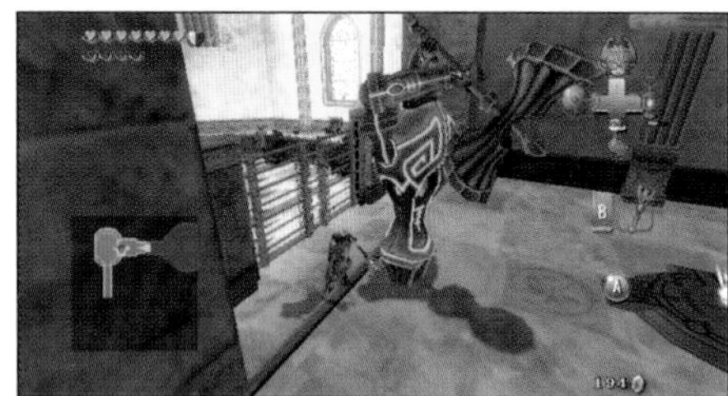

The statue can't climb. Place a pot or a small statue on the floor switch to make the platform near the door sink to your level. Guide the big statue to the platform, then hit the pot with an arrow or possess the little statue with the rod to make the platform rise.

14 The Path to Another Bell

The statue is impervious to electricity and spikes. Have it go ahead of you through the charged field and stop on the switch that makes the field shut off. Then guide the statue through the area that has spiked rollers, letting the rollers run into your indestructible companion.

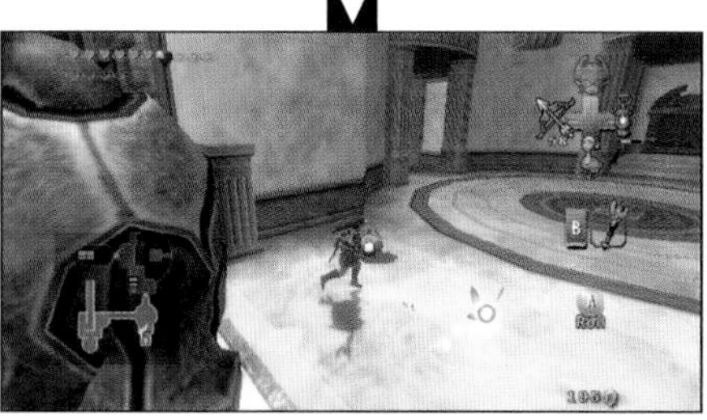

In the south room, have the statue destroy the spiked mechanisms and the Beamos. You'll reveal a floor switch. Guide the statue to the white tiles in the south end of the room. Put a rod-controlled small statue on the switch to make the white-tiled platform rise, then guide the big statue to the bell.

15 New Heights

Guide the big statue onto the scale's first platform. Collect six small statues around the room and toss them onto the same plaform. That will give you the height (while standing on the other platform) to grapple to the spot above the room's big bell. Ride a Spinner track west.

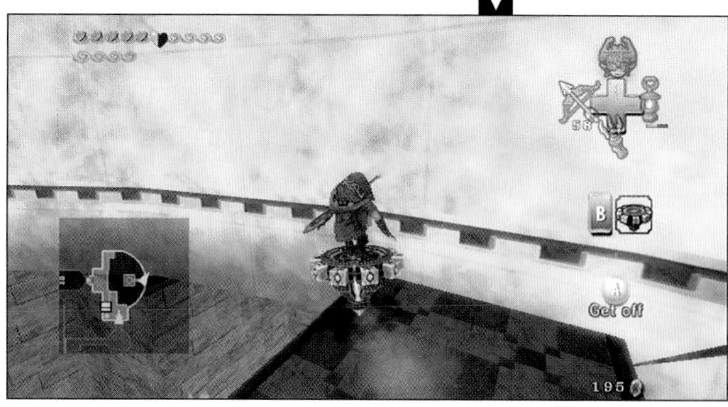

Grapple to the platform above the bell and ride a track to the balcony on the west side of the room. Collect a rupee treasure, fight a Poe for its soul, then move on to the west.

16 Heavy Armor

The gate in the seventh floor's northwest room will lock behind you. Use your Clawshot to pull the armor off the two crawling Helmasaurs in the room, defeat them with your sword, then defeat the Armos. With the enemies gone, the exit will open.

Don't leave the room yet. Grapple up to the balcony and place small statues on three of the four switches. Use the Clawshot to grab a piece of armor from the main floor, and use it to press the fourth switch. That will give you access to the Big Key.

The small statues are scattered throughout the room. You'll find one on a high shelf. Use the Dominion Rod to retrieve it.

17 A Delicate Balance

Return to the room that contains the scale. Lead the large statue to the first platform, then place four small statues on the second platform. That will even out the scale. Move the big statue to the second platform. The scale will tip. Toss the small statues to the first platform, then step off to restore balance. Finally, guide the big guy to the big bell.

18 Treasure Rove

When you reach the room that has the diamond and the sliding barriers, you'll see the statue on the other side of a fence. Use the rod to make your sturdy friend follow your commands, and have it walk past the first barrier. Then hit the diamond with an arrow to make the barriers slide. Guide the statue to the floor switch (turning off the electrical barrier) then advance to the treasure in the northeast corner. It's a Piece of Heart. Guide the big guy to the next room.

19 Break Down the Wall

You're back to the first room in which you encountered the diamond switch and sliding barriers. Have the statue break through the barriers, then lead it to the bell.

20 Heart Operation

There's a Piece of Heart in the room south of the large, round chamber. Starting in the round chamber, push the lever on the pedestal to make it sink to the floor. Pick up a small statue, then take the pedestal back to its starting position.

Place the small statue on one of the floor switches near the southern entrance. Pick up the other small statue (west of the pedestal) and place it on the other floor switch. The white-tile platform will take you to the south door.

Run to the southeastern corner of the south room and use the rod to make a small statue on the other side of a railing come to life. Guide the statue north to a switch. Toss another small statue over the west railing and guide it to another switch. The prize will appear.

21 Smash 'Em Down

Return to the round room and take the pedestal to the top; you'll find the large statue. Give it a Dominion Rod blast and guide it to the pedestal. Sink to the floor and use the statue's hammer to shake the floor and destroy the little spiders. After the last spider is gone, the room's electrical field will shut off.

Before you put the big statue under the bell (to send it to another part of the temple), have it break the golden gate that protects the room's Poe. Transform into a wolf then steal the Poe Soul.

22 Up and Over

Use the Clawshot to get over the gate in the third floor's west room. Bring the big statue to life, have it defeat a smaller Armos, and move on to the bell on the second floor.

23 The Return Home

Go to the first-floor foyer to find the statue waiting for you. Bring it to life once more and guide it to its resting place. The main door will open.

24 Pits and Pendulums

On your way to the boss room, you'll jump over a gap, use arrows to destroy Beamos statues, and run past swinging pendulums. Pick up a small statue and place it on a switch to open a gate. Pass the gate, then use the rod to move the statue. The gate will close and another one will open.

Before you open the door to the boss's chamber, look for a fairy in a pot. Scoop it up with an empty bottle.

Twilit Arachnid—Armogohma

The great spider Armogohma crawls on the ceiling, drops large groups of little spiders, and fires lasers from the eye on its back. Run from the laser, zigzagging as you go, and defeat the little spiders to get hearts and arrows.

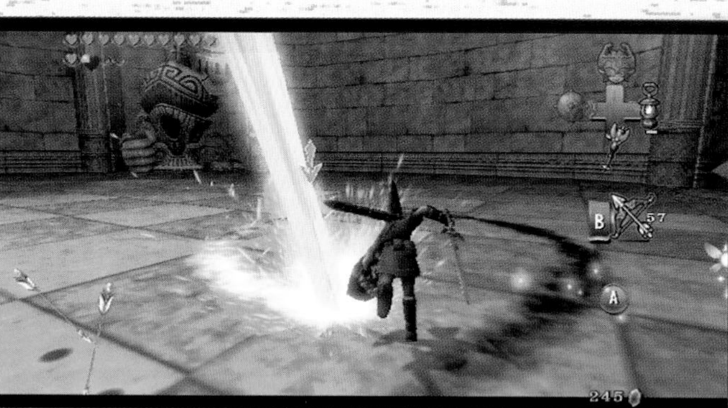

When the spider's eye is open, hit its weak spot with an arrow. A single shot will make the enemy fall to the ground. Run to the statue that is closest to the spider, bring it to life, and have it smash the bug. The spider will get up and go back to the ceiling for another round. You'll destroy the main spider after three rounds, but the eye will remain. Slice it or shoot it with arrows to finish the battle. The spoils of victory are a Mirror Shard and a Heart Container.

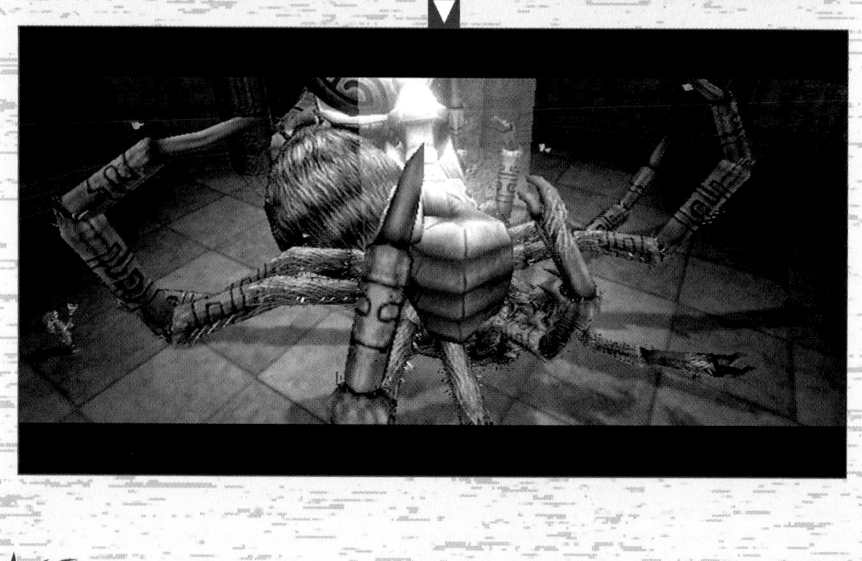

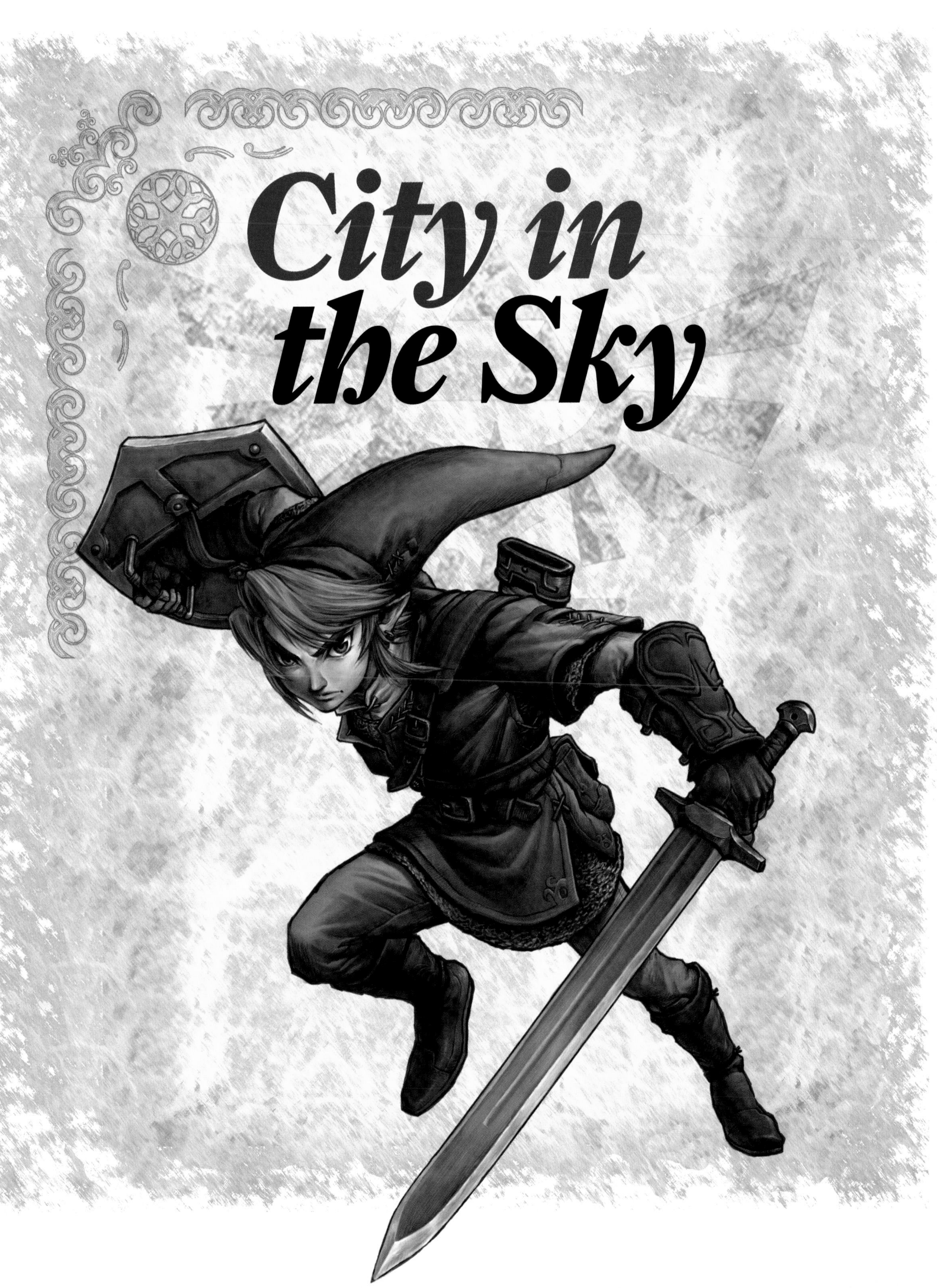
City in the Sky

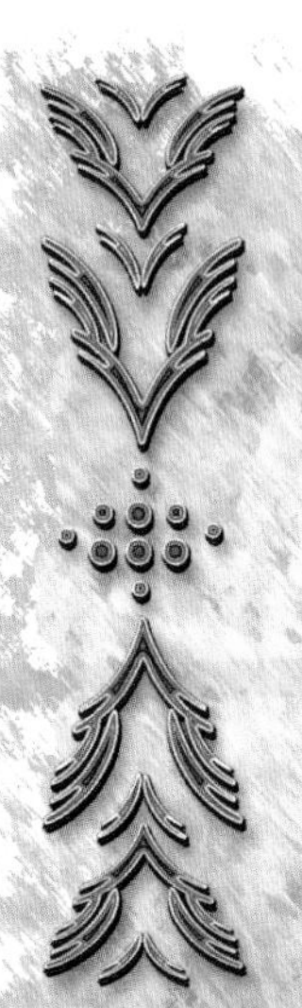

The Oocca's Words

Link's quest to restore Ilia's memory and find six ancient symbols will take him to the far corners of Hyrule.

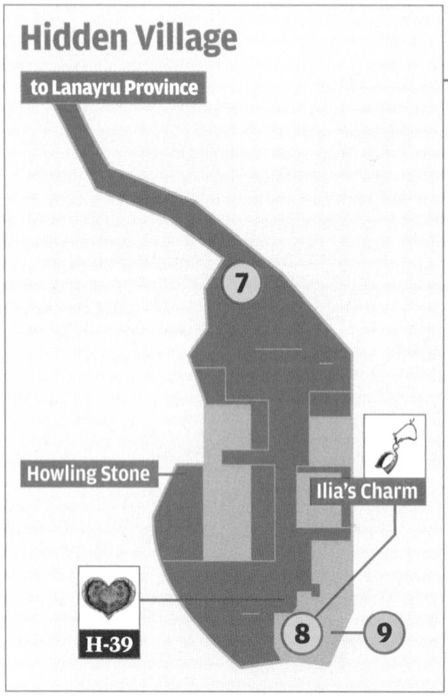

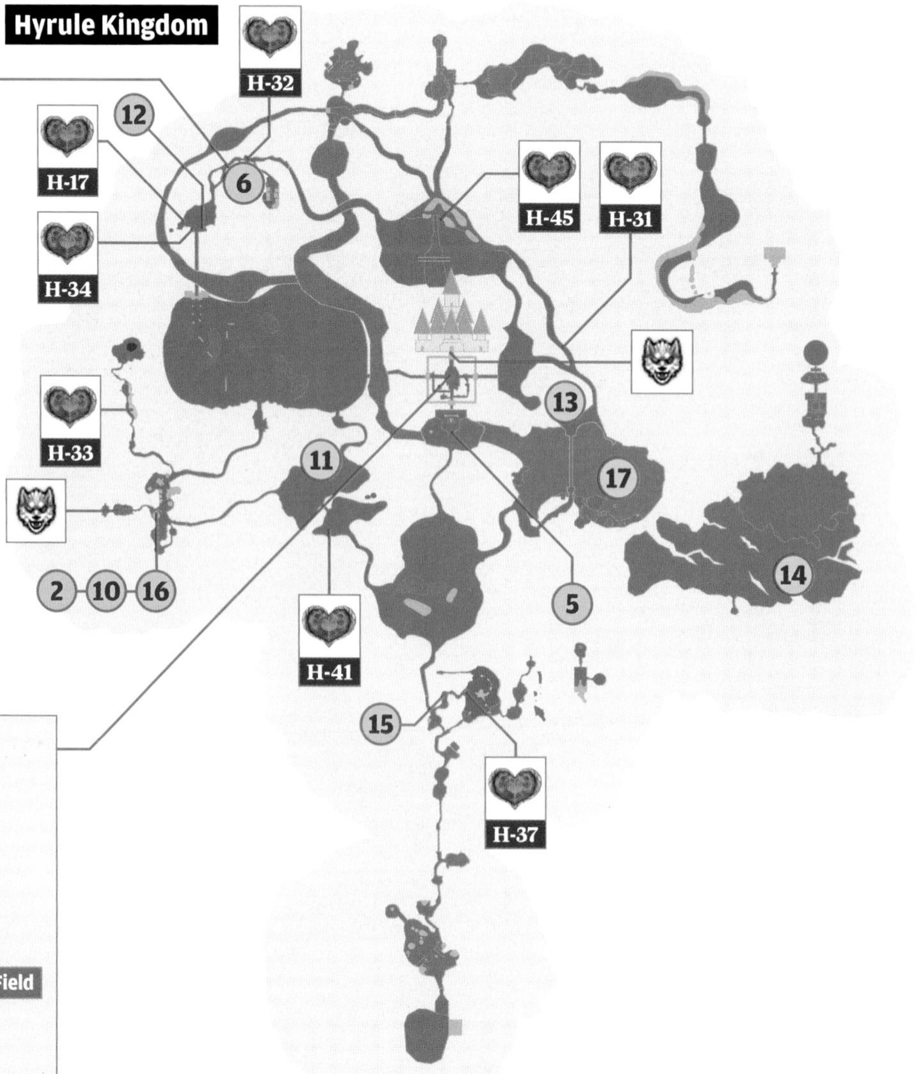

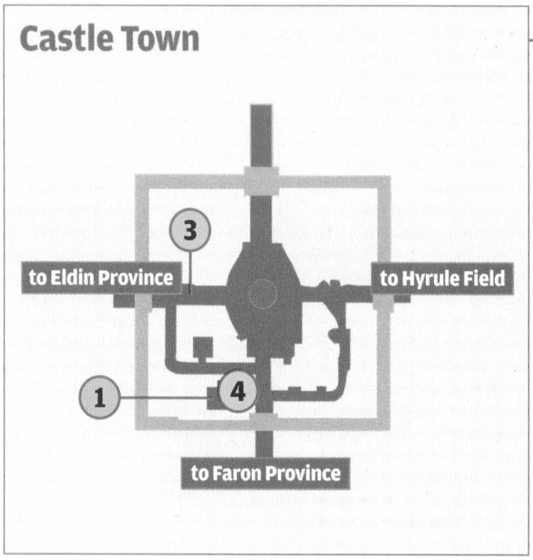

1 Letter for a Friend

With your adventure in the Temple of Time complete, head back to Telma's Bar to find out what your fellow adventurers have been up to. On the way, you'll get a letter from Renado regarding Ilia's memory. As you find out at Telma's, Shad is in Kakariko Village already, so head there to get the scoop from both men.

Grave Importance

If you haven't already met with the golden wolf in Kakariko Village's graveyard to earn a hidden skill, Renado's summons gives you a good excuse to stop by. The mysterious warrior will teach you the Jump Strike, a jumping attack that hits multiple enemies.

2 Memorable Experience

Renado thinks he might know how to get Ilia's memory back, but first you'll have to deliver a letter to Telma that explains the process. It seems that a "rod of the heavens" may have some connection to the memory-restoration process.

Drop into Renado's basement to find Shad admiring a statue. He believes that the statue has something to do with the Oocca people, and that Ilia's memory is tied to finding these lost beings.

3 Medicine Man

Give Renado's letter to Telma; she'll exchange it for the doctor's bar invoice. Locate the doctor's office at the west end of the town's west avenue and deliver the invoice. Unfortunately, the only thing on the doctor's mind is why he can't pay the tab.

Enter the north room in the doctor's office and push the wooden box to reveal a green stain. It appears to be the medicine that he mentioned spilling on Ilia's wooden statue.

Transform into a wolf and learn the medicine's scent, then use your senses to track the scent through Castle Town.

4 The Cat's out of the Bag

The medicine scent leads back to Telma's cat, who you'll find outside the bar. She admits that she stole the wooden statue from the doctor's office, but claims it was taken from her by a pack of skeletal dog beasts that hang out south of the town at night. Take the town's south exit to find the creatures.

5 The Pack Attacks

If you head to the field south of the courtyard outside the town's south entrance at night, the pack of dogs the cat told you about will rise out of the ground. Defeat them all to retrieve the wooden statue.

6 The Gorons Know

Take the statue back to Kakariko Village and show it to Ilia. The statue will bring back a bit of her memory, and the Gorons will recognize that the carving came from a secluded village. Darbus, patriarch of the Gorons, will head to the village entrance, which is north of the Bridge of Eldin; follow him by heading to the red marker that appears on your map.

7 Hidden No More

You may have seen the Hidden Village entrance before, but previously it was blocked by a landslide. Darbus will smash the way open for you and warn you about enemies waiting to ambush you within the village. As he suggests, take them out before they see you.

The wild town is filled with enemies that like to use bows and arrows. Before you proceed through the town, equip your bow with the Hawkeye and use it to take out as many enemies as you can. Look on the upper levels, through windows, and behind boxes.

Check the back alleys to find any lingering enemies. You can use the Clawshot to reach the buildings' upper floors.

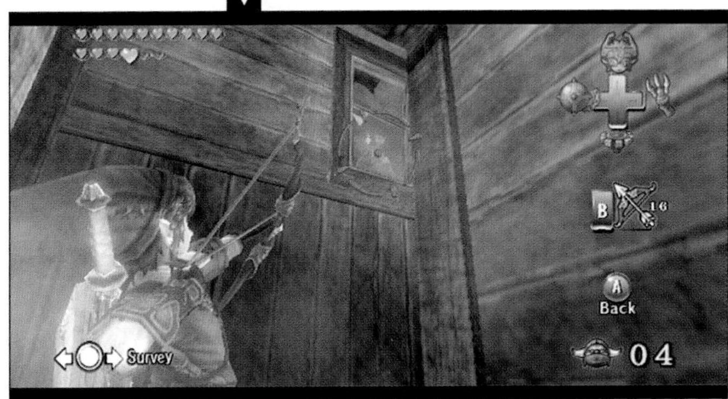

Keep an eye on the onscreen counter to see how many enemies are left. Some of them are hiding inside buildings; you can break the windows to get to them. Try to take out as many enemies as you can from outside the buildings before entering and attacking the foes that are out of bow range.

8 Introducing Impaz

After you've defeated all 20 enemies, an old woman named Impaz will emerge from her home at the rear of the village. She'll explain how she met Ilia and give you Ilia's charm. The charm is key to restoring Ilia's memory.

Last Howling Hurrah

Before heading back to Kakariko Village, locate and activate the Howling Stone behind the western buildings. You'll have to break the building's windows to reach the stone.

Memory Retrieval

When you give Ilia the charm, it will remind her of the times she spent with Link, and her memory will return. She'll give you the Horse Call and some important information about the Dominion Rod.

Horse Call

The Horse Call is a whistle that Ilia created just for Link. It lets him summon Epona from anywhere, even when there's no call grass around.

9 Royal Reading

Return to the Hidden Village and show the Dominion Rod to Impaz. Seeing the rod will convince her that you're worthy of receiving the Ancient Sky Book.

10 Show It to Shad

Go back to Renado's basement. After you show him the Ancient Sky Book, he'll set out to investigate some special symbols near statues; he'll indicate their locations on your map. Seek out the symbols. The magic in the book also restores power to the Dominion Rod.

A Golden Opportunity

Since Link's mission to find the statues takes him all over Hyrule, the task offers a great opportunity to look for Golden Bugs, Pieces of Heart, and Poe Souls if you haven't been searching for them already. After you give Agitha all 24 bugs, she'll reward you with a Giant Wallet that holds 1,000 rupees, and once you collect 20 Poe Souls Jovani will give you a bottle. Since trading in Golden Bugs also generates a lot of cash, it gives you a chance to fund the Gorons' trade route. After you've donated 1,000 rupees to their cause, the west bridge into Castle Town will be rebuilt. If you give them even more rupees, Malo Mart will expand into Castle Town, offering special items and fabulous deals.

11 The First Symbol

The first statue is in the southern section of Eldin Province. Dismount your horse near the north wall and climb up the ledge to find the statue. Use the Dominion Rod to pull the statue from its alcove, and stand on the glowing symbol to learn part of a magic word.

12 The Second Symbol

You'll find the second statue at the north end of Eldin Bridge, along the east side. Use the Dominion Rod to move the statue and learn the next symbol. While you're at it, guide the statue to the southern end of the bridge and use it as a platform to reach a Piece of Heart.

A Great Technique

Head to Castle Town and take the north exit. Behind the door you'll find the spirit of a warrior who will teach you the final hidden skill. The Great Spin is a stronger version of your spin attack; activate it by shaking the nunchuk back and forth while you're at full health.

13 The Third and Fourth Symbols

Head southeast from Castle Town's east exit. You'll find the third statue sitting on a pedestal in an amphitheater. Use the rod to move the statue so it acts as a step between the stone ledge and the pedestal, then hop across it to get the symbol. You can also use the statue to reach a treasure chest.

Another statue is in an alcove north of the Great Bridge of Hylia. Move the statue south and position it beneath the vines. Grapple to the vines with the Clawshot and drop onto the statue, then jump over to the symbol. The statue will help you get the chest in the west alcove, too.

14 The Fifth Symbol

Travel west from the warp point in Gerudo Desert until you reach a set of irregularly shaped stone blocks. Lead the statue off its perch, then jump from the northwest block to the statue, and then to the the block where the symbol is. The nearby chest contains 100 rupees.

15 The Final Symbol

Remember the Lantern Oil salesman in Faron Woods? The last statue is near his abode. Destroy the boulder northeast of his home, then move the statue to collect the final symbol.

16 Big Boomer

With all six symbols collected, return to Kakariko Village. Shad will read the magic word, which will allow you to move the statue with the Dominion Rod. Beyond the statue you'll find an ancient cannon. Talk to Shad again to get him to leave the room, then use Midna to teleport the cannon to Lake Hylia.

17 Fyer It Up

Talk to Fyer at his colorful pagoda. He'll quickly notice your cannon and offer to fix it for 300 rupees. Pay the man and grapple your way into the cannon once it's fixed. You'll be blasted to the City in the Sky.

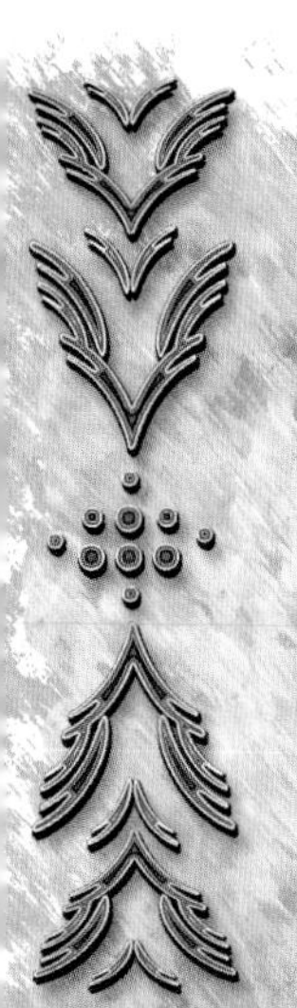

City in the Sky

High above the clouds floats an ancient city. It holds the last Mirror Shard as well as a malevolent dragon.

City in the Sky 1F

Entrance

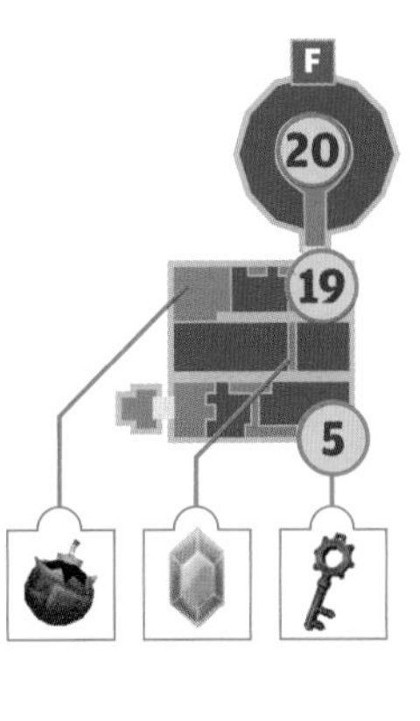

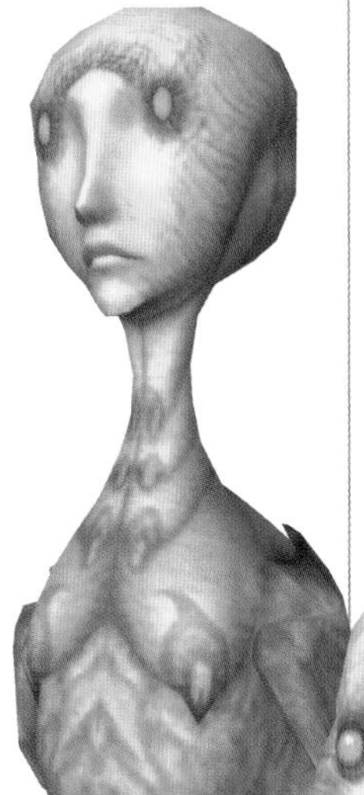

Rock You Like a Hurricane

The City in the Sky is a windy place. The gusts start and stop periodically, and they're especially hazardous when you're near the gaps in the walls. Equip your Iron Boots to ensure you don't get blown over the edge.

1 What's in Store

Before entering the dungeon proper, visit the store to the west—you can stock up on any necessary supplies there instead of returning to the world below.

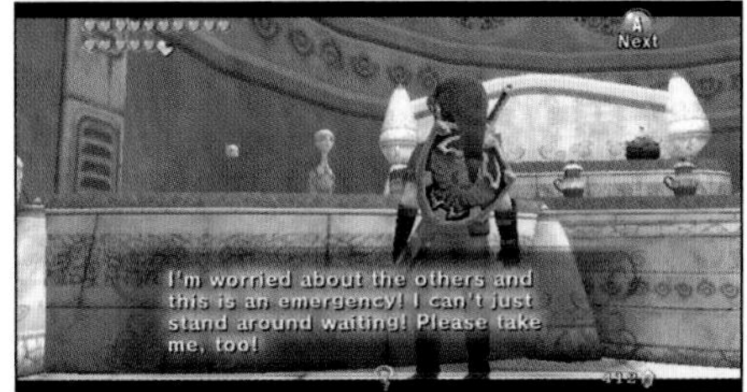

Ooccoo is hanging out in the store. She's at the left side of the counter. Talk to her—she'll join you for your adventure in the City in the Sky.

2 Crystal Shot

Hit the blue crystal above the door to the north to open the way. You can hit it with either your Clawshot or arrows, but the wind may blow the arrows off course.

3 Have Oocca, Will Travel

You'll need the Oocca's help to get through the northern room. The Oocca help you hover just like Cuccoos—just pick one up and you'll glide when you jump.

The blue blocks will fall when you walk on them. If you need to set foot on them, run. Use your Clawshot on the ivy-covered columns to reach higher areas so you can jump the gaps.

The large Helmasauruses in the central room are tougher than their smaller counterparts. Since you can't pull off their armor with the Clawshot, hit them once to stun them, then circle behind them and strike. Alternately, you can use the Back Slice.

4 The East Wing

You need to travel east from the central room, but there's no way to cross the gap to the door. Fortunately, there's an alternate route. Use the Clawshot to grapple to the window grate that's south of the eastern door.

The grate on the window has a hole in it. Go through the hole and drop to the ledge below.

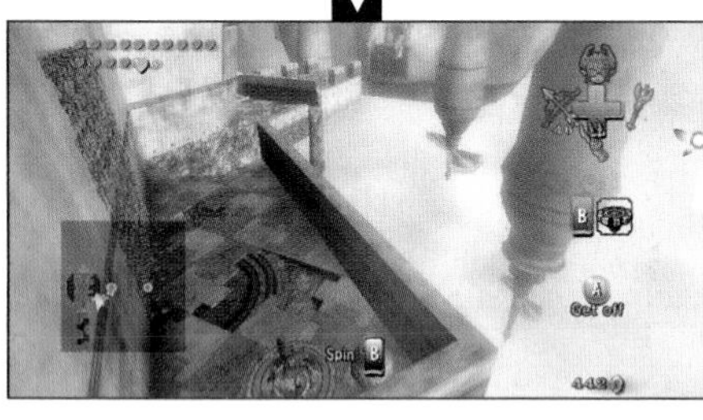

Extend the bridge by using the Spinner in the slot outside (press the B Button repeatedly). Use the Clawshot to grapple to the ivy, then cross the bridge.

5 Enter the Dragon

Jump across the gaps on the north side of the room, then grapple the red target to the southeast. Drop to the platform and retrieve the key from the chest, then use the Clawshot on the grate to get back across the gap. As you head back across the bridge to the central room, a fierce dragon will appear and destroy the bridge. Grapple the ivy on the pillars to return to the center of the chamber.

6 The Wild, Wild West

Run across the blue blocks and enter the west door. Once you're outside, head left and turn another set of gears with the Spinner to activate another bridge. Equip your boots and march across the bridge, then use the key to open the door.

7 City Map

Keep the boots equipped to get past the first wind barrier on the north side of the room, then use the Clawshot on the ivy-covered column to bypass the second. Enter the western door and head left to acquire the dungeon map, then return to the previous room.

8 Wind Breaker

Grapple back across the blue blocks, then drop and make your way to the southeast corner of the room. Walk to the edge of the platform—you'll see a crystal switch behind a pillar.

When you hit the crystal with your Clawshot, the wind barrier in the southwest corner will deactivate.

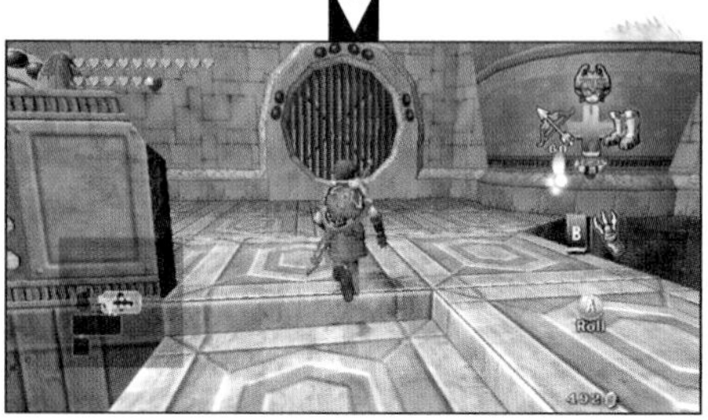

Once the wind has stopped, make your way back to the west side of the room. Remove your Iron Boots and run across the blue blocks to reach the southern door.

9 Watch Your Step

As you jump across the hole-riddled room, time your leaps to avoid the wind funnels that periodically block your path; if you touch one, it will knock you into the abyss below. Use your Clawshot to smash distant pots and grab the resultant treasure.

Tileworms hide under some of the blocks. Use the Gale Boomerang to take them out, or they'll likely knock you off the edge.

City in the Sky 2F

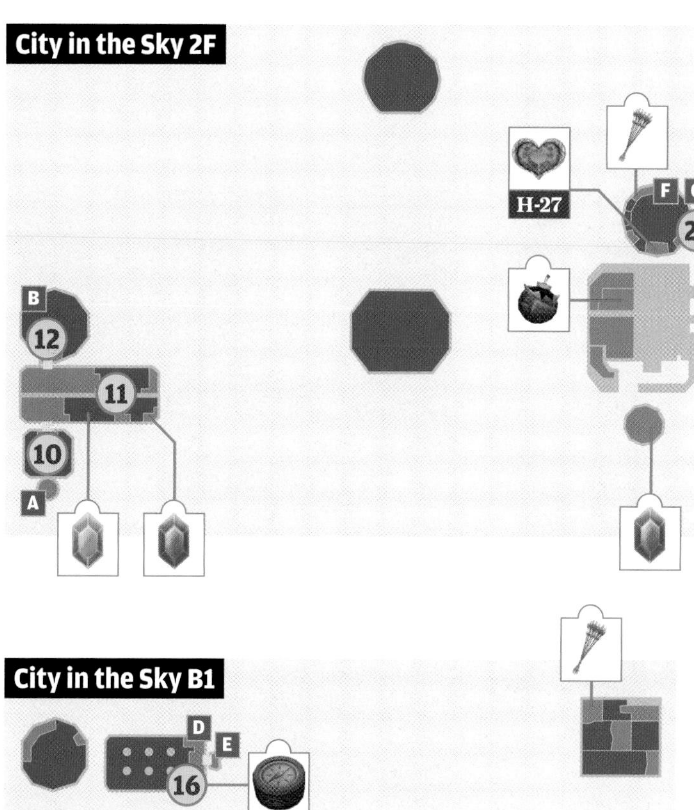

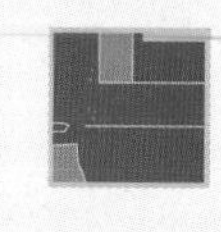

City in the Sky B2

City in the Sky B1

City in the Sky B3

Double Clawshots
14
13
B C

10 Wake the Wind

When you defeat the two large Lizalfos, a gate will open on the second floor. Grapple your way up to the opening, then use the Clawshot on the golden ornament on the ceiling to activate the wind funnel in the center of the room.

The enemies in the room are plenty tough. Use the bomb/arrow combo to take them out from afar (and knock them over the edge if you're lucky).

Once the fan starts turning, grab an Oocca and use it to glide toward the wind funnel, then to the door to the north. Time your jump so you catch the fan's air and get an upward boost.

11 Catch Oocca Air

Before you grab the Oocca and cross to the east side of the gap, grapple the gold ornament on the ceiling to reveal a treasure chest that contains 20 rupees. Grab a 50-rupee prize from the chest at the east end of the room, then use an Oocca to get through the hole in the north wall. Use the Clawshot on another gold ornament to create another wind funnel, then grab an Oocca and fly through the hole in the west wall. Head north through the door.

If you fall to the bottom of the chamber, use the Clawshot to return to the upper floor, or jump into the fan's gust if there's one available (and you have an Oocca).

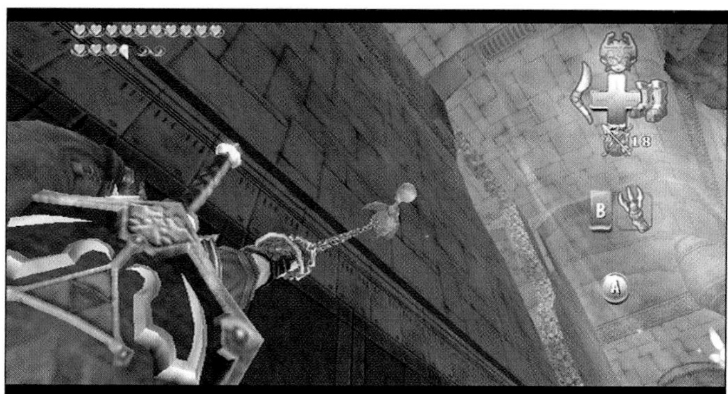

If you don't have an Oocca, you can snag one with the Clawshot.

12 A Long Way Down

Getting to the bottom of the western tower is challenging. Start by grappling to the gold ornament above the platform that's to the right of the door; doing so will open a door you'll need later. Use an Oocca to hover to the platform below and to the west. From there, float to the platform directly below. Hover to the platform in the southeast that has a grapple point next to it, then grapple from ledge to ledge to reach the door.

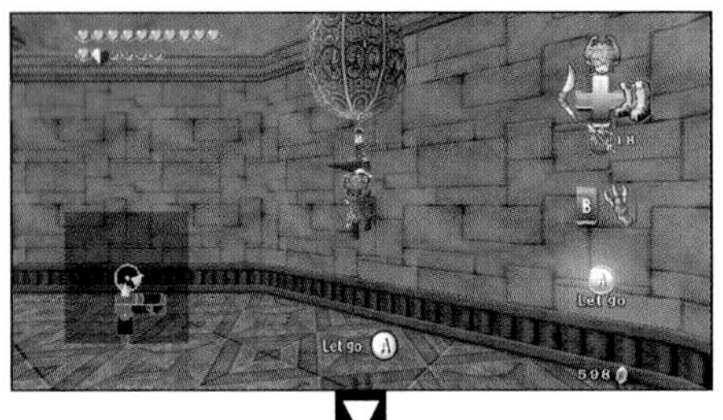

As you travel down through the chamber, avoid the horizontal wind gusts that blow through the tower—they'll push you outside and put an end to your trip. When you need to get past a gusty area, jump only when the wind stops.

City in the Sky 3F

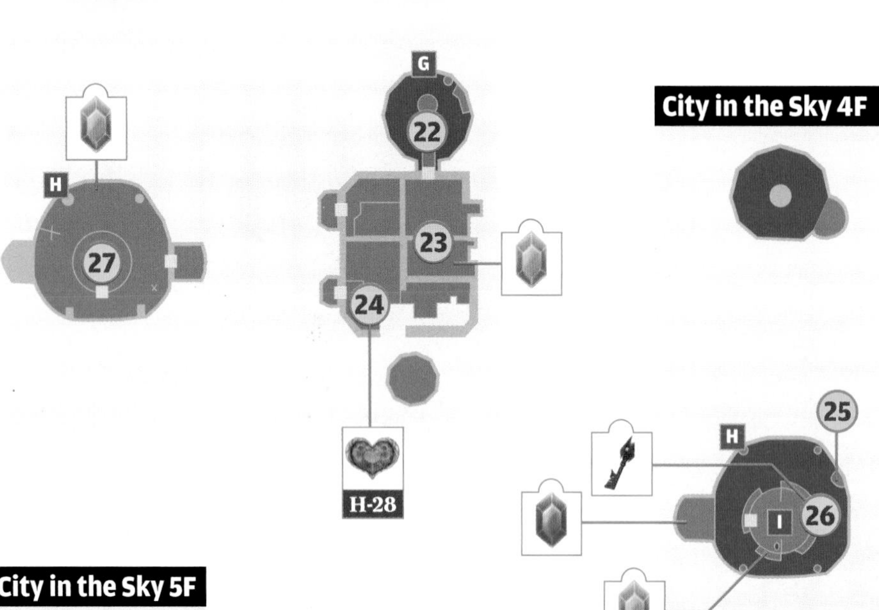

13 Fan-tastic

In the small circular room to the far west, put on the Iron Boots and grapple to the bronze ceiling fixture. The fan will shut down, allowing you to descend to the room below. A mid-dungeon boss awaits.

14 Dragon Warrior

The creature guarding the dungeon's treasure is a small dragon armed with a sword and shield. Draw your Clawshot and aim at the beast as it hovers around. When it puts its shield in front of itself, pull it toward you with the Clawshot, then attack it with your sword. After you hit it several times, it changes attack patterns and begins flying out of the holes in the walls. Scan the room to see where the creature appears, then grapple its shield to bring it close for more sword slashes.

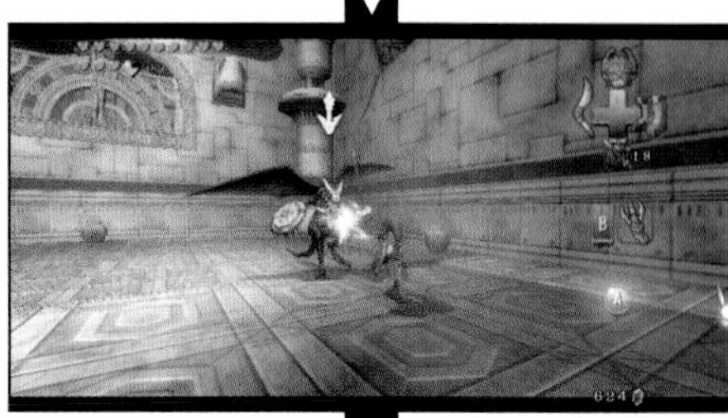

You can also hit the dragon when it swoops down to attack; block the strike, then counterattack. If the creature damages you, however, it will likely knock you onto one of the blue blocks around the edges of the room. Quickly get off of the blue blocks before you fall.

Double Clawshots

Defeating the mid-dungeon boss yields another Clawshot, giving you Double Clawshots. With two Clawshots, you can grapple to a location, then grapple again while hanging.

Practice using the Double Clawshots by grappling your way out of the boss's chamber. After grappling to a spot on the ceiling, lower yourself so you can target another grapple spot or the ivy.

15 Clawful Climb

When you get back to the west tower, use the Double Clawshots to grapple your way up, going clockwise around the room. Partway up you'll see another golden ceiling ornament. Grapple the ornament to open a large door.

After the door opens, lower yourself by pushing down on the Control Stick. When you're lined up with the door, grapple to the red target on the wall to get through the opening just as it shuts.

16 Ready to Crumble

You must grapple from pillar to pillar to get across the room, but each pillar begins to fall apart as soon as you grapple it. Grapple from right to left to right to left before dropping to the ground. (Keep holding Z to target each successive pillar.) A nearby chest contains the compass.

17 Pruning Patrol

When you find yourself beneath the west bridge, you'll need to grapple to get to the other side. Grapple onto the mesh on the bridge's underside, then lower yourself and target the plant enemy on the next-closest mesh area. Hit the enemy with the Clawshot once to stun the foe, then again to cut the stem. When you've reached the end of the bridge, grapple to the vines and climb up, then enter the central chamber.

18 Return Trip

Once you're back in the main room, it's time to put the Double Clawshots to use and head back to the east side of the dungeon.

For your return trip east, you don't need to climb out the window. There's a grapple point hanging on the ceiling between the eastern pillars; latch onto it with the Clawshot, then grapple the target above the door to reach the exit.

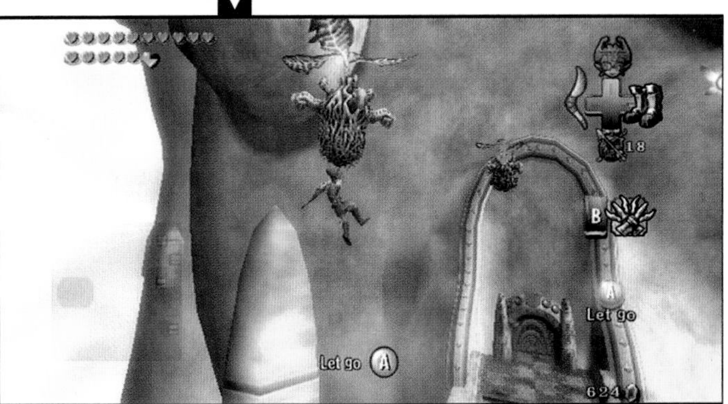

The bridge is out, but the flying plants are still around. Grapple from plant to plant to get across the massive gap. Take off your Iron Boots, though, or you'll drag the plants down.

19 Go Clawshot Crazy

The east wing contains a labyrinthine series of chambers that have fallen into disrepair. Make your way through with the Double Clawshots.

Latch onto the grapple point on the ceiling at the east end of the room, then descend to the next level. Grapple across another series of crumbling pillars then drop to the floor. Walk to the north edge of the platform and grapple the target on the far wall.

While hanging from the north wall on level B2, grapple the target on your right then zip over to the mesh on the wall to reach a treasure chest. Face south and grapple the target to your left then grapple to another mesh screen. Go through the hole in the wall.

Jump or rappel down to the next level. Knock down the plant enemies using the Clawshot or bomb arrows, then grapple to where the plant was hanging. Descend and hit the crystal, then grapple your way through the newly opened gate.

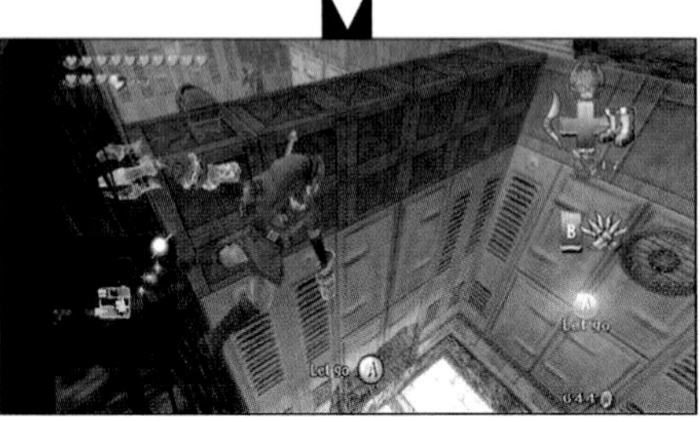

Use the mesh and the grapple points to climb up two levels and reach the door. You can grab two more optional treasure chests in the area, but watch out for the worm enemies that hide beneath the tiles.

20 Herbicidal Maniac

A large plant, much like the one you fought in the Forest Temple, blocks the way. Stun it with the Clawshot, slice it with your sword, and throw a bomb into the center once it's exposed. With the plant gone, grapple to a falling pillar, then to the nearby vines.

21 Walk the Line

Climb around the vine-covered pillar and drop onto the platform. Head counterclockwise and carefully walk along the narrow pathway to reach a treasure chest. Continue onward and grab onto the ledge to your right. Shimmy across the gap to get a Piece of Heart.

While walking along the narrow ledges, keep the enemies at bay with arrows, bomb arrows, and the Gale Boomerang. Don't let them knock you off the edge.

22 Continue the Climb

Shimmy back across the gap and grapple up to a crumbling pillar. From there, grapple to another pillar, then to an ivy-covered column. Grab onto the target hanging from the ceiling, then descend to the platform below, where an enemy is waiting.

The narrow platform doesn't provide much room to fight, but at least it's walled in so you aren't likely to fall. Use skills like the Back Slice to defeat the armored foe.

23 Plants Are the Ticket

The slow, floating plants will get you to the next area. Grapple onto the plant to the east to get over the first wall, then grab onto the western plant to clear the second wall. Snag the flying plant that's traveling toward the island to the south. While hovering, grapple to the plant that floats above the island, then drop to find a Poe and a treasure chest.

If you grab onto the wrong plant, you'll bump into the wall and fall. You'll need to wait until the plant flies past again to give it another try.

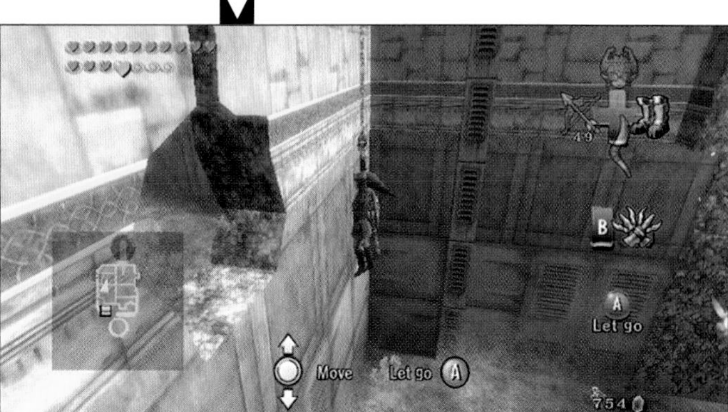

After getting the Poe and the treasure chest, head north via flying plant. Shorten or lengthen the Clawshot's chain to get through the gap in the wall, then transfer to the westernmost flying plant. Ride it to the ledge where the door is.

24 Gotta Have Heart

After exiting the flying-plant-filled ruins, you'll reach a wide-open area that houses even more flying plants. Shoot the flying enemies with arrows, then grapple from plant to plant to reach the balcony to the south. Go through the door to find another Piece of Heart.

25 Wolf on a Wire

Use the hovering plants to grapple to the central structure. Go through the door and take out the enemies, then grapple up the vines in the northeast. Turn into a wolf and head across the ropes. When you get to the middle, head left. Turn back into a human to kill the spiders and cross the vines, then turn into a wolf again and cross more ropes.

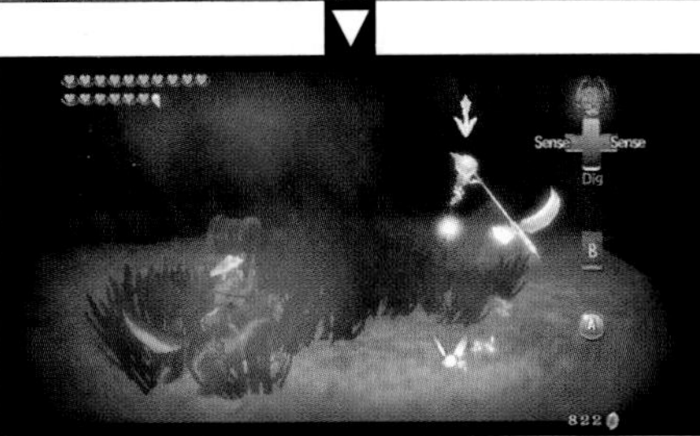

You'll find a Poe near the farthest chest. Enter sense mode to take it out. Be careful due to the precarious footing, and attack only when the Poe dives low.

26 Key to the City

Head back across the ropes and the ivy, and proceed clockwise through the area. Go through the door, then grapple onto the mesh on the ceiling to your right. Put on the Iron Boots and grapple to the ceiling ornament to shut off the fan, then descend to get the Big Key.

27 A Man with a Fan

Drop down the hole in the floor to reach the third level. Open the chest, then grapple the mesh on the ceiling and descend, but don't let go. While you're hanging, grapple to the bronze ceiling ornament, then equip the Iron Boots to start the fan. Drop to the floor and enter the north door.

28 Wind-Powered Panels

Thanks to the wind created by the giant fan, the large panels will be spinning around. Target their mesh sides and grapple across the gap from panel to panel. At the end, grapple the mesh in front of the fan to reach a treasure chest, then drop, and enter the door.

29 Double Dragon

When you enter the far north tower, you'll have to fight two of the small dragon creatures you encountered earlier. After they're defeated, grapple up to the grating on the wall, then to the mesh-covered panel. Use the Clawshot to hit the crystal and start the panels turning. Grapple from panel to panel to climb the tower.

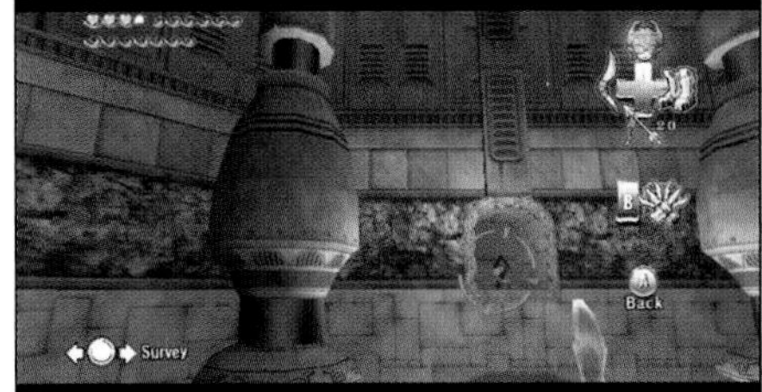

Near the top, you'll have to hit another crystal switch to get the last panel rotating. Once it's spinning, grapple to the target above the door then drop to the ledge and enter the boss's lair.

Twilit Dragon—Argorok

Even after you've entered the boss's lair, you'll need to go a bit farther before the monster shows itself. Grapple onto the grate that's on the pillar near the door, and from there grapple to the vines. Climb the vines to the top of the building, where Argorok will reveal itself.

The boss can hover above the battlefield and flap its wings to try to push you over the edge. Equip the Iron Boots to counter the harsh winds.

The dragon also likes to swoop across the battlefield in an attempt to ram you with its claws or pull you off the edge with its jetstream. You can dodge the ramming attack, and the Iron Boots counter the effects of the gusts.

The key to victory is to pull off Argorok's armor. When the creature swoops down, use the Clawshot to grab onto the end of its tail, then equip the Iron Boots to ground the boss and destroy part of the armor. The easiest way to fight Argorok in the early stages of the battle is to grapple onto one of the pillars around the battlefield, then grapple the beast's tail when it gets close. You can't attack the dragon after you pull it to the ground, but after you ground it a few times it will lose the armor entirely.

Once Argorok has lost its armor and the jewel on its back is exposed, rain begins to fall, causing flying plants to emerge from the ground and hover above the battlefield. Use the Double Clawshots to climb back and forth between the pillars and reach the circle of hovering plants. Wait until the dragon rears its head, then hold down the Z Button and grapple from plant to plant to avoid Argorok's flames. When the fire dies down, use the Clawshot's targeting view to grapple onto Argorok's back, and attack the jewel repeatedly. The beast will fall to the ground, allowing you to climb back up and repeat the process.

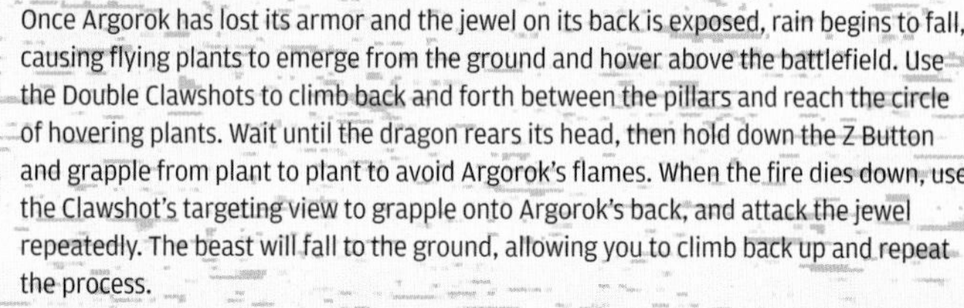

After Argorok takes significant damage, it will breathe fire twice in a row. Turn around and grapple the other direction to avoid the second flame attack, then get ready to jump on its back and strike the jewel. Once you've repeated the jewel-attacking sequence approximately three times, the boss will fly high into the air and explode.

Palace of Twilight

Hyrule Kingdom

It's back to the Mirror Chamber for you. But before you go, spend some time exploring greater Hyrule.

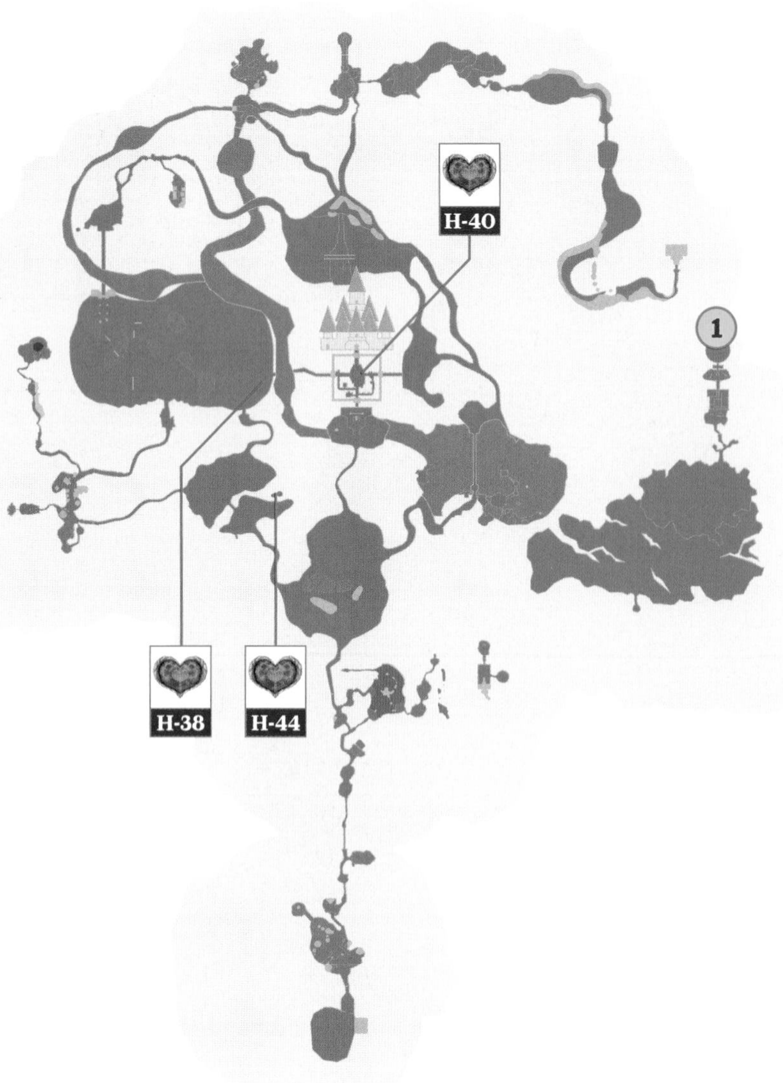

Heart Muscle

Before you head off to the Mirror Chamber, search the kingdom for Pieces of Heart and Poe Souls that you haven't collected yet (see pages 144 and 153 for lists). At this point, you are equipped to collect most of them.

Armor Upgrade

If you haven't given the Kakariko Village Gorons 1,000 rupees to fix the bridge yet, you should have the funds now to make a big contribution. Opening the trade route will lead to the opening of a Malo Mart branch in Castle Town, where you'll be able to buy the rupee-run Magic Armor.

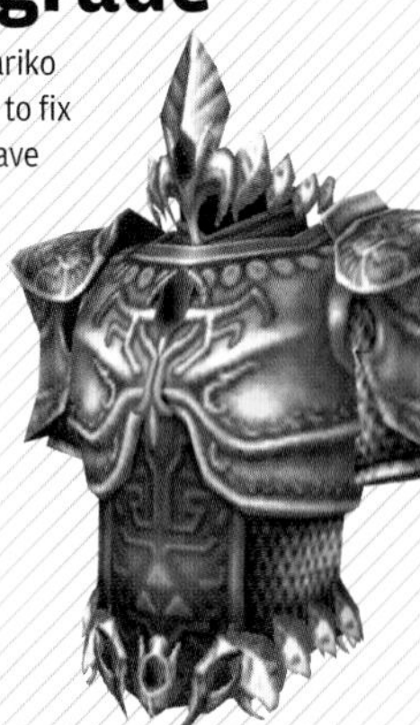

Quite an Ordeal

You now have all the equipment you need to go deep into the Cave of Ordeals (on the Gerudo Mesa); see page 113. Stock up on bombs, potions, and arrows before you enter the 50-floor fairy haunt. See page 163 for details.

1 The Twilight Princess

When you return to the Mirror Chamber and assemble the pieces of the mystic device, the mirror will open a passage to the twilight realm's Palace of Twilight, and the guardians of the mirror will reveal Midna's true identity. She's the Twilight Princess.

Palace of Twilight

Zant rules the world of the Twili. Don't let his ubiquitous image intimidate you as you explore the palace.

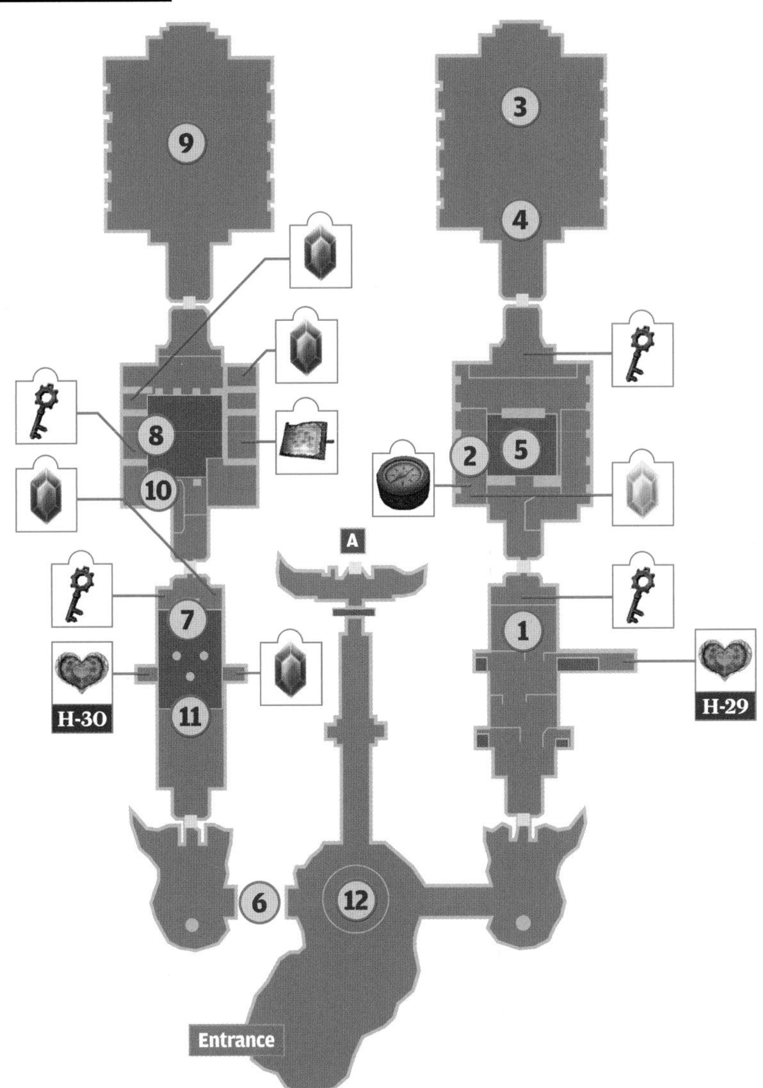

1 Head-Hunting

Travel to the east side of the palace exterior and open the door. You'll go up against a few minor enemies and two magic creatures that look like the head of evil Zant. They'll phase in and out of the room. Use your sword against them. You'll get a Small Key for your troubles.

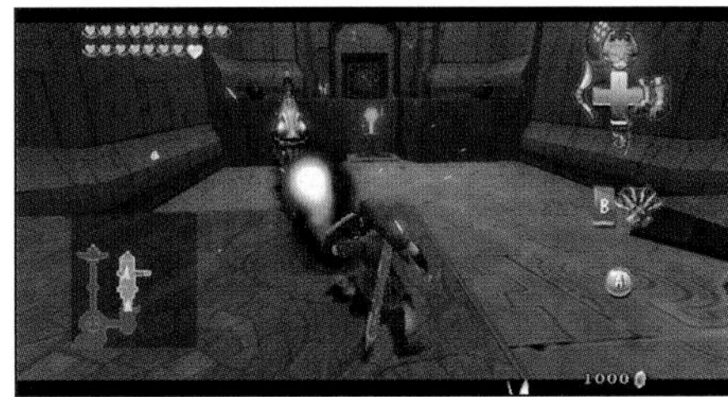

The Zant-head creatures spit damaging magic bullets. Use your Shield Attack skill to deflect them. When the magic hits a head, the creature will be stunned for a moment.

2 Stop for Treasure

Grapple to the door and continue north. There's a key in a chest on the north end of the next room. On your way to it, you'll walk through a black fog that will transform you into a wolf. Use your senses to hunt a Zant-head creature in the fog. By defeating it, you will make two more treasures appear. The one on the floor holds the compass. The one that you must grapple to holds a 100-rupee piece.

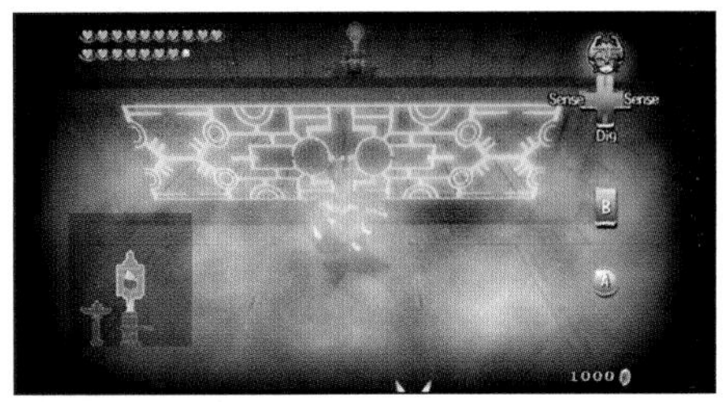

Shadow Beast

The black fog, made from Shadow Crystals, transforms you into your wolf form and it clouds your vision. Use your canine senses to see through the darkness.

3 You versus Zant: Round One

You've been waiting to go up against Zant. You'll do the next best thing in the first floor's northeast chamber. Zant's ghostly image will lock you into the room and conjure enemies, one group at a time. Make Zant your primary target.

Zant's ghostly image phases around the arena, appearing in any one place for only a few seconds. As soon as you see the ghost, go straight for it. If you can hit it before it conjures its minions, you won't have to deal with any other creatures.

Sol Power

The object at the north end of the northeast room is a Sol. It has the power to cut through the black fog and revive the citizens of the twilight realm.

4 Race for the Sun

Attack the hand statue at the north end of the room to make it drop the Sol. Pick up the prize and run to the center of the room. The hand will come to life. It's goal is to steal the Sol from you. Put the Sol into a slot on the floor to make stairs appear. Leave the Sol, run up the stairs, then turn around and use the Clawshot to retrieve the shiny treasure.

The hand will come to life as you approach the slot in the center of the room. Drop the Sol into the slot, run up the stairs, then use the Clawshot to repossess the Sol before the hand can grab it.

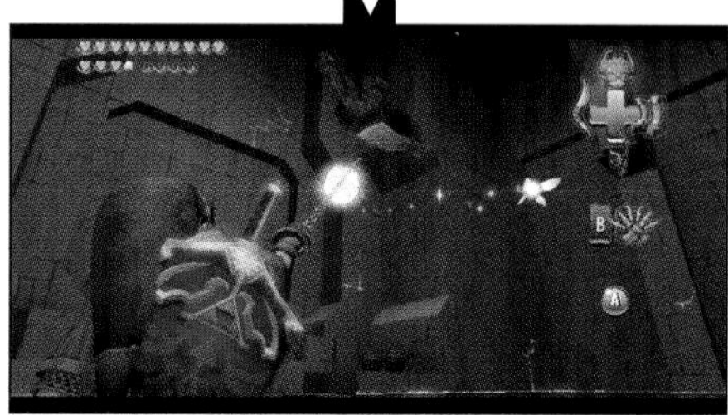

If the hand gets too close for comfort, use the Clawshot to stun it. You can't destroy it, but you can slow it down.

5 Cut Off the Hand

As long as you are inside the palace, the hand will chase after the Sol. Head south. When you're in the middle chamber, place the Sol in the midroom slot to make stairs appear. Climb the stairs then grapple the Sol from above to retrieve it. If the hand picks up your prize before you do, use the Clawshot to steal it away.

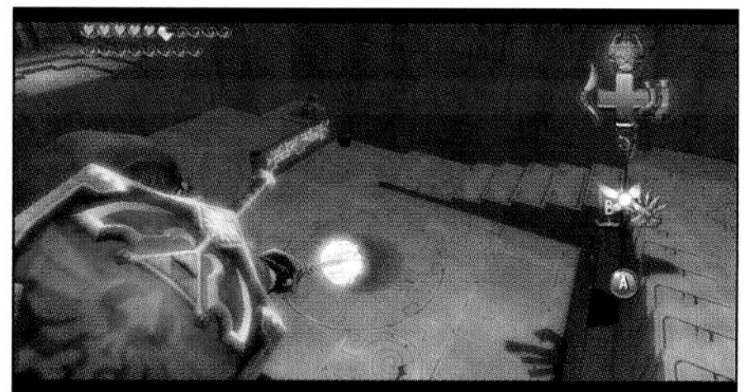

As soon as you get to the top of the glowing stairs, train your Clawshot on the Sol to retrieve it. If the hand is close to the Sol, stun it. On your way along the ledge on the east side of the room, toss the Sol over the high step, then climb to it.

You'll encounter a group of enemies in the southwest section. If the plants grab you, you'll drop the Sol. Run past them then keep running south to avoid the hand.

6 Touch the Twili

The hand can't leave the palace. Once you're outside, the Sol will be safe. Use it to lift the curse from the Twili, then place it in one of the two slots in the area's center section. A square platform will appear. Ride it to the west side.

7 Fly Over the Fog

You'll ride glowing blue platforms on the first step of your journey along the west side of the palace. A Zant head will fire at you as you advance. Use the Shield Attack to deflect the head's shots. Defeat the head (once you're on the north end) to make a Small Key appear.

Grapple to a point on the wall, then to the point on the ceiling. Use the Control Stick to move down just a little to get a view of the platform below you. Once the platform is directly below you, drop onto it. Hop across the platforms, deflect the enemy's shots, and advance to solid ground.

8 Map Trap

Shadow beings will greet you in the midwest room. Walk into the fog to transform into a wolf, then use Midna's dark energy to take care of the beasts. A battle with several Zant-head creatures will follow. You won't have to engage your senses (thus limiting your field of view) to see them—they stick out of the fog. Your prize for beating them is the dungeon map.

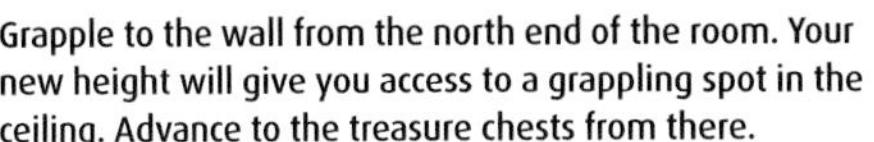

Grapple to the wall from the north end of the room. Your new height will give you access to a grappling spot in the ceiling. Advance to the treasure chests from there.

The dungeon map is in the southeastern chest of the four in the room. The Small Key is in the southwestern chest.

9 You Versus Zant: Round Two

In your second fight for a Sol, Zant will appear in a ghostly form again and send a new group of enemies after you. Once you hit Zant enough to make him regroup, the enemies will disappear. After you steal the Sol and head for the slot in the room's center, you'll take on a few more enemies. Clear them out of the way quickly. The hand is coming.

10 The Western Route

By placing the Sol in the slot in the center of the midwest room, you'll make a tall structure rise. Grapple to the north end of the room, then grapple to the west side. Climb the structure and collect the Sol once you reach the southwest corner.

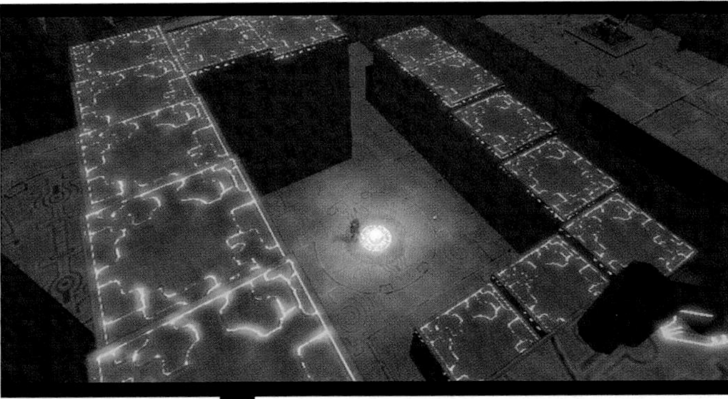

If you get to the slot while the hand is entering the room, the structure that pops up from the floor will block its way. That will give you time for some aerial acrobatics. Grapple to the north wall then grapple to the west. Drop, then climb the structure. Head south then use the Clawshot to retrieve the Sol from the room's southwest corner to retrieve the Sol.

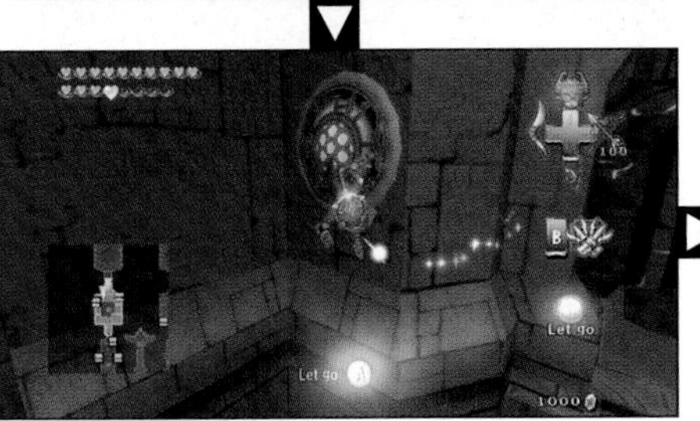

11 Glide to the Finish

You'll need to float above the fog in the southwest room to get to the exit. Ride the platforms to a tower that houses two dark orbs. They will light up when you get close, creating a sliding platform that will take you to the south end.

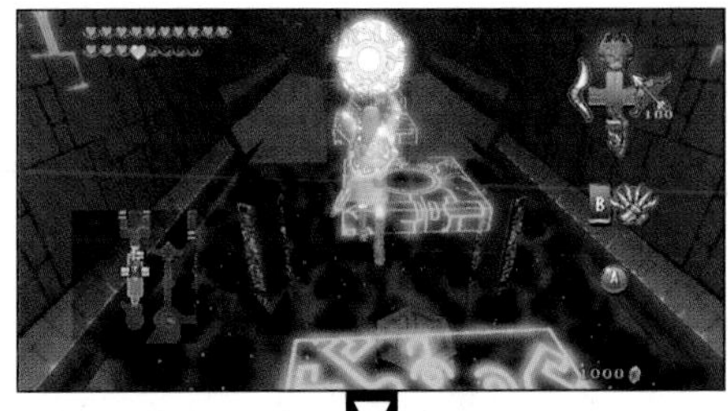

If you fall into the fog, use the Clawshot to stun the hand, then advance to an orb on the north end of the room. Lighting the orb will make a platform appear. Ride it back to your starting point.

12 Illuminate the Sword

When you reach the palace exterior, lift the curse from another Twili citizen, then place the Sol into the other central-section slot. Your reward is the Light Sword.

The Light Sword

The power of the Sols turns the Master Sword into the Light Sword. This new, more-powerful weapon is capable of burning away the dark fog and defeating many of Zant's shadow creatures with a single swipe. Use it to venture into the fog in human form.

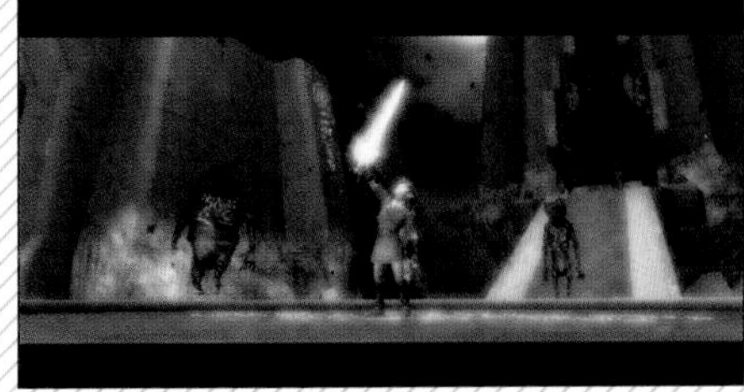

You can test the fog-lifting properties of the Light Sword by returning to the east and west wings of the palace to collect treasures that are surrounded by the darkness. You'll be able to collect two Pieces of Heart.

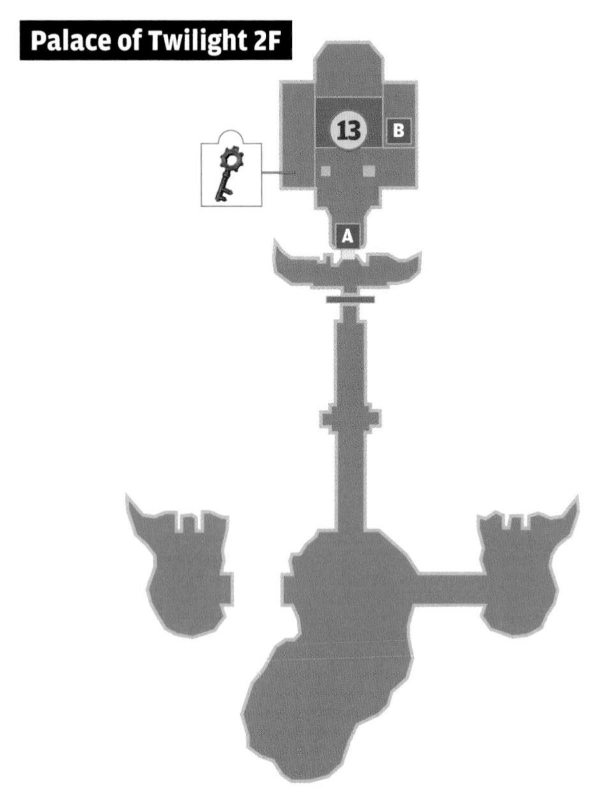

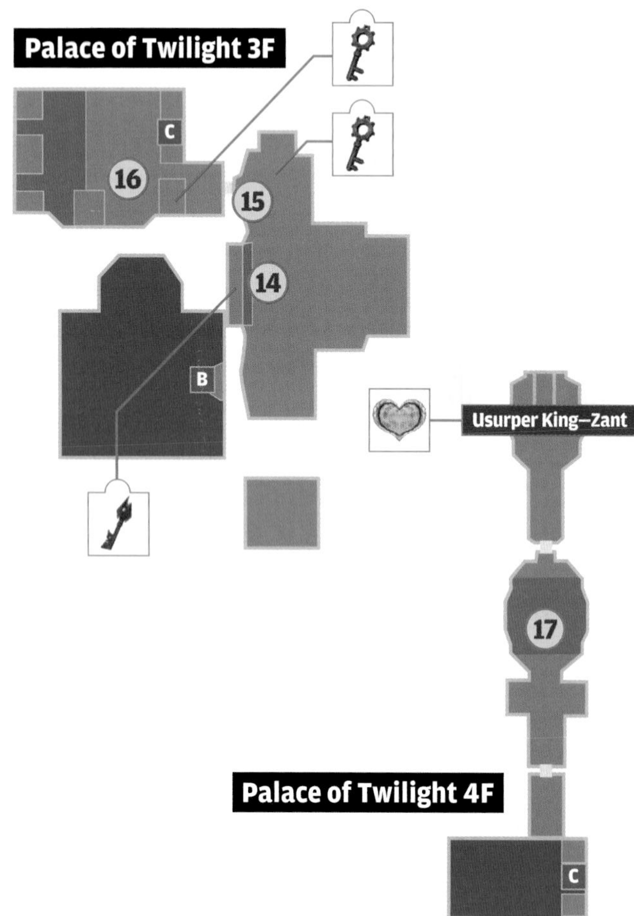

13 Light Up the Room

The spin attack should be your technique of choice to dispel the black fog. Use the move to clear the air in the first chamber of the palace's central section. Place the room's Sols into slots in the floor to make stairs appear. Climb, illuminate an orb to trigger a square platform, and ride it to the northwest corner. Battle Zant heads for a Small Key. Spin to light three more orbs, then ride a platform to the exit.

The room's two Sols are not capable of burning the fog until they're in their slots. Use spin attacks to eliminate the fog and get the Sols into place before the darkness returns.

When you reach the southwest corner, defeat the Zant heads, collect the key, then spin to illuminate three orbs. A platform will appear where you stand and carry you to a locked door on the third floor.

14 Look behind the Curtain

Cut through a curtain of fog on the west side of the first third-floor section, then use the Clawshot to grapple to a high perch where you'll discover the dungeon's Big Key.

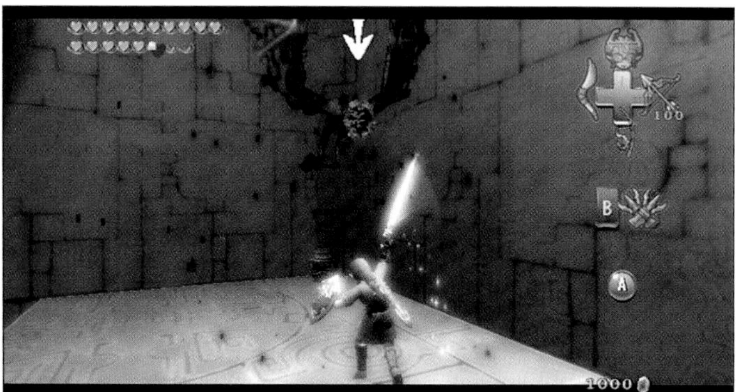

After you leap to the west side of the black-fog curtain, defeat the surrounding enemies. If you try to grapple to the next platform without fighting the creatures, one of them might knock you into the abyss.

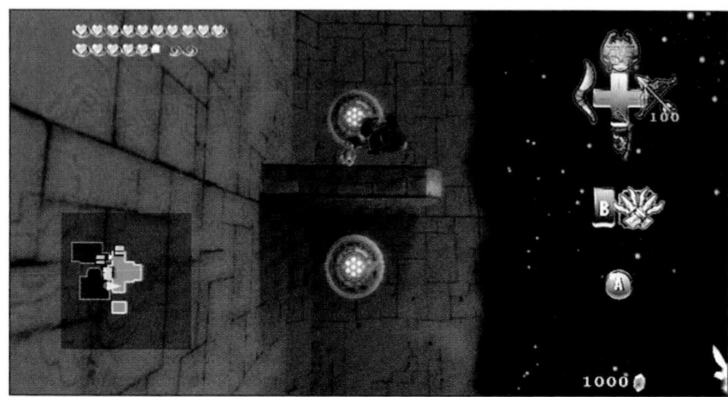

15 Heads First

Before you can collect the Small Key, you'll have to defeat all of the Zant heads in the eastern section of the third floor. Illuminate orbs, float on platforms, and hunt for heads.

Go to the orbs on the eastern edge and perform a spin attack to light them and make a platform appear. It will lift you to the southern balcony, where the first Zant head will be waiting for you.

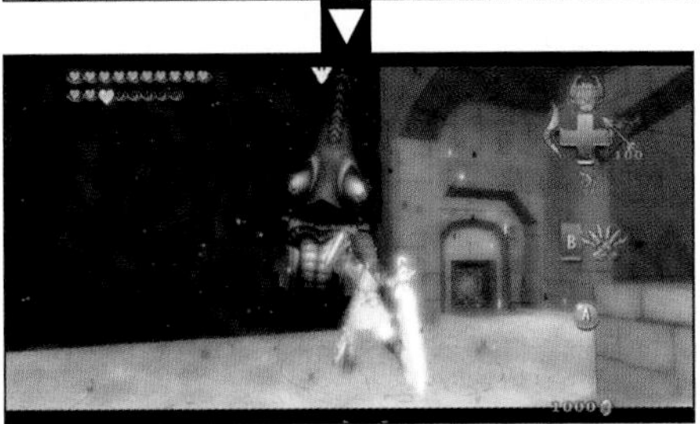

After you defeat the first head, hit two more orbs to trigger the platform for a ride back to the main section. Three heads will attack. Defeat them all. You'll get a Small Key as a reward.

16 It's a Long Way to the Top

A dark fog floats over the floor of the very tall room's north end. Use a spin move to clear the fog, then illuminate the four orbs in the center to begin a jumping and climbing journey to the top of the chamber.

After you light the orbs, a platform will lift you. Hop onto the eastern platform. You'll ride it to two more platforms. Hop onto the north one for a ride to the east ledge. Grapple onto the ledge. Jump to another platform and ride it west. Grapple to a spot on the west wall and defeat a Zant head.

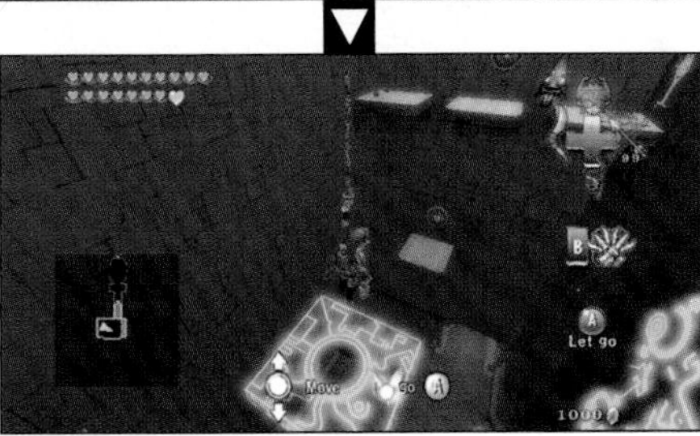

Look up from the ledge on the west-central platform to find a grappling spot. Grapple to the center of the room. Move down just a bit while dangling, then drop to another platform. Ride it to the room's east end to fight a Zant head. Get a Small Key from a chest, then ride to the door.

17 Cut through the Shadows

You'll face a large collection of shadow beings on your way to Zant's chamber. You can defeat them easily—it takes just one slice of the Light Sword for each.

The Madness of King Zant

One of the rewards for trudging all the way to the top of the Palace of Twilight is to discover Zant's back story. What drove him to the darkness? A monologue from the crazed leader will reveal all.

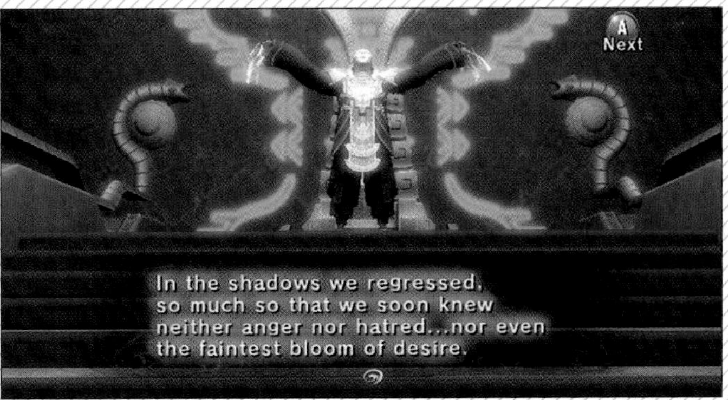

Years of oppression and promises unfulfilled turned Zant into a manic and misunderstood creature. He sought a way to lift himself to a higher place in life.

Zant's depression made him vulnerable to an evil force that wanted to mix darkness with light and forever blanket the kingdom in shadows. That's when he become Hyrule's number-one threat.

Usurper King—Zant

Your fight against Zant is a whirlwind six-stage tour around Hyrule. You'll use a variety of weapons and tools to reach the creature during each phase of the fight, then attack him using the Light Sword. Zant counters with rapid-fire energy blasts that you won't be able to deflect with the Shield Attack (they come too quickly). Avoid the attacks while you prepare for your next hack at the master.

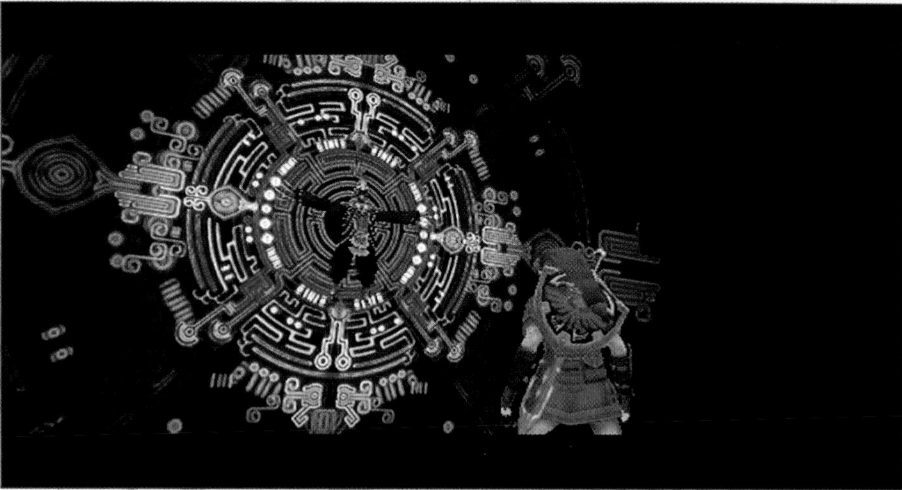

Stage One

The first part of the fight takes place in the Forest Temple boss arena. Zant hovers over the poisonous liquid. Hit him with the Gale Boomerang to draw him near, then slice him with the Light Sword.

As Zant starts his rapid-fire blasts, use your shield to defend yourself, and Z-target the fiend. Throw the Gale Boomerang to bring Zant to the shore, then hit him with a few jump attacks.

Stage Two

The second battle takes place in the Goron Mines, on the giant disc that floats over lava. Zant will warp from place to place along the edge and jump up and down to try to knock you into the hot stuff. Use the Iron Boots to stay anchored. When Zant starts to fire at you, take off the boots, then attack while he's taking a breather.

While Zant is jumping around the edge of the disc, there's nothing for you to do but wait in the center while wearing the Iron Boots. As soon as the disc stops rocking, use your shield for protection as you charge toward your enemy. You should get to him by the time he stops firing. Hit him several times with your sword.

Stage Three

The third section of the battle takes place underwater. You'll need the Zora Armor, the Iron Boots, and the Clawshot. Zant will appear from a giant helmet. After the helmet's door opens, Zant will start firing at you. Avoid his shots, then use the Clawshot to draw him to you. Weigh yourself down with the boots and attack him with the sword.

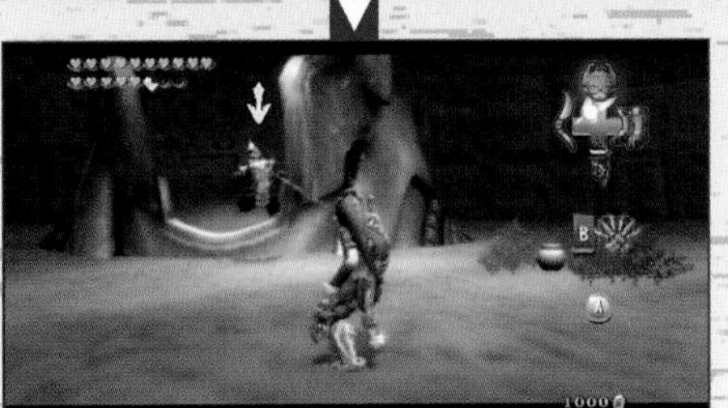

After you hit Zant with a few slices of the sword, four giant helmets will rise from the ocean. Zant will appear in one of the helmets and attack as he did before. Hit him with the Clawshot again, then slice him.

Stage Four

It's off to the Forest Temple again. This time Zant will hop around the baboon's poles. Approach him while he's firing at you, and use the A Button to slam into his pole twice. That will make him fall to the ground. Run up to him and attack him with a few strong sword swipes.

Stage Five

You'll be off to the Snowpeak Ruins boss arena for the fifth phase of the battle. Zant begins the phase as a floating giant. Equip the ball and chain and watch his reflection in the ice; keep moving to ensure that he doesn't land on you. Once he drops, hit one of his feet with the ball. He'll shrink and run. Track him down and hit him with the sword.

After you use the ball and chain to hit the giant, he'll hop around in miniature size. Watch his path and cut him off to get close. Then slice away.

Final Stage

For the last section of the battle, you'll be back outside Hyrule Castle, in an arena defined by a magic barrier. Zant will attack you three different ways. Two of the attacks are designed to push you into the barrier. While he's flailing around to begin the battle, you'll be able to get in quite a few slices and stabs with ease. Next he'll spin like a top. Defend yourself with your shield and keep away from the arena's edges. When Zant stops spinning, he'll stay in one place for a few seconds, too dizzy to fight. That's your cue to hit him with everything you've got. Zant's third attack has him running toward you, waving his blades like a villain in a slasher movie. Again, use your shield to stop his blade and stay away from the arena's edge. A little patience will go a long way in taking care of the beast.

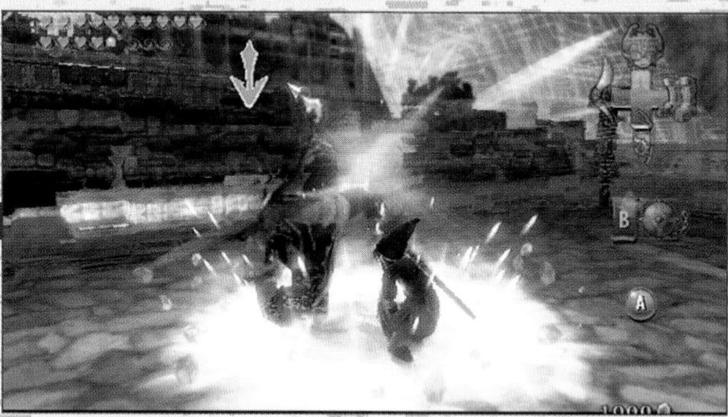

While Zant is spinning around the arena, target him and jump out of the way. You can't do any damage while he's spinning, but you can really knock him for a loop when he's finished spinning and he's trying to regain his composure.

Zant's manic slasher attack, which has him warping around the arena, is one to avoid. Run from him and don't let him corner you. He'll follow it up with another spinning attack.

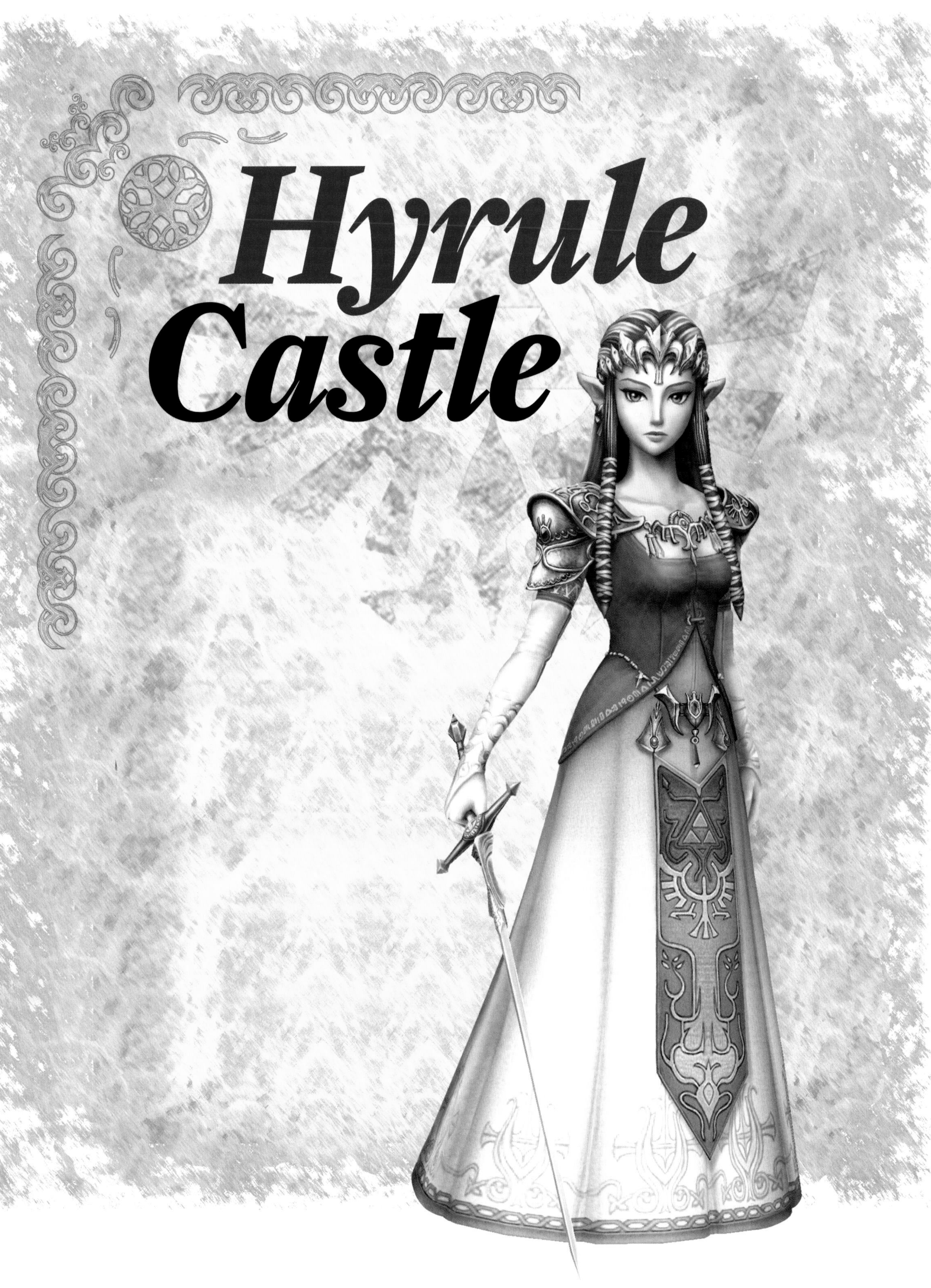
Hyrule
Castle

Hyrule Castle

You've defeated Zant and restored the mirror. Now it's time for the showdown with Ganondorf in Hyrule Castle.

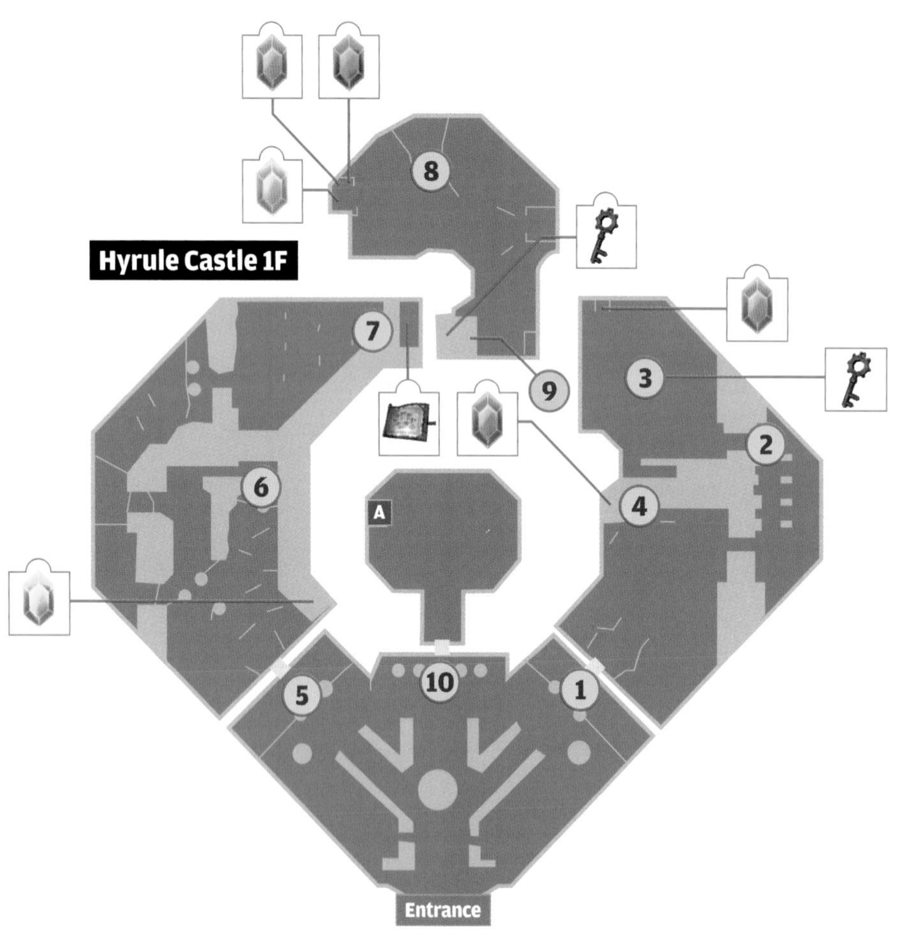

Return to the Castle

Once you've defeated Zant, return to Castle Town and take the north exit to Hyrule Castle. Midna will use the power granted to her by the Fused Shadows to destroy the barrier around the castle.

1 Beasts in the East

Grab onto the massive door handles and push forward to open the way to the castle courtyard. Head toward the eastern exit, but be prepared for enemy ambushes along the way.

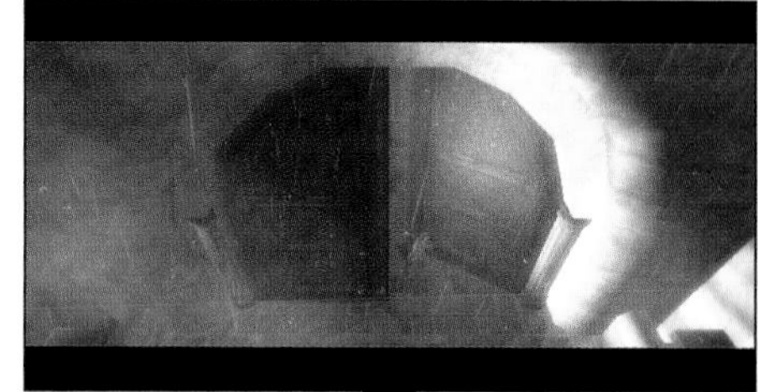

As you head toward the east door, purple Bokoblins will attack you. A barrier will surround you until you've finished them off. Don't touch the barrier or you'll lose health. You'll face more Bokoblins as you cross the east courtyard.

2 Yanking the Chain

To open the gated door in the eastern courtyard, grab onto the chain to the right of the door and pull it to open the way. Head northwest for another fight.

3 Ogre Battle

The big green King Bulblin, and he's just as powerful as before. This time he's got a key you need to proceed, so get ready to fight. Your hidden skills will come in handy as you battle the axe-wielding warrior.

The big guy packs a punch, but he's still slow. Use quick sword attacks to keep him on the defensive, and hit him when he prepares to attack. Use the Back Slice if he keeps blocking frontal attacks.

4 Off the Wall

With key in hand, take a shortcut back to the previous area by climbing the stairs to the south. Jump over the wall and go through the door to get back to the southern courtyard, then head toward the western door.

You can grab the contents of two treasure chests before you head back. One is to the north of where you fought the ogre; you'll find the other when you jump over the wall.

5 Another Ambush

As you head to the west door, you'll have to fight off another group of purple monsters within the confines of an orange barrier. They shouldn't pose much of a threat. Take them out with your spin attack and hidden skills.

6 Go Hog Wild

As soon as you enter the door, you'll be assaulted by enemies. Stay close to the door, where the archers can't hit you, and take them out with your bow. Use the boars north of the entrance to smash through the wood barricades and access the northwestern part of the courtyard.

Destroy the enemies' watchtowers while you're riding the boar through the courtyard. The big pigs are the only way to reach the northwest portion of the area.

7 Take 'Em for a Spin

You'll find six propeller-topped pillars in the northwest portion of the courtyard. Use the boomerang to blow away the leaves in the eastern part of the area and reveal which propellers to activate, then mimic the zigzag pattern with the boomerang to open the door and get the dungeon map.

8 Grave Digger

Change into wolf form and locate the digging spot in the center of the pile of leaves. Use it to burrow into the graveyard. Fend off the enemies and look for the switch that opens the door to the alcove to the west.

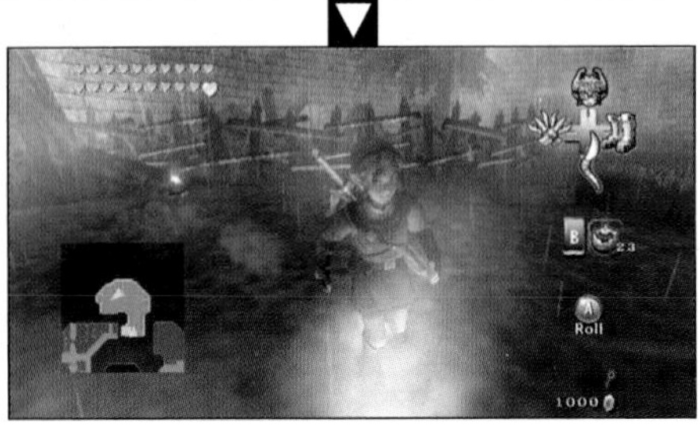

One of the graves south of the alcove hints at a swordsman's grave beneath a sacred tree. Place a bomb on the rock that's next to the northernmost tree. You'll uncover a switch that opens the door to the western alcove. Inside the alcove, you'll find three rupee-containing treasure chests, Lantern Oil, and a torch.

9 Can't Rain All the Time

Lighting the torch in the alcove will make the rain stop temporarily. Immediately run across the graveyard to the eastern alcove and light the torches on either side of the door. With the door open, use the Dominion Rod to move the statues to the southern end of the graveyard.

Lead the two statues into the notches at the southern end of the graveyard. Once they're in place, climb up the nearby stones and use the statues as steps to reach the chamber to the west. Yank the chain to open the door, then retrieve the key from the treasure chest.

10 Through the Front Door

Dig your way back to the western courtyard in wolf form. The goblins have rebuilt their wood barricades, so use another boar to get back to the east side of the area. From the main courtyard, head north and enter Hyrule Castle.

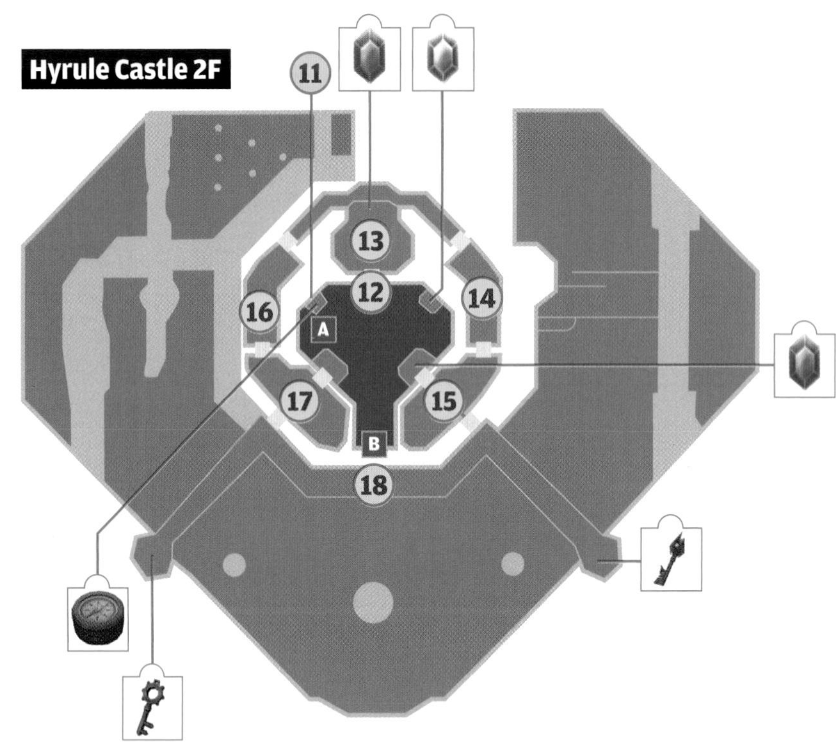

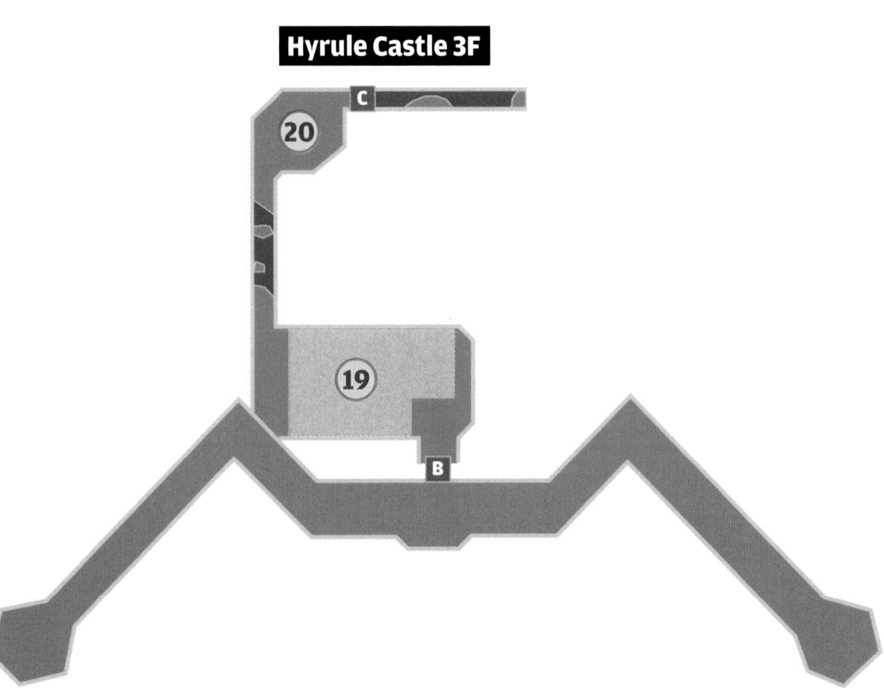

11 Rumpus for the Compass

Shortly after you enter the front hall of the castle, enemies will swarm you. Defeat them to make a treasure chest containing the compass appear on a second-floor balcony.

Climb the small flight of stairs that's next to the balcony where the chest appears. From there, grapple onto the chandelier and drop to the balcony to acquire the compass.

12 To the North Door

From the balcony where you got the compass, grapple to the chandelier to the east. Descend a bit and grapple to the next chandelier. Drop and enter the door to the north.

13 Torch Trick

After you defeat the dark knight, you'll need to get up to the ledge where the treasure chest appeared. If you wish, light the torches on the west side of the room to raise the two lower steps, then climb atop them. Use the Gale Boomerang to extinguish the torch on the east side of the room, then jump onto the rear step as it rises from the floor. You can also stand close to the rear step while you put out the torch and get to the step directly from the floor. Once you're on the upper level, you can go either east or west—both paths lead to the same area.

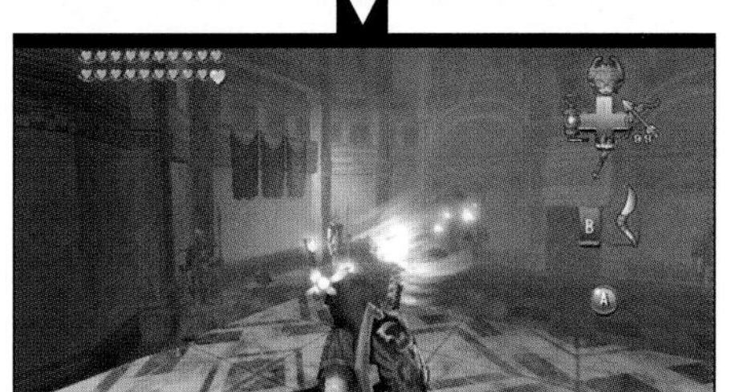

If You Take the East Path . . .

14 Advice from Beyond

If you travel the east path, you can earn some extra rupees and grab some Chu Jelly. As the wolf, you can see ghosts that will help guide you.

Even when you defeat the lizardlike enemies, the door won't budge. Assume your wolf form to see a group of ghosts pointing at a painting; if you shoot down the painting with your bow, you'll reveal a crystal switch. Hit the switch to open the door.

But Is It Art?

You can shoot down other paintings that are hanging on the wall as well. Some of them hide switches that, when shot, cause Chu Jellies to drop from above.

15 Big Fights, Big Money

If you continue along the eastern route, you'll have to take on two Darknuts, but you'll be rewarded with plenty of rupees.

Proceed slowly along one side of the room so that only one Darknut comes after you. Slay him then take down the other one. If you exit via the northwest door, you'll find a switch and a chest that contains 50 rupees. Press the switch to make another chest appear.

To get to the treasure chest, drop to the floor and grapple to the nearby chandelier. Lower yourself a little, grapple to the chandelier above the balcony, then drop to grab the 200-rupee prize. To return to the room with the Darknuts, grapple back up to the north door.

If You Take the West Path . . .

16 Light the Way

You must light four torches to unlock the door. Shoot down the painting in the room to get a clue about the order in which to light the torches: first the southeast one, then the northwest, then the northeast, and finally the southwest.

17 Second-Floor Express

Defeat the armored Dynalfos in the next room to unlock the doors. Beyond the northeast door a switch will lower a chandelier and allow easy grapple access from the front hall.

18 Battles on the Balcony

Whether you took the east or west route, you'll end up on the balcony. Head to the west end, where you'll find a Small Key in a treasure chest after you defeat a flying dragonlike foe. At the east end of the balcony, you'll acquire the Big Key. Once you have the keys, enter the door at the center of the balcony.

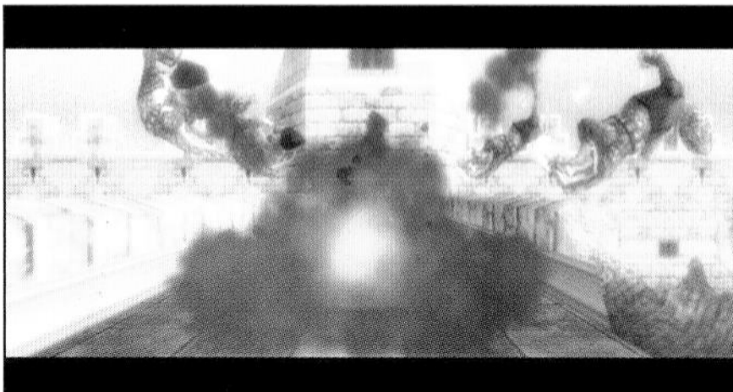

As you head toward the east end of the balcony, a group of enemies springs an ambush, but don't worry—your friends from Castle Town jump in and save the day.

19 Blocked Out

Turn into a wolf and use your senses—they'll let you get rid of the pesky phantom rats and enable you to see ghosts that point the way across the blocks on the floor. If you step on the wrong blocks, you'll fall.

Use your enhanced senses to see the ghosts. Pay attention to the direction they're pointing, and jump directly on the block they're gesturing toward. Keep going in the same direction until you reach another ghost.

20 The Shattered Stairs

After the room with the collapsing-block floor, jump up the broken stairway then defeat the enemies in the room at the top. Once they're gone, grapple your way over the next set of broken stairs.

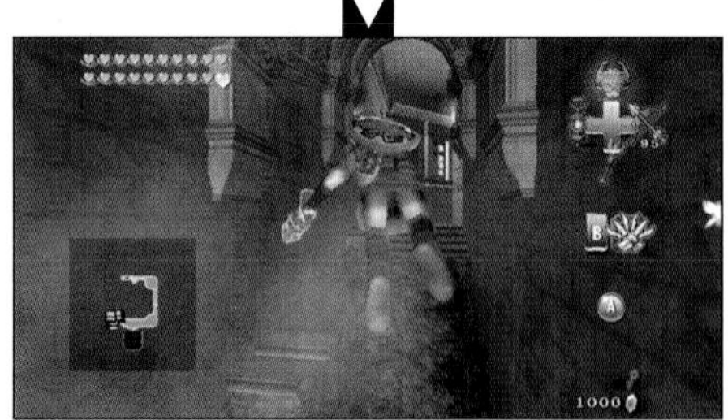

The gaps in the second set of broken stairs are too big to jump over. Use the Double Clawshots to grapple onto the grates over the torches and make your way to the next enemy-filled room.

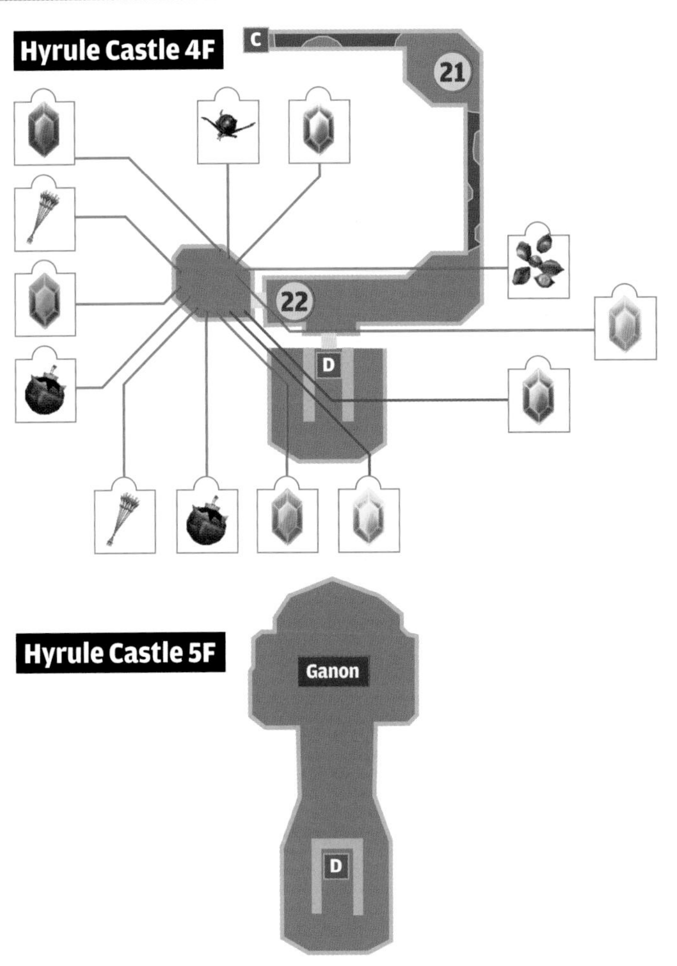

22 Stock Up

Instead of using the Big Key and heading south, use the Small Key on the west door. Inside you'll find tons of supplies and loads of cash.

At Last, Ganondorf

Behind the Big Key door lies the final boss, Ganondorf. Known as the King of Evil, Ganondorf manipulated Zant by arriving before him as a false god and promising him unlimited power in exchange for letting Ganondorf back into the world of light. Before you fight Ganondorf, make sure you're well-stocked with healing items. After you go through the door, head up the stairs and prepare for an epic battle.

21 Go for a Spin

Use the Spinner to clear the third stairway. Start on the left side and bounce from side to side to avoid crashing into the spinning spiked obstacles.

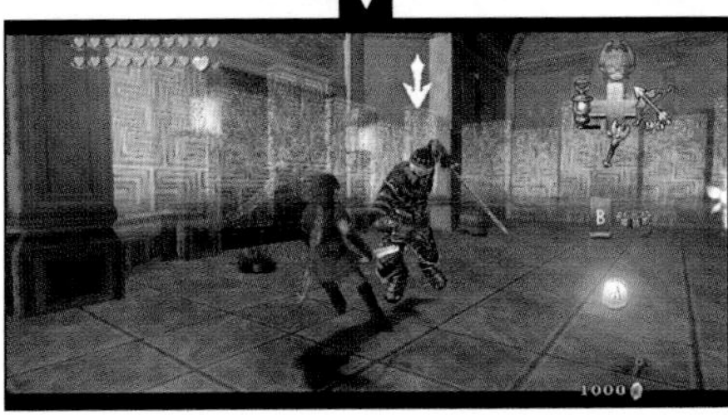

Beyond the third set of stairs is another Darknut. Use the same tactics to defeat him that you used on previous Darknut: dodge his attacks and counter, then use the Back Slice to knock him off balance once his armor is gone.

Ganon's Puppet—Zelda

Before you face Ganon himself, he possesses Zelda and forces you to battle her. Zelda hovers out of your sword's range and uses three types of attacks. Her first offensive is a diving sword attack that yoy can block or dodge. Her second attack is a large triangular energy field that appears below Link; run away to avoid this attack. Her third tactic is to fire an energy ball at Link, which you can block. Deflecting the energy attack is the only way to defeat the possessed Zelda.

When Zelda raises her sword and creates an energy ball, take a few steps back and ready your blade. As the energy ball comes toward you, swing your sword to deflect the attack back at Zelda. When she counterattacks and sends the energy ball back your way, deflect the assault again. Continue the volley until the energy ball hits Zelda. After she's hit three times, she'll be freed of Ganon's influence.

Dark Beast—Ganon

Once Ganon is purged from Zelda's body, he takes on the form of a giant boar. As a boar, Ganon charges straight at you then runs around the perimeter, smashing anything in his path. Ganon's charge can't be blocked, and you can't lock onto him while he's charging. Ganon also jumps into the air occasionally and tries to smash you, so watch for his shadow and run out of the way. After his attack, he warps out of the room then reappears through a portal. After he teleports, stand on either side of the room and watch for where his portals appear. Several false portals appear before before the real one does—the true portal is the one that turns blue. Line up with the true portal and be ready to counter Ganon's charge. The battle has two phases; the method you use to counter Ganon's attacks varies depending on the phase of the battle.

Phase One

During the first phase of the battle, equip the Hero's Bow and shoot Ganon in the glowing white spot on his forehead as he charges. A direct hit will knock the beast down; as he slides along the ground, keep your shield up so you aren't injured by his bulk. Once he comes to a stop, target the white scar on his belly and slash at it with your sword. After you take Ganon down a few times, he'll change attack patterns.

Ganon rarely reappears at the same location he disappeared from, so his disappearance location is the safest vantage point from which to see where he emerges from his portal. Draw your bow and scan the area using the targeting view, then let an arrow fly as soon as you have a shot at the creature's forehead.

Phase Two

Eventually Ganon will teleport away whenever you fire an arrow at him. That's your cue that you need to switch battle tactics. Change to your wolf form and take on Ganon beast to beast. Keep an eye on his warp portals and line up with the blue portal that Ganon emerges from. As he charges, stand your ground; as soon as the indicator appears at the bottom of the screen, press the A Button to grab him, then hold the Control Stick left or right to throw him. After Ganon goes down, pounce onto the weak spot on his belly and hit the A Button repeatedly to inflict damage. You can inflict extra damage if you transform back to human Link.

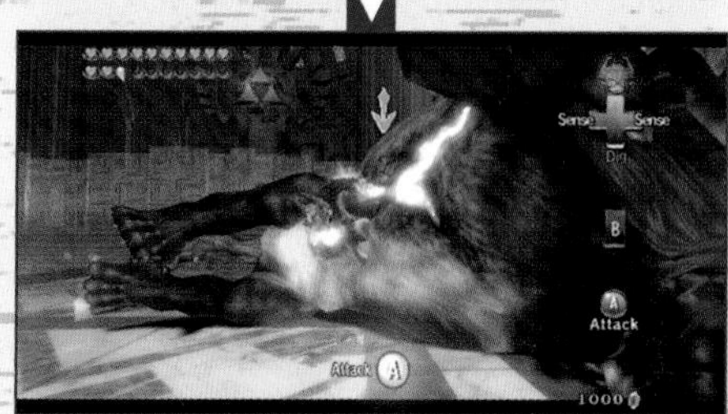

The second phase of the battle is all about positioning and timing. A large hand will emerge from Midna when you're properly lined up. Get into position as soon as you can; Ganon gets faster as the fight progresses.

Dark Lord—Ganondorf

On Horseback

After Ganon clashes with Midna and the villain returns to human form, you'll find yourself on the fields of Hyrule battling on horseback. The goal of the battle is to get close enough to Ganondorf to Z-target him, which will allow Zelda to stun him with a light arrow. While Ganon is stunned, get close to him and slash at him with your sword—a spin attack works nicely. As you try to get Zelda into range, Ganondorf has two attack methods: he can charge you and knock you off your horse directly, and he can shoot out energy that splits into phantom riders. To catch up to Ganondorf, stay inside his turns and try to remain behind him after you strike him with your sword. Make liberal use of Epona's dash, but be sure not to deplete your spur icons entirely.

The trickiest part of the battle is to get into position behind Ganondorf. When you ride toward the boss, he'll often charge and circle around you in an attempt to knock you off Epona. Circle around him in kind.

Ganondorf's phantom riders will knock you off your horse if they touch you. Stay near either side of Ganondorf and veer away when he releases the ghouls. If you're close enough to Ganondorf, they'll go right past you.

Zelda will attempt to pierce Ganon with a light arrow once you're in Z-targeting range. Even if you're locked on, Zelda may miss with her attack; the closer you are to Ganon, the more likely she is to score a direct hit.

Ganon will be stunned after Zelda hits him with a light arrow. Use the opportunity to close in on Ganon and strike him with your sword. You can hit him with a regular attack, but it's easier to connect with the spin attack.

Final Battle

The final battle against Ganondorf is a one-on-one sword fight within an enclosed space. Ganondorf is a master fighter with impressive defensive skills and powerful attacks. His large stature and long weapon also give him a great range advantage over Link. The keys to winning the battle are to keep your guard up at all times and to look for an opening in Ganondorf's defenses. Z-target the Dark Lord and circle him to dodge his sword swings, then counter with quick attacks of your own. Since Ganondorf holds his sword with his left hand, circling him clockwise yields the best results. You can also catch the Dark Lord off guard with the Back Slice. After you hit Ganondorf many times, you'll knock him to the ground, giving you a chance to finish him off with the Ending Blow.

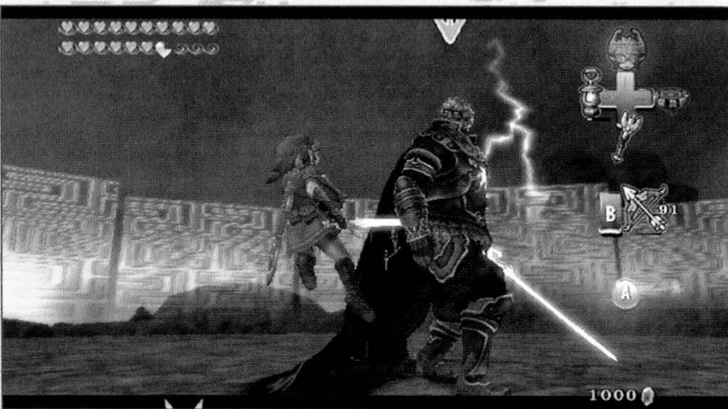

Stay close to Ganondorf as you fight, or you won't be able to take advantage of most attack opportunities. Circle clockwise around the boss while Z-targeting and hit him with the Back Slice, or wait for him to stab, then counter with strikes of your own. His lunging attacks also leave him vulnerable. Only the Master Sword can defeat Ganondorf—your other weapons will have no effect.

Sometimes Ganondorf follows his lunging attack with a quick spin strike. Avoid the lunge—if you block it, it will leave you wide open for the spinning attack. Ganondorf also uses a jumping attack in which he leaps off the screen and reappears behind you. Though you can counter this move with a spin attack, it's safest to run and await the next attack opportunity.

When there's distance between you and Ganondorf, sometimes the villain will lunge and the word "chance" will appear on the screen. If you hit the A Button as soon as the word appears, you'll engage in a close-range sword struggle that requires you to hit the A Button repeatedly as fast as you can. If you win the exchange, Ganondorf will be stunned, allowing you to get in numerous hits. If he's already weakened, the flurry will leave the evildoer vulnerable to the Ending Blow.

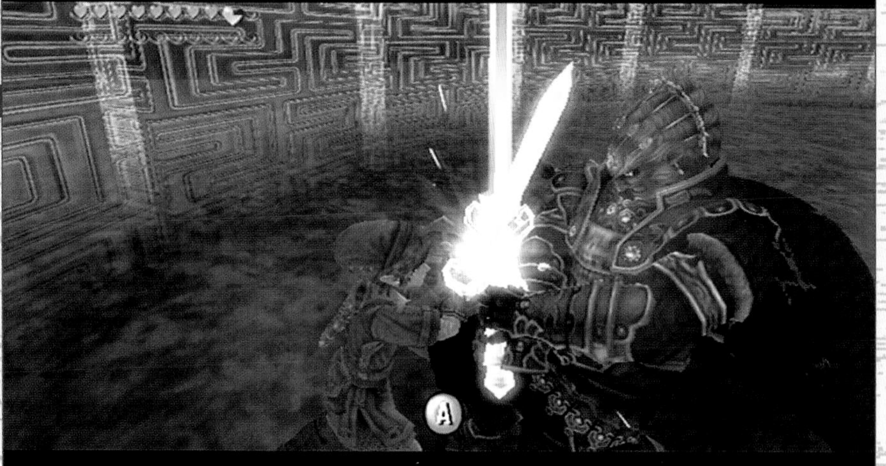

Adventure Appendix

Pieces of Heart

There are 45 Pieces of Heart in the kingdom. For every five you collect, you'll get a Heart Container.

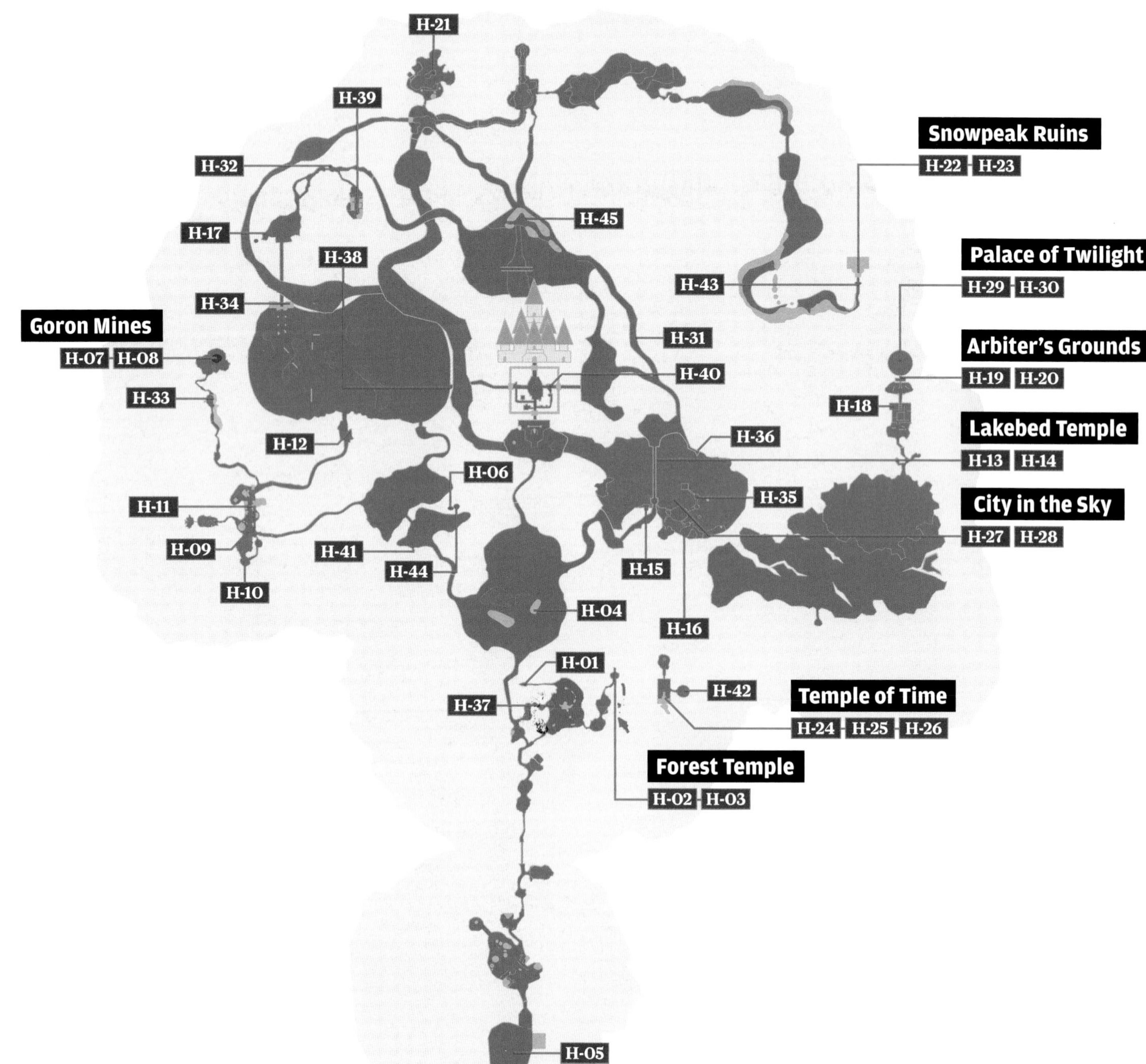

You're All Heart

You'll start the game with three hearts and earn one more in each of the first eight dungeons. To complete the collection of 20 full hearts, you'll have to collect each of the kingdom's 45 Pieces of Heart. You'll get a full Heart Container for every five pieces that you find. Some of the pieces come as prizes for side quests or minigames. The rest are scattered all over the kingdom. You'll go to dark caves, dead ends, and high peaks during your search for all of the life-sustaining treasures.

H-03 Forest Temple

Use the Gale Boomerang to put out the torches in the far east Forest Temple chamber, where creatures wait under floor tiles. The wood platforms in the room will drop, allowing you a clear path to the Piece of Heart.

H-01 Faron Woods

Burn through the Faron Woods swamp's poisonous fog by waving your lantern, and enter the cave in the northwest (where you found the key to the north woods gate). Light two torches at the dead end to make the Piece of Heart appear. Note that if you do this early on, there will be no poisonous fog.

H-04 Hyrule Field

Venture to the south end of the bridge in the middle of Hyrule Field. Equip the Gale Boomerang and investigate the trees in the area with your first-person view. You'll find a heart floating near the branches of one of the trees. Use the boomerang to retrieve it.

H-02 Forest Temple

Drop a bomb into a large plant in the killer-plant-filled chamber that is northeast of the Forest Temple entrance. The giant bud will explode, giving you access to a ground-level alcove and a treasure chest.

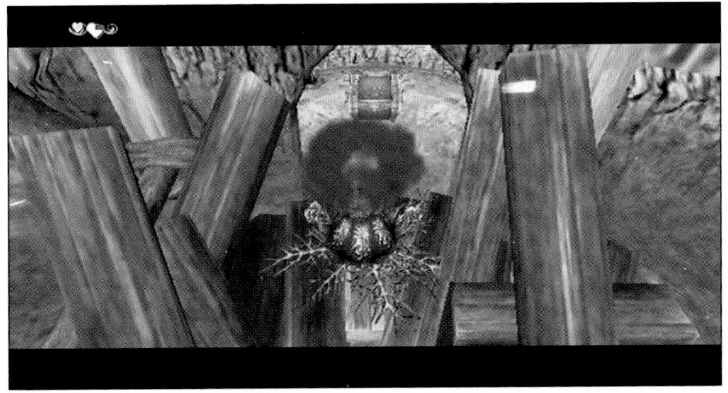

H-05 Ordon Village

Following your adventure in the Goron Mines, you'll regain the use of your horse, Epona. Any time after that, go to the ranch during the day, call Epona and talk to Fado. He'll ask you to herd the goats, and will give you a gift after a successful run.

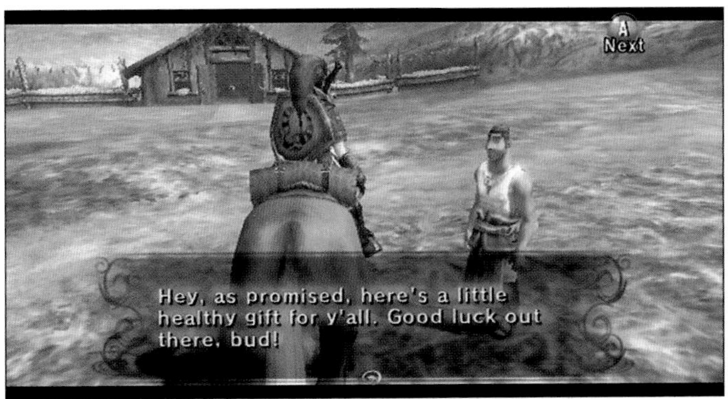

H-06 Hyrule Field

Look for a tall rock formation that towers over the east end of Kakariko Gorge. You'll find a Heart Piece floating above it. Target the prize with your boomerang, then send the boomerang across the gap to add the piece to your collection.

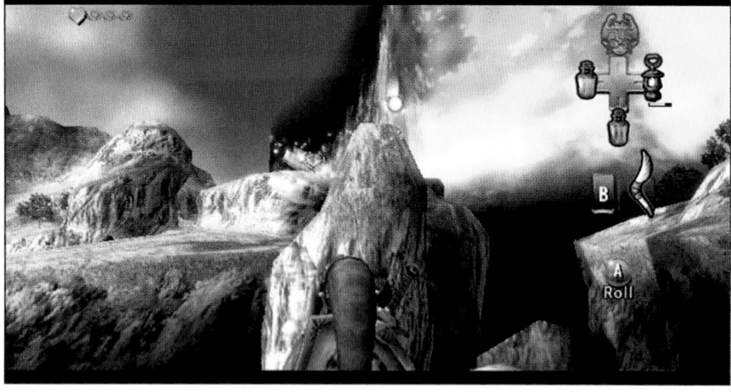

H-07 Goron Mines

Shortly after you speak to Gor Amoto, the first elder in the mines, you'll use the Iron Boots to walk on the ceiling of a large chamber. Advance to the chamber's northwest corner to find a treasure chest that contains a Piece of Heart.

H-08 Goron Mines

After you advance to the second-floor room that houses two turrets and a drawbridge, walk up the magnetic track on the east wall. Follow the track's southern branch to reach a treasure chest on a ledge. Your prize is inside.

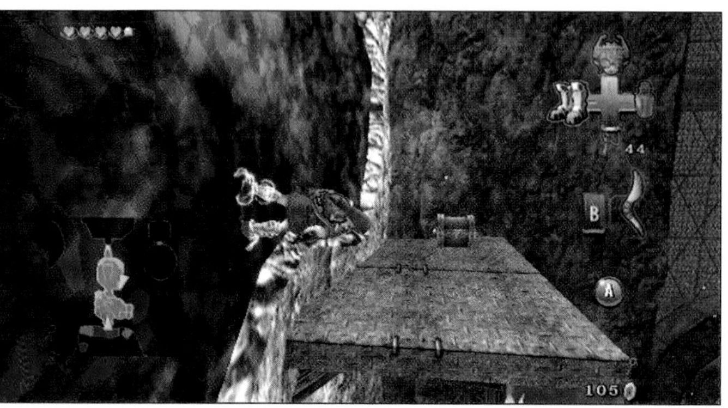

H-09 Kakariko Village

After you complete your adventure in the Goron Mines, get a boost from a Goron at the north end of Kakariko Village, then climb the tower. You'll find Talo at the top. He'll challenge you to an arrow-shooting exercise that will end with you hitting a pole at the top of the tower from the south end of town. That shot will earn you a Piece of Heart—but only if you don't use the Hawkeye.

H-10 Kakariko Village

There's a huge boulder west of the Spirit Spring at the south end of the village. Use a bomb to destroy it and reveal a cave. Follow the path inside, to a pool of water. Dive in, use the Iron Boots to sink to the bottom of the pool, then walk to a treasure chest.

H-11 Kakariko Village

You'll see a grouping of rocks on the cliff above the giant boulder that you bombed to access Piece of Heart H-10. Use a bomb arrow to destroy the rocks and expose another Piece of Heart. Standing close to the cliff, use the boomerang to collect the item.

H-12 Hyrule Field

Travel north of Kakariko Village and use a bomb to destroy a large block on the path's west side. That will give you access to a narrow trail along the rocks. The trail will lead you south. After you destroy a rock with a bomb arrow, climb a vine, then go north to the prize.

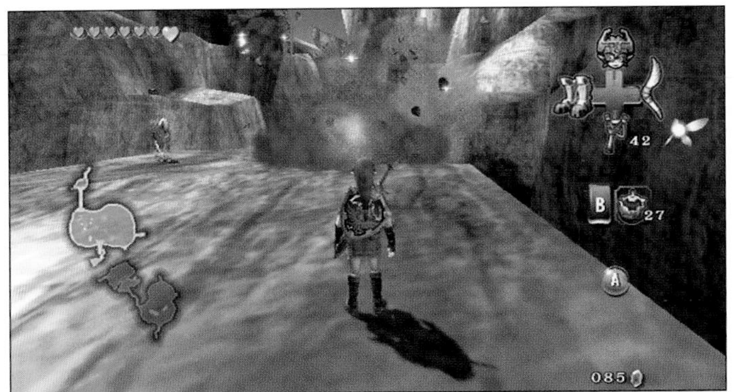

H-13 Lakebed Temple

After you get the Clawshot by defeating the humongous frog, return to the central circular room. From the second floor, use the Clawshot to grapple your way to the chandelier in the middle of the room. You'll find the Piece of Heart in a treasure chest.

H-14 Lakebed Temple

Make sure the water is flowing west in the main chamber, then travel to the westernmost room on the first floor. Cross the bridge to the south, then stand on the switch and grapple to the wall, where you'll find a treasure chest containing a Piece of Heart.

H-15 Lake Hylia

You can reach a room at the back of Lanayru's Spirit Spring by grappling to the ivy with the Clawshot. At the far south end of the room, you'll find two torches. Light the torches with the lantern—a chest with a Piece of Heart inside will appear.

H-16 Lantern Cavern 2

There's a rock-blocked cave south of Lake Hylia's Windstone. Destroy the barrier and venture into the darkness with a full lantern. Your path has many twists, turns, and alcoves. Light two torches in the last chamber to make a Piece of Heart appear.

H-17 Bridge of Eldin

Grapple to a ledge on the west cliff wall north of the Bridge of Eldin. Go south then west into a cavern. As you travel though the cave, you'll leap off ledges for distance then put on your Iron Boots in midair to stick to a wall. After the third time you do that, look for a chest.

H-18 Gerudo Desert

There's a boar on a spit in the northwest corner of the enemy camp. Use a spin attack to destroy the embers under the boar, then attack the boar itself to cut your way through to a Piece of Heart.

H-19 Arbiter's Grounds

Travel to the northwest corner of the Arbiter's Grounds central chamber. Use the Clawshot to fly over a patch of sinking sand and collect the contents of a treasure chest—a Piece of Heart. A grappling point on the west wall will help you get out of the corner.

H-20 Arbiter's Grounds

You'll put the Spinner to the test shortly after you collect it. In the basement's northeast-corner chamber, use your new tool to hook onto a track on the wall. You'll ride up to a mid-room treasure chest and the dungeon's second Piece of Heart.

H-21 Fishing Hole

When you reach the fishing hole in the northwest section of Lanayru Province, talk to Hena in the south hut to rent a canoe and a reel. Paddle out to the middle of the pond, then send out a line to collect the Piece of Heart on the pond's large rock formation.

H-22 Snowpeak Ruins

On the second floor of the foyer, hit the north chandelier with your ball and chain to start it swinging. Hop onto it, then hit and hop onto the two chandeliers to the south. Your goal is to reach the treasure chest on the south ledge.

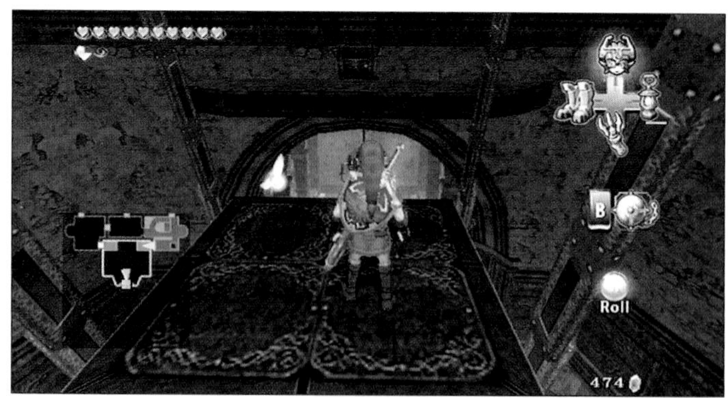

H-23 Snowpeak Ruins

There are cracks in the floor in the southeast corner of the second level. Use a bomb or the ball and chain to blast the floorboards and create a hole. Drop in. You'll find a treasure chest. From there, grapple back to the second level.

H-24 Temple of Time

On your way back to the temple's main door, with the Dominion Rod in hand and a statue under your control, you'll advance through a fifth-floor room that has sliding walls, an electric barrier, and a treasure. Guide the statue to a switch to gain access to the Piece of Heart.

H-25 Temple of Time

Take a slight detour in your journey back to the main door. On the south end of the fifth floor's south room, use the Dominion Rod to guide two small statues along eastern and western paths. After they both hit switches, a treasure chest will appear.

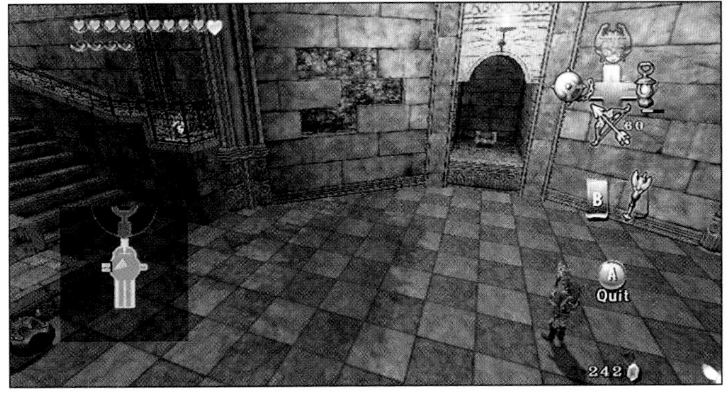

H-26 Temple of Time

When there's power in the Dominion Rod, go to the Temple of Time's main room and use the rod to move a statue that is imbedded in the wall of the southwest corner. You'll reveal a passage that leads to a treasure.

H-27 City in the Sky

After you defeat the large plant on the first floor of the east wing, grapple up to the second floor. Head counterclockwise through the room, carefully walking across the narrow path. Grab onto the ledge to your right and shimmy across the gap to find the Piece of Heart.

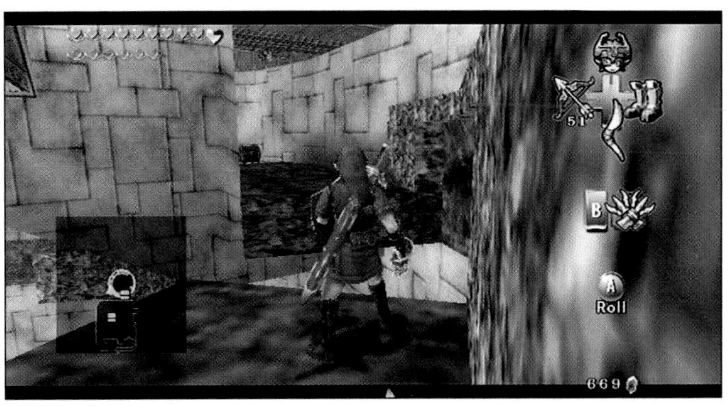

H-28 City in the Sky

There's a Piece of Heart in the chamber filled with flying plants on the east wing's third floor in the City in the Sky. Take the northwest exit from the chamber, then grapple from plant to plant to reach the southern balcony. Go through the door to nab the Piece of Heart.

H-29 Palace of Twilight

Once you have the Light Sword, return to the palace's east wing. Use the sword (or the Sol) to cut through the fog on the east wall of the southeast room, then grapple to a treasure chest.

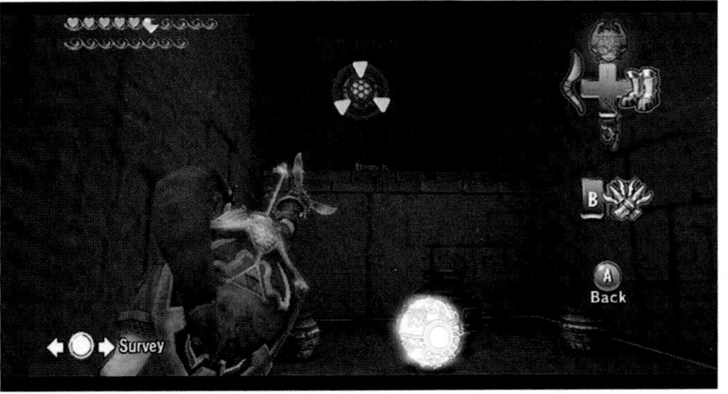

H-30 Palace of Twilight

Go to the palace's west wing with the Light Sword in hand. Cut through the fog in the first room to make a platform appear in the southwest corner of the pit. The platform will carry you to within reach of the treasure chest in the west wall's raised alcove.

H-31 Lanayru Province

A path in the far eastern section of Lanayru Province (east of Castle Town) is blocked by boulders on both ends. After you blast the rocks, use the Spinner to follow a track on the walls (jumping between walls on the upper reaches) to get to a ledge that holds a treasure.

H-32 Eldin Province

In northern Eldin Province, on the east side of the bridge that spans the hidden gulch, use the Spinner on the north wall's track. After you reach a lower ledge, dig into a cave. Destroy three regenerating skeletons inside to make a treasure chest appear.

H-33 Death Mountain

You'll discover a Goron while you're on the Death Mountain trail between Kakariko Village and the Goron camp. Use the Goron for a boost and grab a ledge to the east. Climb up, go north, then drop into a cave to the east. You'll end up near a treasure chest.

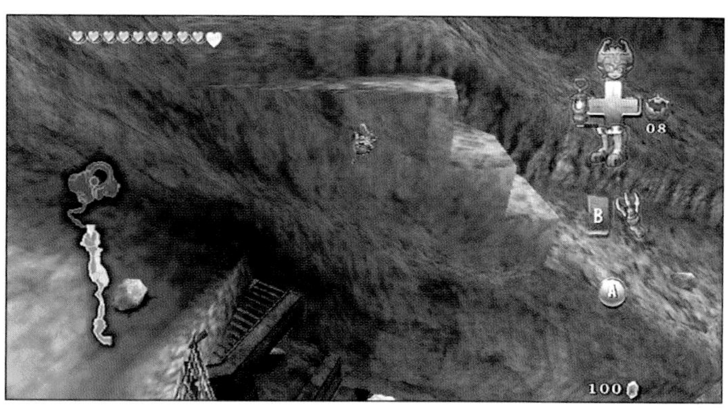

H-34 Bridge of Eldin

After you retrieve the middle of the Bridge of Eldin from the Gerudo Desert. Use the Dominion Rod to guide a statue from the north end to the south end. Drop it into an alcove to the east, then use it as a platform to hop across a gap. Climb a ladder then get a prize.

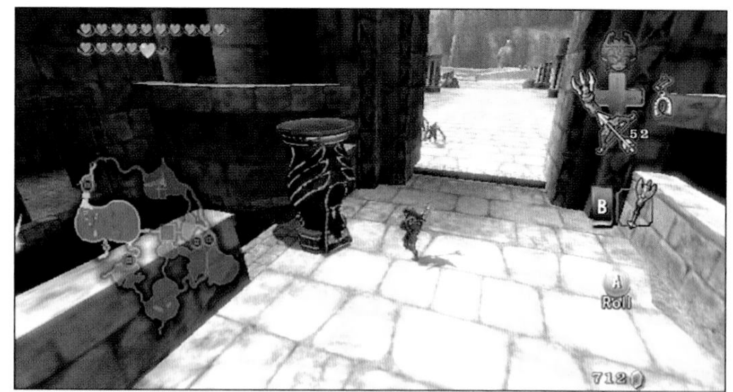

H-35 Lake Hylia

Plumm challenges you to a fruit-balloon-popping challenge on the west side of Lake Hylia. She offers you a mystery prize (it's a Piece of Heart) for a 10,000-point score. The trick is to get score-doubling fruit-matching combos. Go for a long line of strawberries.

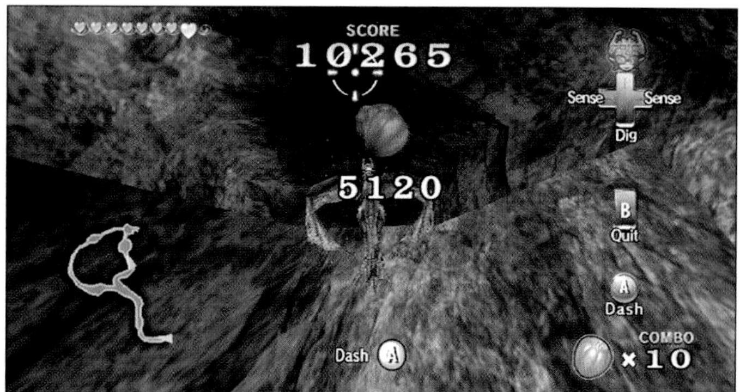

H-36 Lake Hylia

Take Fyer's normal flight to get to Falbi's Flight-by-Fowl challenge. Grab a Cucco and go straight for the floating platforms to the southwest, pressing down on the Control Stick occasionally to decrease your speed. The top stationary platform houses a Piece of Heart.

H-37 Ordon Woods

Go north of Coro's shack, blast a giant boulder, then head north to a statue. Use the Dominion Rod to guide the statue into a shallow hole, then turn into a wolf and use Midna's help to hop onto the statue, and follow a path to a treasure chest.

H-38 Kakariko Village

Once you've donated 1,000 rupees in Malo's shop to rebuild the west bridge to Castle Town, talk to the elder outside the shop. Accept his challenge to bring springwater to the Goron. Zigzag your way through the enemies and douse the Goron to earn a Piece of Heart.

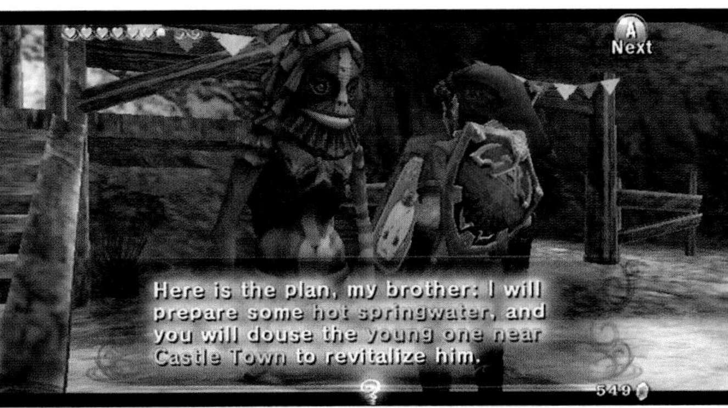

H-39 Hidden Village

Travel south through a cave in Eldin Province's northeast corner to find the hidden village. You'll discover the Cucco leader on the west side. Crash through windows to get to her. Accept her challenge to find and speak to 20 cats. Completion gets you a Piece of Heart.

H-40 Castle Town

A man wearing a green robe on the Castle Town east road accepts your donations in 30- and 50-rupee increments. Once you give him a total of 1,000 rupees, he'll summon a Piece of Heart from the heavens and hand it over.

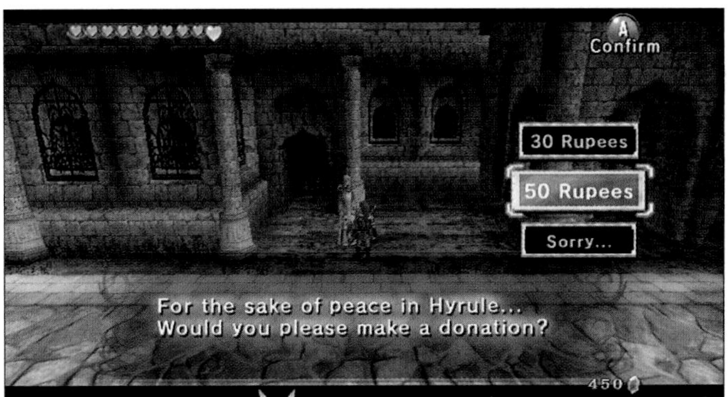

H-41 Lantern Cavern 1

Bombs get you into a lot of places in Twilight Princess. Plant an explosive near a giant boulder southwest of the Kakariko Gorge bridge to gain entry to a sprawling cavern. Light two torches in the cavern's northwest section to make the treasure appear.

H-42 Sacred Grove

Travel east of the temple grounds to one of the places where you faced off with the Skull Kid. Blow up a boulder in the middle of the area, then dig in that place to reach a cave. After you destroy all of the killer plants in the area, you'll discover a Piece of Heart.

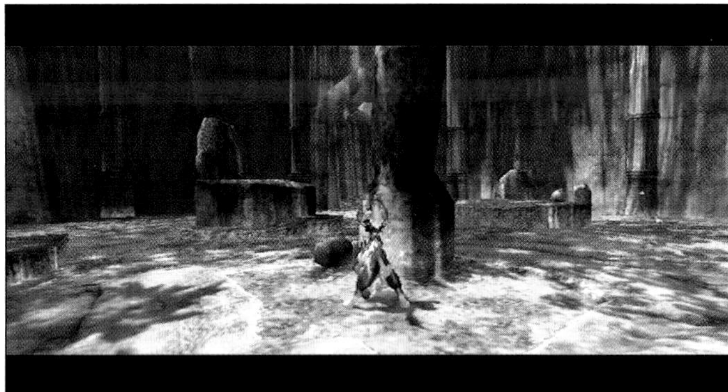

H-43 Snowpeak

Are you ready to yeti? After you've obtained the second Mirror Shard, return to the top of Snowpeak, where you first met Yeto. Challenge him to a snowboard race; if you win you'll get to race his wife, Yeta. Defeat her (use the overpass shortcut) to get a Piece of Heart.

H-44 Hyrule Field

Once you have the Double Clawshots, go to the southeast section of Kakariko Gorge and hit a grappling point in the middle of the large formation. Grapple from there to a point on the south cliff (below the vines), then to the vines on the small formation. Climb to a prize.

H-45 Hyrule Field

In the area north of Hyrule Castle, take the northern rocky path until you reach a clearing with a west-facing cave blocked by a boulder. Destroy the boulder then smash the ice with the ball and chain. Beyond three block-pushing puzzles, you'll find a Piece of Heart.

Poe Souls

Greedy Castle Town resident Jovani has lost his soul. He'll ask you for 20 Poe Souls then 60 Poe Souls to restore it.

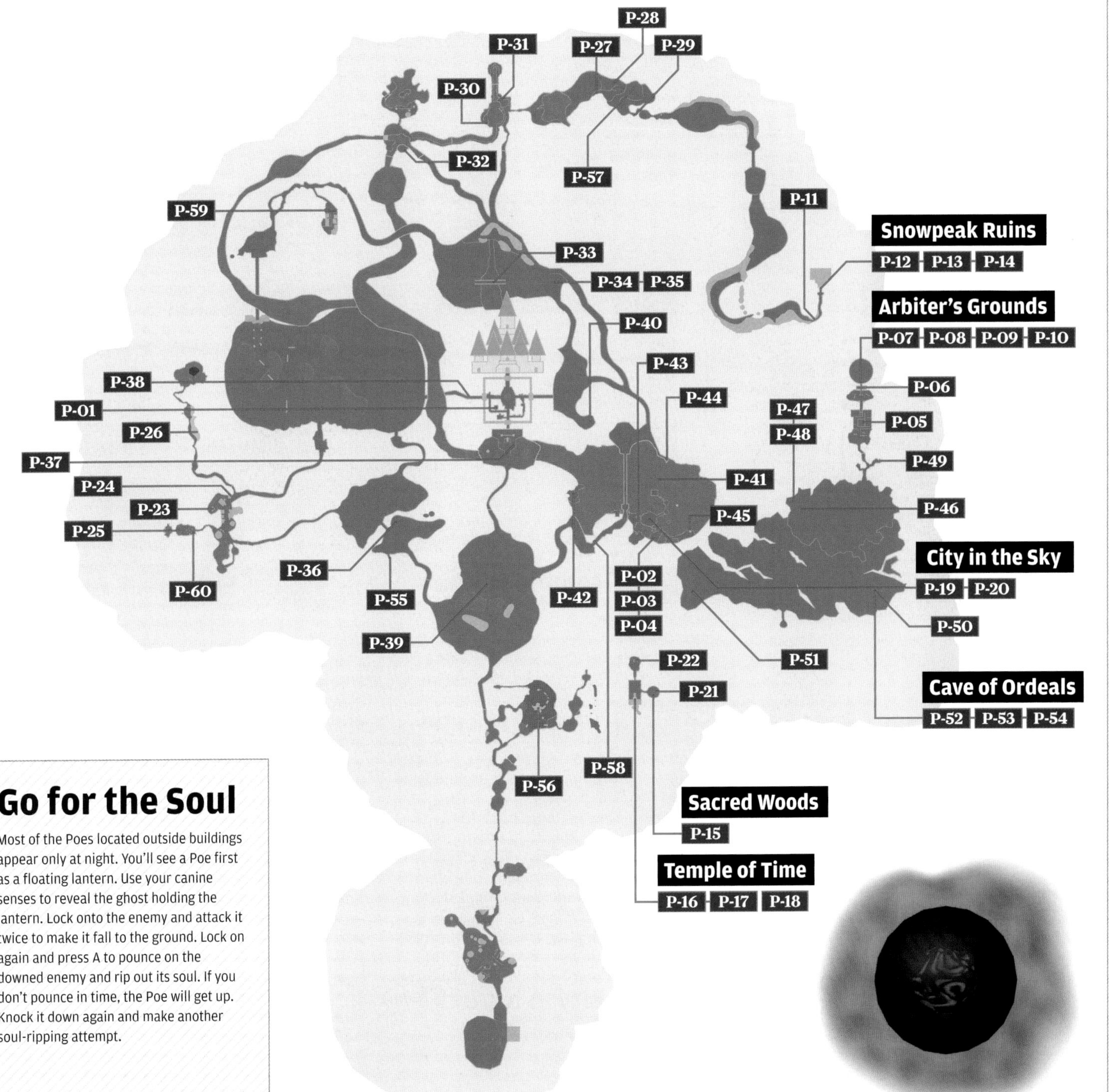

Go for the Soul

Most of the Poes located outside buildings appear only at night. You'll see a Poe first as a floating lantern. Use your canine senses to reveal the ghost holding the lantern. Lock onto the enemy and attack it twice to make it fall to the ground. Lock on again and press A to pounce on the downed enemy and rip out its soul. If you don't pounce in time, the Poe will get up. Knock it down again and make another soul-ripping attempt.

P-01 Castle Town

The first Poe Soul that you will discover belongs to a ghost that haunts Jovani's house on the west side of Castle Town. He'll give you instructions on how to collect it: use your canine senses to track it down, then attack.

P-02 Lantern Cavern 2

The cave south of Lake Hylia's Howling Stone is a winding wonder. Either take a bottle of Lantern Oil with you or collect Chu Jelly that acts as Lantern Oil along the way. You'll find the first of the cave's three Poes early in your journey.

P-03 Lantern Cavern 2

The second Poe in Lake Hylia's lantern cave is about halfway through your journey into the dark. As soon as you see the floating lantern, transform into a wolf, engage your senses, then take on the Poe.

P-04 Lantern Cavern 2

When you reach the final chamber of Lake Hylia's lantern cave, you'll see a third lantern and a glowing exit. Before you leave, transform into a wolf for a final Poe fight.

P-05 Gerudo Desert

After you defeat the axe-carrying King Bulblin in the middle of the enemy camp, return to the scene of the battle (at night) to discover a Poe. You know the drill. Defeat it then rip out its soul.

P-06 Gerudo Desert

While you're walking up the steps to the Arbiter's Grounds entrance, go east at the mezzanine. If it's night, you'll see a floating lantern in the distance. Follow the light to find the Poe.

P-07 Arbiter's Grounds

Four Poes enter the first floor's central chamber. Three Poes leave. Transform into your canine form, engage your senses, then face off with the ghost.

P-08 Arbiter's Grounds

The second Poe that you'll have to defeat to advance through the Arbiter's Grounds is in a round room in the dungeon's northwest section. You'll find it after emerging from the basement.

P-09 Arbiter's Grounds

After you deal with a skeleton crew and two screaming ghouls in a room flooded with sinking sand, you'll dig up a chain. Pull it to move a barrier out of the way, then run past the barrier to the dungeon's third Poe.

P-10 Arbiter's Grounds

You'll discover the last of the four Arbiter's Grounds Poes east of the central chamber. It will make three copies of itself. The real Poe is just a little brighter than the others. Identify it, target it, and steal its soul.

P-11 Snowpeak Area

In canine form, climb to the top of the snow-and-ice bluff that lies southwest of the Snowpeak Ruins entrance. You'll discover a Poe there. As you fight the ghost, avoid falling off the bluff's edge.

P-12 Snowpeak Ruins

There's a lantern in the foyer, often floating over the ice. Transform into a wolf, engage your senses, and attack the Poe who is holding the lantern.

P-13 Snowpeak Ruins

When you get to the southwestern room on the second floor with your ball and chain, use the tool to break the ice barrier on the west wall. You'll reveal a Poe in an alcove. Another bright creature flies around there. Don't mistake it for the ghost.

P-14 Snowpeak Ruins

As soon as you walk into the Snowpeak Ruins, you'll see three suits of armor on each of the east and west entryway walls. Destroy the middle one on the west wall (hitting it twice with the ball and chain) to expose a Poe.

P-15 Sacred Woods

You'll find a Poe in the maze where you chased the Skull Kid. The ghost floats over one of the kid's hiding places: on top of a large, hollowed-out stump. You'll pass under a waterfall and climb roots to get to it.

P-16 Temple of Time

When you get to the sixth-floor scale room, you'll use small statues as weights to make the scales tip and give you enough height to grapple to the middle of the room. Use the Spinner to get to the western ledge, directly above the scale. You'll find a Poe there.

P-17 Temple of Time

A Poe waits behind a gold gate on the east side of the third-floor elevator room. Use the Dominion Rod to activate a small statue on the wall above the gate then guide the statue to a floor switch on the other side. You can attack the Poe after the gate opens.

P-18 Temple of Time

Use the Dominion Rod to move a statue that's embedded in the wall of the opening chamber's southeast corner. A Poe lantern will fly out from behind the animated art. Transform into a wolf and go to work on the ghost.

P-19 City in the Sky

A Poe is hiding on the east wing of the third floor in the City in the Sky. From the northern entrance, use the flying plants to hover over two walls, then grab onto a south-flying plant. While flying, grab onto one more plant and drop to face the Poe.

P-20 City in the Sky

There's a Poe hanging out near the room with the Big Key in the City in the Sky. Climb ivy as a human and walk ropes as a wolf to reach the east side of the fourth floor's central room. You'll find the Poe near a treasure chest on a precarious platform.

P-21 Sacred Grove

Travel east of the main temple grounds to the site of your first Skull Kid standoff. Use a bomb to destroy a giant rock, which exposes a Poe lantern.

P-22 Sacred Grove

After you're out of the Temple of Time, return to the place where you collected the Master Sword. There's a Poe floating out in the open. Grab it in your steely jaws.

P-23 Kakariko Village

Enter Barnes Bomb Shop, climb the stairs, and go through the exit on the top floor. Climb up to the bombed-out storage building from there. If it's nighttime, you'll discover a Poe floating over the wreckage.

P-24 Kakariko Village

Zigzag up the hill from the bombed-out building at night. A Poe will be waiting for you on the porch of the building on top of the hill.

P-25 Kakariko Village

It's a well-known fact that ghosts hang out in graveyards. Go the Kakariko Village graveyard at night to see for yourself. One more Poe Soul will be yours.

P-26 Death Mountain

While you're walking the trail from Kakariko Village to the Goron camp, get a boost from a Goron and grab a ledge to the east. If it's night, you'll see a Poe lantern to the south.

P-27 Snowpeak Area

Since all of the enemies in the Snowpeak area glisten white, it's difficult to distinguish them from the Poe lanterns that float on the slope between the ice floes and the cave at the top. One of the Poes tends to hover near a tree in the southern-central part of the area.

P-28 Snowpeak Area

Just down the slope from Poe P-27, another one of the ghostly creatures haunts the area around a very large rock. Clear away the other enemies in the area before you engage your wolf senses then go after the poltergeist.

P-29 Snowpeak Cave

In the cave at the top of the mountain, you'll discover a Poe on the other side of an icy wall. Set it free by hitting the ice with your ball and chain, then attack it.

P-30 Zora's Waterfall

After you ride down the waterfall, climb up an incline on the west side. If it's dark outside, a Poe lantern will be illuminating the ledge.

P-31 Zora's Domain

When you're in wolf form, use Midna's help to hop up a collection of cliffs, from the east side of the pool to the north side. There's a Poe (which you'll find only at night) in the middle of one of the gaps.

P-32 Zora's River

There's a grassy knoll on the south side of the Zora's River area. A Poe haunts the little hill at night. Climb up and pluck out the Poe Soul.

P-33 Hyrule Field

There's a stone bridge in the Hyrule Field area north of the castle. Wait until night and cross the span to discover a hovering Poe.

P-34 Hyrule Field

Run east of the bridge where you found Poe P-33. There's a ring of tall-grass tufts close to a pair of trees. Engage your canine senses and dig into the soft ground in the center of the ring. You'll drop into a cave where you'll find two Poes (P-34 and P-35).

P-35 Hyrule Field

Poe P-35 is in the same cave as P-34. Use your senses to expose the two ghosts. You may be able to knock both of them to the ground with the same attack. If you do, steal one soul then pounce for the second one before the Poe revives itself.

P-36 Hyrule Field

Walk to the top of a cliff east of the bridge in Kakariko Gorge at night. You'll see a floating lantern near a tree. Engage your canine senses to spy a Poe. Target it and pluck it from the air.

P-37 Hyrule Field

Use Castle Town's southern exit. While you're heading due south, down the stairs of the stone patio area outside of the town you'll confront a Poe. Knock it down and rip out its soul.

P-38 Hyrule Field

A Poe hovers over the wooden bridge outside Castle Town's western exit at night. You can defeat it easily, then add its soul to your collection.

P-39 Hyrule Field

A Poe floats over a small cliff just north of a shallow body of water in the Hyrule Field section that lies between Castle Town and Faron Woods. As is the case with many outdoor-dwelling Poes, you'll find it only at night.

P-40 Hyrule Field

Head southeast from the Castle Town warp portal. After you go over a short hill, you'll come to the amphitheater. Tonight's performance: you fighting a Poe for its soul.

P-41 Lake Hylia

A Poe haunts the first prize platform below Falbi's Flight-by-Fowl challenge. Luckily, both Fyer's cannon and Falbi's challenge are open at night. Use the two concessions to get to the platform. Stay away from the edge while you're fighting the Poe.

P-42 Lake Hylia

You'll find a floating lantern over the patch of land on the west side of Lake Hylia at night. Turn into wolf form and grab another soul for your collection.

P-43 Lake Hylia

Explore the grassy ledges of Lake Hylia's south shore at night. You'll see the Poe lantern light as you approach the southern-central section. Follow the winding path, jump gaps, and close in on your prey.

P-44 Lake Hylia

There's a Poe on a ledge midway up Lake Hylia's north wall, directly below Falbi's Flight-by-Fowl challenge station. Rocket up to Falbi's place, accept the challenge, and do a U-turn as you drop. If it's night, you'll see a lantern on the ledge. Float to it then defeat the Poe.

P-45 Lake Hylia

Climb up to the base of the lookout tower in Lake Hylia's southeast section. You'll find a Poe there, just waiting for you to rip out its soul.

P-46 Gerudo Desert

There's a tree on a bluff due west of the entrance to the enemy encampment (the desert's north-central section). Hit the tree with the Clawshot and grapple to it. If it's nighttime, you'll find a Poe hovering over three skulls.

P-47 Gerudo Desert

Use your canine senses to find a place to dig in the same location where you found Poe P-46. You'll drop into a cave and find a Poe immediately.

P-48 Gerudo Desert

After you find Poe Soul P-47 in an underground cave, another Poe will attack. Use your canine senses to see it, then attack it. Once you have the cave's second soul, climb a boulder that's bathed in light. Midna will lift you out of the cave.

P-49 Gerudo Desert

There are narrow, sandy paths between the main desert and the enemy encampment in the northeast. Follow the path to the east at night. You'll go up against a group of sand-dwelling creatures and a Poe.

P-50 Gerudo Desert

After you transport the center section of the Bridge of Eldin to its rightful place, return to the Gerudo Desert location where you found it. If it's nighttime, you'll find a Poe on the mesa, near the entrance to the now-open Cave of Ordeals.

P-51 Gerudo Desert

South of the place where you land after rocketing to the desert (on the desert's west end), you'll find a large rock. Go there at night to fight a Poe who has another soul for you.

P-52 Cave of Ordeals

After you move a piece of the Bridge of Eldin from the desert back to its rightful place, you'll have access to the Cave of Ordeals on the Gerudo Mesa. You'll find the first of three cave Poes on the 17th floor. Fight bony four-legged beasts before you take on the Poe.

P-53 Cave of Ordeals

The cave's second Poe is on the 33rd floor (of 50). You'll need the Dominion Rod to get past a gate on the 31st floor. Two floors later, you'll be fighting for a Poe Soul.

P-54 Cave of Ordeals

When you venture to the 44th floor, you'll discover the cave's third and final Poe. Keep advancing if you can, though. You'll meet the Great Fairy for the last time on the 50th floor.

P-55 Lantern Cavern 1

The lantern cavern is south of the bridge that spans Kakariko Gorge. Use a bomb to blast your way into it. Once inside, go to the northwest section to discover a Poe.

P-56 Faron Woods

On your way north through the Faron Woods swamp at night, Midna will lead you to a large hollowed-out stump. Fight the Poe there and rip out its soul.

P-57 Snowpeak Area

Explore the Reekfish-scent trail between Poe P-27 and the cave that leads to the Snowpeak summit. Like its lower-slope partner, the ghost haunts a tree.

P-58 Hyrule Field

Travel northeast from Faron into Lanayru Province, and onto a winding path. Before you cross a bridge, examine the eastern cliff for a chest. Use bomb arrows to destroy rocks on the cliffs and expose grappling spots. Climb up to the chest and a Poe.

P-59 Hidden Village

The passage to Hidden Village is in the northeast section of Eldin Province. You'll get there though a cave to the south. There's a Poe lantern on a balcony in the village's northeast corner. Grapple onto a net, climb, transform, then fight the Poe.

P-60 Kakariko Village

Visit the Kakariko Village graveyard at night in your canine form and push the gravestone in the southeast corner. A Poe will pop from the grave. Attack it.

Golden Bugs

Agitha of Castle Town seeks 12 pairs of Golden Bugs for a ball. She'll reward you handsomely for each one.

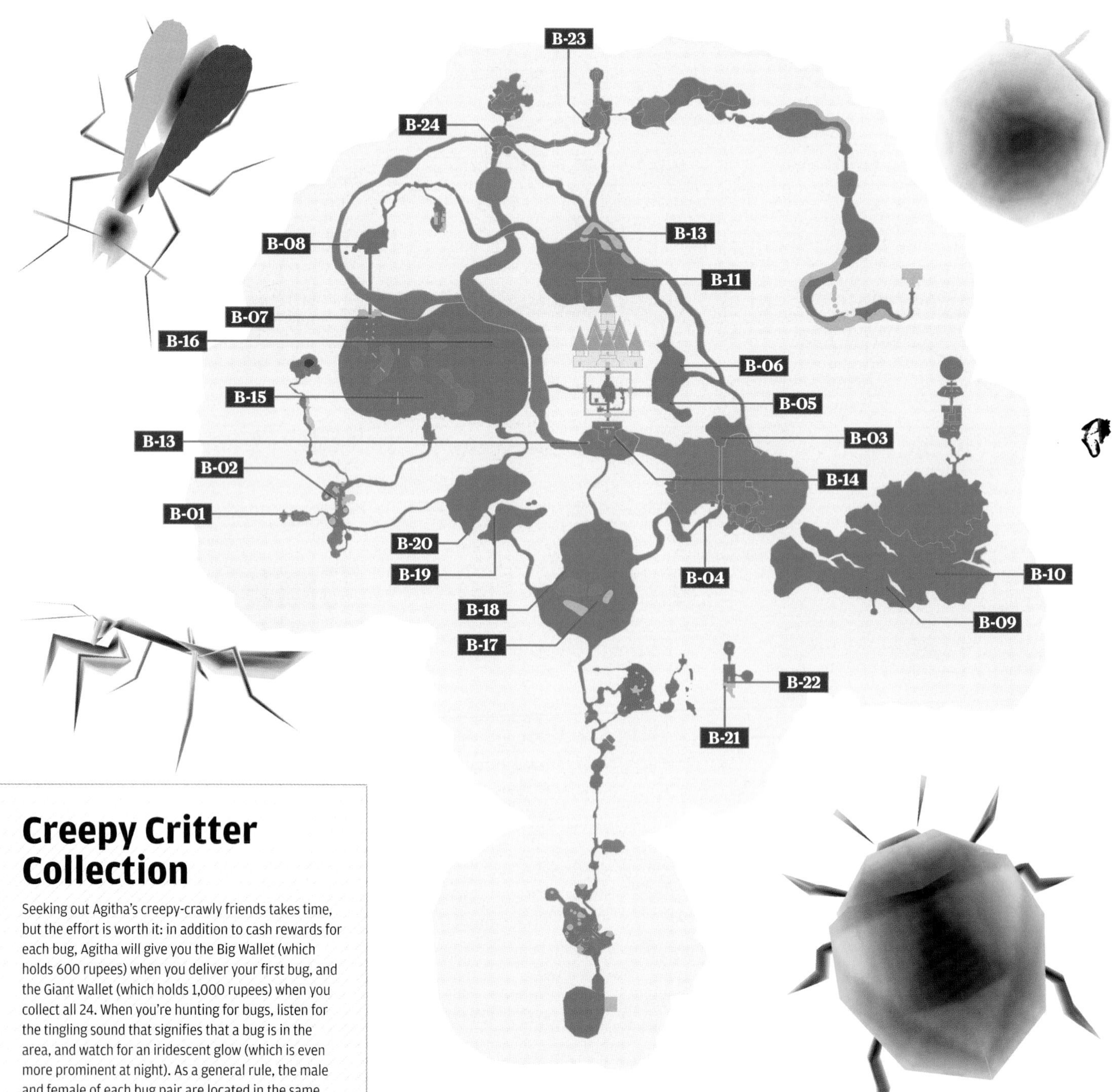

Creepy Critter Collection

Seeking out Agitha's creepy-crawly friends takes time, but the effort is worth it: in addition to cash rewards for each bug, Agitha will give you the Big Wallet (which holds 600 rupees) when you deliver your first bug, and the Giant Wallet (which holds 1,000 rupees) when you collect all 24. When you're hunting for bugs, listen for the tingling sound that signifies that a bug is in the area, and watch for an iridescent glow (which is even more prominent at night). As a general rule, the male and female of each bug pair are located in the same area, usually on the same map.

B-01 Kakariko Village
Male Ant

The male ant is in the graveyard on the west side of Kakariko Village. Look in the back of the graveyard, near the tree on the right side.

B-02 Kakariko Village
Female Ant

You'll find the female ant in a house on the west side of Kakariko Village. Simply walk through the door.

B-03 Lake Hylia
Male Mantis

The male mantis lives at the north end of the Great Bridge of Hylia. The bug often clings to the inner side of the arch—use the Gale Boomerang to grab it if need be.

B-04 Lake Hylia
Female Mantis

South of the Great Bridge of Hylia, giant tree roots sit atop the rocky path. The female mantis is hiding in the southern portion of the root-covered area, usually high on the east side. Snag her with the Gale Boomerang.

B-05 Hyrule Field (Lanayru)
Male Butterfly

Travel south from the east entrance to Castle Town until you reach a path. The male butterfly is in a patch of flowers to the left of the path.

B-06 Hyrule Field (Lanayru)
Female Butterfly

From Castle Town's east entrance, head east along the path until you see an ivy-covered ledge on your left side. Use the Clawshot to reach the top of the ledge. You'll find the insect in a patch of flowers.

B-07 Hyrule Field (Eldin)
Male Phasmid

At the south end of Eldin Bridge, you'll find the male phasmid. It's usually on the inside of the arch. The Gale Boomerang will let you catch him with ease.

B-08 Hyrule Field (Eldin)
Female Phasmid

You can find the female phasmid on the cliff wall to the north of Eldin Bridge. Use the Gale Boomerang to snag the bug from afar.

B-09 Gerudo Desert

Male Dayfly

The male dayfly is in the south-central portion of the Gerudo Desert, slightly north-east of the small, gated alcove. It's easiest to spot at night.

B-10 Gerudo Desert

Female Dayfly

South of the enemy camp and west of the warp portal, you'll find trenches running through the sand. The female dayfly is within one of these trenches.

B-11 Hyrule Field (Lanayru)

Male Stag Beetle

You can find the male stag beetle near a tree in the east side of Hyrule Field, north of Hyrule Castle. If you take the road north from Castle Town's east entrance, you'll see the tree on your right side prior to reaching the bridge.

B-12 Hyrule Field (Lanayru)

Female Stag Beetle

In the section of Hyrule Field located to the north of Hyrule Castle, head to the rocky region north of the river. Take the southern fork when the path splits and look for a bombable west-facing cave entrance. The female stag beetle is above the entrance.

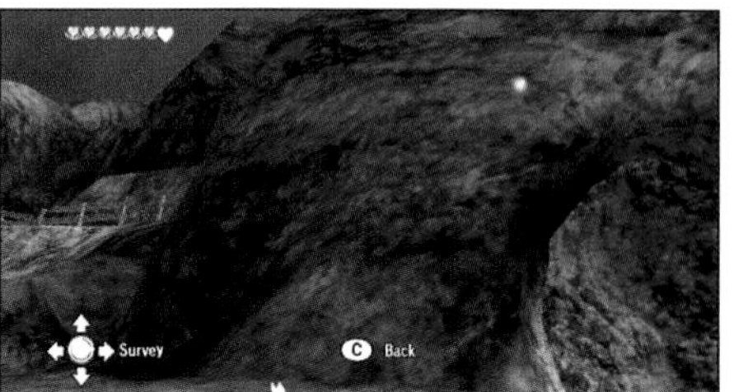

B-13 Hyrule Field (Lanayru)

Male Ladybug

Look for the male ladybug in the small field south of Castle Town. You'll find him near the large ivy-covered rock formation in the western portion of the area, likely near the flowers.

B-14 Hyrule Field (Lanayru)

Female Ladybug

The female ladybug is in the courtyard south of Castle Town, near the trio of trees east of the decorative pool. If the ladybug is startled, it might flutter over the railing, requiring you to grab it from below with the Gale Boomerang.

B-15 Hyrule Field (Eldin)

Male Grasshopper

Head north from Kakariko Village to Hyrule Field; you should see the male grasshopper on the dirt patch in the southern portion of the area. He can be hard to catch since he hops around—use the Gale Boomerang if necessary.

B-16 Hyrule Field (Eldin)

Female Grasshopper

You can find the female grasshopper in the section of Hyrule Field north of Kakariko Village. Look for her in the northeast portion of the area; she's easier to spot at night.

B-17 Hyrule Field (Faron)

Male Beetle

The male beetle is near a tree in the center of Hyrule Field in Faron Province. It's between the two hills that show up as light-green shapes on your map.

B-18 Hyrule Field (Faron)

Female Beetle

Look for the female beetle on the far west of Hyrule Field in Faron Province. She's on a tree trunk on a high ridge across the pathway from the pond. Use the Gale Boomerang to retrieve her.

B-19 Kakariko Gorge

Male Pill Bug

You'll see a golden glow in the grass near the south end of the Kakariko Gorge bridge, Pick it up. It's a small, round pill bug.

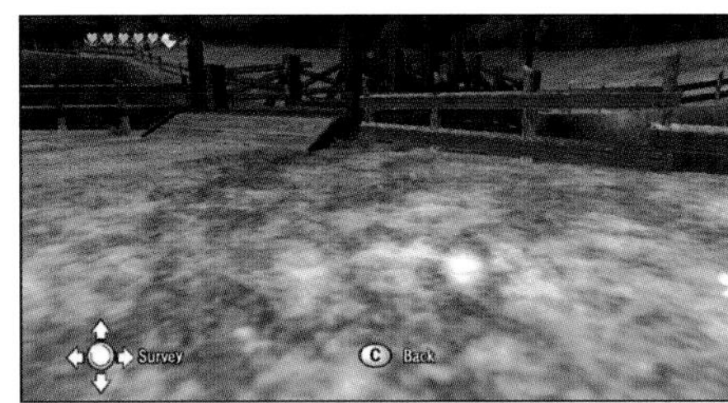

B-20 Kakariko Gorge

Female Pill Big

In the Kakariko Gorge area, head southwest from the north end of the bridge. You'll find the female pill bug in some flowers near a group of trees.

B-21 Sacred Grove

Male Snail

Go to the Sacred Grove entrance where you encountered the the moving-statue puzzle, and enter the alcove to the southwest. Face north and look in the upper-left corner; you'll find the male snail there.

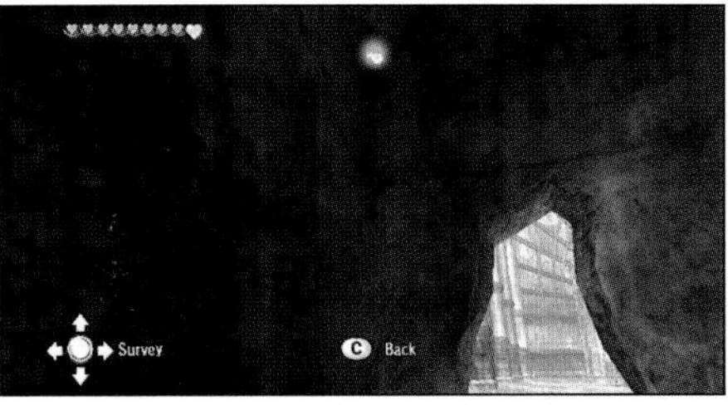

B-22 Temple of Time

Female Snail

From the Sacred Grove, enter the door that leads to the Temple of Time then head down the stairs and to the chamber's southwest corner. The female snail is on the wall next to the stairs.

B-23 Zora's Domain

Male Dragonfly

You'll spot the male dragonfly in the waterfall basin in Zora's Domain. Swim across the basin to the southwest section of the area, where the bug is flying around at the top of a hill.

B-24 Zora's River

Female Dragonfly

The female dragonfly hovers around the base of Iza's boat-rental cabin in the Zora's River area. Since it flies around, it can be tricky to get without using the Gale Boomerang.

Howling Stones

By activating howling stones and finding the golden wolf they unleash, Link can expand his offensive arsenal.

Howling Stone 03

Howling Stone 06

Howling Stone 07

07

03

Howling Stone 02

04

05

06

01

Howling Stone 05

Howling Stone 04

02

Advancing Your Skills

Regardless of the order that you activate the Howling Stones, you'll be taught the hidden skills in a set sequence. When you find a Howling Stone, you must howl into it as a wolf and match the howl pattern by pressing the Control Stick up or down or leaving it neutral. After you match the howl pattern twice, a golden wolf will appear somewhere in Hyrule, as indicated on your map. The number of the Howling Stone corresponds to the number of the golden wolf the stone summons. Since the first wolf appears automatically, there is no Howling Stone 01.

Howling Stone 02

Howling Stone Location

02

Golden Wolf Location

Ending Blow

01

You don't have to activate a Howling Stone to get the first golden wolf to appear; you'll cross his unavoidable path as you're heading to the Forest Temple in the Faron Woods. When you encounter the wolf, it will leap toward you, and you'll see a vision of an undead warrior who will train you to use the Ending Blow. He'll also tell you that you can learn additional skills by summoning him with howling stones.

Howling Stone 02

Shield Attack

02

You'll come across the first Howling Stone as you're heading to Death Mountain while Eldin Province is wrapped in twilight. It's located in a rocky area that's filled with steam geysers. After you match the howl pattern, the golden wolf will appear near the Ordon spring. Once you restore light to Eldin Province and return to human form, visit the wolf to learn the Shield Attack. The skill is good for stunning enemies and deflecting projectiles.

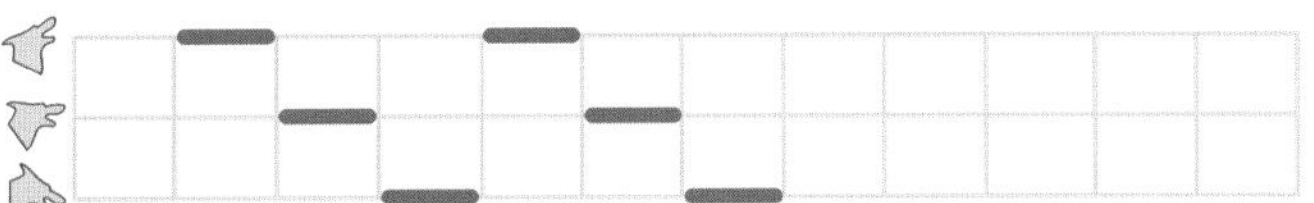

Howling Stone 03

Back Slice

03

Another Howling Stone is located in the Zora's River area of Lanayru Province. You can reach the stone after you've thawed Zora's Domain and the river is flowing again; it's northeast of Iza's cabin. The golden wolf will appear on a platform to the east of Castle Town. When you return to human form and approach the wolf, you'll learn the Back Slice, which lets you quickly circle around enemies and hit them from behind.

Howling Stone 04

Helm Splitter

04

When you return to North Faron Woods on your mission to find the Master Sword, you'll come across another Howling Stone after Midna helps you cross a series of gaps. Activating the stone will summon the golden wolf to the south of Castle Town; take the town's south exit and circle around to the east side of the field. Your reward will be the Helm Splitter, a jumping strike to the head that follows a Shield Attack.

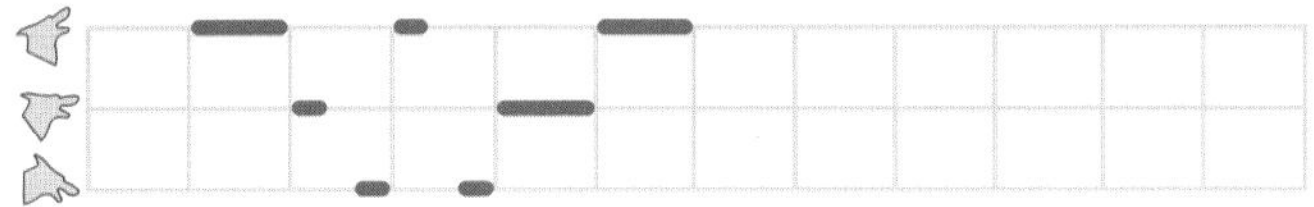

Howling Stone 05

Mortal Draw

05

You'll find another Howling Stone near Lake Hylia basin on a cliff south of the warp spot; you must climb a ladder to reach it. The most opportune time to reach the stone is when you're seeking Auru at the tower. After the stone's activated, you can find the gold wolf in the northeast section of Gerudo Desert, just before you enter the enemy encampment. The undead warrior will teach you the Mortal Draw, a powerful surprise attack.

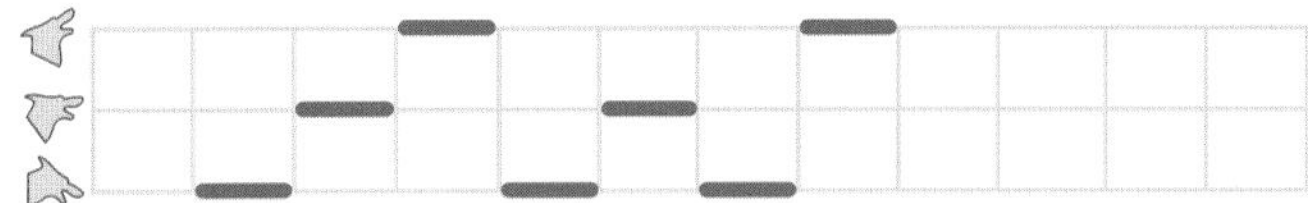

Howling Stone 06

Jump Strike

06

There's a Howling Stone located in the Snowpeak area; it's to the south of the burrow spot that leads to the underground cave. Activating the stone will call the golden wolf to the graveyard in Kakariko Village. When you encounter the wolf, the undead warrior will teach you the Jump Strike, a more powerful version of Link's standard jumping attack. The Jump Strike is capable of hitting multiple enemies at once.

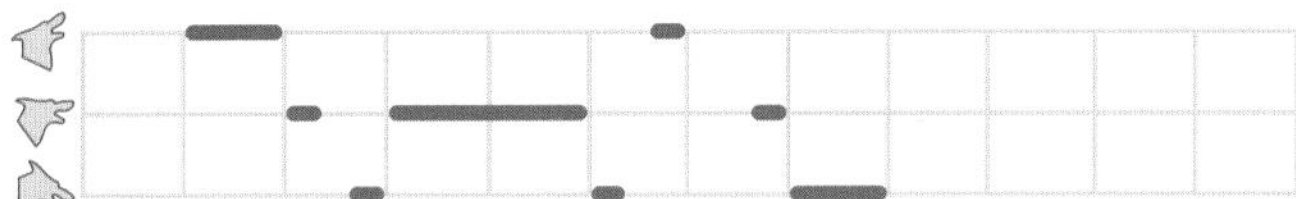

Howling Stone 07

Great Spin

07

The final Howling Stone is on the west side of Hidden Village. To reach it, smash through the windows of the nearby building; the stone is in the backyard. After you activate the stone, the golden wolf will appear in northern Castle Town along the exit that leads to Hyrule Castle. The warrior will teach you the Great Spin, a stronger, farther-reaching version of the standard spin attack. You can activate the Great Spin only when your health is full.

Upgrades

A hero can never have too much stuff. Seek out upgrades to carry additional bombs, arrows, money, and more.

Bomb Bags

You can acquire three regular-sized Bomb Bags during the quest. Buy the first one when you purchase bombs at Barnes Bomb Shop after conquering the Goron Mines. You'll get the second one when you help Iza unblock the river in Lanayru Province. You can find the third one by blowing up the giant underwater rock in the throne room of Zora's Domain with a Water Bomb.

If you score 25 points playing Iza's Rapid Ride minigame, you can earn an upgrade that doubles the capacity of all your Bomb Bags.

Wallets

Agitha in Castle Town will reward you with bigger wallets when you bring her Golden Bugs. She'll give you the Big Wallet (which can hold 600 rupees) when you give her your first bug, and a Giant Wallet (which holds 1,000 rupees) when you give her all 24 insects.

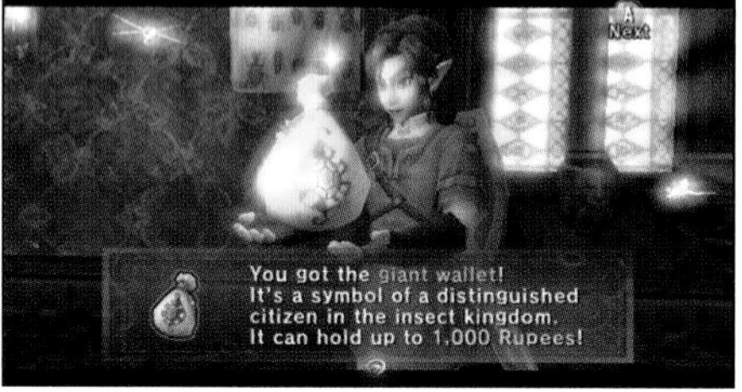

Quivers

Normally you can carry only 30 arrows, but if you succeed at the STAR minigame in Castle Town, you can enhance your carrying capacity. When you beat the STAR minigame the first time, you'll earn the Big Quiver, which allows you to carry 60 arrows. When you beat the game again, you'll get the Giant Quiver, which holds 100. A bigger quiver comes in especially handy when you're exploring the Cave of Ordeals.

You'll need the Clawshot to beat the STAR minigame the first time, and the Double Clawshots to beat it the second time.

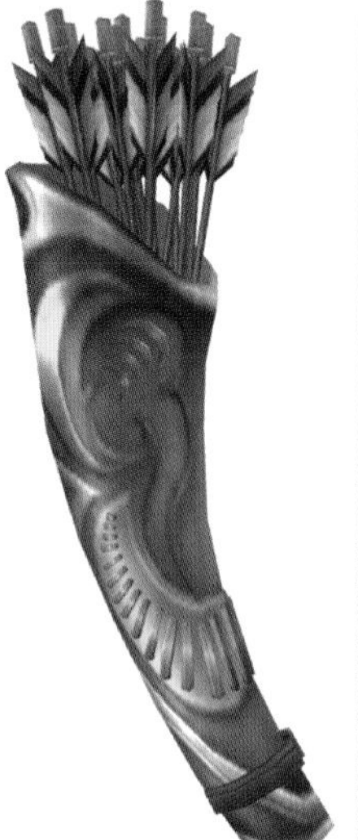

Magic Armor

The magic armor makes Link completely impervious to damage, but it comes at a price—it literally runs on rupees. Your rupees will deplete as long as you wear the armor, and your cash will disappear even faster if you get hit. When you run out of rupees, the armor will stop providing protection, and it will slow Link to a crawl.

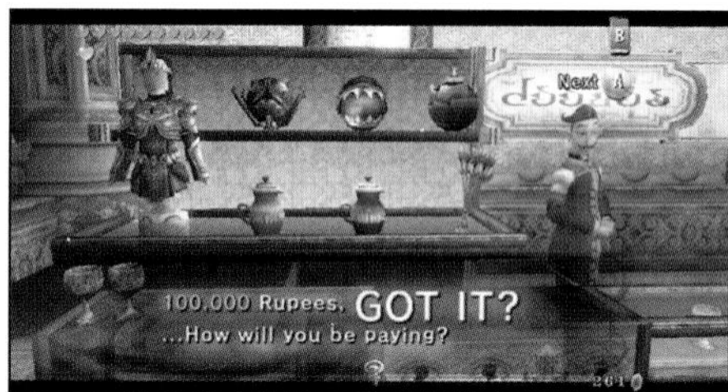

At Malo Mart in Kakariko Village you'll find the Goron elders asking for a 1,000-rupee donation to help restore the west bridge into Castle Town. When you give them the funds they need, they'll request 2,000 more rupees to open a store in Castle Town. After you've given the Gorons the cash they need, Malo Mart will expand into Castle Town and take over the overpriced shop in the southwest corner of the town square, where you can buy the armor for 598 rupees.

Bottles

You can find four bottles as you explore Hyrule. Use them to hold fairies, Chu Jelly, Lantern Oil, and more. To get the first bottle, go to Sera's shop after you catch a fish for Sera's cat in Ordon Village. She'll give you a bottle that's half-filled with milk. You can buy the second bottle from Coro, the Lantern Oil salesman in Faron Woods. He'll sell you a bottle filled with oil for 100 rupees. For the third bottle, visit Hena's Fishing Hole and head to the small bridge on the west side. Bobber-fish on the west side of the bridge, and you'll eventually reel in a bottle. You'll receive the fourth bottle from Jovani. Retrieve at least 20 Poe Souls, then return to his house in Castle Town. He'll reward you with a bottle filled with Fairy Tears.

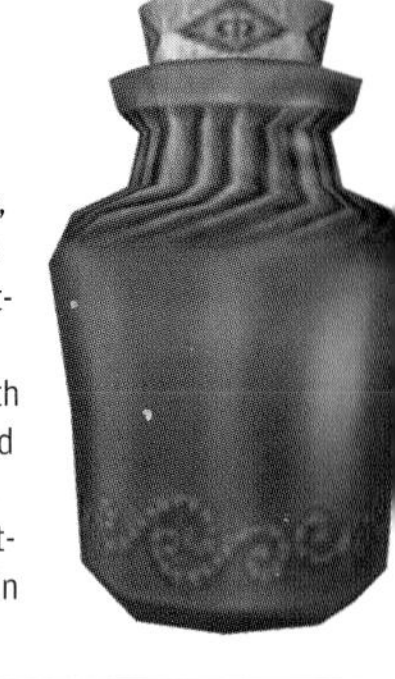

The Cave of Ordeals

With 50 floors of increasingly challenging enemies, the Cave of Ordeals lives up to its name.

Be Prepared

Once you enter the Cave of Ordeals, you're on your own: there's no way to replenish your ammo, and few opportunities to restore your health. Come prepared with bottles full of healing potions, the largest quivers and Bomb Bags available, the Magic Armor, and a wallet full of rupees. You'll also need certain weapons to proceed past every 10th level: the Spinner at level 11, the ball and chain at level 21, the Dominion Rod at level 31, and the Double Clawshots at level 41. If you aren't properly equipped, ask the Great Fairy to warp you back to the surface.

When you speak to the Great Fairy at every 10th floor, she'll praise your strength and release fairies into one of the Spirit Springs in the world above. After you conquer all 50 floors, the Great Fairy will reward you with the Great Fairy Tears, which you can replenish at any Spirit Spring.

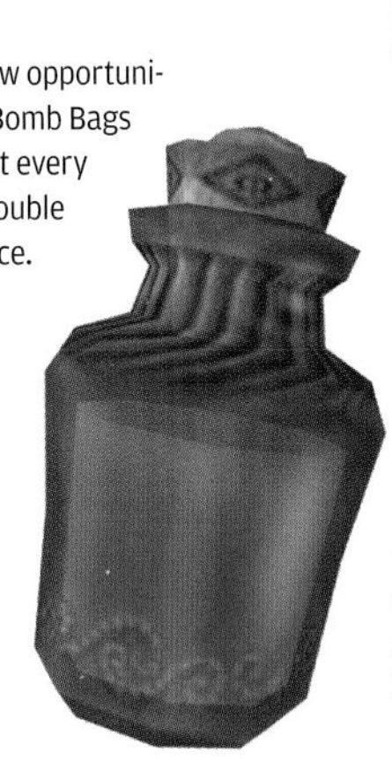

Gerudo Desert

The entrance to the Cave of Ordeals is located at the Gerudo Desert warp spot. You'll be able to enter the cave once you teleport the piece of Eldin Bridge back to where it belongs—in Hyrule Field in Eldin Province.

The Ledge Gives You the Edge

Each floor of the cave has a ledge that you'll leap off of before you face the enemies below. Use the ledge to scope out the situation and to take out enemies with your bow or the Clawshot. If you see especially tough foes, like the ice monsters on floors 35 and 38, equip your Magic Armor.

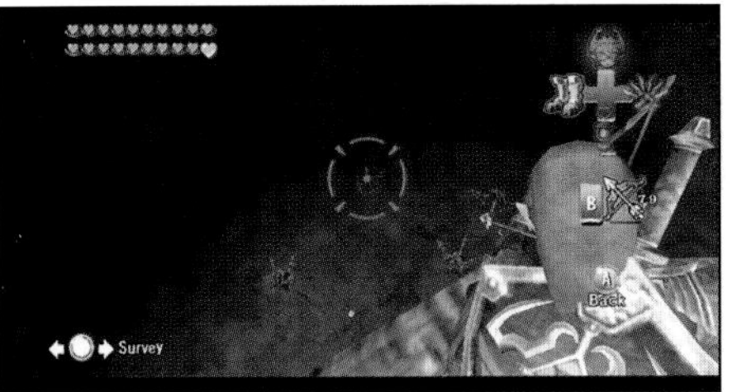

Soul Survivors

If you're trying to track down all of the Poe Souls, a visit to the Cave of Ordeals is a must—three Poes are hiding within. You'll find the Poes on floors 17, 33, and 44 of the cave. Before you wrest the souls from the Poes, it's best to take out the other enemies in the room.

Keep Your Distance

On some floors, certain enemies will remain inert until you get close to them. When you're facing the statues on floor 41 or the dragon knights on floor 48, stay close to the wall when you drop, and maintain your distance so you won't have to fight all the enemies at once.

Dig It!

The cave's floors are generally devoid of helpful items, but if you dig as a wolf, you can find hearts or rupees on some floors. Look for hearts on floors 8, 18, 22, 27, 34, and 45, and rupees on floors 14 and 39.

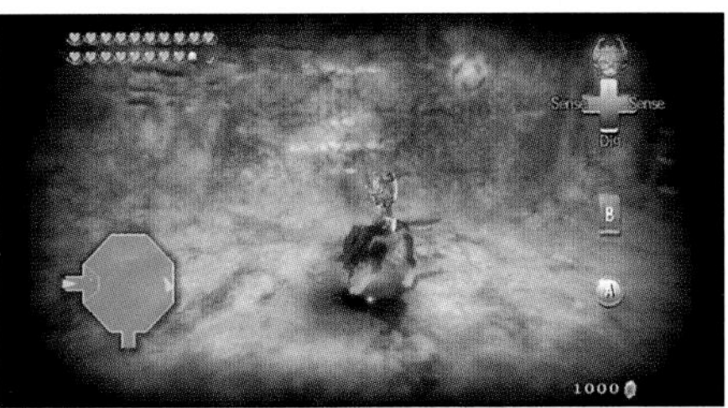

Diversions

Take some time off from saving the kingdom to earn rupees, equipment upgrades, and a few Pieces of Heart.

STAR Minigame

Enter the tent just south of Castle Town's east road to participate in a shiny-orb-collection game. You'll pay 10 rupees to enter the cage for 30 seconds of action. The Clawshot puts the goal in your grasp. The Double Clawshots increase your chances. You'll earn a 60-arrow quiver for your first victory. Play again (for 15 rupees) to try for a 100-arrow quiver.

Start by climbing onto the first platform, turn toward the center, then engage your Clawshot. Grapple to the cage wall while aiming for the orbs. You should be able to grab at least two orbs per flight.

Fruit Pop Flight Challenge

Parrot Plumm oversees a game that takes you on a flight from Lake Hylia to the Zora's River area. You'll initiate the game by howling at Plumm's location on the lake's west shore. The object is to pop fruit-shaped balloons as you fly. You'll rack up a big score by going for a single balloon type. The per-pop maximum for watermelons is 512 points. For oranges it's 1,536 points. For strawberries it's 5,120 points. You'll get a Piece of Heart for scoring 10,000 points or more on a run, and 100 rupees for every score-topping run after that.

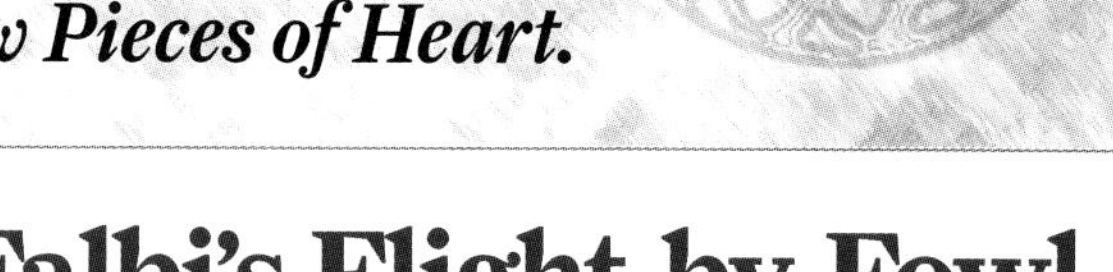

Falbi's Flight-by-Fowl

When you take Fyer's normal cannon flight in Lake Hylia, you'll land at Falbi's clifftop location. There you can pay 20 rupees to fly with a Cucco down to the water and attempt to land on an ascending series of prize platforms. The key to an accurate flight is to regulate your speed as you drop. Press up to increase your speed. Press down to decrease it.

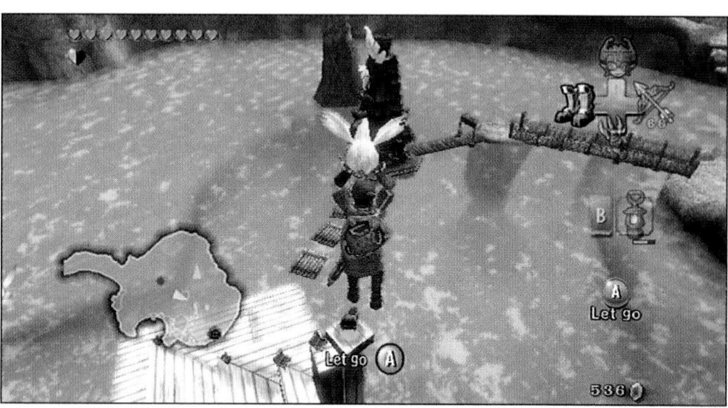

After you jump off the ledge, you'll see rupee symbols to the left and right. Collect them if you wish, but don't lose sight of the platforms straight ahead. Landing on the rotating top platforms earns you 100 rupees. The platform below that has a Piece of Heart.

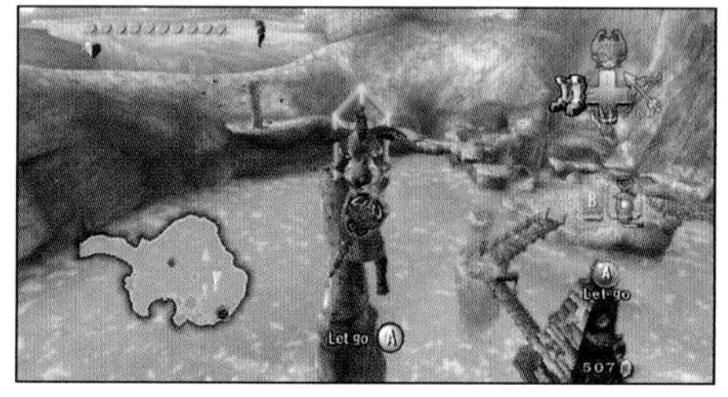

There's a natural-rock tower south and slightly east of the starting place. If you land on the tower then hit all of the Flying Guays in the area with arrows, rupees will rain down into the water below. Dive in and take an 80-rupee swim.

Snowpeak Sledding

After you've conquered the Snowpeak Ruins and claimed the second Mirror Shard, you can race the yetis in a free sledding competition. You'll find the couple at the top of Snowpeak, up the hill next to the warp point. If you talk to Yeto, the male yeti, he'll challenge you to a race. After you beat him, you can race his wife, Yeta, who's much faster. Once you're on your frozen leaf, move left or right with the Control Stick and press the A Button to crouch, then release it to jump.

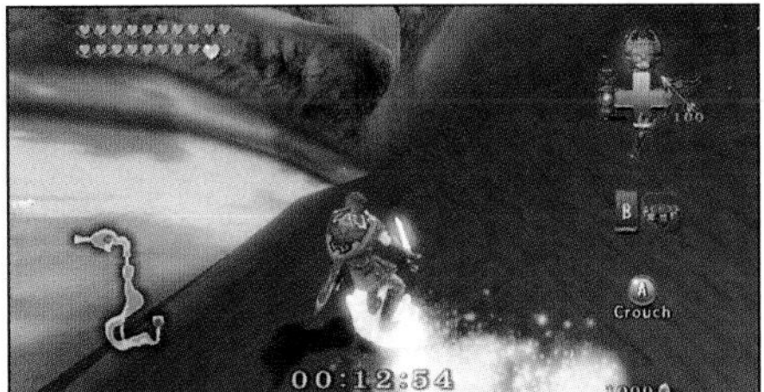

1 There are three sections of the course that you can use to your advantage. The first is right after the initial gap. Crouch as you go down the hill, then jump onto the right snow embankment. Stay on the embankment as you make the right turn, and jump off so you land centered on the course as you near the bridge.

2 The second important spot is right after the tree field. Stay to the right and crouch as you go down the slope, then jump onto the right snow bank. Stay on the snow bank and follow the trail of rupees left onto an overpass—using this shortcut is the only way to beat Yeta.

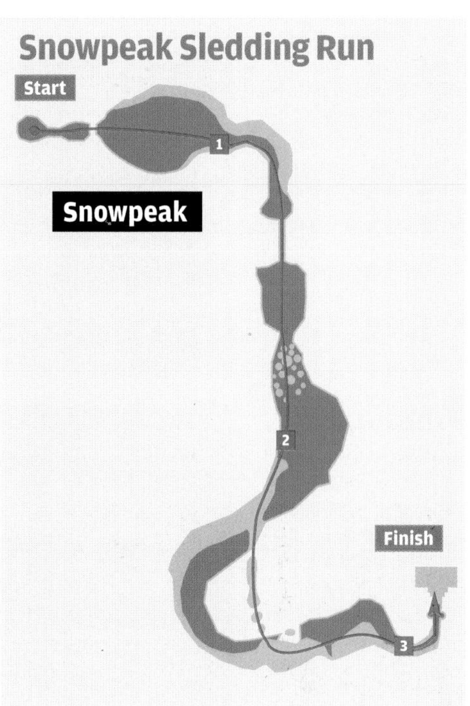

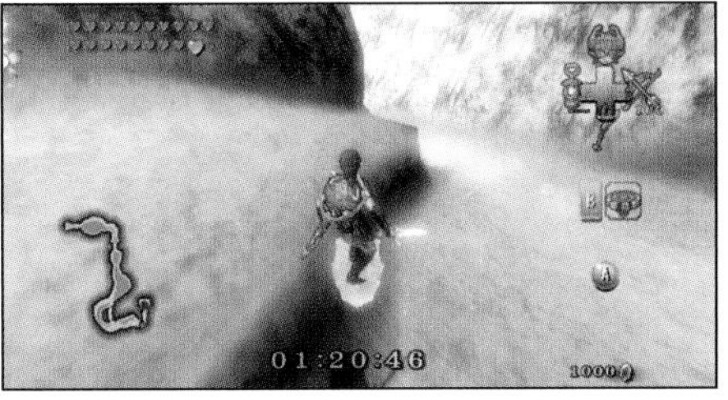

3 The third tricky spot is on the final left curve. As you enter the turn, jump onto the left embankment to maintain your speed without crashing. When you come off the embankment, stay centered and don't hit the guardrails on the bridge or you'll probably get knocked off your leaf. The reward for defeating both yetis is a Piece of Heart.

Iza's Rapid Ride

Iza's boat-rental concession is in the Upper Zora's River area. After you defeat shadow beings in the area then take a ride to clear away rocks for Iza (earning you a Bomb Bag), the stylishly quaffed shopkeeper will challenge you to hit targets while floating downriver. The game costs 20 rupees. A 25-point total earns you a size upgrade for all your Bomb Bags, then 50 rupees.

Green-yellow targets are worth one point. Red targets are worth two. If you hit the wall, you'll lose a point. Concentrate on steering the canoe. If you pass a target while avoiding an obstacle, you'll still have a chance to hit it by pivoting in the canoe.

Catch the Big One

Going up against the villains of Hyrule is one kind of challenge. Fishing for the Hylian loach is an entirely different kind of challenge. When you want to take a breather from your adventure, head up to the fishing hole north of Upper Zora's River or drop a line in any of several bodies of water. With the remote as your rod and the nunchuk as your reel, the game provides an authentic fishing experience.

Finding Fish

Where there's water, there are fish. You can use the standard rod to bobber-fish anywhere you please, including Ordon Village and Upper Zora's River. Bee larva or worms (for bait) will help you catch bigger fish. The only place for lure-fishing (which requires a canoe) is the fishing hole. Give Hena 20 rupees for a lure-rod rental.

Various Lures

There are five types of lure. The standard three are the swimmer (an all-around good lure), the popper (which attracts deep-swimming fish), and the spinner (good for catching skittish fish). You can get the frog lure by playing the Rollgoal game (see below). Once you've lure-fished for a pike, a catfish, and a bass, you'll find the sinking lure in the fishing hole's northwest-corner cove by dropping a bobber line. If Hena sees you using it, though, she'll take it away.

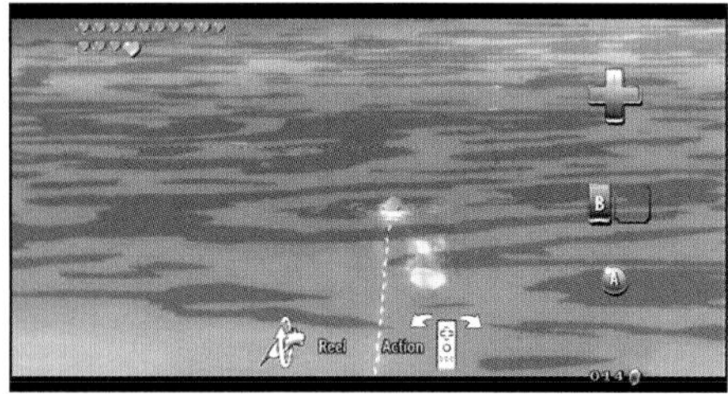

The Rollgoal

By exploring Hena's shop, you'll discover a game that involves rolling a marble on a wooden path. Press C to look at the Rollgoal, and pay five rupees to give it a whirl. If you're successful, you'll earn 10 rupees and a chance to try a trickier puzzle once you've left and returned to the shop. After you've gone through eight puzzles, Hena will give you the frog lure.

The goal of the game is to guide a ball along a narrow path by tilting the remote. Start out slowly. There's a time limit, but it won't be a big factor until you get to the really complex paths. When negotiating tight turns, try stuttered movements to tilt the playing field by small increments, and move the Control Stick to correct the camera. At small hills, rock the remote back and forth to build momentum.

The Fish of Hyrule

You'll catch a Greengill and a Reekfish as part of the story, but there are other fish to catch too. Your finds appear in your fish journal, and the largest examples of fish that you've caught through lure-fishing go into Hena's aquarium. There are some unusual fish (Bomb Fish—which you keep in your Bomb Bag—and Skull Fish) in the Lakebed Temple. You'll throw them back.

Greengill

The Greengill is a common specimen found in the Kakariko Village lake. At the beginning of the adventure, you'll catch one from a dock to make Sera's cat return to the shop.

Hyrule Bass

If you're bobber-fishing around Hyrule, look for bass in Kakariko Village. You'll also find them in the fishing hole. The frog lure and swimmer lure are both good choices to take on bass-fishing trips.

Hylian Loach

Crawl through a hole in the Kakariko Village graveyard to catch a baby loach near Zora's tomb. Or go to the fishing hole's northern cove during the summer to find the big one. (The seasons change every time you enter the fishing hole area.) Use the frog lure or sinking lure for the job.

Hylian Pike

Pike swim around the Upper Zora's River area. When you're lure-fishing for the nervous fish at the fishing hole, the spinner lure will help you.

Ordon Catfish

You'll find catfish in the deepest sections of the Ordon Village waters and in the fishing hole. Use the popper lure at the fishing hole to attract them to the surface.

Reekfish

The red fish of Zora's Domain are a yeti favorite. While you're searching for the Snowpeak Ruins, you'll catch a Reekfish by dropping the coral lure into the water near the area's mother-and-child rock formations.

Nintendo GameCube Version

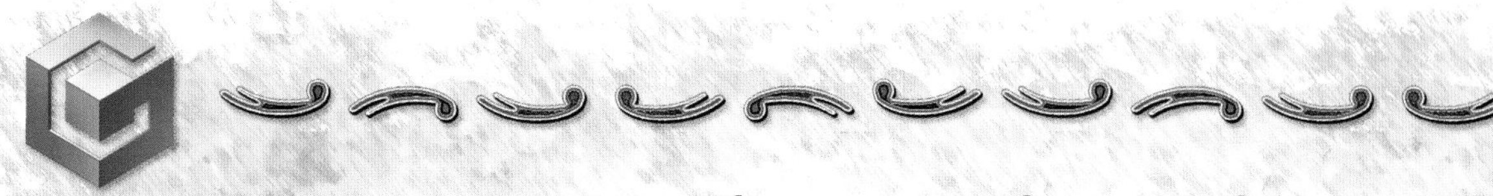

Control Cubed

Though the Wii and GCN versions have strong similarities, they differ greatly in play control. Here's the lowdown.

Nintendo GameCube Controls

Some of the Wii and GCN controls are related. The Control Stick and A Buttons, for example, have the same functions. And whereas pressing C in the Wii game adjusts the camera, you manipulate the C Stick in the GCN version. The biggest differences are in the attacks. The GCN controls are as follows. For Wii controls, turn to page 6.

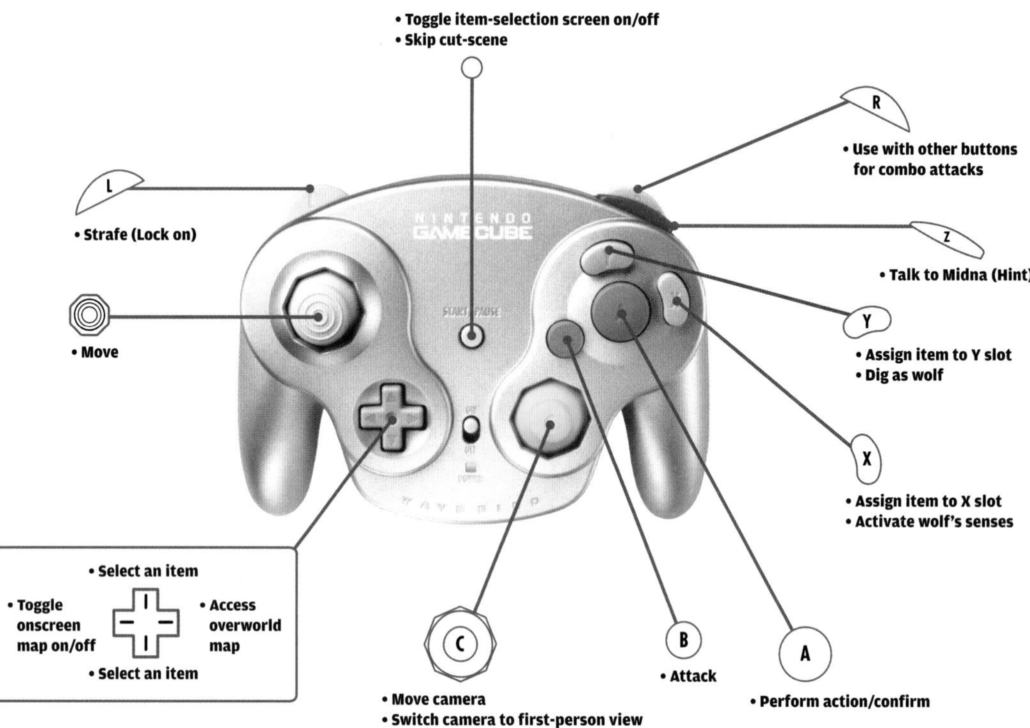

Human Moves

In human form, Link is a sword-wielding, bow-hunting, adventuring hero. There's no stopping him when he's on a roll. He doesn't have animal instincts like his wolf counterpart, but he does have a full arsenal of weapons and tools.

Walk and Roll

The Control Stick handles all basic movement, including climbing over obstacles and jumping over gaps. Press the A Button while you're moving to make Link roll. The A Button alone handles most interactions with people and objects. Use it to converse with villagers, pick up pots, and even crawl into narrow spaces.

Sidestep

The evasive sidestepping maneuver provides a great way for you to avoid attacks but stay on target for counter swipes. Press and hold the L Button then press left or right on the Control Pad and push the A Button.

Backflip

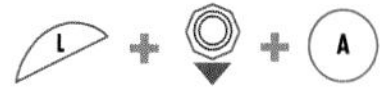

The backflip is closely related to Link's sidestepping move. Press and hold L then press down on the Control Stick and push the A Button. Link will jump back and flip.

Slice

B

Press B to slice with your sword. A quick tap of the button triggers a backhand motion. A slightly longer press of the button triggers a forehand motion.

Stab

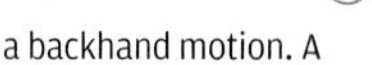

The surprising sword thrust is always right on target. Press and hold L, press up on the Control Pad, and tap B. If you perform the move four times in a row, Link will put a little extra effort into his forward thrust with the last move.

Jump Attack

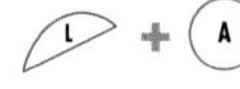

Much more powerful than a standard attack, the jump attack is a great move for when you are within reach of multiple targets. Press and hold L then press A. Link will jump and slice. Keep pressing L after the first foe is down to target the next enemy automatically.

Spin Attack

The 360-degree sword spin and swipe is a very effective way to hit several enemies with one maneuver. Its only drawback is the time that it takes to charge. Press and hold B, wait for a shimmer to travel to the end of Link's sword, then let go. Alternatively, you can spin the Control Stick 360 degrees and press B.

Aim and Fire

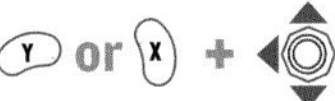

Every projectile weapon or tool uses the same basic controls. Once you have the item mapped to the X or Y Button, press and hold that button to go into aiming mode. Use the Control Stick to aim, then release the button to fire. Some items, such as the Clawshot, show you aiming reticles. Others, such as the bow, don't.

Wolf Moves

The four-legged hero runs quickly and attacks with fury. Passenger Midna rides along for support. Press Z to start a conversation with her or to get her help after she calls. In the Wii version, she giggles. In the GCN version, a whistling sound gets your attention.

Move and Interact

Use the Control Stick to make Link's canine form run and climb. Press A while the dog is moving to have him charge. The A Button alone lets you interact with the environment: talk to animals, crawl through tight openings, pick up objects, and open treasure chests, among other actions.

Sidestep

Whether Link is in human form or canine form, his sidestepping maneuver is a good evasive tactic. Hold the L Button then press left or right on the Control Stick and depress the A Button.

Jump Back/Backflip

The wolf can pull off two backward-moving maneuvers. Hold L then press down and push A once to have the wolf jump back, or double-tap A to make him flip backwards.

Bite

The wolf's basic attack is a lunging bite. Press B to have him surge forth with his teeth and claws. If you pull off a bite move three times in quick succession, the fourth move will be a spinning tail whip.

Jump Attack

The powerful jump attack is feared by both ground-dwelling enemies and hovering foes. Press and hold L to target your enemy then press A to make the wolf pounce. He will grab onto some enemies with his claws. Press A repeatedly to perform a sustained biting attack.

Dark-Energy Attack

The same controls that call Link's spin attack trigger a dark-energy attack when Midna is your passenger. Press and hold B to charge up the attack and spread the dark energy. When you release the button, the wolf will pounce on all enemies touched by the darkness.

Assisted Jumps

Sometimes when you are looking over a wide gap, Midna will call and a Z Button icon will appear, indicating that your companion can help you clear the gap. Press Z, then hold L and press A to jump. If Midna flies off to another location, press A again to keep up.

Canine Specialties

The wolf has enhanced senses that help him detect Poes, special scents, and places where he can dig for treasure or burrow into tunnels. Press X to engage those senses. Then press Y to dig at places where your enhanced vision makes spots on the ground sparkle.

Hidden Skills

Your path will cross with that of the golden wolf several times during the adventure if you take the time to make lupine music at Howling Stones. By getting the shiny wolf's attention, you'll be able to learn seven hidden skills. See page 160 for more details.

Ending Blow

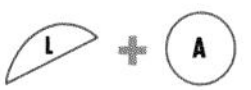

Your first hidden skill (and the only one that you will have to learn as part of the story) is a finishing move. After you've knocked your foe to the ground, hold L to target the creature, then press A to jump and plant the sword in your prey.

Shield Attack

Your sword isn't the only close-contact weapon in your arsenal. You can knock enemies senseless or deflect their projectiles with your shield. Hold L to target the foe then press R to push out with the shield. A direct hit will stun your enemy and make it vulnerable to more attacks.

Back Slice

The Back Slice has you moving around your enemy and hitting it from behind. Press L to target your foe, then press left or right on the Control Stick and push A to jump to the side. Press A again to roll behind the enemy, and finish off with a B-Button swirling slash.

Helm Splitter

You've already learned the Shield Attack. Now take it one step farther. Hold L then press R to hit your enemy with your shield. Once your target is stunned, press A to make Link jump over the foe, hitting its head with his sword as he flies.

Mortal Draw

Approach your foe with your weapon sheathed. Don't target the enemy. Wait for it to lunge toward you, then press A. You'll pull out your sword and defeat the creature with a single slice.

Jump Strike

The ultimate jumping attack allows you to hit one enemy very hard, or strike a group of enemies with a single blow. Target by holding L; then press and hold A, and release A once you're charged up. Link will jump and swing wide, hitting everything in his way.

Great Spin

The Great Spin is a beefed-up spin attack that lets you cut through every enemy within range. Press and hold A then let go once the shimmering light travels to the end of Link's sword. The surrounding enemies will suffer a brutal blow.

Fishing Control

You can fish for fun at several Hyrule locations, and to advance the story in Ordon Village and on your way to Snowpeak Ruins. Your standard rod allows for bobber-fishing. A rented rod (at the fishing hole) allows you to fish with lures.

Bobber-Fishing

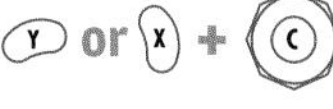

Your first fishing experience will be with a bobber rod. Select it from your list of items and assign it to the X or Y Button. Press that button to equip it, then use the C Stick to cast out and pull in the line.

Lure-Fishing

You'll rent a canoe and a lure rod from Hena at the fishing hole. Manipulate the Control Stick to paddle the canoe, then press B to equip the rod. Pull back the C Stick then let go of it to cast a line. When the line is in the water, move the lure with the Control Stick. Press B to reel it in, or wait for a bite. Once you have a bite, manipulate the Control Stick, the B Button, and the A Button to match the instructions on the bottom of the screen.

Overworld Maps

The GameCube version of Twilight Princess is just as vast as its Wii counterpart. Use the overworld maps to navigate Hyrule's fields and locate hidden items like Pieces of Heart.

Hyrule Kingdom

East Meets West

Link is a lefty in the GCN version of The Legend of Zelda: Twilight Princess (as he has appeared in previous Legend of Zelda adventures), but has become right-handed for the game's Wii version to conform to the remote-swinging control scheme. The difference has led to a direction reversal between the two versions. What is east in the GCN version is west in the Wii version, and vice versa. The following maps for the GCN version reflect that change.

Ordona Province

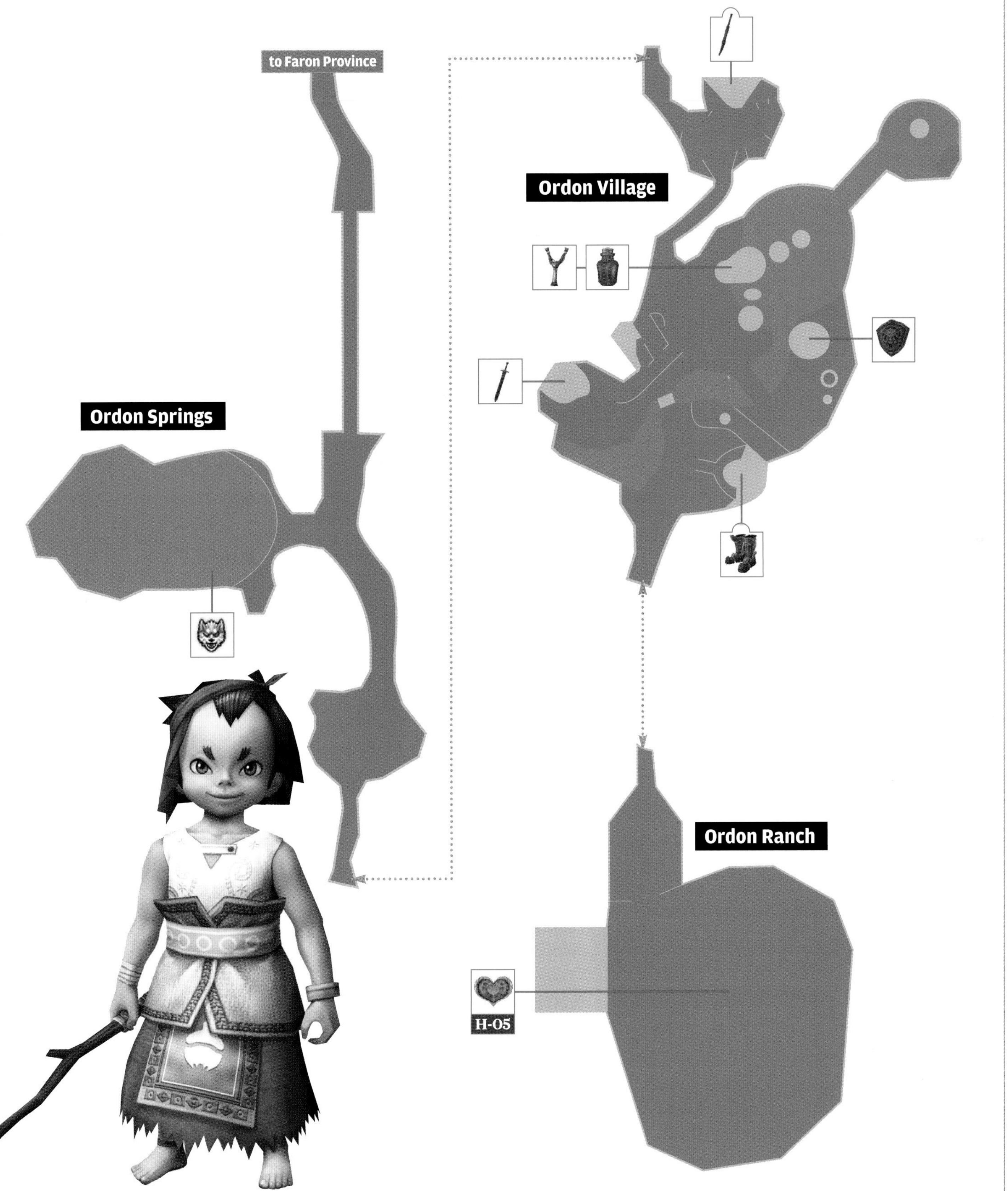

Faron Province

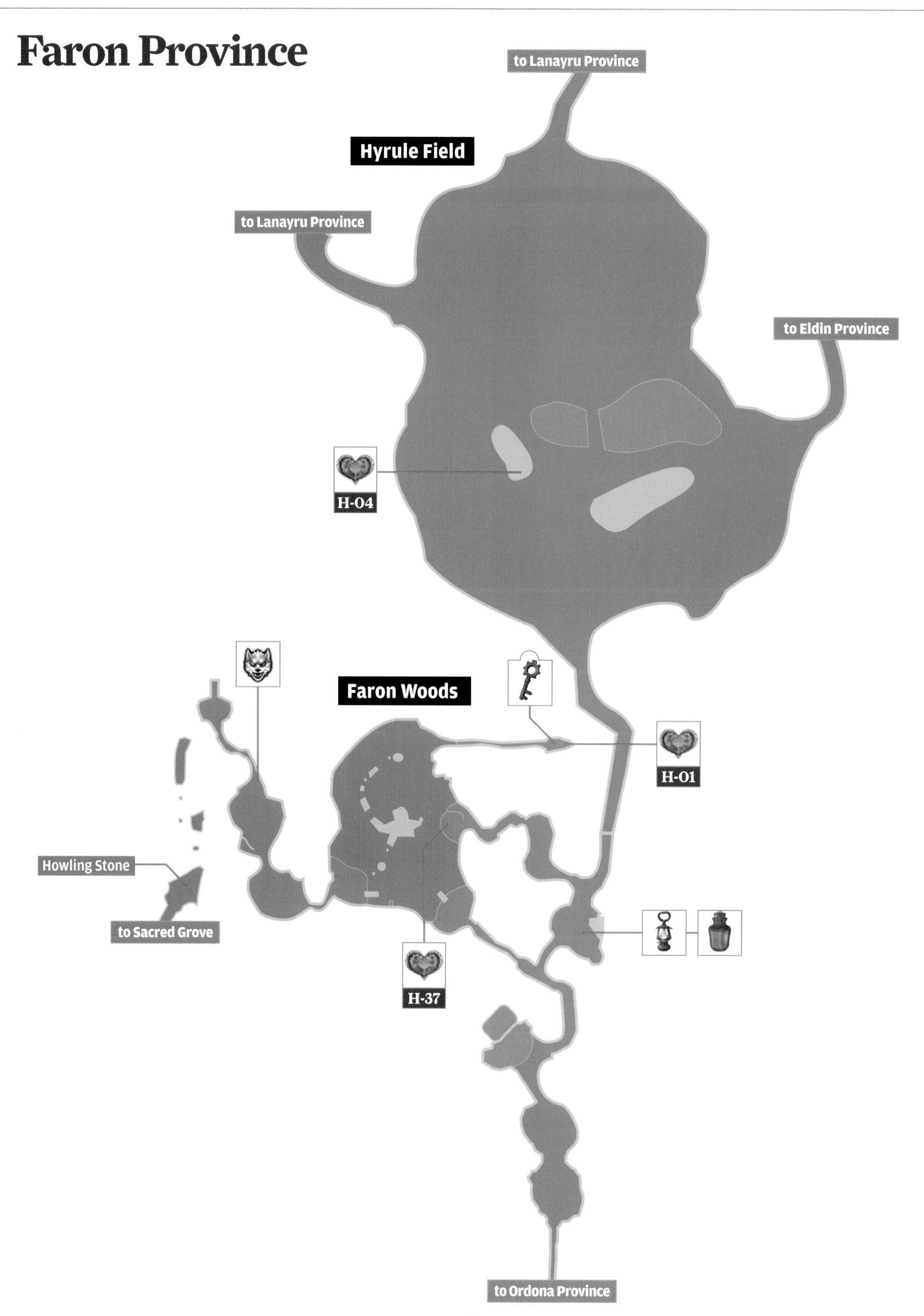

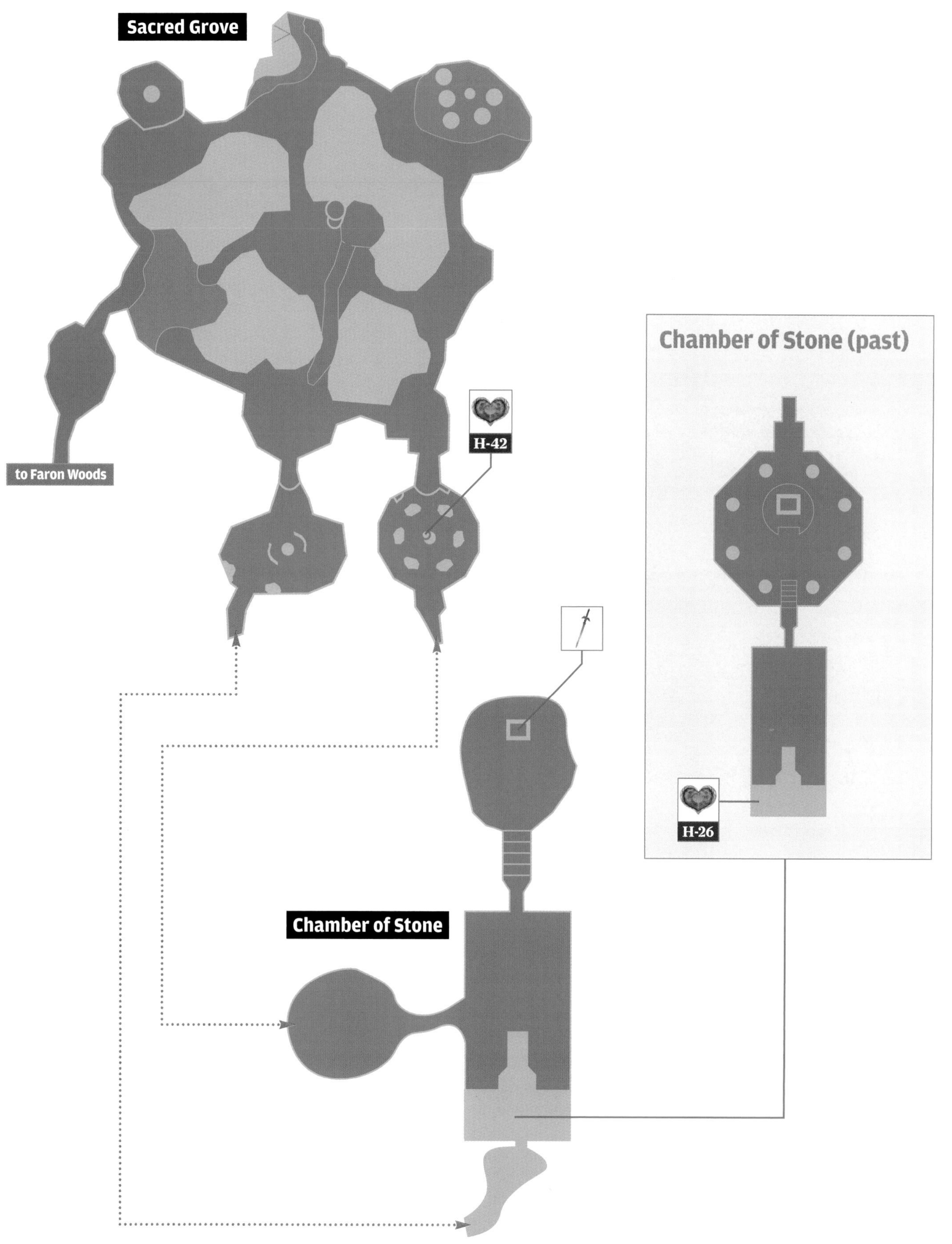
Sacred Grove
to Faron Woods
H-42
Chamber of Stone (past)
H-26
Chamber of Stone

Eldin Province

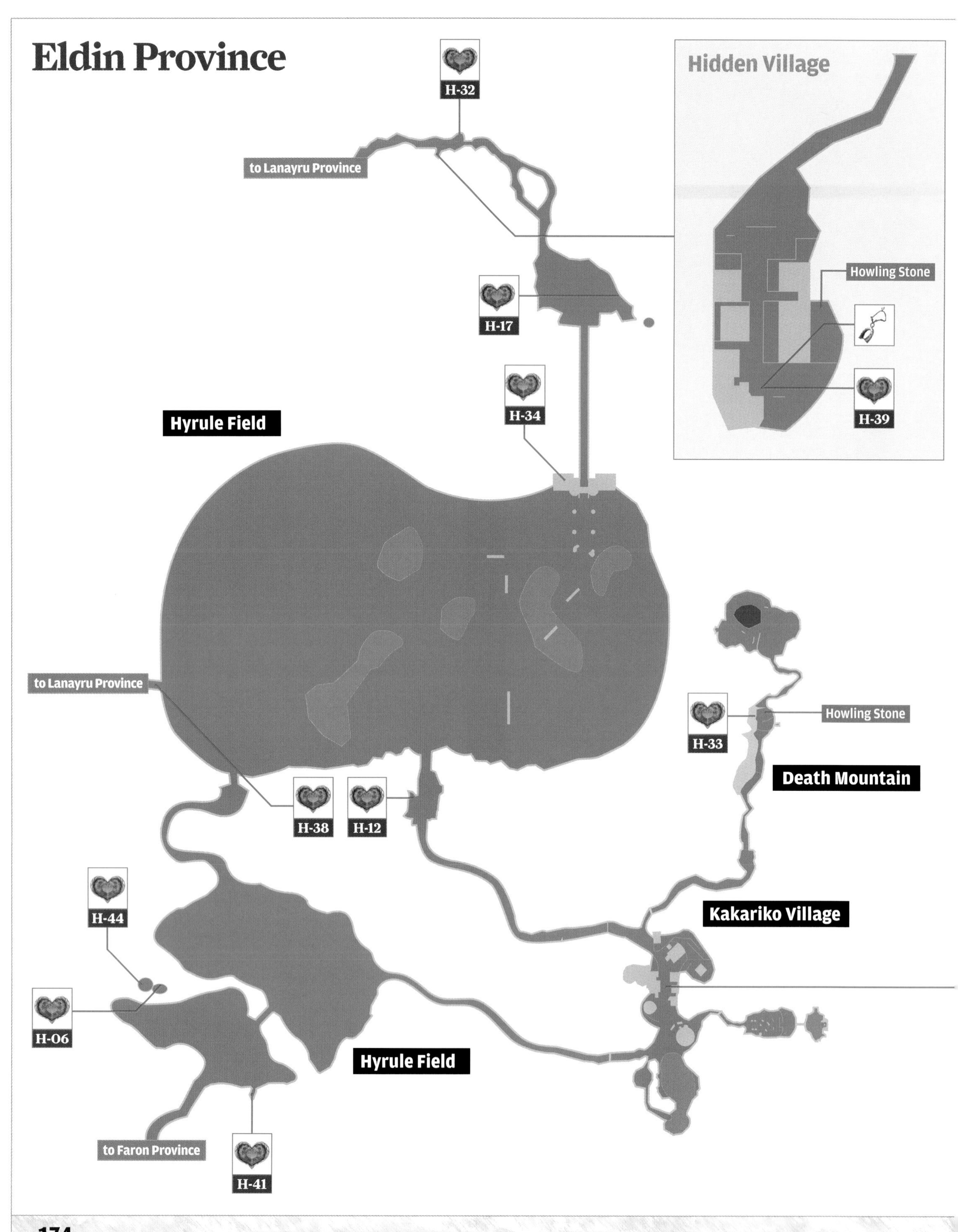

Kakariko Village Detail

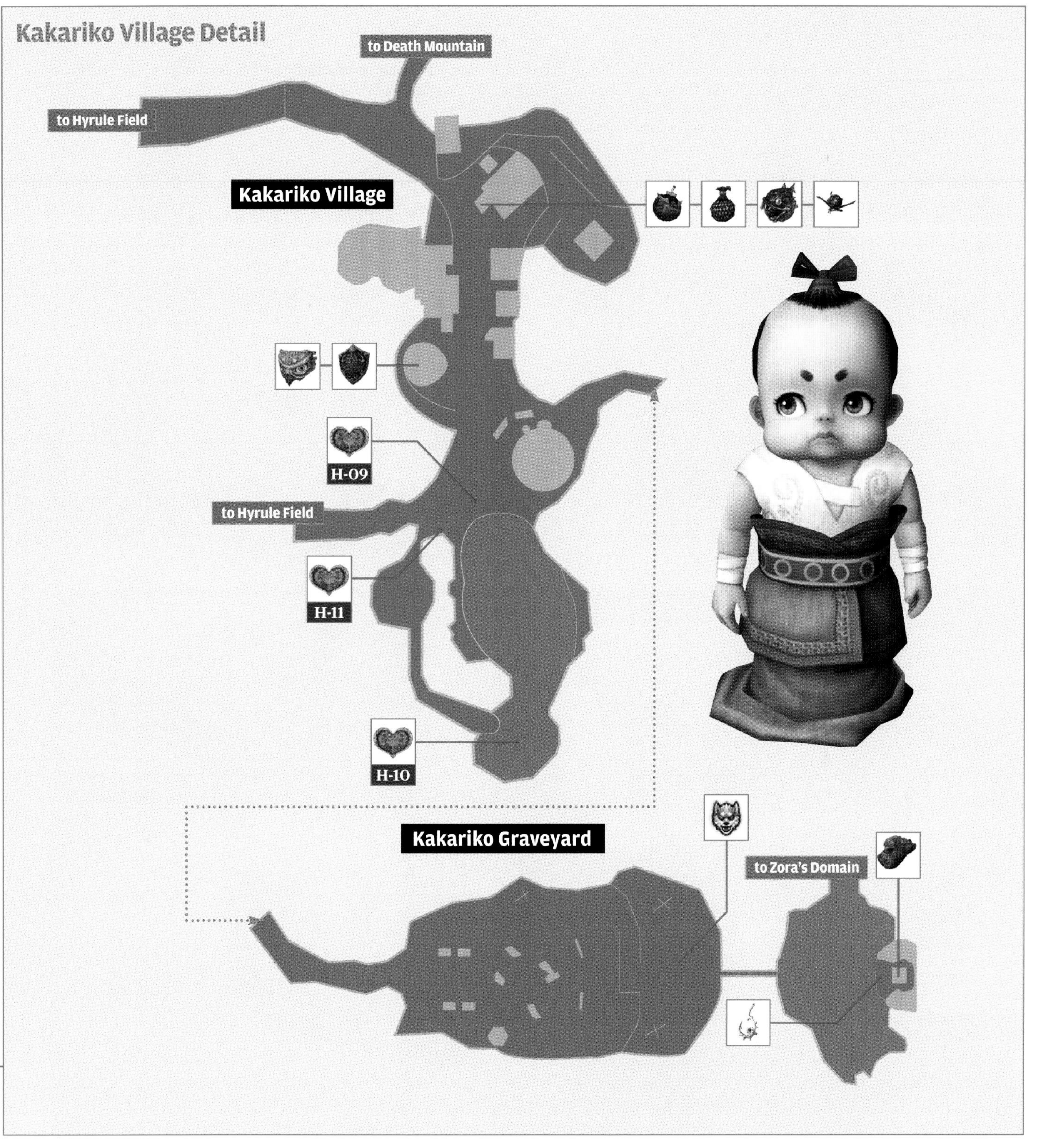

Lanayru Province

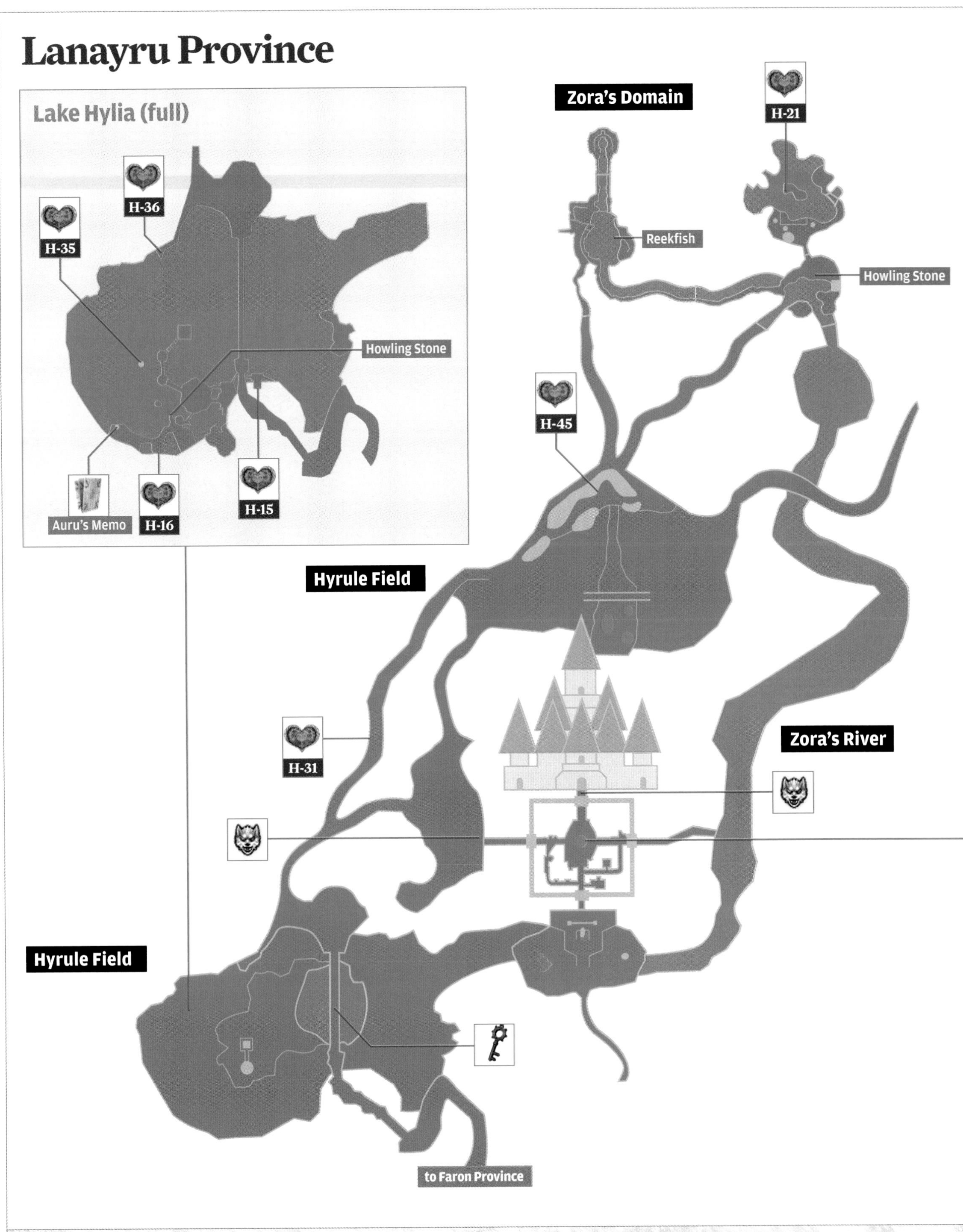

Castle Town

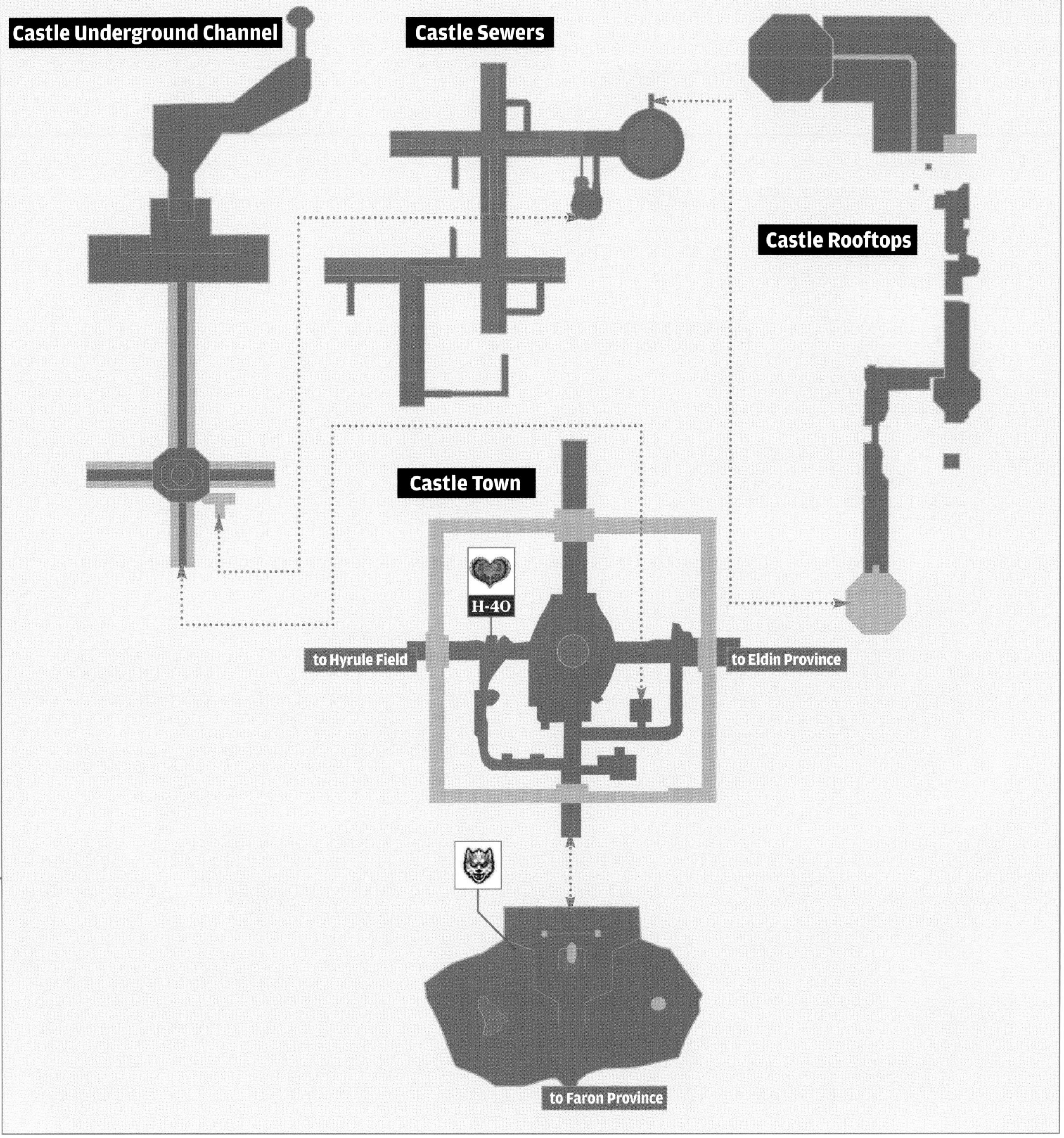

Castle Underground Channel
Castle Sewers
Castle Rooftops
Castle Town
H-40
to Hyrule Field
to Eldin Province
to Faron Province

Gerudo Desert

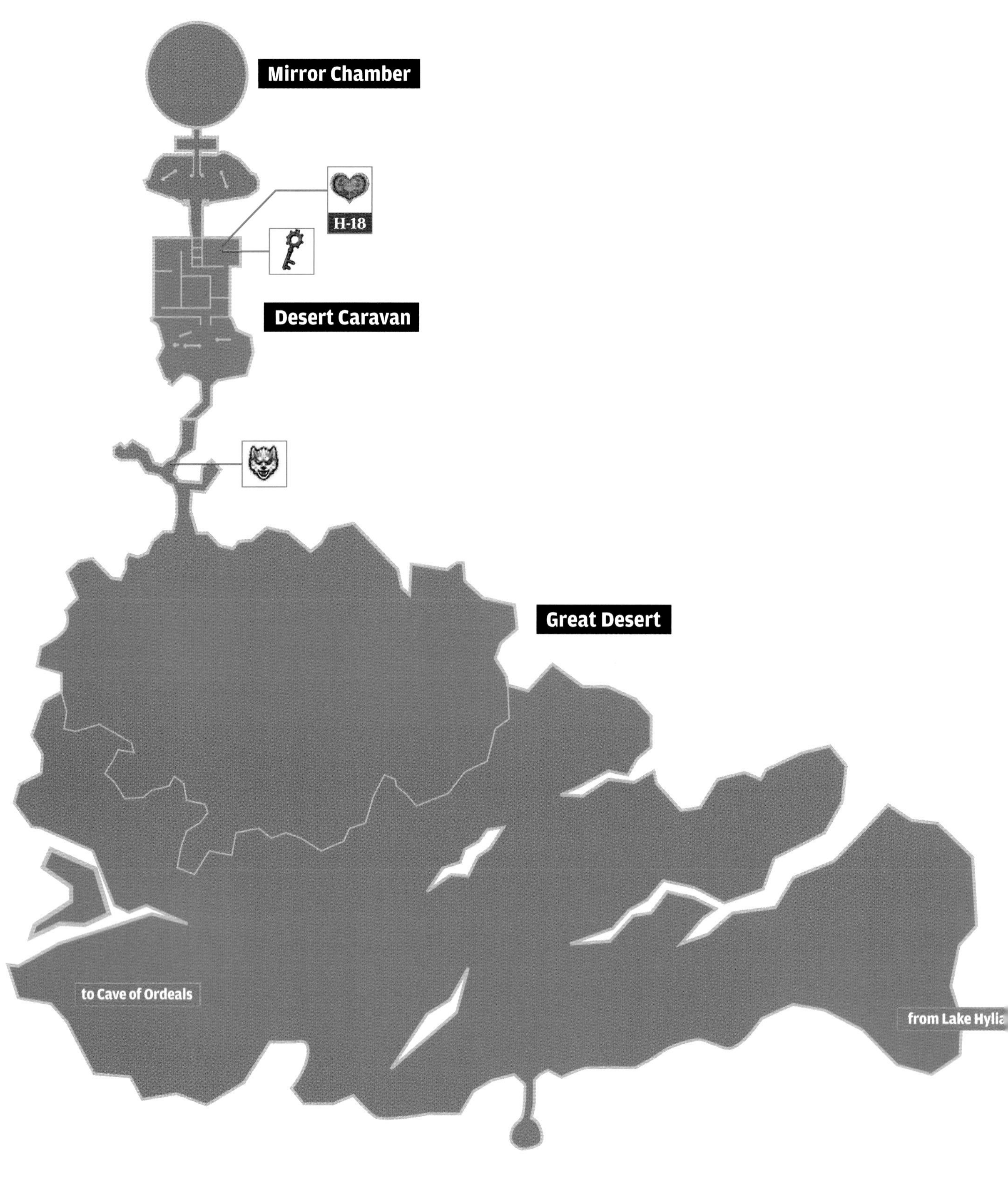

Peak Province

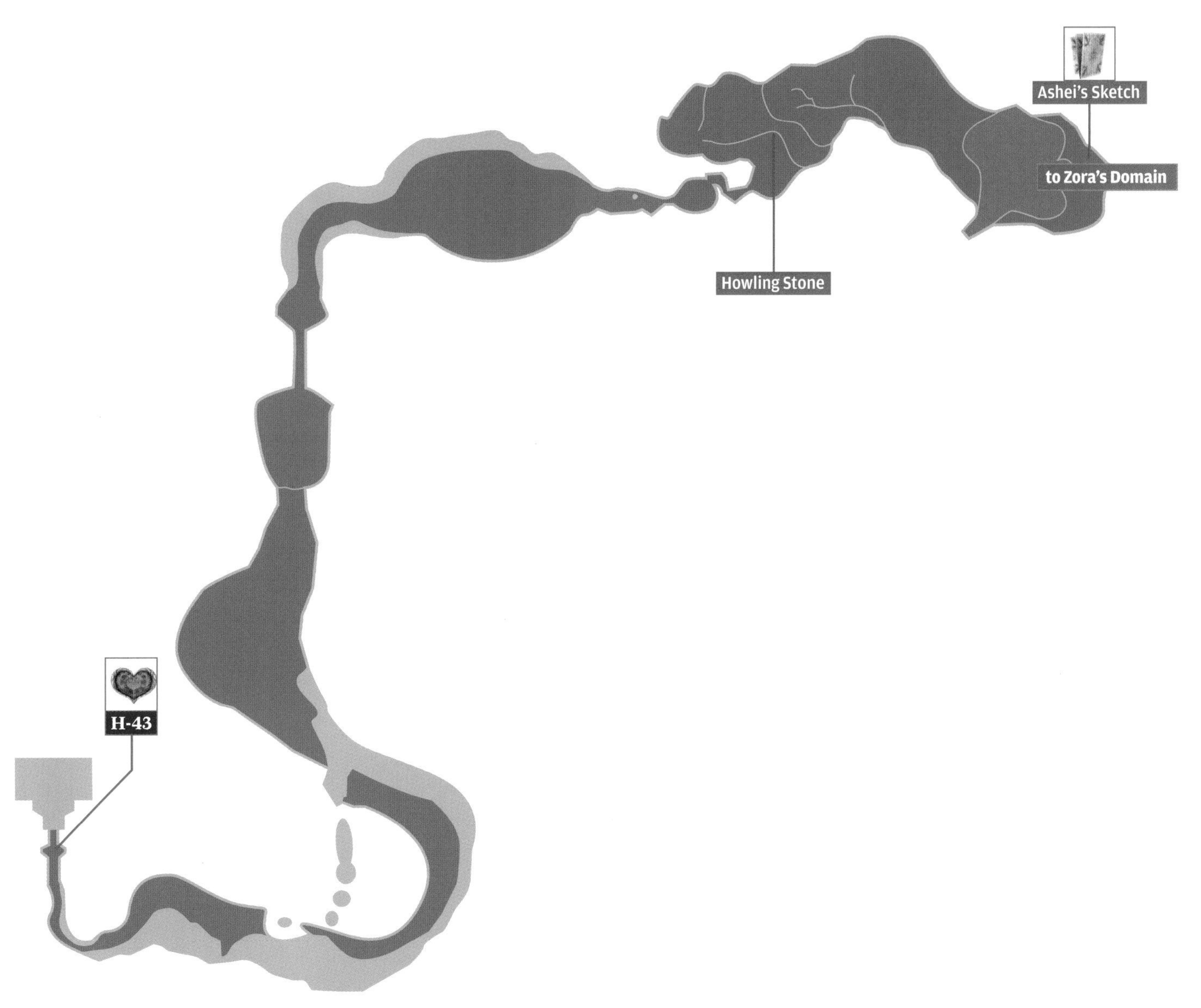

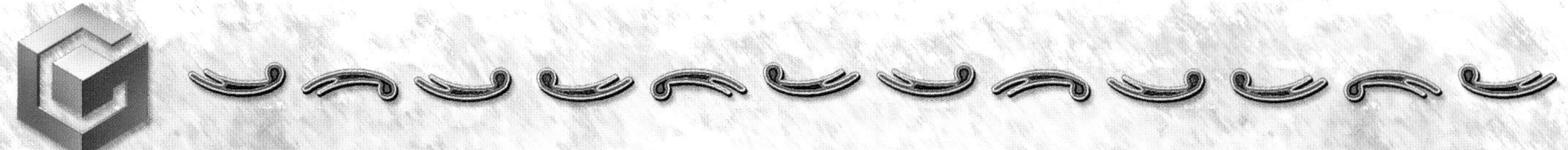

Dungeon Maps

Use the following maps to locate every dungeon in the GameCube version of Twilight Princess, and find the essential items within each.

Dungeon Entrances

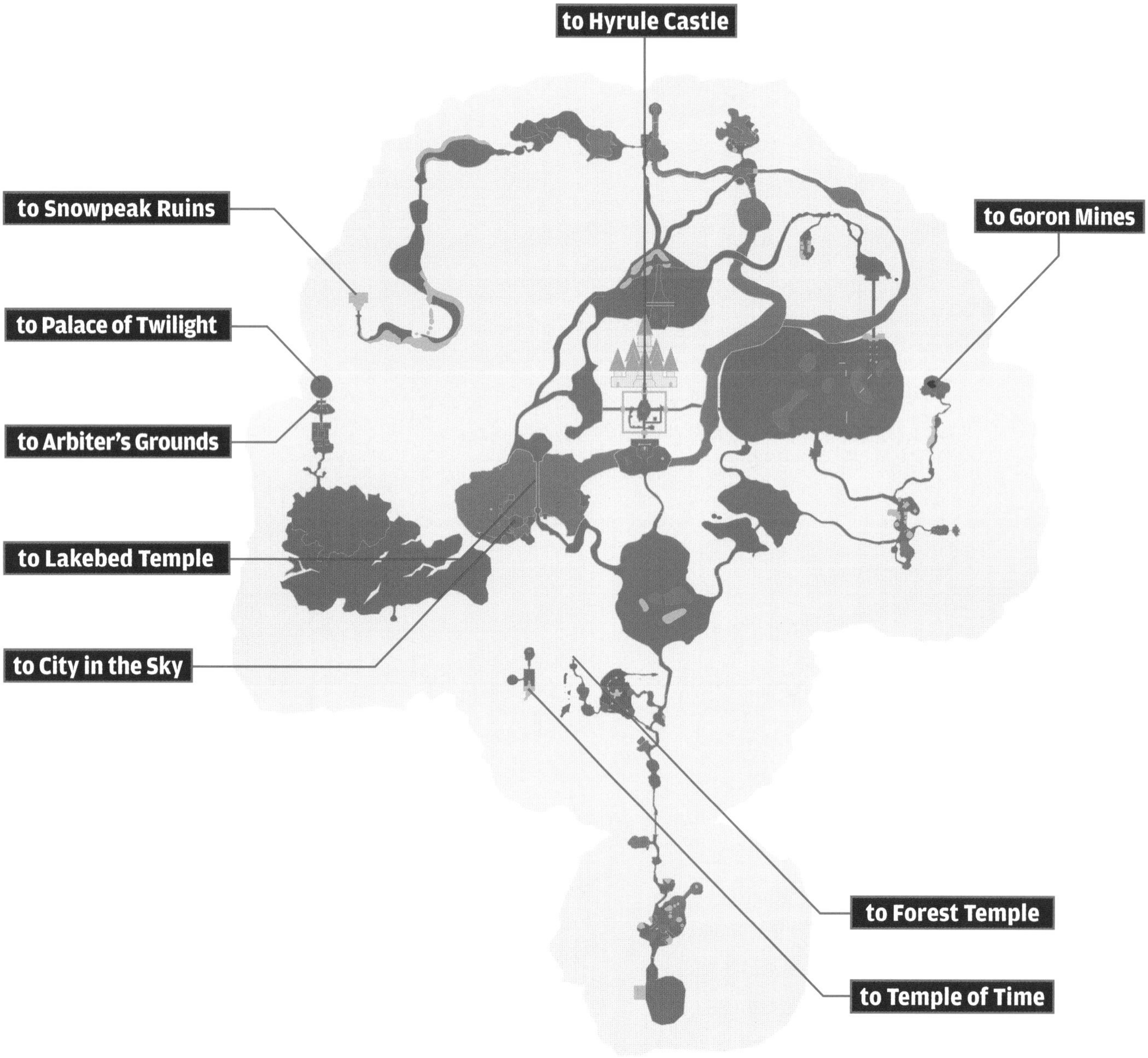

to Hyrule Castle

to Snowpeak Ruins

to Goron Mines

to Palace of Twilight

to Arbiter's Grounds

to Lakebed Temple

to City in the Sky

to Forest Temple

to Temple of Time

Forest Temple

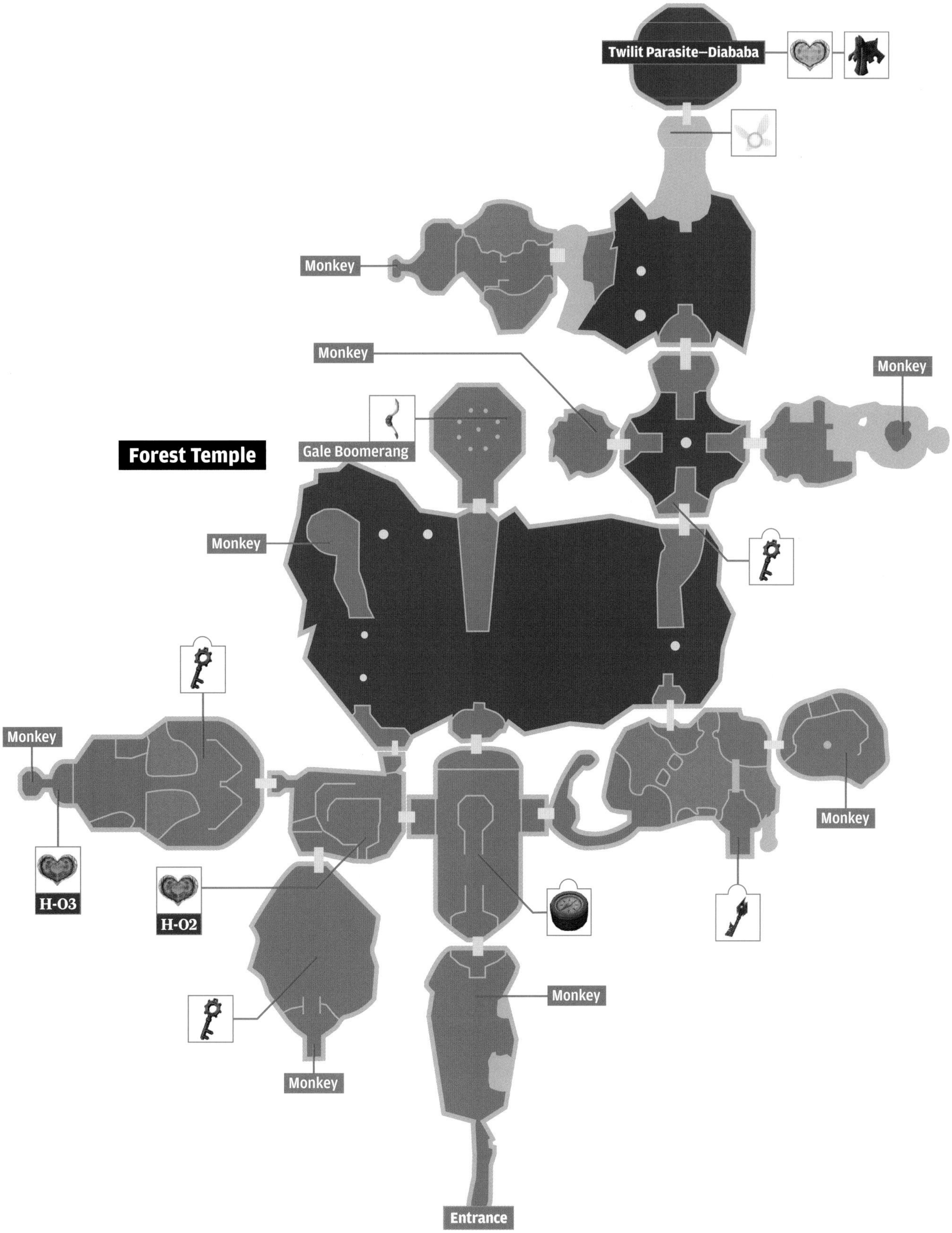

Goron Mines

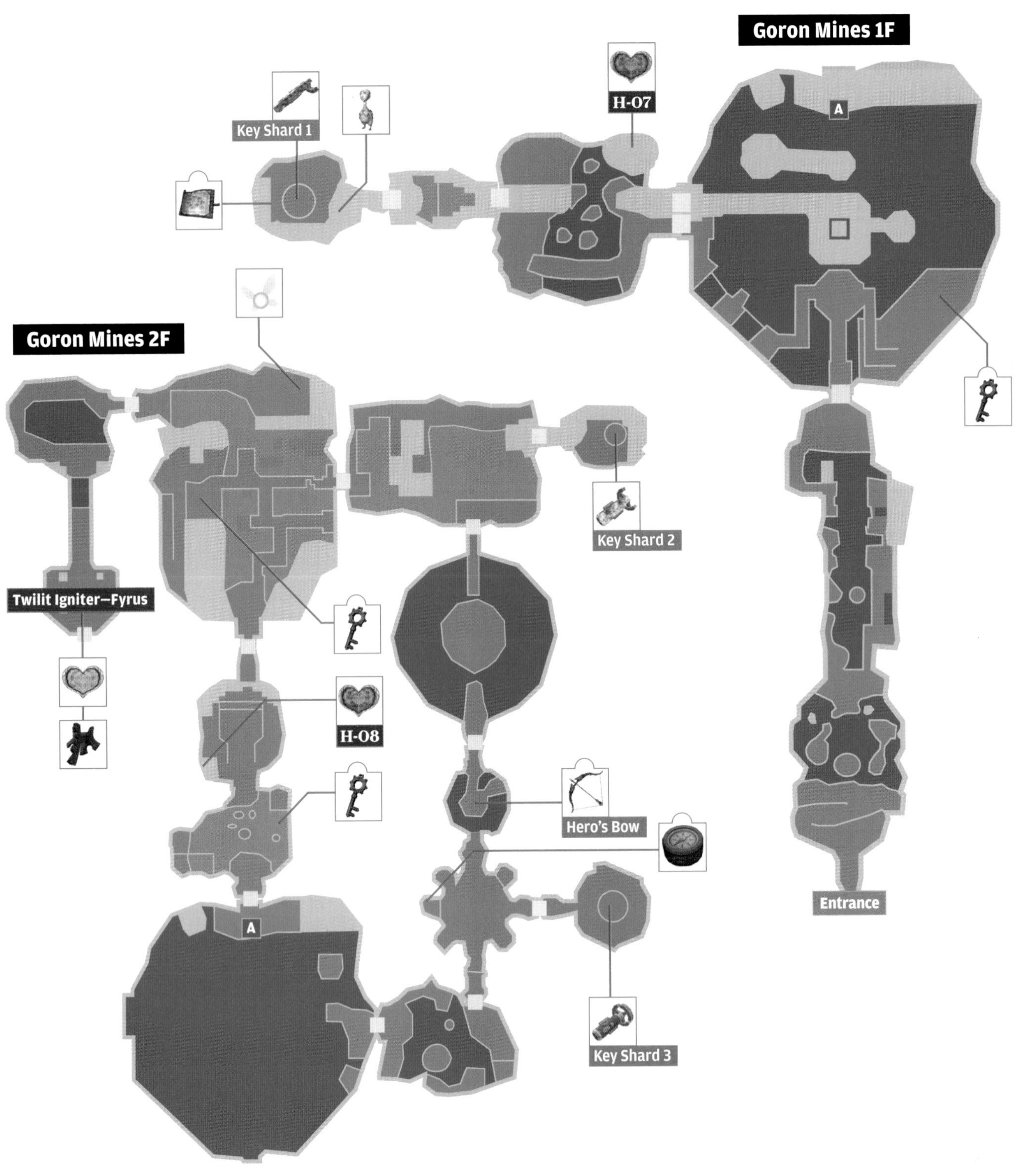

Goron Mines 1F
H-07
Key Shard 1
A
Goron Mines 2F
Key Shard 2
Twilit Igniter—Fyrus
H-08
Hero's Bow
A
Key Shard 3
Entrance

Lakebed Temple

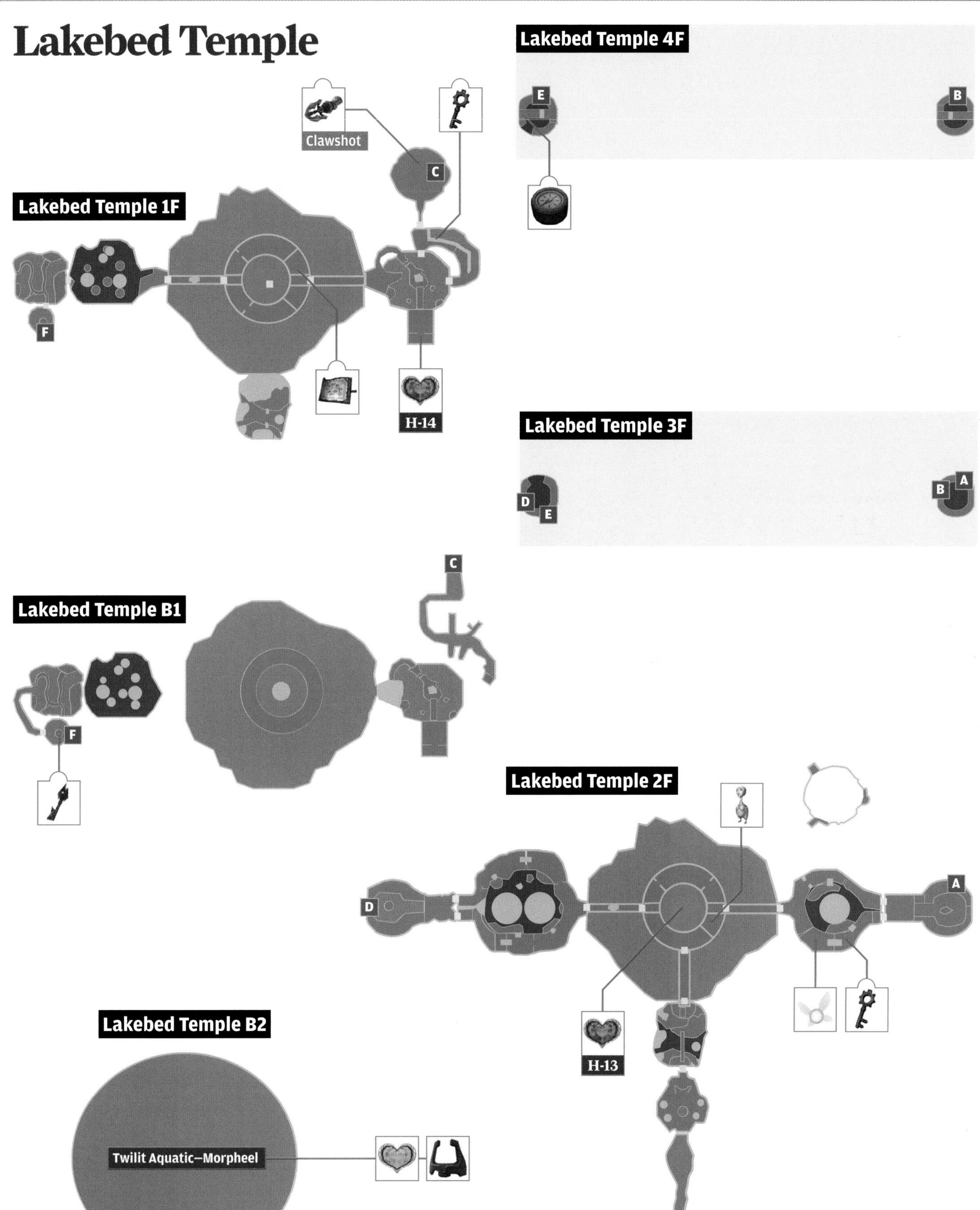

Arbiter's Grounds

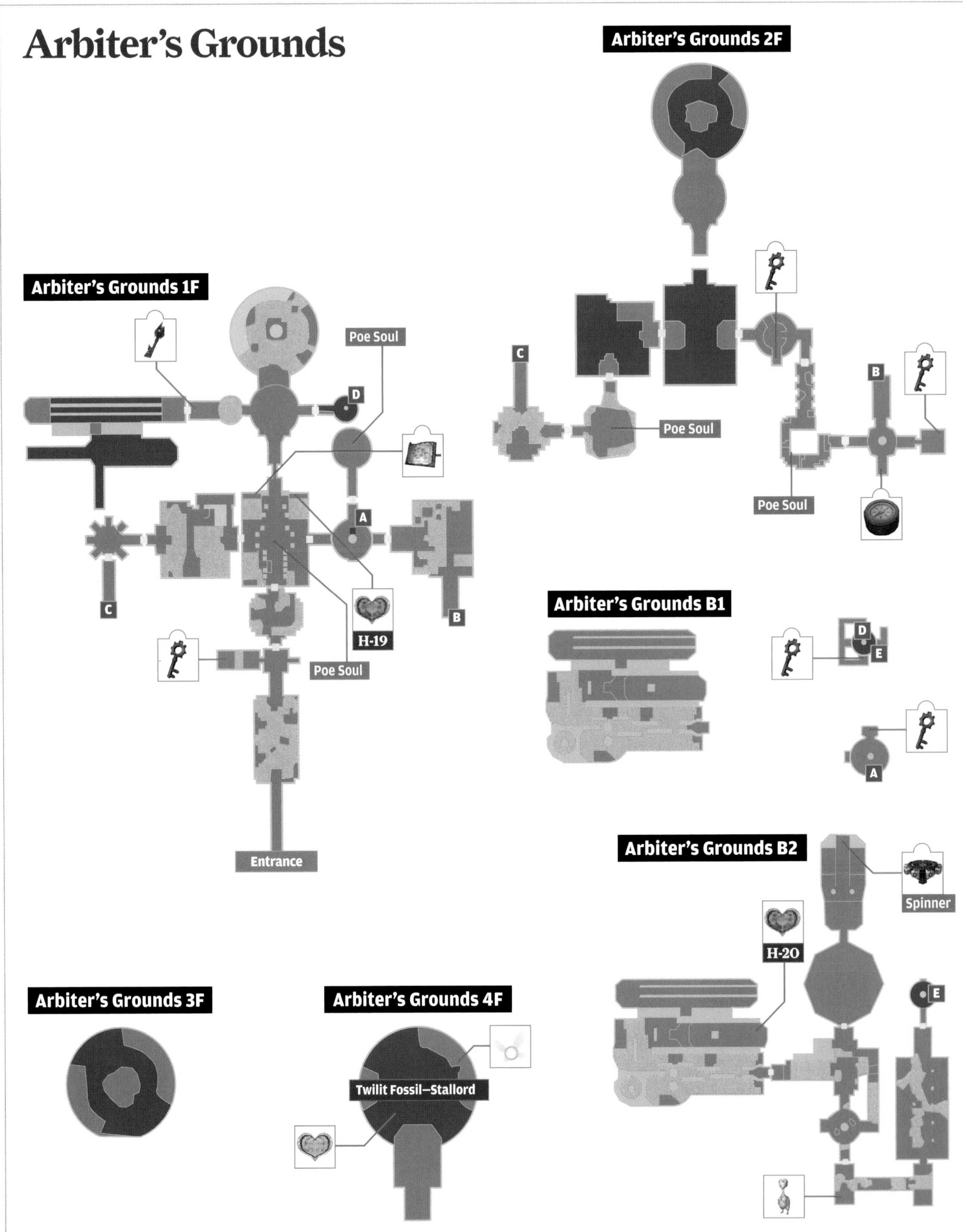

Snowpeak Ruins

Snowpeak Ruins 1F

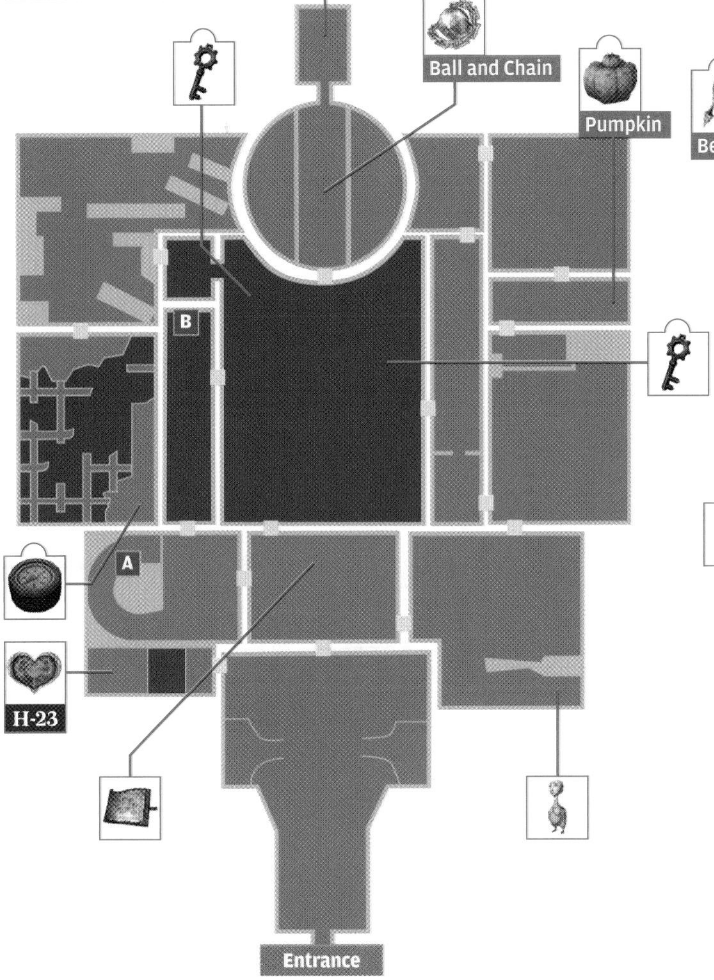
Ordon Goat Cheese
Ball and Chain
Pumpkin
B
A
H-23
Entrance

Snowpeak Ruins 2F

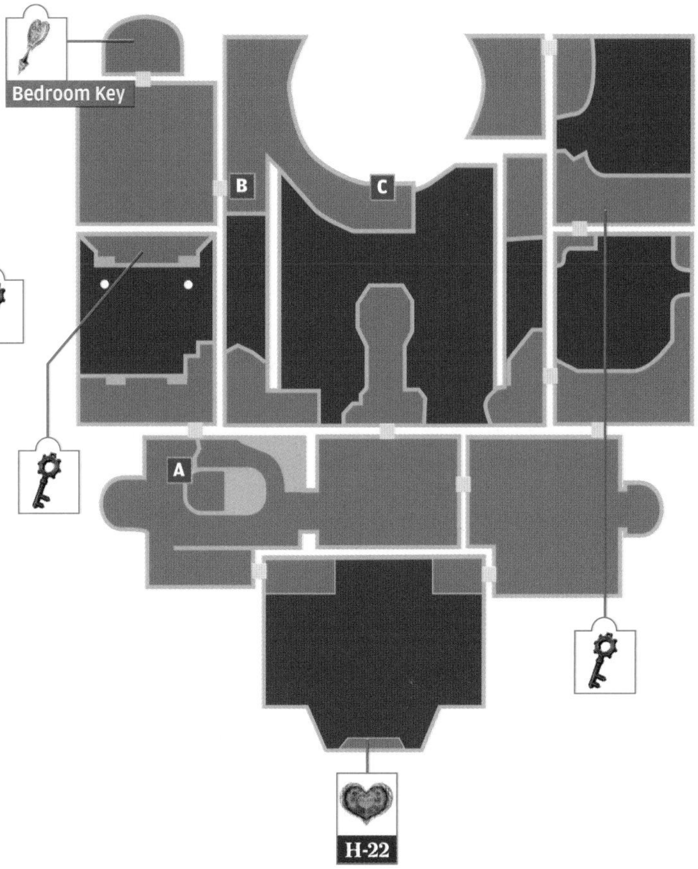
Bedroom Key
B
C
A
H-22

Snowpeak Ruins 3F

Twilit Ice Mass—Blizzeta
C

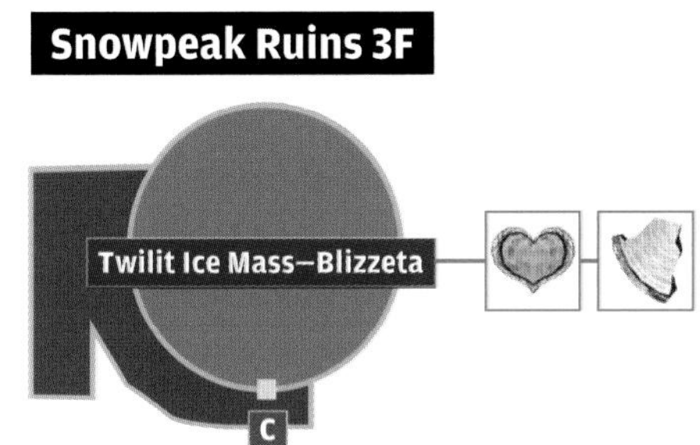

Temple of Time

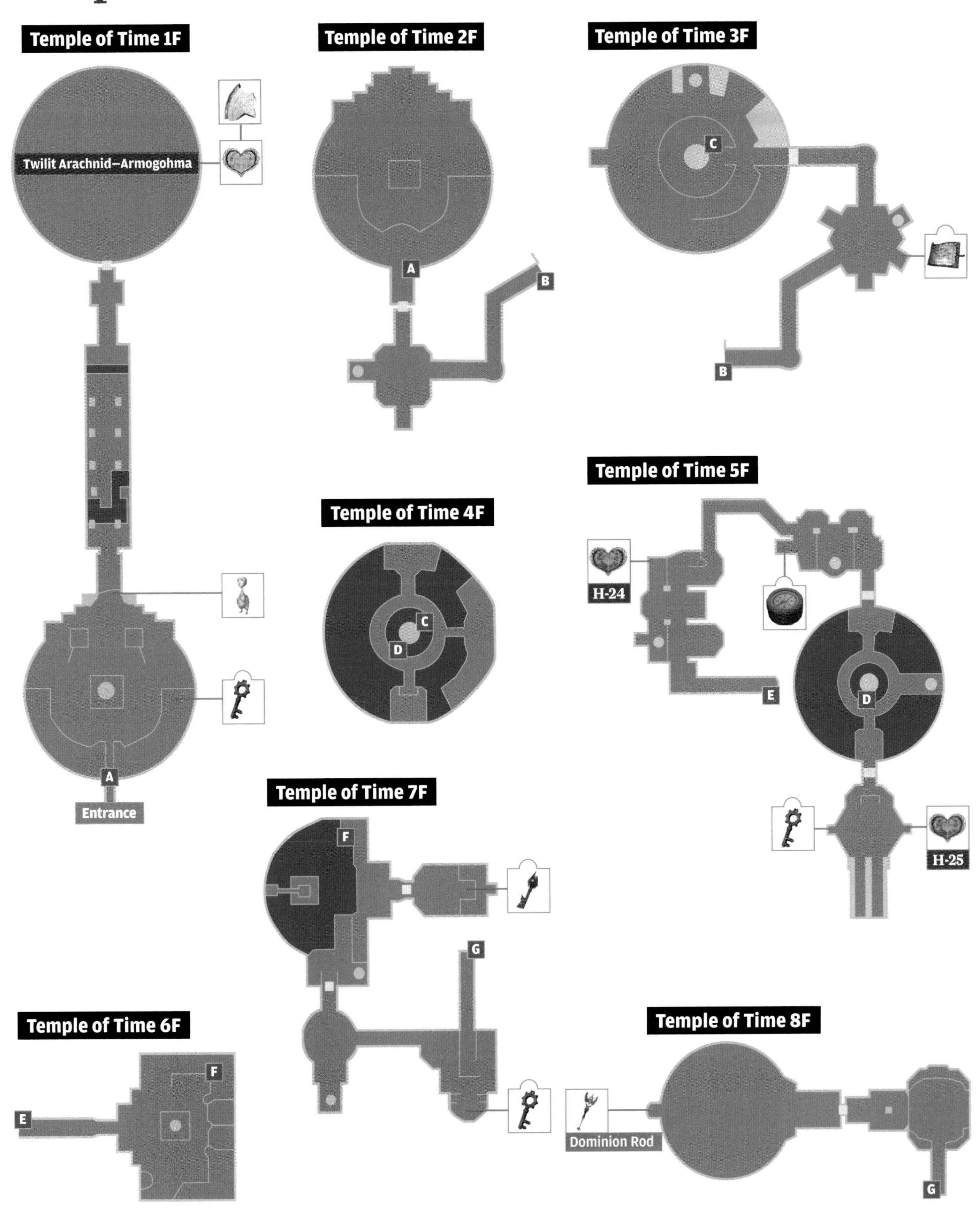

City in the Sky

City in the Sky 1F

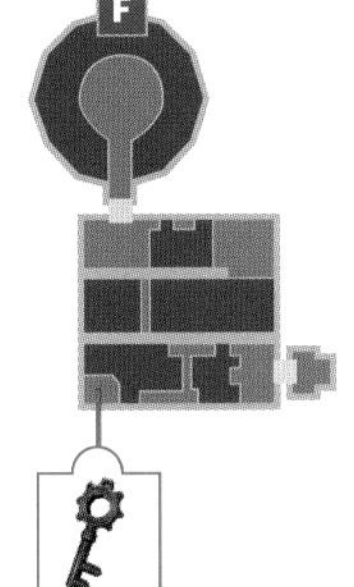

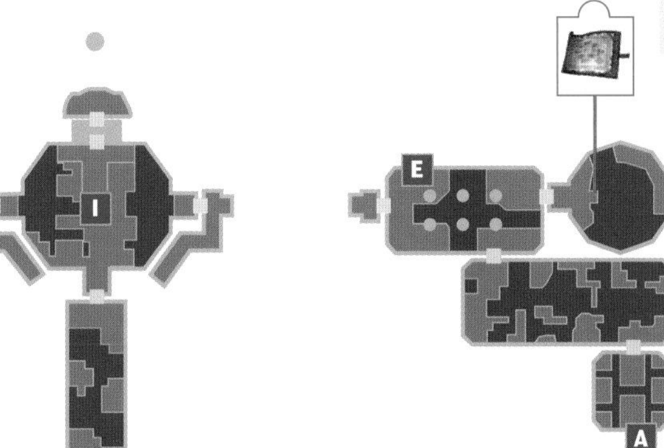

City in the Sky 2F

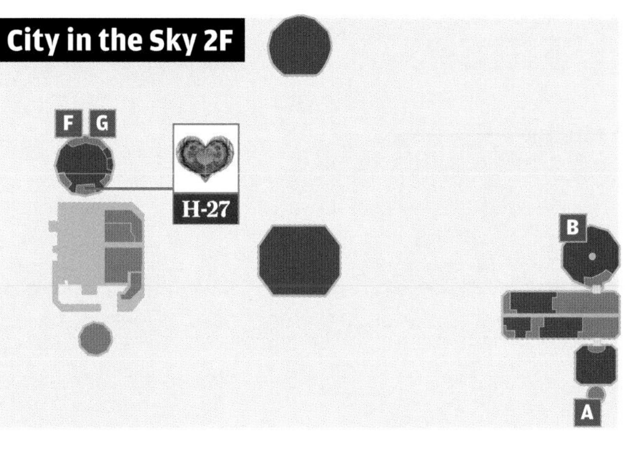

City in the Sky 3F

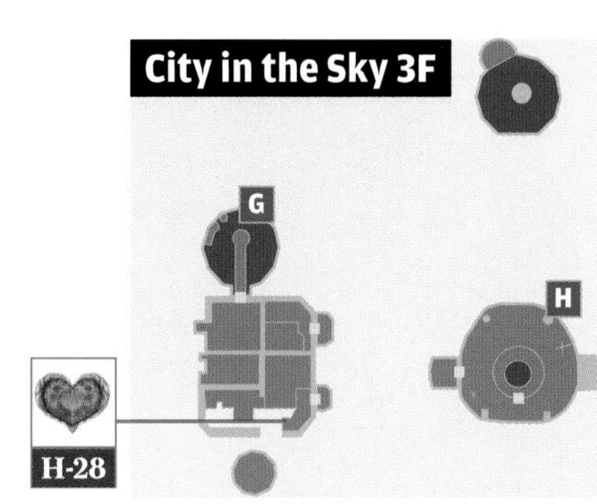

City in the Sky 4F

City in the Sky B1

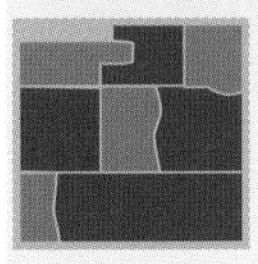

City in the Sky B3

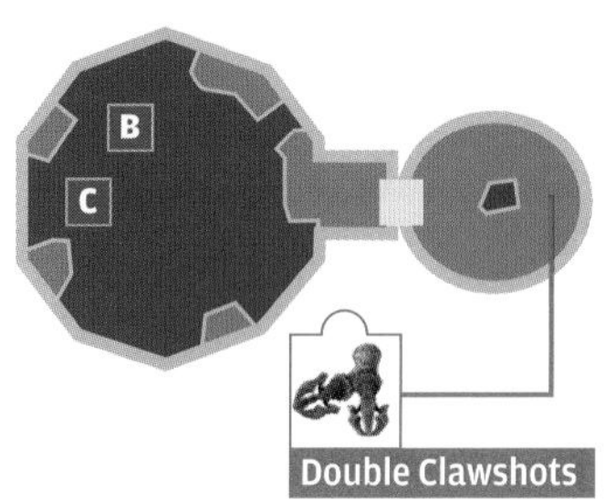

City in the Sky 5F

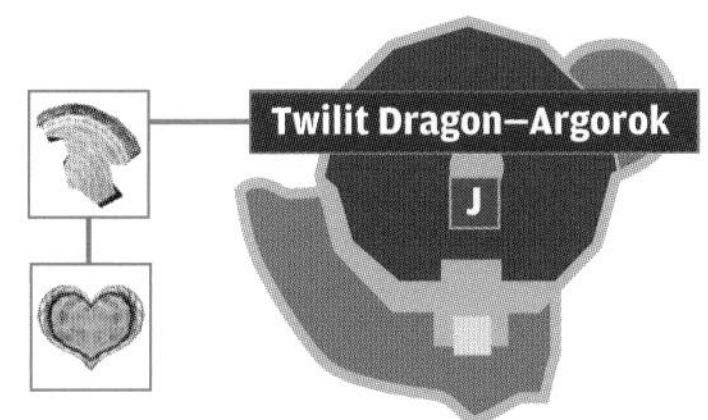

City in the Sky B2

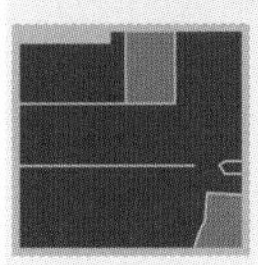

Palace of Twilight

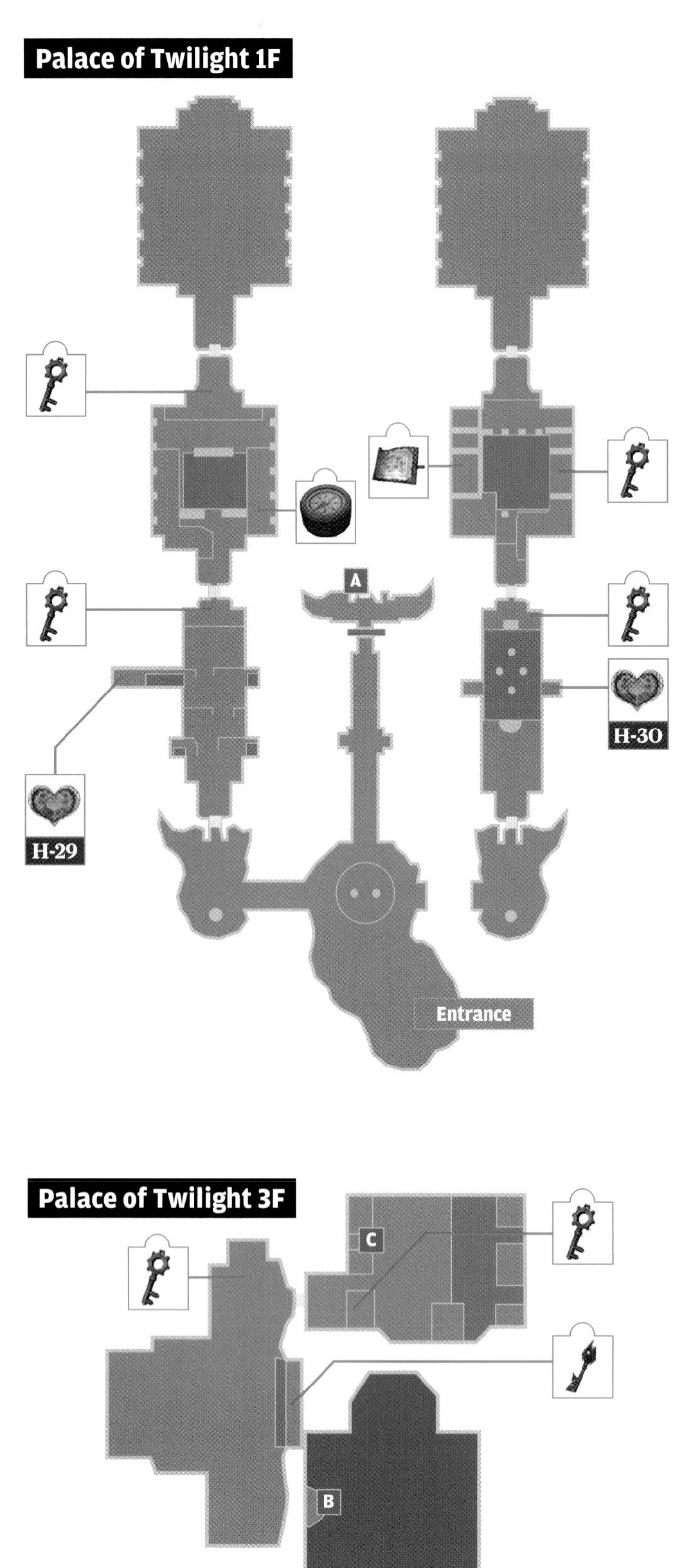

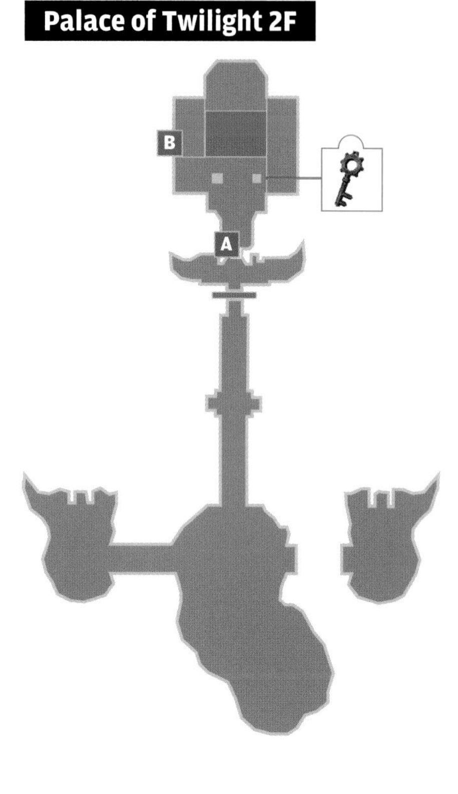

Hyrule Castle

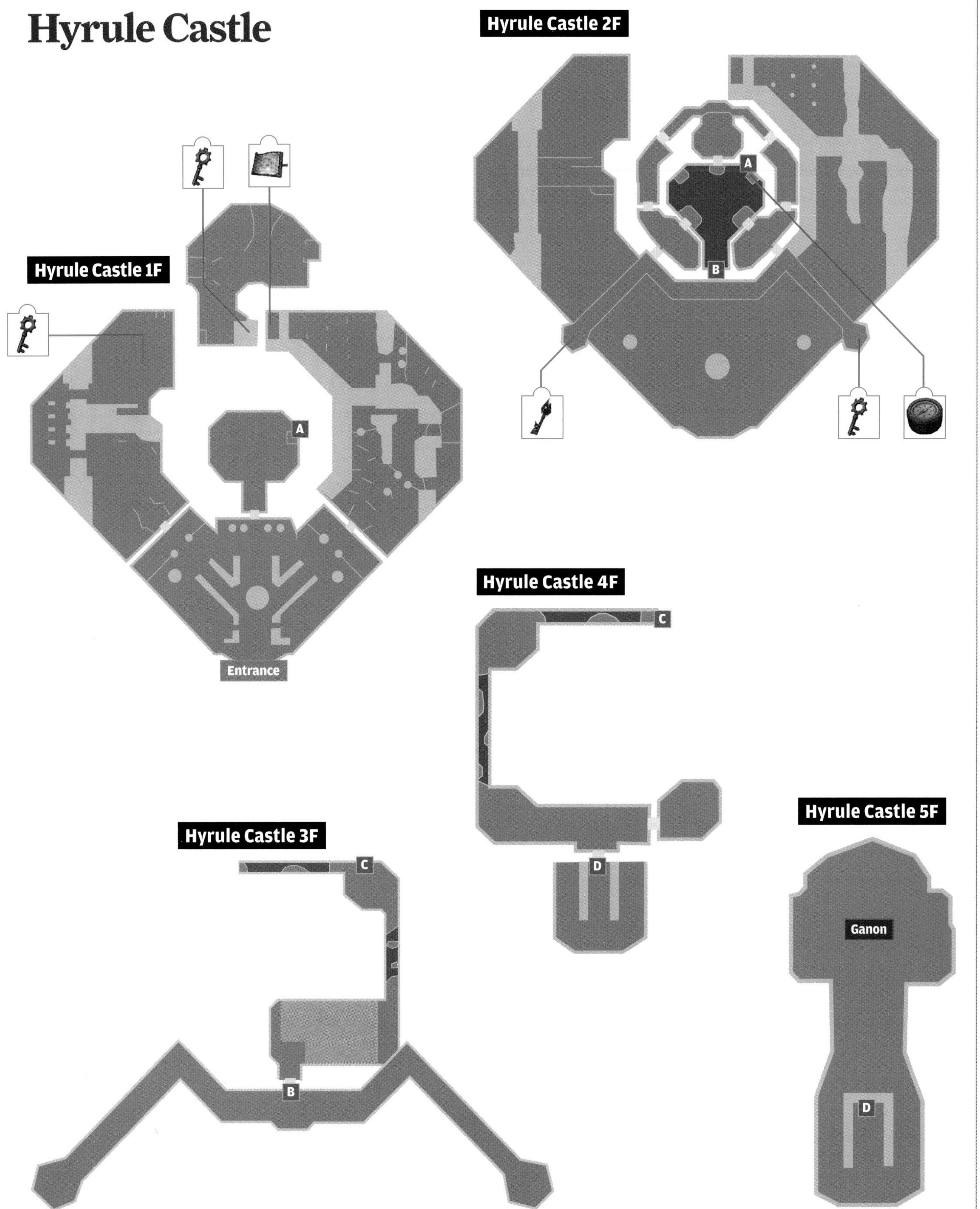

Poe Souls & Golden Bugs

Link will reap great rewards for acquiring 60 Poe Souls and 24 Golden Bugs during his quest. Pinpoint their locations with these maps.

Poe Souls

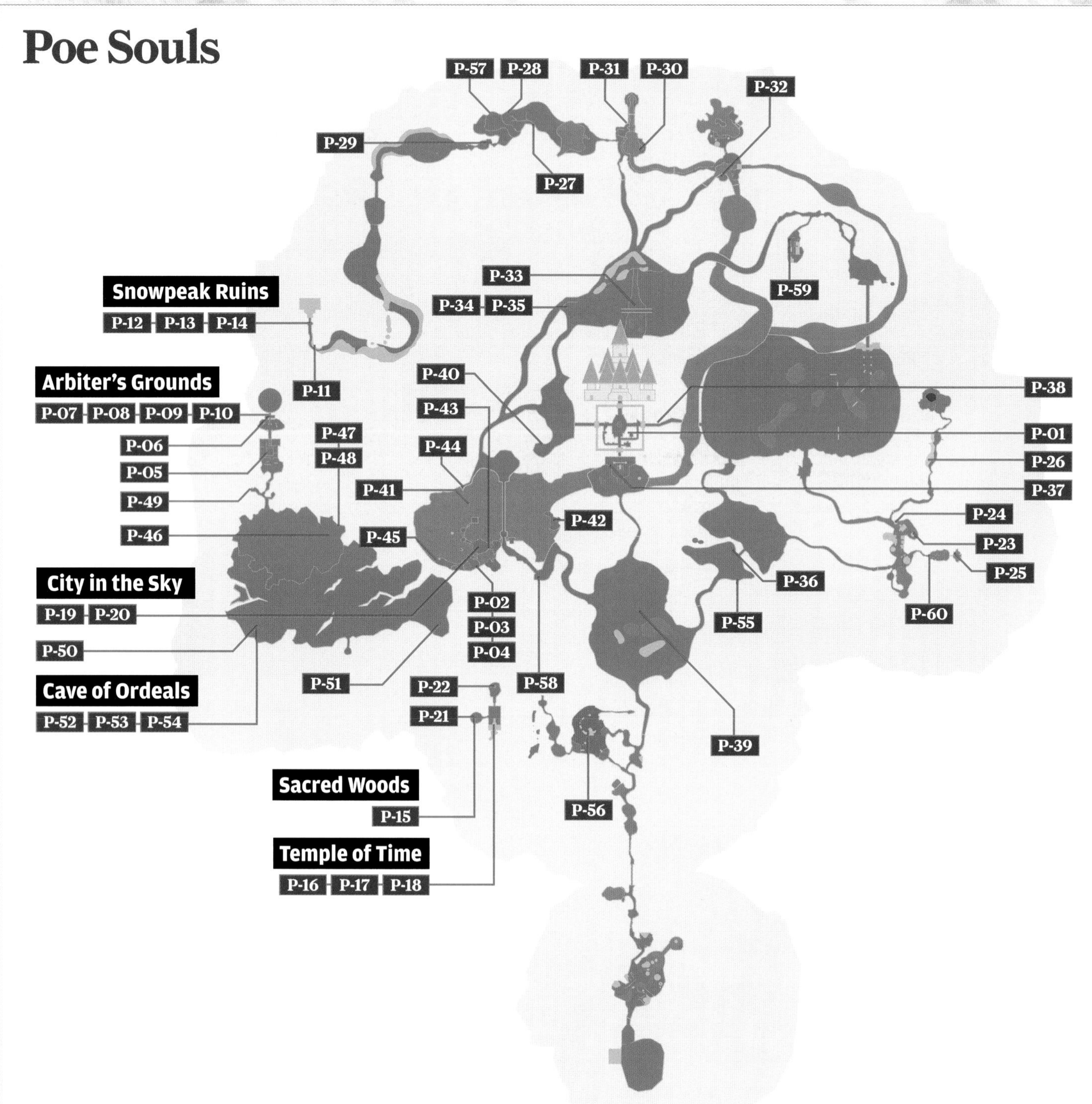

Golden Bugs

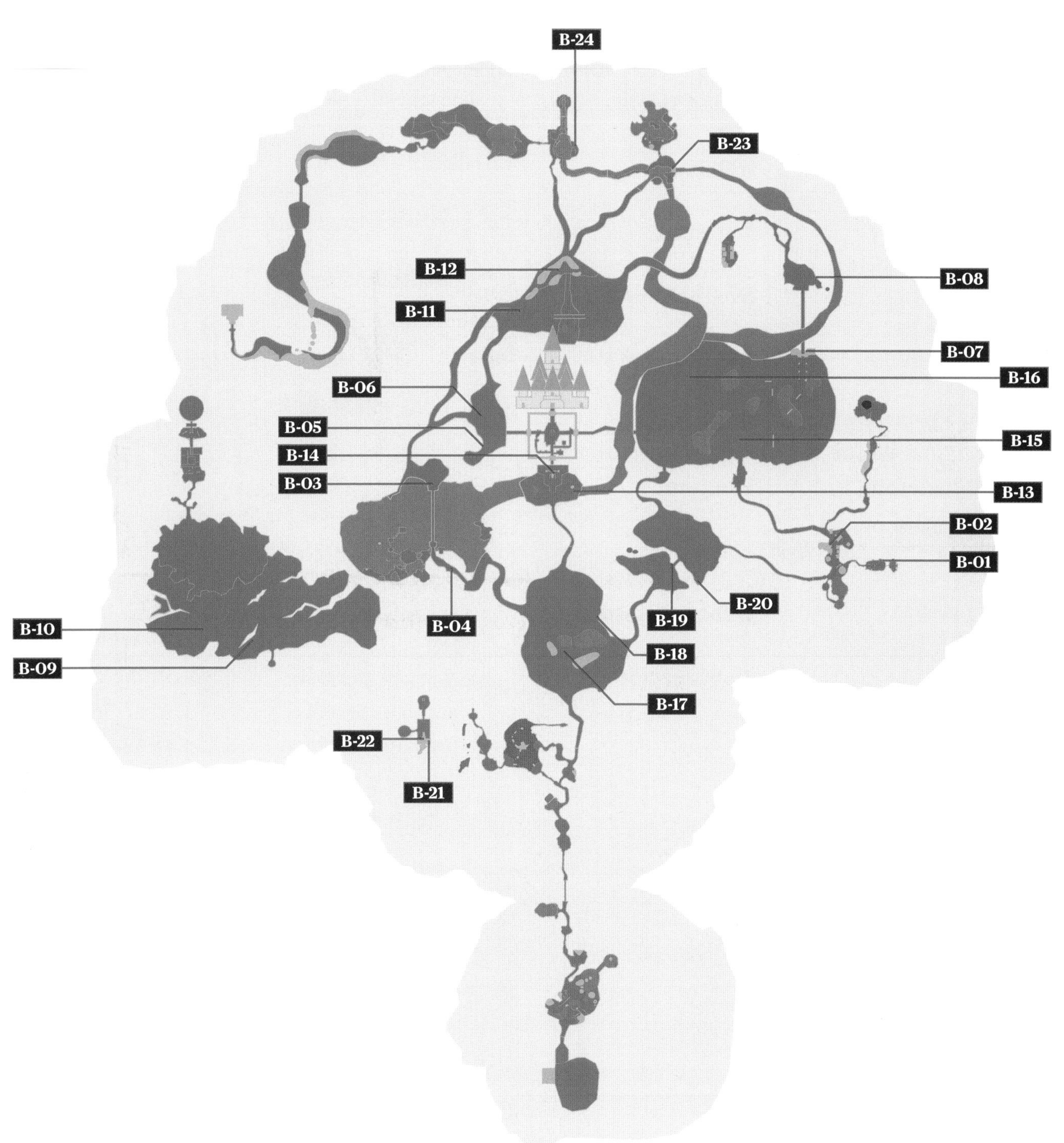
B-24
B-23
B-12
B-08
B-11
B-07
B-16
B-06
B-05
B-15
B-14
B-03
B-13
B-02
B-01
B-20
B-19
B-10
B-04
B-18
B-09
B-17
B-22
B-21

Map Key

Weapons and Tools

 **Ball and Chain**

 **Bottle**

 **Clawshot**

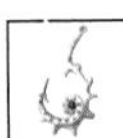 **Coral Earring**

 **Dominion Rod**

 **Double Clawshots**

 **Gale Boomerang**

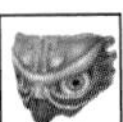 **Hawkeye**

  **Hero's Bow**

 **Horse Call**

 **Hylian Shield**

 **Iron Boots**

 **Lantern**

 **Master Sword**

 **Ordon Shield**

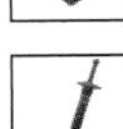 **Ordon Sword**

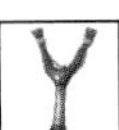 **Slingshot**

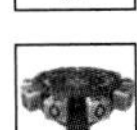 **Spinner**

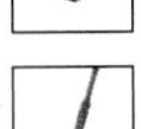  **Wooden Sword**

 **Zora's Armor**

Perishables

 **Arrows**

 **Bombs**

 **Rupees**

 **Bomblings**

 **Water Bombs**

5 10 20 50 100 200

Overworld Items

 **Golden Wolf**

Howling Stone

Item Types

Items found in treasure chests are identified by boxes with a semicircle on top. Square boxes represent items that you'll acquire in other ways.

 H-01 B-01 P-01

You can locate Pieces of Heart (H-01 through H-45), Golden Bugs (B-01 through B-24), and Poe Souls (P-01 through P-60) in boxes like these. See the Adventurer's Appendix for details.

Dungeon Items

 **Big Key**

 **Bedroom Key**

 **Compass**

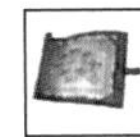 **Dungeon Map**

 **Heart Container**

 **Ooccoo**

 **Small Key**

Quest Items

 **Ashei's Sketch**

 **Auru's Memo**

 **Ancient Sky Book**

 **Doctor's Invoice**

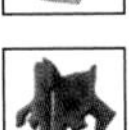 **Fused Shadow**

 **Key Shard**

 **Mirror Shard**

Monkey

 **Ordon Goat Cheese**

Poe Soul

 **Pumpkin**

 **Reekfish**

 **Renado's Letter**

 **Shadow Crystal**

 **Wooden Figure**